Forensic Face Matching

Forensic Face Matching

Research and Practice

Edited by

MARKUS BINDEMANN

Professor of Psychology

School of Psychology

University of Kent

UK

OXFORD

UNIVERSITY PRESS

OXFORD

UNIVERSITY PRESS

Great Clarendon Street, Oxford, OX2 6DP,
United Kingdom

Oxford University Press is a department of the University of Oxford.
It furthers the University's objective of excellence in research, scholarship,
and education by publishing worldwide. Oxford is a registered trade mark of
Oxford University Press in the UK and in certain other countries

Published in the United States of America by Oxford University Press
198 Madison Avenue, New York, NY 10016, United States of America

British Library Cataloguing in Publication Data

Data available

Library of Congress Control Number: 2020944417

ISBN 978–0–19–883774–9

Printed and bound by
CPI Group (UK) Ltd, Croydon, CR0 4YY

Oxford University Press makes no representation, express or implied, that the
drug dosages in this book are correct. Readers must therefore always check
the product information and clinical procedures with the most up-to-date
published product information and data sheets provided by the manufacturers
and the most recent codes of conduct and safety regulations. The authors and
the publishers do not accept responsibility or legal liability for any errors in the
text or for the misuse or misapplication of material in this work. Except where
otherwise stated, drug dosages and recommendations are for the non-pregnant
adult who is not breast-feeding

Links to third party websites are provided by Oxford in good faith and
for information only. Oxford disclaims any responsibility for the materials
contained in any third party website referenced in this work.

Preface

As humans, we are highly tuned to faces. We are very good at finding faces in our visual environment, we enjoy looking at them, and we even find it difficult to ignore them. One reason for this is that we can extract a wealth of social signals by looking at someone's face. Hairstyle, facial hair, and bone structure, for example, can convey a person's gender. Hair colour, skin complexion, and adiposity provide clues to age. Facial expressions can convey a person's emotional state, and the direction a person's eyes are pointing indicates what holds their focus of attention in the immediate environment. Most importantly, however, our faces indicate who we are. They provide the primary visual means by which people can be identified, and for distinguishing one person from another.

In everyday life, we identify faces regularly and seemingly with great ease. Consequently, one might assume this to be a straightforward and highly accurate task. We are certainly very good at recognizing the faces of people that we know, such as those belonging to colleagues, friends, and family. People who are familiar to us in other ways seem to be recognized with great accuracy too, such as the faces of movie stars, famous sports people, and politicians. Contrary to the identification of familiar people, however, we are poor at identifying the faces of unfamiliar people, whom we have never met before, despite the fact that important tasks depend on this. Passport control at airports and borders, for example, depends on the identification of people who are not known to the observer, by comparing their faces to photo-identity documents. And police investigations frequently require the comparison of footage of a target person with the faces of suspects to make an identification. In these applied settings, these identification tasks are referred to as facial (image) comparison and are utilized widely on a national and international scale. However, the systematic study and validation of these identification processes by practitioners has not kept pace with their application in the field.

In psychology, a similar identification task is known as 'forensic' or 'unfamiliar face matching', because it requires the comparison of two or more instances of a face to decide if these provide an identity match, by depicting the same person, or a mismatch, comprising of similar-looking but different people. In recent years, this task has come to the fore as a field of study in its own right because face matching differs from other ways in which people can be identified. The recognition of familiar faces, for example, has been studied extensively in psychology, and theories of this process have been in existence for more than 30 years. Similarly, face–memory paradigms, in which observers have to recognize newly learned faces after an interval, have been applied extensively in the study of eyewitness testimony. Face matching, on the other hand, does not involve prior exposure to a face, to generate familiarity or an eyewitness memory, at all.

It is identification in its purest form, based solely on the visual comparison of the similarity of two or more concurrent faces.

Contrary to the occupational settings in which facial comparison is of great relevance but investigated little, face matching has now been studied extensively in the psychological domain. As a consequence, face matching in psychology has, de facto, become the science of facial comparison. Almost all available, systematic, peer-reviewed research in this domain has, and continues to be, carried out by scientists in psychology working at universities internationally. Psychologists are therefore playing a pivotal role, not only in furthering understanding of the cognitive task of face matching but also of the analogous applied task of facial comparison.

In this context, the aim of this book is to provide an overview of what is currently known about these processes, by bringing together the latest expert knowledge. The bulk of research in this field has only been conducted in the past decade and is therefore very recent, but the volume of work is now substantial and a book of this kind is a timely necessity to draw together what has been learned so far. As the psychology of face matching is important for understanding person identification at passport control and criminal identification in police investigations, the book covers evidence that speaks to both these tasks. Of course, some clear differences exist in how facial comparison is implemented and performed in these different applied settings. Passport control, for example, normally requires the rapid identification of a high volume of people, who are presented under good viewing conditions. Facial comparison in police settings, on the other hand, typically focuses on individual cases, which are examined in great detail over a prolonged, documented process. However, many similarities also exist across facial comparison at passport control and in police investigations, and much of the existing research on face matching is relevant to both. These topics are therefore combined in this book.

Chapter 1 provides important context for understanding facial comparison at passport control, by reflecting on the development of international standards for travel documents and how improvements in this field have given way to the problem of identity impostors. Chapter 2 dissects key factors that have an impact on the accuracy of facial comparison, both at passport control and in policing, based on a substantial body of scientific knowledge from laboratory experiments on face matching. Chapter 3 then draws together a wide range of psychological evidence on face matching to support the development of a theoretical account of this task.

The middle section of this book focuses heavily on understanding the accuracy and impact of facial comparison in practice. In Chapter 4, the face-matching performance of different practitioner groups is reviewed systematically to give insight into the extent to which these outperform untrained lay observers, and considers how expertise in face matching might be acquired. This is followed by an in-depth examination in Chapter 5 of whether face identification ability can be trained for occupations that rely on this task. Chapter 6 then focuses on the differences that exist between individuals in face-matching performance, their potential underpinnings, and the reliability of the assessment tools that are currently in use for determining a person's competence in facial identification. In Chapter 7, the procedures and application of facial comparison in the police are reviewed critically, drawing on the extensive occupational experience of an expert examiner. This is complemented in Chapter 8 by a legal perspective, in order to consider the evidential rules and principles that regulate the admissibility of facial-comparison evidence by experts in criminal trials.

The book comes to a close by considering two key developments that are likely to have a great impact on the future of facial comparison in occupational settings. Chapter 9 focuses on automatic face recognition and reviews the effectiveness of current systems, both when operating in isolation and in conjunction with supervision by human observers. Chapter 10 then introduces the emerging threat of hyper-realistic face masks, systematically reviewing evidence of how these have an impact on person identification under controlled laboratory conditions and in the field.

My hope is that the book will provide readers with a wide-ranging, detailed and critical overview of facial comparison and face matching, to give insight into their application, efficacy, and limitations in occupational settings, and of current scientific knowledge of this task. In the making of this book, I wanted to give contributors the freedom to pick their own points of emphasis. As a consequence, this volume inevitably gives up some parsimony and integration across chapters. The advantage, however, is that the book samples knowledge and expertise from a much wider spectrum than a more restricted approach would afford. It is this variety of knowledge and experience that has gone into the production of the book that makes up its value. I am enormously grateful to the contributors, their time and expertise, and their willingness to share their latest insights in this way.

Markus Bindemann
Canterbury, January 2020

Contents

Contributors

Sarah Bate is Professor of Psychology in the Face Processing Research Group at Bournemouth University. She is interested in individual differences in face recognition ability, and works with people who experience face recognition difficulties, those who have facilitated face recognition skills, and the typical population. Sarah is particularly interested in methods for assessing and enhancing face recognition skills.

Markus Bindemann is Professor of Cognitive Psychology at the University of Kent in England. He has been researching face perception for nearly 20 years, with particular emphasis on person identification over the past decade. He holds numerous scientific publications in this field and has edited several special journal issues on this topic. He is the editor as well as a contributing author to this book, which he conceived to bring together the latest knowledge of key experts in the rapidly expanding field of unfamiliar face matching.

A. Mike Burton is Professor of Psychology at the University of York, UK. He is a Fellow of the British Academy and a past President of the Experimental Psychology Society. In collaboration with many colleagues, he has studied face recognition across a variety of contexts, both in the lab and in real-world contexts. He has published research using diverse approaches, including experimental psychology, computer modelling, and neuroimaging.

Matthew C. Fysh is a Psychologist and Research Fellow at the University of Kent, who specializes in facial identity matching. He has previously worked with Border Force UK to assess the face-matching accuracy of passport control personnel at airports and is lead author of the Kent Face Matching Test. He is currently dedicated to the development of future technologies to study face matching, such as the simulation of airport security tasks within virtual environments.

Matthew Q. Hill is a PhD student studying cognition and neuroscience at the University of Texas at Dallas. He works under Professor Alice O'Toole, using a cognitive neuroscience perspective to investigate the ways modern face recognition algorithms encode information. He previously worked as part of a team competing in the IARPA Janus program to evaluate convolutional neural networks trained for face identification. Currently, his focus is on the ways in which facial familiarity can be modelled by these neural networks.

Rob Jenkins is a Cognitive Psychologist at the University of York, UK. His main interest is in how people identify each other from faces seen live or in photographs. His research includes behavioural experiments, computational modelling, and image analysis. Rob was a member of the Young Academy of Scotland and the Global Young Academy.

Richard I. Kemp is Professor of Forensic Psychology working at UNSW Sydney in Australia, who seeks to apply research in the fields of memory and perception to aspects of the legal system. His current research interests include identity verification and face perception, eyewitness memory, police interviewing, and forensic science evidence. Richard has undertaken his research in collaboration with various partner organizations, including state and federal government agencies, police and emergency service organizations, and banks and financial service providers. He has provided expert evidence in a number of significant court cases, and provides training to judges, lawyers, police, and other legal professionals.

Natalie Mestry is a Cognitive Psychologist and Senior Lecturer in the Face Processing Research Group at Bournemouth University. She was previously a postdoctoral researcher at the University of Southampton where she also completed her PhD on configural face processing. Natalie is researching challenges in visual search for unfamiliar faces and individual differences in face processing.

Reuben Moreton is the Identity and Biometrics lead at Qumodo and a postgraduate researcher in Psychology at the Open University. Previously the senior face examiner for forensics in the Metropolitan Police Service in the UK, he regularly attended court as an expert witness and designed and implemented face-matching systems and processes for the police. Reuben has co-authored international guidance and research in face matching. He provides consultancy on the introduction and use of face-matching systems, and delivers training in identification from images.

Eilidh Noyes is a Cognitive Psychologist at the University of Huddersfield. She was educated at the University of York and the University of Glasgow, and has previously worked at the University of Texas at Dallas. Her expertise is in human and machine face recognition, with a particular interest in achieving the best of face recognition in both optimal and challenging image conditions. She has been involved in an international study of human and machine face expertise, and has conducted research on the face recognition abilities of officers from the Metropolitan Police super-recognizer unit.

Emma Portch completed research posts at both the University of Leeds and Manchester before taking up a lecturing position in the Psychology Department at Bournemouth University. Emma is interested in the individual differences that underpin the ability to perceive identity and emotional expression from faces. She is also involved in facial composite research, exploring how the interaction between witness-constructors and computerized systems can be improved to produce better-quality facial likenesses.

Andrew Roberts is Associate Professor at Melbourne Law School, the University of Melbourne, where he teaches courses in the law of evidence and the process of proof. He has published widely on various aspects of criminal process, and has a long-standing interest in eyewitness identification evidence and the law governing the reception of expert evidence. He is co-author of a text on Australian evidence law (*Uniform Evidence*, 3rd edition, 2019: OUP) and was convening editor of the first collection of essays on that body of law (*Critical Perspective on the Uniform Evidence Law*, 2017: Federation Press).

Jet G. Sanders is an Experimental Psychologist at the Department of Psychological and Behavioural Sciences of the London School of Economics. Her research has focused on hyper-realistic masks and face perception. She looks at science through an applied lens, and uses secondary data analysis, laboratory and field experiments to propose and test practical solutions. Jet is currently an honorary academic advisor for the Center for Advanced Hindsight at Duke University and the European Behavioural Insights Network.

Charlie Stevens is a former Head of the UK's National Document Fraud Unit. He was closely involved with the development of international standards for secure identity verification by the International Civil Aviation Organization (ICAO) to facilitate passenger movements through airports. He served as UK delegate to the ICAO's New Technologies Working Group for over a decade, during the development of specifications for the inclusion of verifiable biometric identifiers in travel documents for facial recognition. He is an expert on security and immigration threats at borders and airports, such as the problem posed by impostors.

Alice Towler is a Cognitive Psychologist at UNSW Sydney in Australia. Her research focuses on improving the accuracy and efficiency of face identification systems. She has worked closely with the Australian Passport Office and Metropolitan Police Service to evaluate the effectiveness of professional training courses and develop new evidence-based training for facial image comparison. She also has a broader interest in improving the evidence base in the forensic sciences through her work with the Evidence-Based Forensics Initiative.

David White is a Cognitive Psychologist at UNSW Sydney in Australia. His research focuses on factors that determine accuracy in face identification tasks and he has published foundational tests of professional staff who perform these tasks in their daily work. He has worked for over a decade with interdisciplinary teams from academia, government, and industry on improving performance in these tasks in forensic and security settings.

1

Person Identification at Airports During Passport Control

Charlie Stevens

1.1 Introduction

The growth of air travel was one of the major global developments of the twentieth century. This trend has continued into the twenty-first century and into the foreseeable future. Major international airports, such as London's Heathrow Airport, now handle tens of millions of passengers annually. This has had enormous impact on airport infrastructure and border security checks, and creates a constant pressure between commercial entities and control authorities. Airlines and airport operators seek rapid movement of passengers through arrival and departure to meet consumer demand, and to increase passenger satisfaction and profitability. As a result, government authorities are under political and financial pressure to facilitate the movement of passengers through passport control, but must also meet the requirements of immigration law and maintain border and national security. In this context, passport control is a frontline security task of fundamental importance, because it provides the primary means to quickly determine the nationality and identity of passengers seeking to enter a state. Once this information has been established, the control authorities can proceed to determine eligibility of the passengers to enter under the immigration laws of the state.

To establish identity and nationality of passengers, personal information from travel documents such as passports is scrutinized by immigration officers, who must be satisfied that the person presenting the document is also its rightful holder. This centres on comparing the facial image displayed in a passport with its bearer to verify that these depict the same person. This process can be supported by other biographical data about the holder contained in the document, such as information about age, height, and eye colour. This examination process must be carried out quickly in busy control situations, and now it is usually assisted at major airports by document machine readers.

1.1.1 The Development of Machine-Readable Travel Documents

At the beginning of the twentieth century, with mass migration within Europe and between Europe and North America, states realized that international guidelines were necessary for passports. In 1920, the League of Nations International Conference on

Charlie Stevens, *Person Identification at Airports During Passport Control* In: *Forensic Face Matching.* Edited by: Markus Bindemann, Oxford University Press (2021). © Oxford University Press. DOI: 10.1093/oso/9780198837749.003.0001.

Passports agreed such guidelines with the formulation of a general booklet design incorporating the inclusion of a photograph of the document holder. The document specifications were only basic, resulting in great variation in size, format, and security safeguards in passports (see Figure 1.1), but remained in use for many decades.

By the late 1960s, the international aviation industry, as a result of rapid growth in international air travel, began to investigate solutions to improve passenger flow and passport control processing times through airports. This work included a review of travel documents. At that time, individual states still chose their own unique designs, formats, and materials for their travel documents, because there was still no agreed international standard. Biographical details of document holders were usually entered by hand by issuing offices and could cover three or more pages of a document, including a wide variety of information. Some states, for example, would include information about the holder's occupation status, height, and eye or hair colour as well as any other distinguishing features. All documents included a photograph of the holder, but this was often insecurely attached by issuing authorities. Authenticating seals were often lacking in security and could easily be copied.

Around the same time, and in part also as a consequence of the increase in affordable air travel, states were experiencing increased inflows of migrants. More stringent border and visa controls were implemented to restrict access to persons with correct documentation and clearances. In turn, this led to many people who might not qualify for such clearances to look to illegal means to cross borders, such as forged or counterfeit travel and identity documents. This combination, of a continued lack of standardization of identity documents across countries and the simple ways in which these documents could be altered and misused, led to inefficient and ineffective passport control. These checks often resulted in long delays and allowed a range of opportunities for inadmissible persons to illegally enter other states.

In the 1970s, the International Civil Aviation Organization (ICAO), with its membership of 192 states, took over responsibility for the development of global standard specifications for passports and travel documents. The ICAO's Technical Advisory Group (TAG) on Machine Readable Travel Documents explored the development of a machine-assisted international passport inspection standard to assist passport control officials with the verification of passenger identity, and in the examination and registration of passport data by computer. The work was delegated by the TAG to its New Technologies Working Group. This group consisted of international technical experts, government representatives from border control agencies, travel document issuing authorities and representatives of the International Organization for Standardization.

The work of the group led to recommended standards for content and format of travel document holders' data. It also resulted in cost-effective and reliable machine-readable technology in the form of optical character recognition, which could be used to scan and encode information from a new machine-readable zone in passport documents. This zone provided information such as a person's name, nationality, and

Figure 1.1 Examples of passports from the early twentieth century.

Source: Images retrieved from Fram Museum (top) and Pixabay (bottom).

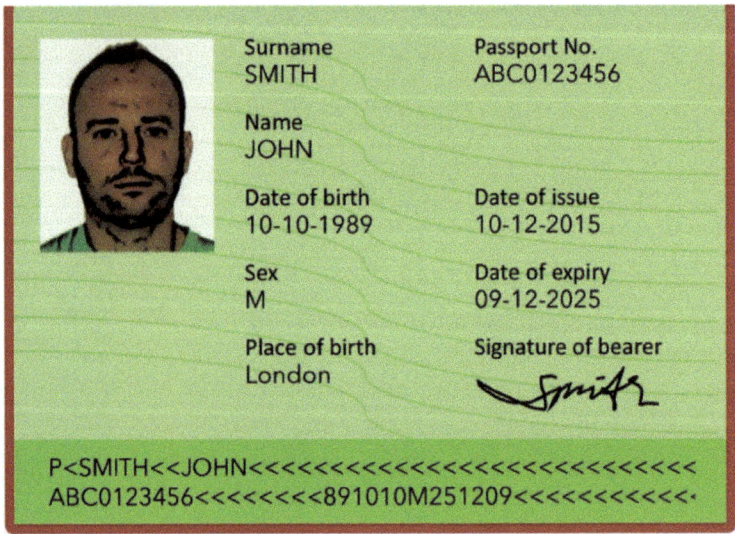

Figure 1.2 An illustration of a passport with a machine-readable zone at the bottom of the document.

passport number. Machine reading of this information enabled the more accurate and faster processing of passports than human operators could support, and faster entry of a traveller's data for comparison against person watchlists and immigration databases. The standardized format and layout of these machine-readable travel documents would also mean that the documents of all complying states could be easily recognized, read, and verified by properly trained and equipped passport control officials anywhere in the world. An illustration of a machine-readable passport is provided in Figure 1.2.

An international specification for modern passports was finally agreed and a manual of guidance material for states was published by the ICAO in 1980 as the first edition of *Document 9303*. This content evolved over subsequent years into a three-part reference covering specifications and standards for machine-readable passports (Part 1), visas (Part 2), and other travel documents (Part 3)[1], including those in card format. Over the years since, these three parts of *Document 9303* have been reviewed and revised on a number of occasions to reflect both changes in member states' needs and improvements in secure document technology. In 2006, Part 1 was split into two further volumes for standard specifications and to cover the addition of specifications for biometric e-Passports. This new type of passport resembles the traditional passport format physically, but contains embedded electronic microprocessor chips with information to authenticate the identity of the passport holder, such as a digital variant of the passport photograph, the holder's name, and date of birth.

---

[1] ICAO (International Civil Aviation Organization) (2015). *Doc 9303. Machine readable travel documents*, 7th edn. Available at: https://www.icao.int/publications/Documents/9303_p3_cons_en.pdf (accessed 4 May 2020).

1.1.2 Document Security Standards

The ICAO recognized the criminal and national security threats posed by the abuse of travel documents. Therefore, minimum specifications were built into the *Document 9303* standards to cover the physical security of new travel documents. This involved the incorporation of high-security features that could be checked and tested by properly trained border control officials, while at the same time frustrating forgers or counterfeiters attempting to compromise documents. Security features recommended for passports ranged from high-quality paper incorporating intricate watermarks produced by high-security paper manufacturers to sophisticated printing techniques provided by secure government-approved printing works that were not available to non-government purchasers. Many of the recommended security features were deliberately designed to be read and tested using either vision or touch, with the minimum amount of basic equipment required by properly trained passport control officials. Such equipment included handheld magnifiers and ultraviolet scanners that could be used in operational passport control situations, and skills such as holding a document up to ordinary white light to check for features such as watermarks.

While these specifications were designed and implemented to prevent the forging and counterfeiting of travel documents, the ICAO became concerned in the 1990s that *genuine* documents could also be used for fraudulent purposes. This was because, while machine readers verified the contents of the printed machine-readable zone in travel documents, this process could not confirm that the document concerned was properly issued to the person presenting it. Stolen blank documents, fraudulently made to look official, could deceive the conventional document-reading devices and border control officials. Identity theft at the passport-issuing stage could also be used to acquire a clean passport fraudulently—for example, by submitting a photograph of a person other than the existing holder during document renewal. This could allow documented criminals to acquire a clean passport that would allow them to travel without raising alarm. And genuine documents presented by impostors, who are of similar appearance to the passport holder, could be used to pass through border control.

Consequently, the ICAO began to look at new technologies that could provide additional layers to assist the document security and verification process. The ICAO's New Technologies Working Group started to consider the technical feasibility of introducing biometric technology into travel documents. Suitable biometric identifiers that were looked at for use in future e-Passports included fingerprints and iris biometrics. After in-depth research into the various technologies, facial recognition was selected as the designated mandatory biometric system for e-Passports. Specifications for these biometric systems were completed in 2006, with the introduction of standards for new e-Travel documentation and the production of the first e-Passports. In addition to traditional facial identification by passport control officers, current e-Passports can be used for passenger identification by using facial recognition technology to verify a traveller's identity against the electronic facial image stored in the chip of the biometric passport.

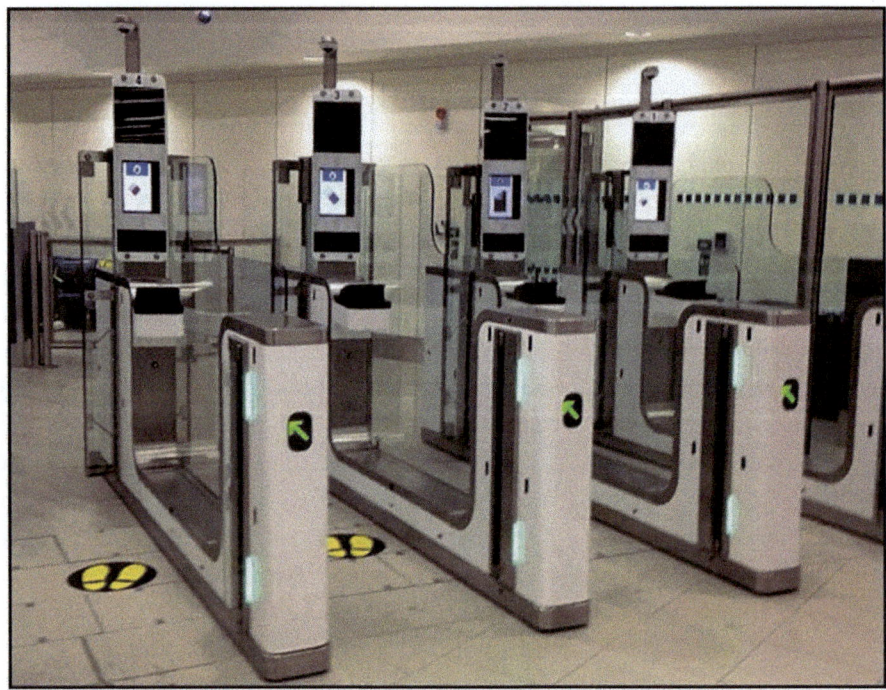

Figure 1.3 Illustration of an Automatic Border Control Point at a UK airport.
Source: Elliott Killingbeck / CC BY-SA (https://creativecommons.org/licenses/by-sa/3.0). Adapted by Markus Bindemann from https://commons.wikimedia.org/wiki/File:GAT_South_eGates.JPG.

Travellers pass through *Automatic Border Control systems*—commonly referred to as 'e-Gates'—that capture their facial image and match it to the one contained in their passport with sophisticated algorithms (see Noyes & Hill, this volume). An example of an Automatic Border Control point is provided in Figure 1.3.

1.1.3 The Current Situation with e-Passports

The intention of the ICAO was to provide a globally interoperable passport examination and verification system. Having achieved the technical specifications for this, the problems then faced by the ICAO and its member states were the uptake of the passport specifications and the widespread deployment of the requisite technical tools, such as computer-assisted passport readers. One of the most significant barriers to uptake was the higher cost of producing the new e-Passports compared with the previous non-chip passports. This meant that governments either had to increase charges for passport applications and renewals or subsidize those costs with public funds. States also had to fund the cost of installing machine readers for e-Passports at control points and of training passport control officers in the use of the new equipment. In addition, chip and reader technology was still new and developing. Because of these challenges, the ICAO expected the transition to e-Passport biometric verification readers to take many years.

The uptake of ICAO specification e-Passports is now improving rapidly. In 2014, more than 100 countries were issuing chip-based ICAO specification passports and more than 500 million e-Passports were in circulation. The ICAO has continued to lead in the promotion of e-Passport issuing by states and the introduction of e-Passport reading capabilities at border controls. In 2013, it launched the Traveller Identification Programme strategy. The aim of this was to provide an international framework for the production and deployment of e-Passports by states. The ICAO has carried this work forward by organizing international workshops and seminars to cover all technical issues involved with e-Passports, such as the systems required for their introduction, security and checking at borders, and guidance in important related issues such as passport application processes and civil registration procedures.

Despite much progress in the implementation of e-Passport and Automated Border Control technology, checking times to this day remain challenging in meeting the need for rapid processing of passengers through busy airports. Further, the levels of false acceptances of fraudulent travel documents and false rejection of legitimate documents still mean that automated systems have a less than 100% success rate, and require monitoring by skilled officers to deter and prevent illegal passage through passport control. In addition, if a genuine chip in an e-Passport fails to read, other than due to malicious damage, then the passport remains valid for travel, as well as for certifying the identity and nationality of the holder. In such circumstances, control officials rely on conventional physical document security safeguards and personal face-checking identity verification skills to confirm the veracity of personal data and the entitlement of the person presenting the document to hold it. Furthermore, whereas facial recognition technology continues to develop rapidly, technological solutions to determine the *intentions* of a traveller do not form part of the passport control specification at Automated Border Control points. The examination skills of properly trained and skilled passport personnel therefore continue to remain essential.

1.2 Threats to Passport Control

Passport or immigration controls, most especially at airports, continue to be vital to the defence of security, the way of life, and the economies of all states. Given the state of the world in the twenty-first century of globalization and ease of international travel and communication, states' passport controls need to protect citizens from illegal immigration and, more importantly, from internationally organized groups wishing to conduct cross-border criminal activity. In addition, and most significantly, states face a constant and high-level threat of international acts of terrorism and cross-border travel by persons encouraging, or wishing to carry out, terrorist atrocities against innocent people. It remains necessary and of vital importance to ensure that resources are available within border control agencies to meet and combat the persistent and increasing threats being faced at passport control.

The most significant trend in document abuse in many Western countries in recent years has been a marked *decline* in the numbers of false documents detected at
the border. Detection rates at United Kingdom border controls in 2008, for example,
were barely a third of the numbers of 2004 and there has been a continued decline since.
There are numerous reasons for this. Increased detection of document abuse abroad
before passengers embark for the UK, thanks to a network of airline and immigration
liaison officers working closely with carriers and control authorities in source or transit
countries, has led to thousands of inadequately or improperly documented persons
being denied boarding annually. The increasing use of international standard machine-
readable travel documents and the willingness to use more sophisticated and varied
high-quality security features in documents has presented serious challenges to forgers
and counterfeiters. This has been recognized by many of the organized criminal groups
responsible for the vast majority of document fraud, and has created a shift away from
forged and counterfeit documents towards the use of genuine documents by impostors.

1.2.1 The Problem of Impostors

The use of documents by impostors, or look-alikes, is one of the simplest methods of
passport fraud. An impostor will simply attempt to pass inspection at passport control by presenting a genuine, unaltered document issued to someone similar in facial
appearance, and pretend to be that person to deceive the control officer. Impostors attempt to conceal their true identities and nationalities for a variety of reasons. These
include adverse travel or immigration histories or a criminal record. They might also
want to use the real passport holder's document to avoid a visa requirement or because
it provides a favourable immigration status into the target state for entry. Finally, they
may seek to avoid detection to engage in criminal or terrorism-related activities.

Using the passport of another person as an impostor is a cheaper and lower-risk alternative to high-cost forgery factories using expensive skilled forgers and high-tech
printing and computer equipment. Furthermore, impostors are problematic for passport control because this type of fraud is difficult to detect and requires a high level
of skill and professionalism in the examining officer. If a document is unaltered, then
the examining officer risks facing legal action for wrongful arrest and detention if evidence that the person presenting the document is not the rightful holder cannot be
produced.

In recent years, impostors have represented one of the fastest growing and most serious methods of fraud involving passports and identity and travel documents. The extent of the problem can be demonstrated by the statistics from a number of countries.
In the UK, for example, impostors accounted for 24% of all cases of travel document
abuse detected at the border in 2005. By 2009, this figure had risen to 37% and it has
since exceeded 50%. The United States of America recently estimated that impostors
represented 80% to 85% of all fraudulent document intercepts at its borders. This is not
a problem confined to Western countries. Impostors now constitute one of the biggest

immigration control threats at third-world airports, particularly where passengers are embarking for Western countries.

1.2.2 A Real-World Example of Impostors: Flight MH370

A widely reported example of identity impostors at passport control is the case of Malaysian Airlines flight MH370.[2] On 8 March 2014, this flight departed from Kuala Lumpur International Airport in Malaysia with 227 passengers and 12 crew on board to Beijing Capital International Airport in China. Last communications with the aircraft occurred 38 minutes after take-off. Thereafter, the plane deviated from its flight path and was tracked by military radar for another hour before disappearing over the Indian Ocean. A large-scale search for the aircraft was unsuccessful, but debris from the plane washed ashore in the Western Indian Ocean during 2015.

Following the mysterious disappearance of the aircraft, the BBC reported that investigators had discovered that two passengers had boarded flight MH370 with stolen passports. The passengers, who were both Iranian, had used passports stolen in Thailand. One of these belonged to an Australian and the other to an Austrian man. The Iranians had not been properly checked before boarding the Malaysian flight and were bound for Europe, where it is believed they sought to apply for asylum.

Border security officials and airline staff had clearly failed to detect these identity impostors at passport control. In addition, passport nationality and number details for both the stolen passports had been reported and placed on the Interpol Stolen and Lost Travel Documents database but airline staff had not made the necessary checks that would have identified them. The Interpol database had been established in 2001 and, by 2014, held details of more than 40 million records of lost or stolen passports. The database is available to all of the 190 member states of Interpol, but at that time (2014) only three states—the USA, UK, and the United Arab Emirates—were systematically searching it at passport control points.

1.2.3 Acquisition of Documents by Impostors

The tragedy of flight MH370 provides a poignant example of the threat of identity impostors, demonstrating that it is possible for several to board the same plane. In turn, such cases raise questions about the process by which identity documents can be acquired for such criminal use, and which requirements they must meet.

Inevitably, the identity documents employed by impostors must provide a reasonable match to their own profile. Thus, the original holder should be of the same sex as the impostor, and should also approximate them in terms of ethnicity, age, and general appearance. The identity document must also be suitable for the purpose required by

---

[2] https://www.bbc.co.uk/news/world-asia-26531175 (accessed 10 April 2020).

the impostor—for example, by belonging to a nationality that enables the impostor to pass through control points without raising undue suspicion. The most favoured documents are those that are readily accepted in the end destination state without undue scrutiny and without the necessity of the document holder requiring to obtain a visa prior to travel.

In the UK, police detected a number of major cases where organized criminals targeted burglaries at properties occupied by persons who possessed passports or other travel or identity documents that matched the profiles of the intended eventual impostors. Another classic example of such impostor identity fraud is when passports or travel documents are passed on from one family member to another. This strategy may prove particularly effective in cases where one family member has managed to gain immigration status or citizenship of the desired destination state. That person's documents can then be sold or passed on to another, similar-looking family member. In a situation such as this, the person allowing their document to be used by another will invariably not declare the document to be lost or stolen until after the impostor has travelled and gained entry to the target destination. As a result, the misused document will not appear on databases of lost or stolen documents in time to enable it to be intercepted at passport control.

An alternative route for impostors to acquire the identity documents of another person is at the passport-issuance stage, by submitting bogus applications for a passport in the identity of a genuine citizen of a country. These criminal activities are at further risk of going undetected if supported by corrupt passport-issuance staff. The authorities must therefore vet all employees carefully and install secure administrative procedures to combat risks associated with staff corruption. The threat posed as a result of the successful impersonation at the document-issuing stage is the most serious of all, because it enables the impostor to obtain a document that then actually contains their biometric data. Consequently, the fraudulent use of these documents will be impossible to detect even by biometrics verification.

1.2.4 The Human Observer and Impostor Detection

To operate passport control efficiently and effectively, and to combat travel document abuse, the UK has identified two key areas as part of its strategic and structural approach. These are professionally skilled immigration control officers and technology. Passport control officers carry out routine frontline control procedures, which should lead to impostors being detected. If the identity document presented by a traveller is an ICAO standard machine-readable travel document and an appropriate reader for this type of document is available, then the control officer checks whether the document scans properly and is the subject of an intelligence alert. Many impostors will try and use documents that are on watchlist databases such as the Interpol International Stolen and Lost Travel Documents database, which can be checked within seconds at the start of a border control examination. It is vital, therefore, that states secure access to such databases at the frontline control if any document fraud, let alone the threat posed by impostors, is to be tackled. For wider effectiveness, frontline database checks of intelligence watchlists require that integration of many databases is possible. This necessitates a two-way process of supplying as well as accessing data, as well as cooperation *between* states' organizations to ensure that information is exchanged securely and in formats that meet national and international privacy and data protection laws.

Alongside these checks, border control officials must also conduct a personal *face-matching* check to compare the image on the document with the person presenting it. By scanning the passport, the officer will have access on a computer screen to the image captured in the passport chip. The officer will then manually compare this image with the passport biodata page image in the document he is holding and with the passenger standing in front of them. These images should be identical. When undertaking a systematic facial comparison of the passenger to the passport image, the officer should compare the shapes and positions of the face, chin, lips, eyes, and nose displayed in the passport image with those of the person presenting the document.

A careful facial comparison following a systematic process can be carried out in a matter of seconds, while asking the passenger a few basic questions. These can also help to determine whether the passenger matches the biographical data and nationality displayed in the passport. The questioning skills of border control officials are of particular importance for the detection of impostors who have acquired documents fraudulently at the issuance stage. At passport control or other security control points, such fraud will only be successfully detected by access to and use of intelligence data, and by the professional skills of highly trained and experienced control staff in determining that the person presenting the document does not match the profile given by the document. For example, the holder can be demonstrated not to be a national of the country issuing the passport.

In addition to the long-standing passport control checks by border control officials, an alternative route to person identification is now becoming widespread through new technology. If a presented passport document is an ICAO specification e-Passport, then the passenger can be checked through the Automated Border Control system. In this system, the stored facial image in the chip is biometrically compared by face recognition algorithms with a live image of the person presenting the document to an e-Gate. In the case of an impostor, the person presenting the e-Passport should fail this biometrics check. Automated Border Control systems are now widely in use at major airports but are not infallible (see Noyes & Hill, this volume). As many travellers have discovered when attempting to clear passport control, these systems frequently produce false rejections due to technical failure to read a document or correctly match the stored biometric face data in the passport to its owner. Such technical failure can occur if passengers present their passports or themselves incorrectly in accordance with the Automated Border Control machine-reading requirements—for example, by failing to face directly forward, or without a neutral facial expression, or by partially occluding the face with glasses, scarves, or hats.

Despite the development of face recognition capabilities at Automated Border Control points, it is notable that this process remains supervised by border control officers rather than fully automated for determining the identity of document holders. Passport officers at control stations behind e-Gates continue to check that the image captured by the camera matches the one on each traveller's passport. In addition, in the event of a failure to accept a passenger at an Automated Border Control point, the passenger is unable to proceed through the e-Gate and is redirected to a manned passport control point for examination. The passport control officer will then carry out checks using machine document readers and scanners, and will personally check the passenger against the passport image. Thus, even at Automated Border Control points, passport control officers retain ultimate responsibility for verifying the identity of the person presenting the passport and for determining whether they are entitled to be granted entry to the state concerned.

1.2.5 Selection, Training, and Monitoring of Passport Control Staff

Considering the central role that human operators continue to play to verify travellers' identities at passport control, it is essential that states recognize the need for effective personnel selection, training, and monitoring of performance. In addition, checking individual passengers and their supporting travel documentation with professional skilled staff is the only effective way of properly determining intentions and bona fides. Human observers also play a vital role in identifying new or growing threats against immigration controls.

Passport control officers are required to be intelligent and generally expected to be educated to degree level. They must also possess good interpersonal and communication skills, and be able to interface with the travelling public in the crowded, often stressful conditions of immigration control points in busy international airports. Ideally, they should have experience in communicating with and understanding people from a range of ethnic and cultural backgrounds, and have a working knowledge of one or more foreign languages. Selected applicants for passport control staff who meet these initial criteria are then required to pass the scrutiny interview boards, which will include senior experienced passport control managers, before achieving selection.

Successful applicants will then attend initial training, extending to several weeks, when they will be tutored in the immigration law and rules of the state, and how these regulations are to be used by passport control officers. The training will also incorporate development of interviewing skills, and a range of passenger assessment and analysis skills. Skills will also be taught in travel document security and document fraud detection sufficient for frontline control purposes. Trainees will be tested and their progress reviewed to ensure that they meet the important qualities of frontline staff, who are the first members of officialdom of state that passengers will encounter. As such, it is important that they will operate a firm but fair immigration control under the laws of the state irrespective of gender, sexual orientation, ethnic background, or creed of passengers.

Following initial training, new recruits will be posted to their destination ports of entry. There they will be mentored by senior, experienced officers on a one-to-one basis until they are deemed by local managers to have sufficient skills and competence to examine passengers. All passport control staff always work under the supervision of senior managers, who are constantly present at passport control to ensure that security procedures are followed correctly and that high standards of customer service are being provided. The officers are also monitored to ensure that their competence and skill levels are meeting required legal and ethical standards. Passport control staff are subject to regular one-to-one reviews with line managers to discuss their performance and professional progress. Managers look for further training needs to meet any weaknesses or to encourage career development by acquisition of additional specific skills, such as in-depth suspect document examination.

In times of economic constraint, as has been deemed necessary in the UK and many other countries since the 2008 financial crisis, there can be a temptation by governments to scale back training. This is regarded by operational passport control staff as false economy because regular training programmes are required to develop and maintain high levels of professional expertise to ensure effective control operations and to stay ahead of those carrying out fraud.

1.3 Summary

Global phenomena, such as mass migration and the expansion of affordable air travel, have provided a crucial impetus for the creation of modern-day passport and travel documents. The ICAO has held a key role in this work by developing internationally interoperable standards and the technology to process these documents. Current identity documents are sophisticated and highly secure, enabling fast machine reading of passenger information and the increasingly more widespread application of automated face recognition technology at airports and border control points. These developments have led to the creation of travel documents that can be issued and processed globally by internationally recognized states, and have made it very difficult for people with criminal intentions to forge and counterfeit passports and travel documents, leading to a marked decline in the detection of false documents at borders.

At the same time, a new security threat has emerged in the form of identity impostors, who use unaltered travel documents of someone similar in appearance to pass inspection at passport control. These impostors are problematic for passport control because this type of fraud is difficult to detect. Border control officers are central to impostor detection by carrying out routine frontline control procedures, such as document scans, checking of watchlists and security databases, and the facial identity comparison of the passenger to the passport image. Skilled and experienced control staff can also apply intelligent questioning in an effort to determine whether the person presenting a document is the rightful holder. These identification processes have changed in recent years with the widespread introduction of facial recognition technology at Automated Border Control points. However, even when automatic face recognition is used, this process remains supervised by border control officers. Thus, border security personnel remain central to establishing the identity and nationality of travellers, and hence their eligibility for entry to or exit from states.

Author's Note

The contents of this chapter are based on extensive occupational experience by the author in the field of airport security, passport control, and document fraud, at a national and international level.

2

Factors Limiting Face Matching at Passport Control and in Police Investigations

Matthew C. Fysh

2.1 Introduction

Face matching refers to the process of comparing two faces that are unfamiliar to the viewer to establish whether they depict the same person or different people (Fysh & Bindemann, 2017a; Johnston & Bindemann, 2013). This task has been studied extensively due to its practical importance in applied settings. In airports, banks, and supermarkets, for example, a comparison between a live person and a photographic document often comprises the principle means of establishing identity. In these settings, a key challenge is to ensure that the document bearer corresponds to the person depicted in the photograph. This is particularly important for passport control, where the occurrence of impostors—people who attempt to illegally enter a country by using somebody else's passport—represents a primary concern (see Stevens, 2012; Stevens, this volume). Moreover, recent reports of impostors attempting to evade detection at passport control indicate that the identification of these individuals represents an ongoing challenge for modern security (Richards, 2018). Yet, because of challenges associated with effectively monitoring impostor prevalence, the true scale of this problem is difficult to reliably estimate. In addition to passport control, face matching is also conducted in police settings. For instance, forensic facial examiners often study surveillance footage alongside a photograph of a suspect to establish their involvement in a crime, or to verify their innocence (see Moreton, this volume; see also Mileva & Burton, 2019; Robertson et al., 2016).

These real-world applications of face matching might lead one to expect that this is a reliable and accurate process. Yet, the study of this task within experimental settings suggests otherwise. In these studies, observers typically view two simultaneously presented photographs of unfamiliar faces (see Figure 2.1 for an example), and decide whether these depict the same person (an identity *match*) or different individuals (a *mismatch*). These studies measure accuracy on a scale from 50% (chance performance) to 100% (ceiling), and consistently report a surprising number of errors for this task. For instance, when examining high-quality images of the same person that were taken on the same day, observers mistakenly identified around 20% of these as separate identities (Burton et al., 2010). Comparable error rates are observed on mismatch trials, whereby observers study high-quality images of two different individuals and falsely

Matthew C. Fysh, *Factors Limiting Face Matching at Passport Control and in Police Investigations* In: *Forensic Face Matching.* Edited by: Markus Bindemann, Oxford University Press (2021). © Oxford University Press. DOI: 10.1093/oso/9780198837749.003.0002.

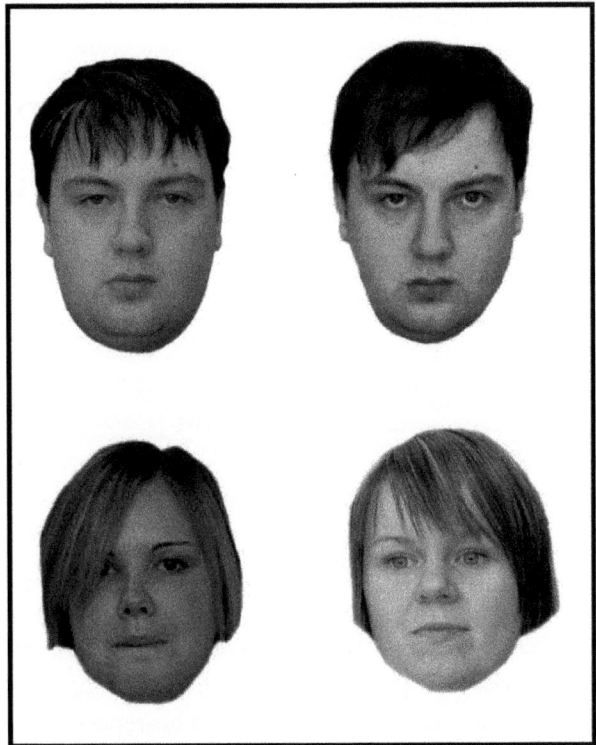

Figure 2.1 An example match (top) and mismatch (bottom) from the Glasgow Face Matching Test.

Source: Reproduced from the 'Glasgow Unfamiliar Face Database', http://www.facevar.com/glasgow-unfamiliar-face-database. Copyright © 2010, A. Mike Burton.

classify around 20% of these as the same person (Bindemann et al., 2010). In other words, even under conditions that are designed to maximize accuracy in face matching, observers respond incorrectly on one in every five instances.

Why do such errors occur? One explanation is that face-matching performance is contingent upon the quantity and quality of visual information that is available within to-be-compared faces (see Burton, 2013; Fysh & Bindemann, 2017a; Jenkins & Burton, 2011). A key challenge for researchers is therefore to understand the factors that limit the availability of such identity-relevant information within to-be-matched faces by investigating these in experimental settings in order to subsequently overcome these obstacles in the real world.

2.2 Face Identity Matching in the Real World

The matching of unfamiliar faces in real-world settings is accompanied by a number of practical challenges that vary from one context to another (Robertson et al., 2015, 2019). For instance, matching faces at passport control involves comparing a live individual to a small passport photograph that could have been acquired up to 10 years earlier (Jenkins et al., 2011). The difficulty of this process is likely to be further compounded by factors such as time pressure (Bindemann et al., 2016; Fysh & Bindemann, 2017b) and sophisticated impersonation attempts from impostors (Noyes & Jenkins, 2019). By contrast, forensic examiners in police settings often attempt to establish the identity of a suspect based on a comparison between a high-quality photograph and images or video clips retrieved from closed-circuit television (CCTV) that place the suspect at the scene of a crime. Such material is understood to suffer from low image quality, as well as partial lighting and problematic viewing angles (e.g., Burton et al., 1999; Mileva & Burton, 2019).

These practical challenges to face matching in applied settings have been explored extensively under laboratory conditions. A key aim of these studies is to understand which factors impose limits on face-matching accuracy, and to explore strategies for overcoming the obstacles that such limits present. The remainder of this chapter will review the factors that are likely to influence face matching in the real-world contexts of passport control and police settings. Table 2.1 provides an at-a-glance reference guide for these factors, and indicates whether each given factor is likely to influence face matching in one of these settings or both. In the next section, the factors that are relevant to face matching at passport control are reviewed first.

2.3 Matching Faces at Passport Control

In border security settings, passport officers visually compare a live individual to a passport photograph. Because passports remain valid for up to 10 years, a person's passport photograph can fail to incorporate important variations in their appearance that occur naturally over time, such as changes in hairstyle, weight, and complexion (Jenkins et al., 2011). Moreover, this task must be performed in rapid succession for hundreds of passengers, some of whom might be impostors who have altered their appearance to more closely resemble that of the person whose passport they have acquired (Noyes & Jenkins, 2019; Sanders et al., 2017). As a consequence, face matching at passport control is subject to a range of factors that reduce the degree of visual correspondence between a traveller and their photograph, or prevent personnel from acquiring sufficient visual data to accurately match faces to passport photographs. These factors are reviewed below.

2.3.1 Comparing Photographs to People

When studying face matching in experimental settings, participants typically compare two face *photographs* to one another (Burton et al., 2010). By contrast, person identification in airports entails live-to-photo matching—that is, a comparison between a live person's face and a passport photograph. The dynamic visual information afforded

Table 2.1 An at-a-glance reference guide

Factor	Relevant Studies	Relevant Setting
Passenger volume and time pressure	Bindemann et al. (2016) Fysh & Bindemann (2017b) Özbek & Bindemann (2011)	👮
Impersonation attempts	Noyes & Jenkins (2019) Robertson et al. (2018) Sanders et al. (2017)	👮
Impostor frequency	Bindemann et al. (2010) Papesh & Goldinger (2014) Papesh et al. (2018)	👮
Changes in appearance over time	Bindemann & Sandford (2011) Jenkins et al. (2011) Megreya et al. (2013)	👮 📹
Live-to-photo comparison	Kemp et al. (1997) Megreya & Burton (2008) Ritchie et al. (2020)	👮 📹
Expression	Bruce et al. (1999) Chen et al. (2011) Mileva & Burton (2019)	👮 📹
Camera lens distortion	Noyes & Jenkins (2017)	👮 📹
Changes in lighting	Hill & Bruce (1996) Liu et al. (2013)	📹
Image quality	Bindemann et al. (2013) Henderson et al. (2001) Ritchie et al. (2018)	📹
Changes in viewpoint	Estudillo & Bindemann (2014) Favelle et al. (2017) Hill & Bruce (1996)	📹
Disguise attempts	Davis & Valentine (2009) Meissner et al. (2013) Kramer & Ritchie (2016)	📹

Key:

👮 Factor is likely to influence face matching at passport control

📹 Factor is likely to influence face matching in police settings

Note: This table is not an exhaustive list of studies, but rather is simply intended to guide readers towards studies on some of the key factors that relate to matching faces in real-world settings. The right-hand column provides an indication of whether the factor in question is relevant to passport control, police settings, or both.

by a live person's face and body, such as motion, depth, and texture, might reasonably be presumed to offset some of the limitations within static face images (e.g., Knight & Johnston, 1997). Contrary to this expectation, however, numerous errors have been observed when a live person is compared with a photograph. This is observed irrespective of whether the task is performed by student participants (Megreya & Burton, 2008; Ritchie et al., 2020), passport officers (White, Kemp, Jenkins, Matheson, et al., 2014), or supermarket cashiers (Kemp et al., 1997), suggesting that substituting one photograph for a live person does not eliminate identification errors.

Direct comparisons between live-to-photo and photo-to-photo matching support this assertion, and also indicate that comparable error rates arise in both conditions. In one study, for instance, Megreya and Burton (2008) found that accuracy on mismatch trials deteriorated from 84%, when viewers matched pairs of face images, to 77%, when comparing a single face photograph to a live person. This reduction in mismatch accuracy coincided with a numerically small but significant increase in match accuracy from 85% in the photo-to-photo condition to 89% in the live-to-photo condition, indicating that the presence of a live individual might bias observers to erroneously perceive different individuals as the same person (see also Davis & Valentine, 2009). These findings converge with other studies that have attempted to establish whether substituting a live individual for close-up video footage of that person's face, for comparison with a facial image, can improve matching accuracy (see, e.g., Davis & Valentine, 2009; Lander et al., 2004). Converging with live-to-photo matching paradigms (e.g., Megreya & Burton, 2008), these studies also find that video-to-photo matching produces accuracy rates that are comparable to when both stimuli are photo-bound (Bruce et al., 1999), or that are even slightly worse (Lander et al., 2004). Together, these findings communicate that the additional information in dynamic faces is not directly useful for face matching.

The presence of a live person in face matching also allows observers to utilize information from the body. Studies have suggested that when the visual information within to-be-matched faces is particularly limited, observers may use information from the body to supplement identity decisions (Hahn et al., 2016; Rice, Phillips, & O'Toole, 2013; Rice, Phillips, Natu, et al., 2013). This was demonstrated in one study, for example, in which observers matched faces to videos of targets who were portrayed at different distances (Hahn et al., 2016). The findings revealed that, when targets were farthest away, accuracy benefitted most when observers' decisions were based on both the face and body, as opposed to the face or body alone. These results converge with another study, in which the inclusion of the body in identity photographs appeared to boost matching performance when processing highly dissimilar images of the same person, as well as highly similar images of different individuals (Rice, Phillips, Natu, et al., 2013). These studies therefore indicate that, when facial information is particularly limited, the body may be used to aid identification.

Taken together, the available literature implies that, when faces can be easily studied, the information supplied by a live face does not enhance face-matching accuracy (e.g., Megreya & Burton, 2008; Ritchie et al., 2020). On the other hand, information from the body may promote identification when information from the face is limited (Rice, Phillips, Natu, et al., 2013; Rice, Phillips, & O'Toole, 2013). One way to utilize these findings to reduce the likelihood of errors at passport control might therefore be to include the body in passport photographs, in order to increase the amount of person information that can be analysed to facilitate identification.

2.3.2 Changes in Appearance over Time

One of the key challenges for matching faces at passport control, but also in police settings, comprises the extent to which faces vary over time (Burton, 2013; Jenkins et al., 2011). As people age, for instance, skin elasticity decreases, while hair might thin, recede or lose colour. These variations in appearance, which typically occur over many years, coincide with changes that are more superficial in nature, such as variations in hairstyle, make-up, or glasses. Such variability represents a key challenge for person identification at passport control, given that passport photographs remain valid for up to 10 years in many countries and can thus fail to incorporate critical variations in a person's appearance that occur within this time frame (for an example, see Figure 2.2).

Laboratory experiments have demonstrated that this within-person variability substantially increases the difficulty of matching unfamiliar face photographs. In one study, accuracy deteriorated from around 90%, when comparing images of the same person that were taken on the same day, to around 70% when these were acquired several months apart (Megreya et al., 2013). Similar accuracy rates of around 66% are also observed for both match and mismatch trials when observers compare a high-quality digital face photograph captured under controlled conditions to a counterpart image that was taken a number of months earlier, and which was not constrained in terms of lighting, expression, or pose (Fysh & Bindemann, 2018). Still further errors are

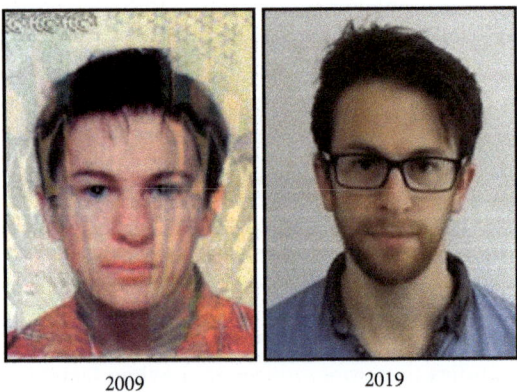

2009   2019

Figure 2.2 Passport photographs remain valid over a 10-year period, meaning that these can fail to accommodate changes in appearance that occur naturally over time.

Note: These are both images of Matthew C. Fysh. The left-hand image was obtained from his old and expired passport.

observed when comparing images of faces that were taken 24 to 26 years apart, whereby the mean accuracy rate for observers unfamiliar with the identities depicted was only 33% (Bruck et al., 1991). Together, these studies show that the natural changes in appearance that occur over time substantially increase the difficulty of face matching.

While it makes sense that variations in appearance as people age increase the difficulty of matching unfamiliar faces, there is evidence to suggest that this effect is not necessarily unitary across time. In one study, observers attempted to match a target face that was located within an array to one of three photo identification cards, of which one had been acquired 19 months prior to testing, whereas the other two depicted the target from three months prior to testing (Bindemann & Sandford, 2011). Interestingly, the 19-month-old ID card produced the highest accuracy rate of 67% compared to the second and third ID cards, for which accuracy was at 46% and 58%. This finding may seem counter-intuitive given that one might anticipate the lowest accuracy rate for the oldest image. On the other hand, these scores indicate instead that lengthening the time interval between images of the same person does not exert a linear effect on face-matching performance, and that the changes in appearance that occur over time can be superseded by other sources of noise, such as a change in pose, lighting, and expression (see also Jenkins et al., 2011).

At the same time, there is some evidence to suggest that such variability can also be harnessed to improve identification. For instance, Bindemann and Sandford (2011) found that, when participants viewed all three photo-ID cards simultaneously alongside the target face, accuracy improved to 85%. This multi-photo advantage has since been replicated (see Ritchie & Burton, 2017; White, Burton, et al., 2014), but only seems to emerge when same-face arrays consist of images that were acquired across several months or years, as opposed to images that were taken over several minutes (Ritchie & Burton, 2017). Given that most passports are now equipped with an electronic chip that holds a digital copy of the physical photograph, it should be possible to electronically store multiple images of the bearer as they age. Based on the available evidence (Bindemann & Sandford, 2011; Ritchie & Burton, 2017; White, Burton, et al., 2014), this approach might present a possible route to reducing identification errors at passport control.

2.3.3 Impersonation Attempts

While genuine passport bearers tend to become less similar to their passport photograph over time, identity impostors may attempt to minimize the likelihood of being detected by superficially altering their appearance to more closely resemble whomever they are impersonating. Such alterations may include changes to hairstyle and hair colour, as well as the addition or removal of facial paraphernalia and the application of make-up. One recent study explored the effects of impersonation on face matching by creating identity mismatches that comprised one individual attempting to resemble somebody else, whereby they were provided with a reference photograph depicting the target identity and were instructed to alter their appearance in such a way as to re-semble that person (Noyes & Jenkins, 2019). The results showed that mismatches based on impersonation attempts were more likely to be falsely accepted as identity matches, by around 8%, than when mismatches comprised randomly paired face images of the same sex. This effect was diminished but still emerged in a subsequent experiment when participants were warned about the disguise manipulation, suggesting that dis-guises are difficult to detect even when anticipated. These findings converge with an-other recent investigation in which mismatches were less likely to be detected if these stimuli were digitally altered to more closely resemble each other in terms of either hairstyle, distinctive features (i.e., scars and moles), or glasses (Wirth & Carbon, 2017). This effect was most pronounced for hairstyle, indicating that similarity of this feature particularly inflates the perception of similar identities.

Some identity impostors have also started resorting to more sophisticated methods of impersonation. One such method comprises the use of highly realistic silicone masks that are worn over the entire head and are crafted to resemble a specific person. Some recent studies have investigated the effectiveness of these masks at disguising identity (see Sanders & Jenkins, this volume; Sanders et al., 2017; Sanders & Jenkins, 2018). In one study, it was demonstrated that observers could not reliably distinguish a realistic mask within an array of real faces, and were poor at identifying if a live person was wearing such a mask even when viewed from the close distance of five metres (Sanders et al., 2017). Subsequent research has further demonstrated the difficulty of this task, but suggests also that considerable individual differences exist between observers in their ability to detect these masks, whereby some observers are able to identify that a person is wearing a mask with ceiling-level accuracy. This finding indicates that highly realistic masks do not fully eliminate the information that is present within faces, but that at the same time not all observers process this information effectively (Sanders & Jenkins, 2018).

Impersonation attempts have also been observed at the passport-issuance stage by using identity morphs to obtain a fraudulent passport (see Robertson et al., 2018, 2019). These morphs involve digitally fusing, or 'morphing', one person's face to re-semble another individual, while simultaneously resembling the original identity (see Figure 2.3). The final product is a face that is sufficiently similar to the existing passport holder to be accepted as a valid likeness at document renewal, while also being of suf-ficient resemblance to the impostor so that they can present the passport document at border control without being detected. Research has demonstrated the difficulty of detecting morphed identities. For instance, in one study, observers viewed pairs of faces that comprised either matches, mismatches, or identity morphs (see Robertson et al., 2017). This latter stimulus category consisted of a face image that was presented along-side an image of the same person but which had been morphed with a different person and should therefore be rejected. Accuracy on unaltered mismatch trials in this study was at 92%, indicating that observers were generally good at distinguishing different identities. However, these observers also accepted 68% of identity morphs, signalling that this new approach to impersonation might be particularly challenging to detect.

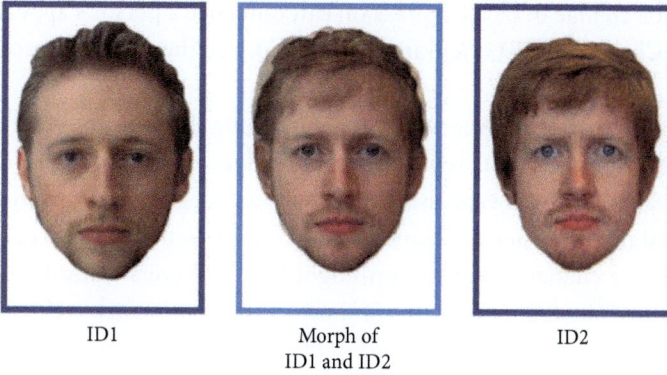

| ID1 | Morph of ID1 and ID2 | ID2 |

Figure 2.3 Two images of different people (left and right), and a facial morph (middle) depicting how these would look when combined.

Source: Adapted from Robertson et al. (2017) 'Fraudulent ID using face morphs: Experiments on human and automatic recognition', *PLoS ONE*, *12*(3), e0173319, Figure 2. https://doi.org/10.1371/journal.pone.0173319 © 2017 Robertson et al.

Performance improved dramatically when observers were informed in advance that some images might comprise morphs of separate identities, with accuracy increasing to 79%. Converging with this finding, a more recent study demonstrated that training observers with morph exemplars and trial-by-trial feedback dramatically improved morph detection accuracy, from 45% to 79% (Robertson et al., 2018), suggesting that errors can also be substantially reduced through training.

Overall, these findings demonstrate how impersonation attempts at passport control increase the difficulty of detecting identity mismatches. Modest increments in error rates are observed following superficial attempts to impersonate somebody different by changing one's hair, make-up, and facial attire (Noyes & Jenkins, 2019; Wirth & Carbon, 2017). More sophisticated impersonation attempts, via realistic facial masks (Sanders et al., 2017) and facial morphs (Robertson et al., 2018), promote higher error rates still. Evidence suggests that these errors might be offset through personnel selection and training (Robertson et al., 2018), although further research is necessary to fully understand how mismatch detection under such conditions can be optimized.

2.3.4 Expression

Most passport applications require applicants to adopt a neutral expression in their photograph (Australian Passport Office, 2019; Her Majesty's Passport Office, 2011). The ubiquity of this requirement might suggest that neutral expressions are easier to match than when people are smiling or frowning. In fact, this is asserted directly by the Australian Passport Office in their guidelines for submitting a passport photograph (Australian Passport Office, 2019). Studies that have investigated this assertion confirm that a change in facial expression can influence a person's appearance (Bruce et al., 1999; Chen et al., 2011; Jenkins et al., 2011). Yet, the precise nature of this effect is unclear.

In one study, observers were worse at determining that a smiling unfamiliar target face was absent from a concurrent array of neutral faces, compared to when the target was also bearing a neutral expression. However, a change in expression from smiling to neutral did not influence performance on target-present arrays (Bruce et al., 1999), indicating that a change in expression might lead observers towards conflating separate identities. Converging with this finding, subsequent work has demonstrated that a change in facial expression can reduce matching accuracy. For instance, Chen et al. (2011) found that sequentially presented faces were matched more accurately when they displayed the same expression, regardless of the expression that was depicted. By contrast, matching the identities of faces with different emotional expressions reduced accuracy considerably, from around 90% when observers compared two disgusted faces, to around 76% when one of these faces was neutral. In addition, this effect was further exacerbated following a change in pose, suggesting that these separable factors can exert combined effects on performance.

More recently, research has shown that, when comparing simultaneously presented pairs of unfamiliar faces, accuracy improved by 9% on match and 7% on mismatch trials when observers studied two smiling instead of two neutral faces (Mileva & Burton, 2018). However, this advantage seemed to be based on open-mouth as opposed to closed-mouth smiles. In addition, an accuracy enhancement of around 20% was observed on match, but not mismatch, trials when only the lower face regions were visible. These findings may therefore be interpreted as signifying that open-mouth smiles amplify specific identity characteristics that occur within faces (see also Jenkins et al., 2011), making it easier to decide that images portray the same person, as well as enhancing the detection of impostors.

Overall, the available research therefore suggests that the current requirement to hold a neutral expression in passport photographs might only be useful if this expression is matched by the bearer at the point of inspection (Chen et al., 2011). Moreover, a change in expression might increase the difficulty of detecting identity impostors (Bruce et al., 1999). On the other hand, if photograph requirements were altered to require applicants to smile, then possible gains in accuracy might be observed in practical settings (Mileva & Burton, 2018), although the true extent to which this factor interacts with other practical elements of the task remains to be seen.

2.3.5   Camera Lens Distortion

In the UK, passport photograph regulations require that the photograph is clear and in focus, but do not provide any indication of the distance from which photographs should be taken. Yet, research has found that this variable influences identity perception. These changes are characterized by an outwardly curved (i.e., convex) face when

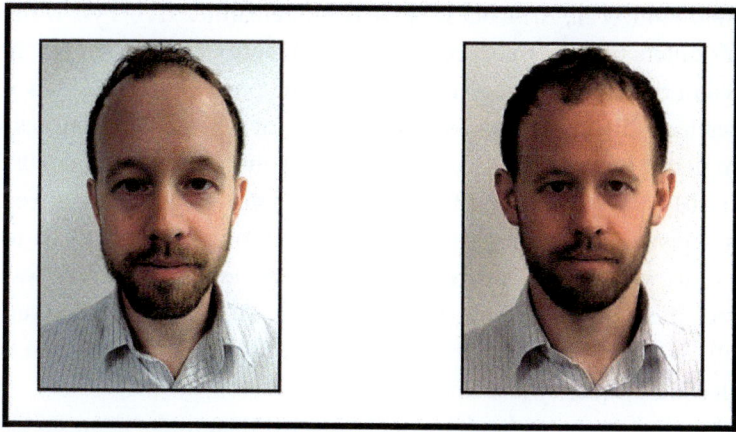

Figure 2.4 Two images of the same person taken a few seconds apart, but from near (left) and far (right) distances.

photographed from close distances (e.g., <1 metre), but a flatter facial surface when photographed from further away (see Figure 2.4).

In an investigation of how this influences identity matching, it was demonstrated that altering the distance from which unfamiliar targets were photographed produced a marked decrease in accuracy on match trials from 97%, when face images were acquired from the same distance, to 69%, when photographs were captured from different distances (Noyes & Jenkins, 2017). By contrast, accuracy on mismatch trials improved from 84% under same-distance conditions to 92% when the distance at which images were taken varied. These reductions in accuracy on match trials were observed alongside measurable differences between two images of the same person's face when photographed from near (0.32 metres) and far (2.70 metres) camera distances. A further experiment also indicated that these effects may be partially offset by reducing the size of face images that were taken from far away while maintaining the original size of faces that were photographed from close distances.

Considered together, these findings provide a basis for standardizing camera-to-subject distance for passport applications, which currently do not provide any strict guidelines on the distance from which subjects are photographed. This is particularly important when considering the extent to which accuracy on match trials suffered when subjects were photographed from close distances (Noyes & Jenkins, 2017). If such performance effects were to arise at passport control as a result of non-standardized camera-to-subject distances, then this would likely place greater demands on passport officers.

2.3.6 Impostor Frequency

Laboratory studies of face matching typically feature an equal number of match and mismatch trials (see, e.g., Bindemann et al., 2016; Burton et al., 2010; White, Kemp,

Jenkins, Matheson, et al., 2014, but see Fysh & Bindemann, 2017b; Fysh & Bindemann, 2018). This differs from passport control, where identity mismatches (i.e. impostors) typically comprise a very small percentage of to-be-processed individuals. Only very few studies have directly examined the question of whether mismatches are more difficult to detect when these occur infrequently (Bindemann et al., 2010; Papesh & Goldinger, 2014; Papesh et al., 2018). These studies reveal mixed findings. For instance, one study showed that, when participants were informed in advance as to whether impostor trials would be common or rare, the detection of such trials was comparable between these two conditions (Bindemann et al., 2010). This finding suggests that infrequently occurring mismatches are not more difficult to identify than when they occur with equal frequency to match trials.

However, more recent studies have demonstrated that, under some conditions, the frequency with which mismatches occur can have an impact on the accuracy with which observers are able to classify these trials (Papesh & Goldinger, 2014; Papesh et al., 2018). These studies show that, when observers are not informed as to whether mismatches are rare or common, but receive trial-by-trial feedback following each incorrect identification decision, mismatch accuracy declines considerably, from 77% under equal match–mismatch frequency to 48% when mismatches are rare (Papesh & Goldinger, 2014). However, one possible explanation for these differences in findings might be that the administration of trial-by-trial feedback in Papesh and Goldinger's (2014) study effectively encouraged a decline in the detection of mismatches when these occurred only infrequently, by reinforcing a response pattern that was dominated by one outcome—identity-match responses. In line with this reasoning, a recent investigation also demonstrated that, in the absence of trial-by-trial feedback, identification accuracy for infrequently occurring mismatches improves (Papesh et al., 2018).

In summary, the current research on the detection of infrequent mismatches indicates that, when observers are informed in advance, rare mismatches are still detected with similar accuracy rates to when mismatches are common (Bindemann et al., 2010). On the other hand, the administration of trial-by-trial feedback under low mismatch prevalence appears to compound the detection of impostors greatly (Papesh & Goldinger, 2014; Papesh et al., 2018). One question that arises then is whether passport control personnel might be administering such 'feedback' intrinsically, based on the assumptions that nearly all travellers will constitute identity matches and that, therefore, the overwhelming majority of match decisions must also be correct. If this were to be the case, then the frequency of mismatches might profoundly affect their detection in these security settings. The available evidence is still far too limited in scope to resolve such key issues, so these remain important topics for further research.

2.3.7 Passenger Volume and Time Pressure

When processing travellers at international borders, passport officers might only have a few seconds to compare a person to their photograph. This is due to the high volume of passengers who must often be processed within a very limited time frame (Home Affairs Committee, 2012). Studies suggest that restricting the duration for which faces can be viewed in matching tasks reduces accuracy considerably, with noticeable drop-offs in performance occurring when fewer than two seconds are available per trial (Bindemann et al., 2010; O'Toole et al., 2007; Özbek & Bindemann, 2011). In addition, studies have shown that under more realistically challenging conditions, whereby observers must process a block of face-matching trials within a set time target, at least six to eight seconds must be available on average for face identification to reach typical (i.e., baseline) performance (Bindemann et al., 2016; Fysh & Bindemann, 2017b; Wirth & Carbon, 2017). Importantly, these studies also indicated that time pressure specifically has an impact on the detection of mismatches. Yet, it is not clear as to whether the sort of time advocated by these studies (i.e. six to eight seconds) is available for processing travellers in the field or, indeed, whether passport officers utilize this time effectively even if it *is* available.

Perhaps counter-intuitively, there is also evidence to suggest that additional time in face matching may not be beneficial to all observers. Student participants do not show performance differences between enforced viewing durations of three, six, or nine seconds, for example (White, Burton, et al., 2014). On the other hand, highly trained facial examiners show enhanced accuracy when permitted to view face stimuli for up to 30 seconds (White et al., 2015). Still higher rates of accuracy are observed when the time course for face matching approximates that which is available in police settings, which can encompass several months (see Phillips et al., 2018). While such time frames cannot be implemented at passport control, these findings advocate that, in police settings, fully utilizing the available time may represent a reliable route to minimizing identification errors.

Together, these studies provide compelling evidence that time pressure is likely to be detrimental to face-matching performance at passport control (Bindemann et al., 2016; Fysh & Bindemann, 2017b; Wirth & Carbon, 2017). This effect is closely related to the number of to-be-processed identities in that, as the volume of passengers increases, the available time to match each person to their passport photograph is reduced if time targets are to be met. Most importantly, these research findings suggest that pressure to meet time targets specifically reduces one's ability to distinguish mismatching identities, increasing the likelihood that impostors may go undetected (Fysh & Bindemann, 2017b). Finally, there is evidence to suggest that maximizing the available time to process faces enhances matching accuracy for select personnel who are trained to utilize this time effectively (Phillips et al., 2018; White et al., 2015).

2.4 Matching Faces in Police Settings

The previous section reviewed factors that limit the visual information within faces that are of particular relevance to passport control. However, face matching is also performed in police settings to identify suspects (see Moreton, this volume). This process

is often facilitated by comparing static images or brief video clips retrieved from surveillance footage that depict a target identity to a corresponding photograph of a suspect (e.g., Mileva & Burton, 2019). However, the quality of such footage is often limited
by factors such as low image resolution (Burton et al., 1999; Bindemann et al., 2013),
problematic lighting (Hill & Bruce, 1996), and the distance at which suspects are recorded (Hahn et al., 2016). At the same time, suspects may also attempt to disguise
their identity (Noyes & Jenkins, 2019), and avoid looking at the camera, thereby providing only partial facial views for analysis (Estudillo & Bindemann, 2014; Favelle et al.,
2017). The effects of these factors on face matching are reviewed below.

2.4.1 Image Quality

Surveillance footage is commonly utilized in police investigations to verify a person's
involvement in a crime. To accomplish this, facial examiners, who are specialists in
the analysis of facial images (see Moreton, this volume; White, Towler, & Kemp, this
volume), might compare a photograph of the suspected criminal identity to a static
frame from surveillance footage that provides a clear shot of the person's face. However,
such footage is often limited by low image resolution, which can result in images that
are pixelated—that is to say, images that appear 'blocky' (for an artificial rendition
of this effect, see Figure 2.5. See also Burton et al., 1999; Henderson et al., 2001, for
real-world examples). Studies investigating this aspect of surveillance footage consistently show that faces are considerably more difficult to match if one image is pixelated
(Bindemann et al., 2013; Henderson et al., 2001; Ritchie et al., 2018).

   In one study, participants compared a high-quality face photograph to a static face
image that had been extracted from heavily pixelated surveillance footage. Participants
in this study were able to match images of the same person with approximately 55%
accuracy, while accuracy for distinguishing different identities was around 73%
(Henderson et al., 2001). These levels of performance are comparable to those observed
in more recent work in which participants matched high-quality face photographs to

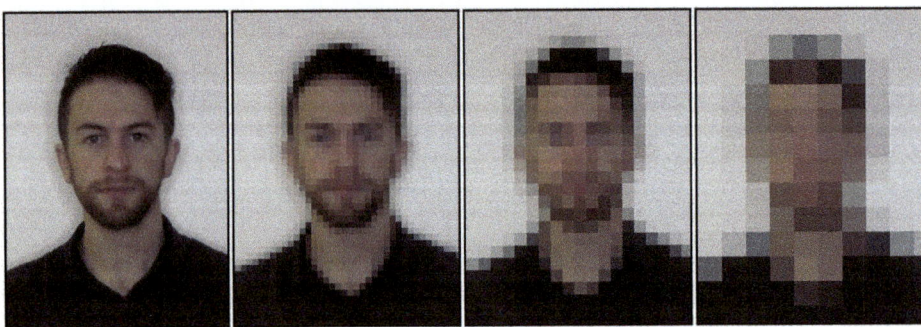

Figure 2.5 A high-quality face photograph followed by an example of light, moderate, and
heavy image pixelation.

low-quality images retrieved from drone footage (Bindemann et al., 2017) and corneal reflections (Jenkins & Kerr, 2013), demonstrating that facial matching is considerably more challenging when based on degraded material.

Other work has systematically manipulated the quality of face stimuli to understand how identification rates diminish as image pixelation increases. In one such study, accuracy was at 90% and 85% on match and mismatch trials respectively, when both face stimuli were presented in high resolution (Bindemann et al., 2013). Subsequently lowering the horizontal resolution of one face stimulus to 20, 14, and 8 pixels in width diminished accuracy on match trials to 66%, 59%, and 48%, respectively. On the other hand, accuracy on mismatch trials declined to around 60% across all pixelation conditions.

These findings imply that the identification of unfamiliar people in police settings using surveillance footage, which can be prone to these types of heavy degradation (see Burton et al., 1999; Henderson et al., 2001) is particularly difficult. However, some studies have indicated that it is possible to partially offset some of the performance limits imposed by pixelated face images. For instance, identification accuracy may be enhanced by either reducing the size of the pixelated image (Bindemann et al., 2013) or increasing the distance between the observer and the stimulus (Lander et al., 2001). These gains in accuracy may seem counter-intuitive when considering evidence that faces are more difficult to identify in video footage when viewed from further away, and become easier to identify as they move closer to the camera (Hahn et al., 2016). However, it has been demonstrated that blurring pixelated images smoothens the blocked nature of the representation and subsequently enhances the quality of the perceived image (Harmon & Julesz, 1973). Such a blurring effect can be superficially achieved by squinting at the image, but may also be accomplished by *decreasing* the size of the image or *increasing* the observer-to-image distance.

An alternative strategy to overcoming errors that derive from low image quality may be to generate an 'average' facial image, which is created by aggregating many different images of the same person. These facial averages effectively preserve the stable visual characteristics of a person's face, while eliminating 'noisy' aspects, such as a change in expression or lighting, which may vary from one image to the next (Burton et al., 2005). One recent study explored the question of whether facial averages might present a viable route to offsetting face-matching errors that derive from low image quality (Ritchie et al., 2018). In this study, an accuracy improvement of around 10% was observed on identity match trials when observers compared a high-quality face image to a facial average that was generated from multiple pixelated images. However, this approach did not improve performance on mismatch trials.

Together, these studies demonstrate that reductions in image quality reduce face-matching accuracy (Bindemann et al., 2013; Henderson et al., 2001). This effect seems to be particularly detrimental to performance on match trials as opposed to reducing accuracy generally, indicating that the loss of visual information specifically fosters dissimilarity between faces. In other words, observers are more likely to mistake images of the same person for two different people when the quality of images is compromised.

2.4.2 Lighting

Under natural viewing conditions, the angle from which faces are illuminated often varies depending on the time of day, as well as the presence of artificial lighting. This raises some potential challenges for matching the face of a suspect from a photograph or moving footage that was obtained under natural lighting to an evenly lit counter-part, given that changes in facial lighting can influence the proportion of a face that is visible. When a face is illuminated from below, for example, the resulting shadows can obscure large segments of the person's nose, forehead, and eyes. Alternatively, when the direction of lighting originates from the left- or right-hand side, the opposing half of the face can be hidden entirely. Studies investigating the effects of lighting in relation to face matching have suggested that this task is best facilitated when both faces are illuminated from above (Hill & Bruce, 1996) or the front (Favelle et al., 2017). On the other hand, bottom-lit faces appear to be more difficult to identify. For instance, Hill and Bruce (1996) found that accuracy on match trials declined when the direction of lighting originated from below stimuli, suggesting that the lower regions of the face, which would typically be shadowed under such conditions, carry useful information for diagnosing identity matches. A similar pattern of results was observed when the direction of lighting was different for both faces within a pair. This latter finding makes some sense when considering that changes in illumination alter the areas of a face that are visible, and would therefore lead observers to base their comparison on different sources of facial information.

Recent evidence has demonstrated that it is possible to computationally adjust or 'pre-process' facial stimuli to eliminate the effects of problematic lighting while preserving the properties of the original image. One study found that pre-processing methods elevated matching accuracy from 73%, when the direction of illumination differed between sequentially viewed faces, to 84%, when images were pre-processed to increase the luminance of shaded areas (Liu et al., 2013). These studies therefore indicate that difficulties caused by illumination may be potentially offset by artificially balancing lighting information within stimuli. However, it remains unclear as to how effective pre-processing might be on non-controlled face images derived from surveillance footage. An alternative strategy may also be to explore facial averages as a route to offsetting errors that derive from changes in lighting (Burton et al., 2005), thus presenting a potential avenue for further research in this area.

In sum, these studies demonstrate that lighting non-trivially influences face matching. These findings are relevant to police settings, where facial examiners must identify the faces of suspects from photographs and surveillance footage that may be affected by natural or artificial lighting. In addition, this information also carries some relevance to face matching at passport control, given that travellers are illuminated from the front at e-Gates but lit from above at passport control desks. While both these lighting directions have been indicated to be beneficial for face matching (Favelle et al., 2017; Hill & Bruce, 1996), when conditions contrive an illumination mismatch between the live person and their photograph, identification errors are likely to increase (Hill & Bruce, 1996; Liu et al., 2013).

2.4.3 Facial Orientation

Similar to variations in lighting, changes in facial orientation also affect the information that can be utilized for face matching. Faces viewed from the front, for example, provide visual access to a person's eyes, nose, and mouth. Conversely, viewing a face from the side (i.e. in profile) limits the available information to only one side of the face, but also grants access to different facial characteristics such as the length of a person's nose and eye depth. Consequently, when comparing a frontally oriented face to a profile face, observers must base their identity decisions on different facial aspects.

Converging with this assertion, studies show that accuracy for matching two profile faces is comparable to when both faces are presented in frontal (Kramer & Reynolds, 2018) or three-quarter views (Hill & Bruce, 1996), thereby implying that observers are similarly proficient at equating information between face images that are matched for pose. However, a change in orientation between to-be-compared faces reduces accuracy considerably (Estudillo & Bindemann, 2014; Favelle et al., 2017; Favelle & Palmisano, 2018; Hill & Bruce, 1996). For instance, overall accuracy in one study was around 88% when observers were comparing two frontally oriented faces, but deteriorated to around 77% when comparing a frontal face to a profile-oriented counterpart (Estudillo & Bindemann, 2014). These error rates resonate with more recent work in which accuracy deteriorated from 89%, when observers matched sequentially presented frontal faces, to 79% and 80%, when frontally oriented faces were paired with three-quarter-right and -left counterparts, respectively (Favelle et al., 2017). These studies therefore reflect that even fairly modest changes in orientation between faces introduce visually relevant discrepancies by altering the information that is available from one face to the other.

The orientation of a face can also vary along the vertical (i.e., pitch) axis. This is particularly relevant to instances when police may attempt to compare a photograph of an unfamiliar suspect to footage that was acquired from a higher vantage point, such as a CCTV tower, camera pole, or drone. Research suggests that changes of this sort can also increase task difficulty. In one study, accuracy for matching frontally aligned faces was around 91% but declined to around 72% when a face was rotated upwards (Favelle et al., 2017; see also Favelle & Palmisano, 2018).

Together, these findings raise concern for the identification of suspects from surveillance footage, which is often acquired from a high vantage point and may therefore provide only limited access to a person's face. Additional evidence suggests that accuracy for matching faces across different views declines further following a change in lighting direction (Favelle & Palmisano, 2018), indicating that attempts to identify poorly lit suspects from problematic angles may be particularly likely to facilitate identification errors.

2.4.4 Disguise Attempts

To avoid identification in police settings, a criminal suspect may sometimes attempt to conceal or alter their facial appearance to look less like themselves. Several studies have demonstrated that even simple disguises can promote errors in identity matching tasks (see, e.g., Davis & Valentine, 2009; Henderson et al., 2001; Strathie & McNeill, 2016). In one study, for example, the addition of glasses for one face within a pair reduced accuracy from 80% to 74% (Kramer & Ritchie, 2016). These findings converge with earlier work in which accuracy declined from 82%, when observers matched non-disguised faces, to 73%, when targets were depicted wearing a hat and sunglasses (Meissner et al., 2013). In both these studies, this decline in accuracy was qualified by a shift in response criterion, whereby observers became more likely to classify face pairs as depicting different individuals. In other words, these disguises reduced the degree to which images of the same person resembled one another.

One interesting aspect of studies examining the effects of concealing one's appearance is that the disguises employed are typically simplistic in nature, usually comprising a hat or hood to cover the hair, or sunglasses to cover the eyes (Davis & Valentine, 2009; Henderson et al., 2001; Meissner et al., 2013; Strathie & McNeill, 2016). Yet, these disguises are generally sufficient to reduce accuracy by between 9% and 21%, thereby implying that the features they conceal are important for successful identification. This interpretation aligns with evidence that observers utilize hair when attempting to match unfamiliar faces, and that occluding this feature increases errors for participants who are accustomed to utilizing this cue for identification (Megreya & Bindemann, 2009). However, this limitation is not observed for participants residing in Middle Eastern countries, where headscarves are often worn and cover an individual's hair and facial outline (Megreya & Bindemann, 2009). These findings indicate that the inner facial regions, encompassing the eyes, nose, and mouth, contain sufficient visual information for face matching. More recent findings support this interpretation by demonstrating that accuracy can actually be improved by occluding hair under circumstances where a change in hairstyle has occurred (Kemp et al., 2016), but also that examining facial outlines between face images is unlikely to enhance accuracy (Towler et al., 2014).

A key overlap between these studies is that external regions of the face, such as facial outline and hair, are unreliable markers of identity (Kemp et al., 2016; Megreya & Bindemann, 2009; Towler et al., 2014). Yet, it is unclear as to which internal features are most useful for enhancing accuracy. Converging with the general finding that disguising the eye regions via sunglasses reduces accuracy (Davis & Valentine, 2009; Meissner et al., 2013), there is some evidence to suggest that specifically focusing on the eyebrows can improve performance (Megreya & Bindemann, 2018). At the same time, other studies have demonstrated the importance of alternative features, such as the nose (Bobak et al., 2017; Rice, Phillips, Natu, et al., 2013) and mouth (Mileva & Burton, 2018). One interpretation of these mixed findings might be that a range of facial features *can* be useful for face matching, but the relative contribution of each feature varies from one face to the next, or from one face set to another (see also Bindemann & Burton, this volume).

2.5 Conclusion

The factors reviewed in this chapter reflect that identity matching is strongly influenced by the availability of visual information within faces, or the time frame within which such information must be acquired and processed. Based on the current evidence reviewed here, there are also several potential avenues to improving person identification in operational settings. At passport control, the available evidence suggests that this identification process would benefit greatly from the inclusion of additional photographs of the bearer that were obtained over several months or years (Bindemann & Sandford, 2011; White, Kemp, Jenkins, Matheson, et al., 2014). Alternatively, passport photographs could be replaced by a facial average, which may provide a more faithful representation of the bearer than a single photograph that was taken up to a decade earlier (Burton et al., 2005). Alongside these recommendations, passport regulations need not enforce a neutral expression at the application stage, given that smiling faces seem to be more easily matched than neutral faces (Mileva & Burton, 2018). At the same time, these guidelines *should* specify distance parameters from which passport photographs are obtained, based on evidence that these also have an impact on identity matching (Noyes & Jenkins, 2017).

The psychological evidence reviewed here also provides some recommendations for the matching of unfamiliar faces in police investigations. For instance, when comparing degraded face images, accuracy may be enhanced by reducing the size of the pixelated image (Bindemann et al., 2013), or by generating a facial average (Ritchie et al., 2018). Alongside these suggestions, research also advocates that person identification is most reliable when to-be-matched faces are viewed in the same pose (Hill & Bruce, 1996), and when targets are similarly illuminated (Favelle et al., 2017). Following these recommendations will assist in ensuring observers' matching decisions are based on an analysis of the same information between face images, and should boost their accuracy. Importantly, understanding how these various factors are likely to affect face matching also provides some scope for evaluating experts' judgements by establishing the parameters under which identification is *most* and *least* likely to succeed.

Finally, it is important to note that many of the visual characteristics of to-be-compared face stimuli that were covered in this chapter do not fully account for errors in face matching. This is based on studies showing that, even under conditions that are designed to maximize performance, the accuracy of individual observers varies substantially, from chance level (i.e., 50%) to perfect accuracy (Bindemann et al., 2012; Burton et al., 2010; White, Kemp, Jenkins, Matheson, et al., 2014). Such individual differences reflect that, alongside visual characteristics of the *stimuli*, many errors may also be attributed to the capacity of the *matcher*, whereby observers misidentify to-be-matched faces because of a failure to process the visual data within stimuli effectively. This is in line with evidence that fluctuations in face-matching performance are likely to be driven by a combination of the visual information in stimuli and the latent ability of the person who is performing the comparison. Some observers, for example, are able to match faces with near-perfect accuracy even when a change in facial orientation has occurred (Estudillo & Bindemann, 2014), as well as when stimuli are heavily pixelated (Robertson et al., 2016), and when images of the same person are taken many months apart (Fysh & Bindemann, 2018). On the other hand, some observers fail to match faces even under highly optimized viewing conditions (Bindemann et al., 2012). Together, these studies indicate that alongside the visual characteristics of to-be-compared face stimuli, the latent ability of the observer is also crucial for facilitating the matching of unfamiliar faces.

References

Australian Passport Office (2019). *Passport Photo Guidelines*. Department of Foreign Affairs and Trade. Available at: https://www.passports.gov.au/passports-explained/how-apply/passport-photo-guidelines (accessed 2 May 2020).

Bindemann, M., Attard, J., Leach, A., & Johnston, R. A. (2013). The effect of image pixelation on unfamiliar face matching. *Applied Cognitive Psychology*, 27, 707–717. doi:10.1002/acp.2970

Bindemann, M., Avetisyan, M., & Blackwell, K. A. (2010). Finding needles in haystacks: Identity mismatch frequency and facial identity verification. *Journal of Experimental Psychology: Applied*, 16, 378–386. doi:10.1037/a0021893

Bindemann, M., Avetisyan, M., & Rakow, T. (2012). Who can recognize unfamiliar faces? Individual differences and observer consistency in person identification. *Journal of Experimental Psychology: Applied*, 18, 277–291. doi:10.1037/a0029635

Bindemann, M., Fysh, M. C., Cross, K., & Watts, R. (2016). Matching faces against the clock. *i-Perception*, 7(5), 2041669516672219. doi:10.1177/2041669516672219

Bindemann, M., Fysh, M. C., Sage, S. S. K., Douglas, K., & Tummon, H. M. (2017). Person identification from aerial footage by a remote-controlled drone. *Scientific Reports*, 7, 13629. doi:10.1038/s41598-017-14026-3

Bindemann, M. & Sandford, A. (2011). Me, myself, and I: Different recognition rates for three photo-IDs of the same person. *Perception*, 40, 625–627. doi:10.1068/p7008

Bobak, A. K., Parris, B. A., Gregory, N. J., Bennetts, R. J., & Bate, S. (2017). Eye-movement strategies in developmental prosopagnosia and 'super' face recognition. *Quarterly Journal of Experimental Psychology*, 70, 201–217. doi:10.1080/17470218.2016.1161059

Bruce, V., Henderson, Z., Greenwood, K., Hancock, P. J. B., Burton, A. M., & Miller, P. (1999). Verification of face identities from images captured on video. *Journal of Experimental Psychology: Applied*, 5, 339–360. doi:10.1037/1076-898X.5.4.339

Bruck, M., Cavanagh, P., & Ceci, S. J. (1991). Fortysomething: Recognizing faces at one's 25th reunion. *Memory & Cognition*, 19, 221–228. doi:10.3758/BF03211146

Burton, A. M. (2013). Why has research in face recognition progressed so slowly? The importance of variability. *Quarterly Journal of Experimental Psychology*, 66, 1467–1485. doi:10.1080/17470218.2013.800125

Burton, A. M., Jenkins, R., Hancock, P. J. B., & White, D. (2005). Robust representations for face recognition: The power of averages. *Cognitive Psychology*, 51, 256–284. doi:10.1016/j.cogpsych.2005.06.003

Burton, A. M., White, D., & McNeill, A. (2010). The Glasgow Face Matching Test. *Behavior Research Methods*, 42, 286–291. doi:10.3758/BRM.42.1.286

Burton, A. M., Wilson, S., Cowan, M., & Bruce, V. (1999). Face recognition in poor-quality video: Evidence from security surveillance. *Psychological Science*, 10, 243–248. doi:10.1111/1467-9280.00144

Chen, W., Lander, K., & Liu, C. H. (2011). Matching faces with emotional expressions. *Frontiers in Psychology, 2*, 206. doi:10.3389/fpsyg.2011.00206

Davis, J. P. & Valentine, T. (2009). CCTV on trial: Matching video images with the defendant in the dock. *Applied Cognitive Psychology, 23*, 482–505. doi:10.1002/acp.1490

Estudillo, A. J. & Bindemann, M. (2014). Generalization across view in face memory and face matching. *i-Perception, 5*, 589–601. doi:10.1068/i0669

Favelle, S., Hill, H., & Claes, P. (2017). About face: Matching unfamiliar faces across rotations of view and lighting. *i-Perception, 8*(6), 2041669517744221. doi:10.1177/2041669517744221

Favelle, S. & Palmisano, S. (2018). View specific generalisation effects in face recognition: Front and yaw comparison views are better than pitch. *PLoS ONE, 13*(12), e0209927. doi:10.1371/journal. pone.0209927

Fysh, M. C. & Bindemann, M. (2017a). Forensic face matching: A review. In M. Bindemann & A. M. Megreya (eds), *Face processing: Systems, disorders and cultural differences*, 3rd edn (pp. 1–20). New York: Nova Science Publishers.

Fysh, M. C. & Bindemann, M. (2017b). Effects of time pressure and time passage on face matching accuracy. *Royal Society Open Science, 4*(6), 170249. doi:10.1098/rsos.170249

Fysh, M. C. & Bindemann, M. (2018). The Kent Face Matching Test. *British Journal of Psychology, 109*, 219–231. doi:10.1111/bjop.12260

Hahn, C. A., O'Toole, A. J., & Phillips, P. J. (2016). Dissecting the time course of person recognition in natural viewing environments. *British Journal of Psychology, 107*, 117–134. doi:10.1111/bjop. 12125

Harmon, L. D. & Julesz, B. (1973). Masking in visual recognition: Effects of two-dimensional filtered noise. *Science, 180*, 1194–1197. doi:10.1126/science.180.4091.1194

Henderson, Z., Bruce, V., & Burton, A. M. (2001). Matching the faces of robbers captured on video. *Applied Cognitive Psychology, 15*, 445–464. doi:10.1002/acp.718

Her Majesty's Passport Office (2011). *Passport photo guidance.* Available at: https://assets.publishing.service.gov.uk/government/uploads/system/uploads/attachment_data/file/303780/ Photoguidance_v7.pdf (accessed 10 April 2020).

Hill, H. & Bruce, V. (1996). Effects of lighting on the perception of facial surfaces. *Journal of Experimental Psychology: Human Perception and Performance, 22*, 986–1004. doi:10.1037/ 0096-1523.22.4.986

Home Affairs Committee (2012). The work of the UK Border Force Agency (December 2011– March 2012). *Fifth Report of Session 2012–13.* Available at: https://publications.parliament.uk/pa/ cm201213/cmselect/cmhaff/71/71.pdf (accessed 10 April 2020).

Jenkins, R. & Burton, A. M. (2011). Stable face representations. *Philosophical Transactions of the Royal Society B: Biological Sciences, 366*, 1671–1683. doi:10.1098/rstb.2010.0379

Jenkins, R. & Kerr, C. (2013). Identifiable images of bystanders extracted from corneal reflections. *PLoS ONE, 8*(12), e83325. doi:10.1371/journal.pone.0083325

Jenkins, R., White, D., van Montfort, X., & Burton, A. M. (2011). Variability in photos of the same face. *Cognition, 121*, 313–323. doi:10.1016/j.cognition.2011.08.001

Johnston, R. A. & Bindemann, M. (2013). Introduction to forensic face matching. *Applied Cognitive Psychology, 27*, 697–699. doi:10.1002/acp.2963

Kemp, R. I., Caon, A., Howard, M., & Brooks, K. R. (2016). Improving unfamiliar face matching by masking the external facial features. *Applied Cognitive Psychology, 30*, 622–627. doi:10.1002/ acp.3239

Kemp, R. I., Towell, N., & Pike, G. (1997). When seeing should not be believing: Photographs, credit cards and fraud. *Applied Cognitive Psychology, 11*, 211–222. doi:10.1002/ (SICI)1099-0720(199706)11:3<211::AID-ACP430>3.0.CO;2-O

Knight, B. & Johnston, R. A. (1997). The role of movement in face recognition. *Visual Cognition, 4*, 265–273. doi:10.1080/713756764

Kramer, R. S. S. & Reynolds, M. G. (2018). Unfamiliar face matching with frontal and profile views. *Perception, 47*, 414–431. doi:10.1177/0301006618756809

Kramer, R. S. S. & Ritchie, K. L. (2016). Disguising Superman: How glasses affect unfamiliar face matching. *Applied Cognitive Psychology, 30*, 841–845. doi:10.1002/acp.3261

Lander, K., Bruce, V., & Hill, H. (2001). Evaluating the effectiveness of pixelation and blurring on masking the identity of familiar faces. *Applied Cognitive Psychology*, *15*, 101–116. doi:10.1002/1099-0720(200101/02)15:1<101::AID-ACP697>3.0.CO;2-7

Lander, K., Humphreys, G., & Bruce, V. (2004). Exploring the role of motion in prosopagnosia: Recognizing, learning and matching faces. *Neurocase*, *10*, 462–470. doi:10.1080/13554790490900761

Liu, C. H., Chen, W., Han, H., & Shan, S. (2013). Effects of image preprocessing on face matching and recognition in human observers. *Applied Cognitive Psychology*, *27*, 718–724. doi:10.1002/acp.2967

Megreya, A. M. & Bindemann, M. (2009). Revisiting the processing of internal and external features of unfamiliar faces: The headscarf effect. *Perception*, *38*, 1831–1848. doi:10.1068/p6385

Megreya, A. M. & Bindemann, M. (2018). Feature instructions improve face-matching accuracy. *PLoS ONE*, *13*(3), e0193455. doi:10.1371/journal.pone.0193455

Megreya, A. M. & Burton, A. M. (2008). Matching faces to photographs: Poor performance in eyewitness memory (without the memory). *Journal of Experimental Psychology: Applied*, *14*, 364–372. doi:10.1037/a0013464

Megreya, A. M., Sandford, A., & Burton, A. M. (2013). Matching face images taken on the same day or months apart: The limitations of photo ID. *Applied Cognitive Psychology*, *27*, 700–706. doi:10.1002/acp.2965

Meissner, C. A., Susa, K. J., & Ross, A. B. (2013). Can I see your passport please? Perceptual discrimination of own- and other-race faces. *Visual Cognition*, *21*, 1287–1305. doi:10.1080/13506285.2013.832451

Mileva, M. & Burton, A. M. (2018). Smiles in face matching: Idiosyncratic information revealed through a smile improves unfamiliar face matching performance. *British Journal of Psychology*, *109*, 799–811. doi:10.1111/bjop.12318

Mileva, M. & Burton, A. M. (2019). Face search in CCTV surveillance. *Cognitive Research: Principles and Implications*, *4*, 37. doi:10.1186/s41235-019-0193-0

Noyes, E. & Jenkins, R. (2017). Camera-to-subject distance affects face configuration and perceived identity. *Cognition*, *165*, 97–104. doi:10.1016/j.cognition.2017.05.012

Noyes, E. & Jenkins, R. (2019). Deliberate disguise in face identification. *Journal of Experimental Psychology: Applied*, *25*, 280–290. doi:10.1037/xap0000213

O'Toole, A. J., Phillips, P. J., Jiang, F., Ayyad, J., Pénard, N., & Abdi, H. (2007). Face recognition algorithms surpass humans matching faces over changes in illumination. *IEEE Transactions on Pattern Analysis and Machine Intelligence*, *29*, 1642–1646. doi:10.1109/TPAMI.2007.1107

Özbek, M. & Bindemann, M. (2011). Exploring the time course of face matching: Temporal constraints impair unfamiliar face identification under temporally unconstrained viewing. *Vision Research*, *51*, 2145–2155. doi:10.1016/j.visres.2011.08.009

Papesh, M. H. & Goldinger, S. D. (2014). Infrequent identity mismatches are frequently undetected. *Attention, Perception & Psychophysics*, *76*, 1335–1349. doi:10.3758/s13414-014-0630-6

Papesh, M. H., Heisick, L. L., & Warner, K. A. (2018). The persistent low-prevalence effect in unfamiliar face-matching: The roles of feedback and criterion shifting. *Journal of Experimental Psychology: Applied*, *24*, 416–430. doi:10.1037/xap0000156

Phillips, P. J., Yates, A. N., Hu, Y., Hahn, C. A., Noyes, E., Jackson, K., et al. (2018). Face recognition accuracy of forensic examiners, superrecognizers, and face recognition algorithms. *Proceedings of the National Academy of Sciences*, *115*, 6171–6176. doi:10.1073/pnas.1721355115

Rice, A., Phillips, P. J., Natu, V., An, X., & O'Toole, A. J. (2013). Unaware person recognition from the body when face identification fails. *Psychological Science*, *24*, 2235–2243. doi:10.1177/0956797613492986

Rice, A., Phillips, P. J., & O'Toole, A. J. (2013). The role of the face and body in unfamiliar person identification. *Applied Cognitive Psychology*, *27*, 761–768. doi:10.1002/acp.2969

Richards, K. (2018). New facial recognition technology caught 'impostor' using someone else's passport, US officials say. *The Independent*, 24 August. Available at: https://www.independent.co.uk/news/world/americas/facial-recognition-technology-man-intercepted-passport-airport-us-customs-border-protection-a8507186.html (accessed 10 April 2020).

Ritchie, K. L. & Burton, A. M. (2017). Learning faces from variability. *Quarterly Journal of Experimental Psychology, 70*, 897–905. doi:10.1080/17470218.2015.1136656

Ritchie, K. L., Mireku, M. O., & Kramer, R. S. S. (2020). Face averages and multiple images in a live matching task. *British Journal of Psychology, 111*, 92–102. doi:10.1111/bjop.12388

Ritchie, K. L., White, D., Kramer, R. S. S., Noyes, E., Jenkins, R., & Burton, A. M. (2018). Enhancing CCTV: Averages improve face identification from poor-quality images. *Applied Cognitive Psychology, 32*, 671–680. doi:10.1002/acp.3449

Robertson, D. J., Kramer, R. S. S., & Burton, A. M. (2017). Fraudulent ID using face morphs: Experiments on human and automatic recognition. *PLoS ONE, 12*(3), e0173319. doi:10.1371/journal.pone.0173319

Robertson, D. J., Middleton, R., & Burton, A. M. (2015). From policing to passport control: The limitations of photo ID. *Keesing Journal of Documents and Identity, 46* (February), 3–7.

Robertson, D. J., Mungall, A., Watson, D. G., Wade, K. A., Nightingale, S. J., & Butler, S. (2018). Detecting morphed passport photos: A training and individual differences approach. *Cognitive Research: Principles and Implications, 3*, 27. doi:10.1186/s41235-018-0113-8

Robertson, D. J., Noyes, E., Dowsett, A. J., Jenkins, R., & Burton, A. M. (2016). Face recognition by Metropolitan Police super-recognisers. *PLoS ONE, 11*(2), e0150036. doi:10.1371/journal.pone.0150036

Sanders, J. G. & Jenkins, R. (2018). Individual differences in hyper-realistic mask detection. *Cognitive Research: Principles and Implications, 3*, 10. doi:10.1186/S41235-018-0118-3

Sanders, J. G., Ueda, Y., Minemoto, K., Noyes, E., Yoshikawa, S., & Jenkins, R. (2017). Hyper-realistic face masks: A new challenge in person identification. *Cognitive Research: Principles and Implications, 2*, 43. doi:10.1186/s41235-017-0079-y

Strathie, A. & McNeill, A. (2016). Facial wipes don't wash: Facial image comparison by video superimposition reduces the accuracy of face matching decisions. *Applied Cognitive Psychology, 30*, 504–513. doi:10.1002/acp.3218

Towler, A., White, D., & Kemp, R. I. (2014). Evaluating training methods for facial image comparison: The face shape strategy does not work. *Perception, 43*, 214–218. doi:10.1068/p7676

White, D., Burton, A. M., Jenkins, R., & Kemp, R. I. (2014). Redesigning photo-ID to improve unfamiliar face matching performance. *Journal of Experimental Psychology: Applied, 20*, 166–173. doi:10.1037/xap0000009

White, D., Kemp, R. I., Jenkins, R., & Burton, A. M. (2014). Feedback training for facial image comparison. *Psychonomic Bulletin & Review, 21*, 100–106. doi:10.3758/s13423-013-0475-3

White, D., Kemp, R. I., Jenkins, R., Matheson, M., & Burton, A. M. (2014). Passport officers' errors in face matching. *PLoS ONE, 9*(8), e103510. doi:10.1371/journal.pone.0103510

White, D., Phillips, P. J., Hahn, C. A., Hill, M., & O'Toole, A. J. (2015). Perceptual expertise in forensic facial image comparison. *Proceedings of the Royal Society B: Biological Sciences, 282*(1814), 20151292. doi:10.1098/rspb.2015.1292

Wirth, B. E. & Carbon, C. C. (2017). An easy game for frauds? Effects of professional experience and time pressure on passport-matching performance. *Journal of Experimental Psychology: Applied, 23*, 138–157. doi:10.1037/xap0000114

3

Steps Towards a Cognitive Theory
of Unfamiliar Face Matching

Markus Bindemann and A. Mike Burton

3.1 Introduction

The visual comparison of unfamiliar faces, that are not known to an observer, is utilized widely for the identification of people in security settings, such as passport control at airports and in criminal investigations. Alongside these important applications, a substantial volume of laboratory research has emerged in the field of cognitive psychology to study the identification of unfamiliar faces. Despite this concentration of effort, a cognitive theory to explain how human observers perform these identifications does not exist. The aim of this chapter is to aid the development of such a theory, by outlining issues of importance that should be considered in the construction of a cognitive account of facial identity comparison. The chapter is divided into sections that are structured around three overarching components of this process: The *face* as the visual input upon which all cognitive processes must build, the *observer* as the processor for performing the identity comparison, and the *context* within which identifications are made.

3.2 The Face

In its most basic and most studied form, facial identity comparison appears to be a deceptively simple task. Observers are shown two face photographs side by side and must determine whether they depict the same person or different people (Fysh & Bindemann, 2017a). This identity comparison is frequently referred to as forensic or unfamiliar *face matching* in psychology, with same-person photograph pairs described as identity matches and different-person pairs as mismatches. Variants of this task may also involve comparing a photograph with a live person or video footage, such as that provided by closed-circuit television (CCTV) (Bruce et al., 1999; Davis & Valentine, 2009; Megreya & Burton, 2008). Irrespective of the exact format, these tasks all require visual comparison of faces to make an identification. Because the tasks deal with the identification of people who are not known to the observer, additional person-specific knowledge stored within the cognitive system is not at hand. Thus, facial identity

Markus Bindemann and A. Mike Burton, *Steps Towards a Cognitive Theory of Unfamiliar Face Matching* In: *Forensic Face Matching*. Edited by: Markus Bindemann, Oxford University Press (2021). © Oxford University Press.
DOI: 10.1093/oso/9780198837749.003.0003.

comparison—or unfamiliar face matching—is based primarily, and typically solely, on a direct visual analysis of the face.

3.2.1 Similarity

The routine usage of these matching tasks in applied settings implies that faces provide an accessible, distinctive, and stable source of a person's identity that lends itself well to this process. Common sense also dictates a simple solution to the task of face matching: Human beings are unique individuals and so it seems sensible to assume that the closest identity match to a person is their own face, not any other. The effect of this should be that the visual *similarity* of two face photographs of the same person consistently exceeds that of two different people. This difference should allow match versus mismatch decisions to be made with high accuracy.

There is some scientific evidence to support this reasoning. People are good, for example, at determining that two face photographs are identical images (see Burton, 2013; Jenkins & Burton, 2011) and also at discriminating face images that are not visually identical by depicting different faces (see Rossion, 2014; Xu et al., 2017; Yan et al., 2019). However, these elementary demands are the same for virtually any visual perception task (Posner & Mitchell, 1967), and therefore do not reveal particularly useful information about face matching. The challenge of this process is that it must operate across *different* images of the *same* people. During person identification at passport control, for example, a traveller's facial appearance will never provide an exact image match for comparison with their passport photograph. Similarly, the expertise of forensic facial examiners in the police is required because identifications must be made across multiple sources of face images, such as different clips of CCTV, surveillance photos, and custody mugshots.

There is clear evidence that similarity is important for solving face matching under these more realistic conditions too. The identity-matching process is more accurate, for example, when it is based on photographs of faces taken on the same day, from the same viewpoint, and under similar viewing conditions (Burton et al., 2010) than those of faces recorded on different days (Megreya et al., 2013), from different viewpoints (Estudillo & Bindemann, 2014), and under more variable viewing conditions (Fysh & Bindemann, 2018; Jenkins et al., 2011). Likewise, factors that manipulate similarity of two images of a face in a consistent and metrically quantifiable manner influence matching accuracy incrementally. Facial appearance varies, for example, due to lens distortion when portrait photographs are systematically captured at different distances (Noyes & Jenkins, 2017), or when one face identity is morphed gradually into another (Robertson et al., 2017). As the differences between to-be-compared face images increase, these manipulations incur corresponding reductions in accuracy during identification. In light of such findings, the cognitive mechanisms underpinning face matching appear to be relatively straightforward, operating monotonically on the visual overlap between faces, whereby similar pairings are identified as matches and dissimilar pairs as mismatches.

3.2.2 Variability

What makes face matching challenging is that people naturally exhibit substantial variance in visual appearance through changes in emotional expression, pose, ageing, lighting, and so forth (see Fysh, this volume). Demonstrations aplenty now exist to show the effect of the variability that such factors introduce between different images of the same face. For example, identification accuracy declines by around 20% when observers are asked to match pairs of face photographs that were recorded several months apart, compared with images recorded on the same day (Megreya et al., 2013). Matching an image of a person that is unconstrained in terms of lighting, facial expression, and image-capture device to a more standardized portrait taken several months later similarly reduces identification accuracy compared with highly controlled same-day face pairings (Fysh & Bindemann, 2018). In such circumstances, accuracy can also vary dramatically for individual face pairs. An illustration of such variability is provided in Figure 3.1, which shows an identity match and mismatch from the Kent Face Matching Test (Fysh & Bindemann, 2018). These example face pairs are classified incorrectly by three in every four observers and illustrate the *similarity paradox* of face matching: Although this task must rely on the visual resemblance between different images of the same face to establish identity, observers can be profoundly confused by the accompanying natural variability in a person's appearance.

For lay observers and practitioners who do not have access to such scientific demonstrations, the challenge that *within-person variability* in appearance poses for face matching might be surprising. We are, after all, surrounded by a wealth of facial information from birth and throughout life, and are generally good at recognizing the people whom we know. Thus, one might assume that we should have plenty of experience for understanding how faces can vary in appearance (Ritchie et al., 2015). Our high ability to recognize familiar faces is, in fact, based on the experience of such within-person variability, which plays a key role in enabling the robust recognition of known persons (Burton et al., 2005; Jenkins & Burton, 2011). However, from the study of familiar faces, it is now also emerging that within-person variation in visual appearance is *idiosyncratic* (see Burton et al., 2011; Burton et al., 2016). Thus, how one person varies in their facial appearance differs from how other people vary, and therefore the visual patterns that accurately capture anyone's facial identity are very difficult to pin down. This makes it challenging to determine systematically whether two unfamiliar faces depict the same person based on the faces that we already know. It is perhaps for this reason that, even with lifelong experience of social interaction with other people in the general population, or extensive occupational experience in relevant security professions, within-person variability continues to impair the matching of unfamiliar faces (e.g., Papesh, 2018; White, Kemp, Jenkins, Matheson, et al., 2014; Wirth & Carbon, 2017).

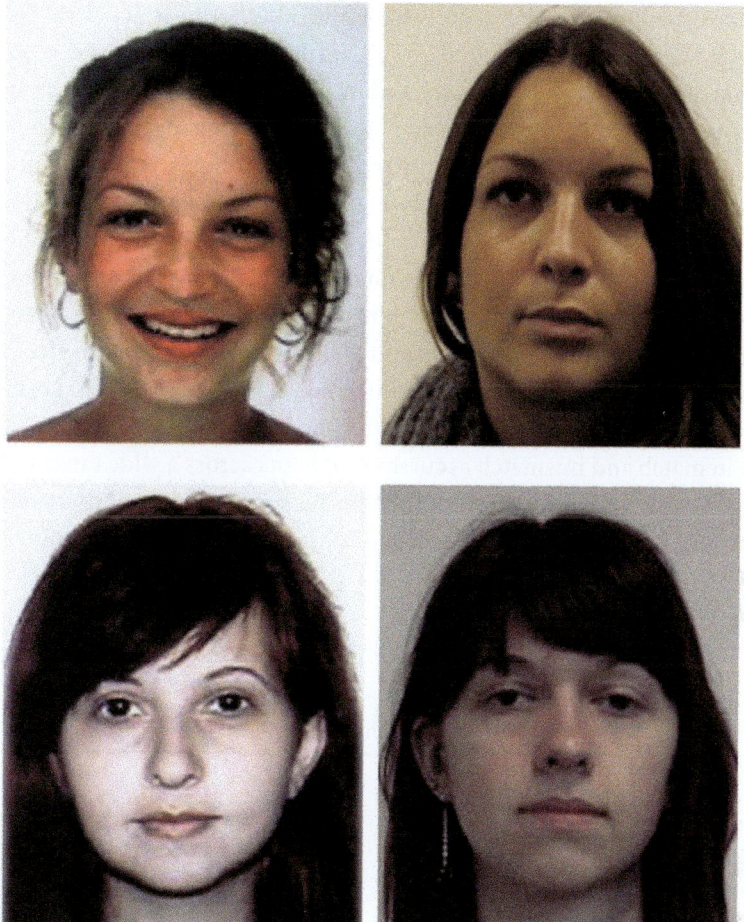

Figure 3.1 An example match face pair (top) and mismatch face pair (bottom) from the Kent Face Matching Test (KFMT).

Source: Adapted from Fysh & Bindemann (2018) 'The Kent Face Matching Test' *British Journal of Psychology, 109,* 219–231, Figure 1. https://doi.org/10.1111/bjop.12260 © 2018, Wiley.

3.2.3 Matches and Mismatches

Whereas the within-person variability that a person can exhibit in appearance is difficult to predict, this variability also plays different roles in the processing of identity matches and mismatches. In the classification of identity matches, observers must see through variability in appearance to detect similarities between faces. In the case of mismatches, on the other hand, variability in identity must be detected despite similarities in appearance that different people can share. This may create the impression that match and mismatch identification are obverse aspects of a unitary cognitive process so that, if one outcome is not determined, the other must be (Glanzer & Adams, 1985; Glanzer et al., 1993). Contrary to this impression, correlational studies demonstrate that observers who are good at classifying either one of identity matches or mismatches are not consistently also good at classifying the other (Bate et al., 2018, 2019; Kokje et al., 2018; Megreya & Burton, 2007). This surprising finding indicates that distinct abilities are required to solve the match and mismatch aspect of face matching.

One visual factor that may contribute to this match–mismatch dissociation is that different sources of variability are at play for both stimulus types. As illustrated in Figure 3.2, the classification of identity matches requires an understanding of variability in the facial appearance of only a single person. Mismatch classification, on the other hand, involves the detection of coincidental between-person similarity in the context of two underlying sources of within-person variability—the two people under comparison. This indicates that match and mismatch classifications are based on separable visual processing requirements, which may be linked to the dissociation in the identification of these stimulus pairings during face matching. However, the broad variance in match and mismatch accuracy that exists across a wide range of face pairings suggests also that this interplay of within-person variability and between-person similarity may be intricate and difficult to disentangle (Fysh & Bindemann, 2018).

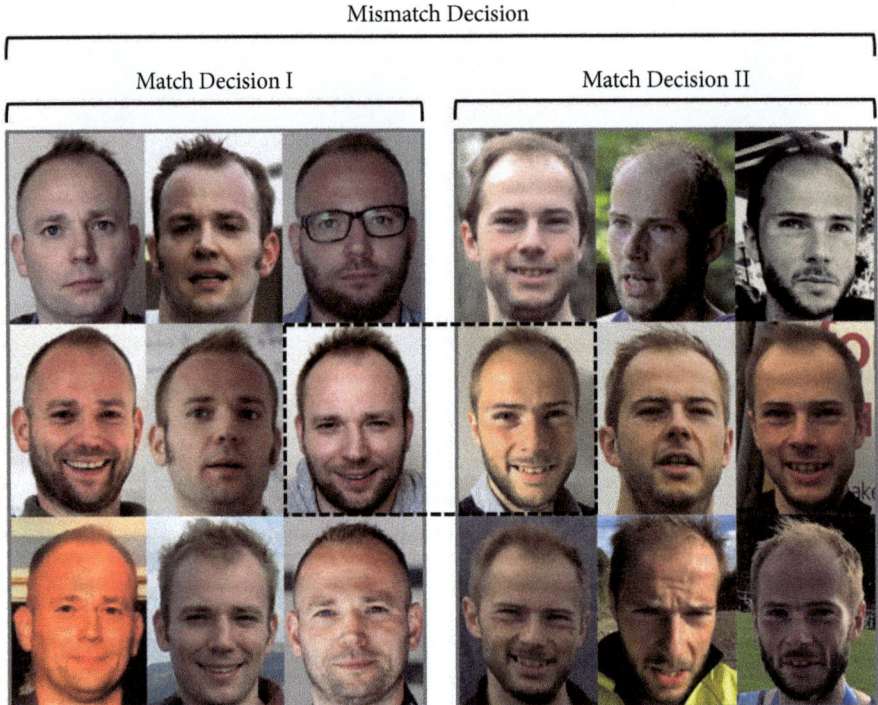

Figure 3.2 Illustration of within-person variability and between-person similarity.

Note: Classification of identity matches requires similarity detection between faces in the context of natural variability in appearance from only a single person. In identity mismatches, two such sources of within-person variability exist, creating possible resemblance between identities depending on the images under comparison.

3.3 The Observer

Whereas the face provides the data input for identity comparison, it is the *observer* who processes this information. The challenge of within-person variability and between-person similarity in facial appearance, and the idiosyncratic nature of these factors, suggests that observers must apply sophisticated cognitive strategies to solve this task. When complex cognitive strategies are at play, variation is also likely to exist across people in their abilities to exercise these strategies. In line with this reasoning, substantial individual differences between observers in the ability to match faces have now been reported across many studies (for a review, see Bate, Mestry, & Portch, this volume; Lander et al., 2018). A theory of face matching must therefore not only explain how facial identity is determined in the light of within-person variability and between-person similarity in visual appearance, but also provide a mechanism for capturing variation in performance across individuals. In this section, four cognitive components are discussed that might underpin face matching and the individual differences in this task.

3.3.1 Attention

Visual information from the face must be acquired first to support facial comparison processing, and this initial data acquisition is determined inevitably by what observers can see. Parts of a face that are not visible (e.g., that are occluded by hair) or not discernible (e.g., from a low-grade image) cannot contribute to the matching process. Similarly, the visual system puts limits on what can be seen, because the acuity of vision is best in the centre of the eye (the fovea) and deteriorates sharply in the periphery. Consequently, observers must move their eyes so that the visual information they seek to process in detail falls on the foveal region of the eyes (Henderson, 2003). This process is mediated by visual attention, which determines the selection of task-relevant information from complex stimuli to direct where observers look (Henderson, 2007).

3.3.1.1 Data Acquisition from Faces

There is now considerable evidence that observers' eye movements are involved in the processing of a face. It has been demonstrated, for example, that eye movements to faces are task specific, with more fixations directed at upper regions of the face during the processing of identity compared with emotional expression (Malcolm et al., 2008). The active control of such eye movements also plays a functional role in face perception, because the encoding of identity from unfamiliar faces into memory is impaired when natural movements of the eyes are not permitted and gaze has to be held steady on a central location in a face (Henderson et al., 2005). Thus, data acquisition from faces is determined by how faces are scanned, and this appears to influence identification processes directly. This indicates that the viewing patterns employed to allocate attention to different face regions, as evidenced from the study of eye movements, are also likely to be important early components of the face matching process.

3.3.1.2 Holistic Processing or Feature Analysis

A key question here concerns the type of data that might be sampled through these viewing strategies. The accurate recognition of familiar faces—of friends and family or famous people—is typically attributed to holistic processing mechanisms, by which facial features are integrated into a single percept that can be processed at a glance (Maurer et al., 2002; Rezlescu et al., 2017; Richler & Gauthier, 2014). There is some evidence that such holistic processing is also involved in face matching. In a pairwise matching task, for example, accuracy exceeds 70% when faces are displayed so briefly that only a single fixation to each identity under comparison is possible (Özbek & Bindemann, 2011) or the total time to view both faces is restricted to only one second (Bindemann et al., 2010; see also Bindemann et al., 2016).

However, holistic processes also appear to be less important for the identity comparison of unfamiliar faces than for the recognition of familiar faces. There is evidence, for example, that unfamiliar face matching dissociates from familiar face processing (Megreya & Burton, 2006; Ritchie et al., 2015), does not correlate with indexes of holistic processing, such as the Composite Face Test (Verhallen et al., 2017), and does not exhibit effects that are considered markers of holistic face processing, such as impaired processing with stimulus inversion (Megreya & Burton, 2006). In turn, whereas matching is above chance when only a single fixation can be made on faces, accuracy improves substantially when more viewing time is available, and is best when observers can perform a self-terminating face scan (Özbek & Bindemann, 2011; see also Bindemann et al., 2016; Fysh & Bindemann, 2017b). This indicates that the holistic visual overlap comparison that a single glance on a face provides is superseded by a more analytical comparison of specific stimulus features. Finally, unfamiliar face matching also correlates with object matching tests in which accuracy relies on the identification of features (Burton et al., 2010; Megreya & Burton, 2006).

In occupational settings outside the laboratory, there is also a strong emphasis on featural processing in face-matching practice. Facial examiners in the police, for example, are specifically trained to apply morphological analysis in which individual features are compared systematically (Moreton et al., 2018). In these settings, guidelines as to which features should be considered during identification must be followed as a matter of routine, ranging from the perception of main features to sub-components, such as the specific shape of the nostrils, wrinkles, or facial marks (see Moreton, this volume). In contrast to such professional guidelines, the scientific evidence about how features should be compared during face matching is much less clear, and there are limited data on the diagnosticity of different features. What evidence exists is somewhat mixed—for example, sometimes emphasizing eyebrows (Megreya & Bindemann, 2018), eye shape (Abudarham & Yovel, 2016), or ears (Towler et al., 2017) as particularly useful features. This suggests that diagnostic features might vary across different facial identities and stimulus sets, which corresponds with the idiosyncratic variation that faces seem to exhibit in appearance (Burton et al., 2011; Burton et al., 2016) and the case-by-case handling of the search for diagnostic featural detail in forensic practice (Moreton et al., 2018).

3.3.1.3 Individual Differences in Viewing Strategies

The ways in which features are studied during face matching are likely to vary across individuals, and diverse viewing *strategies* may lead to differences in information acquisition at the attention stage. For example, viewers seem to differ in where they look first during face identification, with the location of these fixations corresponding to points on a face that maximize individual performance (Peterson & Eckstein, 2013). Observers who tend to look lower on a face spontaneously, for example, also perform better in tasks that force them to look at the lower facial areas first. Thus, people seem to enact individualistic viewing strategies that correlate with their own identification style (Peterson & Eckstein, 2013). These idiosyncratic scanpath routines are consistent over many months, indicating that they reflect intrinsic and stable viewing strategies that observers possess for faces (Mehoudar et al., 2014).

These findings suggest that one factor that might contribute to large individual differences in face matching reflects observers' viewing strategies, which modulate the allocation of attention to specific features. If this is the case, then some viewing strategies should enhance accuracy whereas others might limit face-matching performance, so that the fixation points of observers might not necessarily map onto where diagnostic identity information lies. This could explain why the location of fixations on a face is not always associated with accurate recognition (Mehoudar et al., 2014). In turn, giving observers instruction to attend to diagnostic features should generate a performance gain. In support of this reasoning, it has been demonstrated that manipulations that direct attention to specific features can increase identification accuracy for faces in recognition (Hills et al., 2013; Hills & Pake, 2013) and matching tasks (Megreya & Bindemann, 2018).

In face matching, these improvements were obtained primarily for identity-match pairings (Megreya & Bindemann, 2018; see also Towler et al., 2017). This suggests that viewing strategies differentially affect the classification of identity matches and mismatches, and provide a possible locus for the dissociation in accuracy between these distinct types of face pairings. When observers can view faces freely, however, it seems unlikely that systematic differences in eye movements to matches and mismatches emerge during early viewing, when the nature of a face pair is not yet known. Viewing strategies might then diverge as a face pair is analysed further and observers start accumulating evidence towards one type of identity classification or the other.

While studies manipulating attention to facial features emphasize that a range of viewing strategies could be applied to face matching (Hills et al., 2013; Hills & Pake, 2013; Megreya & Bindemann, 2018), it also seems likely that observers have more than one viewing strategy at their disposal (Miellet et al., 2011). In turn, it is also possible that salient or unusual facial features command attention irrespective of viewing strategies, which may attenuate differences between observers (Godoy et al., 2011; Ishii et al.,

2009; Meyer-Marcotty et al., 2010). Attention can also be allocated covertly, without accompanying eye movements (Luck & Vecera, 2002; but see Findlay, 2004), or eye movements to specific features may not be required when faces are presented at small sizes that fall fully within foveal vision (Bindemann et al., 2013; Noyes & Jenkins, 2017). Thus, eye movements cannot be equated with attentional allocation or analytic featural viewing strategies during face matching per se. It is clear, however, that much progress can still be made by utilizing eye-tracking methodology to gain insight into the visual aspects of faces that are utilized for identity comparison.

In summary, the wider face perception literature suggests that accuracy of the face matching process may be determined by the attention-allocation strategies that are employed for data acquisition. If these strategies rely on the processing of facial features, then this can provide flexibility for the differential viewing of diverse types of faces, depending on the stimuli at hand. In turn, there is evidence that individual observers possess their own scanpath routines to view faces, and that these routines appear to be linked to identification accuracy. Very few studies exist, however, that have combined the eye-tracking approach directly with face matching, leaving much room for knowledge gain here.

3.3.2 Perception

3.3.2.1 Looking and Seeing

Once attention is allocated to a specific face region, the information that this can provide towards an identity comparison is perceived. Identity judgements for individual features must be initiated at this point. Such judgements are not interdependent, so that a mixture of 'same' and 'different' decisions can occur across features (Abudarham & Yovel, 2016; Towler et al., 2017). This perception process appears distinct from an attention component in that it involves *interpretation* of what is viewed. This distinction is supported by the individual differences that are observed in face-matching studies. For example, whereas poor performance in face matching indicates that many individuals have a limited idea of what constitutes a match or mismatch (Bindemann et al., 2012; Burton et al., 2010; Estudillo & Bindemann, 2014), *some* individuals also perform exceptionally well in this task (Bindemann et al., 2012; Bobak, Dowsett, et al., 2016; Bobak, Hancock, et al., 2016; Bobak, Pampoulov, et al., 2016; Burton et al., 2010; Robertson et al., 2016). Similar inter-observer inconsistencies arise at the featural level, whereby people vary in the classification of the same face regions (Ritz-Timme et al., 2011; Towler et al., 2014). Thus, the viewing of a face generally, and of individual features more specifically, does not give rise consistently to the same percept across observers. Consequently, some see similarity in identity where others do not.

3.3.2.2 Observers' Identification Criteria

Individual differences between observers indicate that, even when a face pair contains the necessary visual information for a correct identification, some individuals simply do not know how to utilize this information effectively (Fysh & Bindemann, 2017a; Jenkins & Burton, 2011). Such individual differences in face perception might be rooted in the internal *criteria* that observers hold for making such identity comparisons, whereby people vary in their idea of what constitutes sameness or dissimilarity of identity. In support of this idea, it seems that observers have limited insight into their ability to process unfamiliar faces (Bindemann et al., 2014; Bobak et al., 2018; Palermo et al., 2017), which also makes it likely that they possess inadequate criteria for identification. This notion receives further support from studies of facial feature categorization, which show that observers' repeat classifications of the same features are often inconsistent (Ritz-Timme et al., 2011; Towler et al., 2014). Similarly, the phenomenon of choice blindness shows that individuals will unwittingly justify a matching decision for face pairs, even if originally they did, in fact, make a different identification decision about the same stimuli (Sauerland et al., 2016). These phenomena should simply not present for people who have definitive, stable criteria for categorizing identity matches and mismatches.

Providing criteria of some kind also seems to improve matching accuracy. In a sorting task, for example, in which observers divide a set of photographs into different identities, many errors are typically made (Jenkins et al., 2011). Accuracy improves sharply, however, when observers are informed in advance of how many target identities the photographs should be sorted into (Andrews et al., 2015). Trial-by-trial feedback for an observer's responses can also improve their face-matching accuracy subsequently (White, Kemp, Jenkins, & Burton, 2014), but only if this feedback is delivered while the stimuli remain on display (cf., Alenezi & Bindemann, 2013). These findings appear distinct from studies that improve face matching with attention-directing instructions (Megreya & Bindemann, 2018), because observers are not pointed to specific regions of a face in feedback paradigms. This suggests that the provision of attention-directing strategies can produce distinct effects from manipulations that provide criteria for what constitutes an identity match or mismatch.

These ideas require direct testing, but the fact that some observers perceive similarity in identity when others do not provides good reason to suggest that a distinction in 'seeing' and 'perceiving' must be made in theorizing about face matching, whereby one process refers to what is viewed in a face and the other reflects the interpretation of the looked-at visual information. Whereas observers may view the same content during face matching, there is evidence that this can be interpreted differently, contributing to individual differences in identification accuracy. An underlying source of these individual differences must be the internal criteria that observers hold for interpreting similarities and differences between faces.

3.3.3 Evaluation

3.3.3.1 Probability and Meaning
It seems unlikely that the perception of a feature to be the same or different across to-be-compared faces is sufficient for reaching an identification decision. The observer

must also decide whether the detected similarities or differences are meaningful, by evaluating the *probability* that these point to the correct overall identification decision. The necessity of including such a quantitative process in face matching can be illustrated with examples of a specific feature, such as the eyes. Observers appear to be particularly sensitive to information from the eyes under strictly controlled laboratory conditions, such as the colour of the iris (Abudarham & Yovel, 2016). However, whether the accurate perception of eye colour information might be useful for face matching depends on the probability value that such information holds. When to-be-compared faces display the same eye colour, then the convergence of this information may point to an identity match. In turn, considering that eye colour is a phenotypic trait, one might think that the probability that faces with distinct eye colours are different people should be high.

However, such inferences are complicated by additional factors. For example, only a limited number of discrete eye colours exist (six), meaning that many different people can exhibit the same eye colour. Thus, an eye colour match is unlikely to be indicative of an identity match. On the other hand, the majority of the world population are estimated to have brown eyes whereas very few people are estimated to have green eyes.[1] Thus, the probability that to-be-compared faces are the same person varies also by the eye-colour match that presents—for example, in that the occurrence of brown eyes between two faces may carry less evaluative bearing on the final decision than the occurrence of green eyes. In addition, eye colour is determined by other factors, such as the scattering of light in the iris, and therefore depends on lighting conditions and the medium of face presentation. Face photographs, for example, may capture eye colour poorly, depending on factors such as camera white-balance settings and image size.

These considerations illustrate that observers can be sensitive to specific facial features, but that evaluating the identity relevance of such information can be complex nonetheless. The eyes provide a useful example here because of the limited number of eye colour categories that exist. For other facial features, categories of subtypes are harder to pin down because of continuous and complex variability in shape across people, making illustrations of probability estimation even more obscure. On the other hand, there are features that may also produce very clear probabilities in support of an identity match or mismatch. In cases where to-be-compared face photos share distinctive blemishes, for example, the probability that these are of the same person could be high. In turn, the presence of such distinctive information in one face and its absence in another might also indicate a high probability that different identities are shown. An illustration of such a case is provided in Figure 3.3. This identity match from the Kent Face Matching Test is frequently misclassified as a mismatch, with average accuracy at just 30% (Fysh & Bindemann, 2018). Despite many differences in appearance between the faces in this pair, the pattern of moles marked up in Figure 3.3 can provide distinctive information towards reaching the correct identification decision.

---

[1] https://www.worldatlas.com/articles/which-eye-color-is-the-most-common-in-the-world.html (accessed 8 April, 2020).

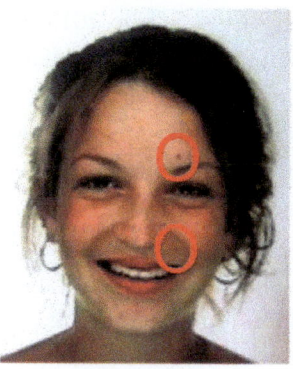

Figure 3.3 Example face pair from the Kent Face Matching Test (KFMT) illustrating the role of blemishes in signalling identity matches.

Source: Adapted from Fysh & Bindemann (2018) 'The Kent Face Matching Test' *British Journal of Psychology, 109,* 219–231, Figure 1. https://doi.org/10.1111/bjop.12260 © 2018, Wiley.

These examples illustrate the importance of evaluating whether the detected similarities and differences between faces' features are meaningful by pointing to the correct *overall* identification decision, but they also demonstrate the difficulty of this process. Observers must balance the perceived similarity (or dissimilarity) of two faces against the prior probability of obtaining that similarity, in order to decide whether there exists sufficient evidence that both faces reflect the same person source. A key issue here is how observers know such probabilities or whether these can, in fact, be known accurately at all. Returning to the example of eye colour, most observers may well be unaware of basic facts about this feature, such as percentage prevalence of different colour categories in the general population. This problem extends to professionals working in the domain of facial comparison, with a lack of empirical databases to inform probability evaluations of features (see Moreton, this volume; for legal implications, see Roberts, this volume). An analogue problem exists in other criminal identification tasks, such as fingerprint analysis (see Busey & Loftus, 2007; Busey & Parada, 2010), and demonstrates that this is not an easy question to study.

3.3.3.2 Individual Differences and Experience

Without databases to support quantitative statistical evaluation of facial comparison evidence, knowledge of the extent to which similarities and differences between various features are indicative of identity matches or mismatches must fall back on observers' *experience* with faces. Theories of familiar person recognition demonstrate how experience shapes stored representations of individual faces (Burton et al., 2005; Burton et al., 2016; Jenkins & Burton, 2011). In a similar vein, there is evidence that experience can influence facial identification at the level of the individual observer. It is already known, for example, that the ability to process faces of different ages (Harrison & Hole, 2009; Hills, 2012; Rhodes & Anastasi, 2012) or ethnicities (Brigham et al., 1982; Chiroro & Valentine, 1995; Cross et al., 1971) is shaped by a person's experience with these face types. More broadly, face recognition ability has also been related to the number of faces that a person comes into contact with (Balas & Saville, 2015, 2017; Sunday et al., 2018). This suggests a link between individual experience and variation in the appreciation of commonalities and differences during face matching.

Experience in itself, however, may be insufficient to acquire knowledge of probabilities. A number of reports demonstrate, for example, that professionals can perform poorly at face matching despite substantial occupational experience (e.g., Papesh, 2018; Phillips et al., 2018; White, Kemp, Jenkins, Matheson, et al., 2014), highlighting that many expert decisions may be based on subjective experience and epistemic beliefs (see Moreton, this volume; Roberts, this volume; Towler, Kemp, & White, this volume). It seems that for experience to inform face-matching decisions, this must be accompanied by feedback information about the true nature of a to-be-matched face pair (i.e., whether it is actually an identity match or mismatch). Otherwise, this experience might serve to sustain misconceptions that lead to over- or under-estimates of particular probabilities. Studies that provide feedback (White, Kemp, Jenkins, & Burton, 2014) or labelled example face pairs to support matching decisions (Gentry & Bindemann, 2019) demonstrate how experience can improve identification when truth is known. In these studies, these improvements persisted after feedback and examples were no longer present, indicating an experience effect that lasted beyond comparison of a set of concurrent faces. However, these effects also showed little or no transfer across different stimulus sets, which suggests that experience may be specific to particular types of faces. This further emphasizes the importance of experience for understanding the different ways in which distinct types of faces can vary.

In sum, for judgements on the similarity of facial features to inform matching decisions, probabilistic evaluation that these point to the correct overall identification decision must come into play. Such calculations are difficult and no scientifically vetted databases currently exist to support such a quantitative statistical evaluation of face-matching evidence. Therefore, such judgements are based inevitably on the prior experience that observers have with faces. While there is some evidence of experience shaping face identification ability, the subjective nature that this imposes on probability judgements emphasizes concerns about the accuracy of the face-matching process and its application in real-world settings (see Roberts, this volume). Very little is known about probability judgements in face processing generally and in face matching more specifically.

3.3.4 Decision Making

If face matching relies on the perception of individual features, and the probabilistic evaluation of the information that such features can provide, then a decision-making process is also required in which this information is integrated to reach an overall identity match or mismatch decision. At present, the nature of the processing framework that is applied to combine information to reach an overall matching decision is largely unknown. However, a basic assumption that can be made is that such identity decisions are based on a continuous information-sampling process by which evidence is gradually gathered in favour of either a match or mismatch response. Based on the study of decision-making processes for other psychological tasks, it is possible to speculate on some decisional styles that may be available to observers to achieve this.

3.3.4.1 Counting Strategies

One strategy might reflect an internal counter that records whether features are pointing to a particular outcome (see Ratcliff & Smith, 2004). In such a counting strategy, if the features of a face pair are consistently pointing to the same outcome, then this information can be combined in a straightforward cumulative manner. Similarly, it is also possible that the majority of features point toward one outcome (e.g., an identity match) but a few features do not (e.g., indicating differences between faces). If this minority of features is associated with low probabilities of pointing to the correct overall identification decision during the evaluation stage, then they could simply be omitted from the counting process during information accumulation. The mouth region, for example, could vary in appearance through differences in emotional expression during face matching. If this limits its contribution to the overall decision that two faces represent an identity match, then this may be omitted from the decision process during counting.

A number of problems emerge with this strategy, however, that suggest this approach is insufficient without modification. For example, it is not known how many facial elements contribute to an identity comparison but, considering the idiosyncratic variability that faces exhibit, the number is likely to vary across different face pairings. As a consequence, the total number that one is counting towards is not known, making predictions difficult about when the process should be terminated to reach an identification decision. A variant of this approach might be a diffusion strategy, whereby the continuous accumulation of information during face matching drives the overall identification decision up or down towards either a match or mismatch response (Ratcliff et al., 2016; Voss et al., 2013). However, the self-terminating nature of a diffusion process also gives rise to the possibility that a decision is made before sufficient evidence to make the correct identification is accumulated.

A second problem arises from the match–mismatch dissociation in face matching (Bate et al., 2018, 2019; Kokje et al., 2018; Megreya & Burton, 2007). The locus at which this distinction arises between match and mismatch processing is not clear. It is possible that it reflects attention and perceptual factors, leading to early processing differences, but it also may not because the nature of the stimuli under comparison is not yet known at this point. This would move the locus of the match–mismatch dissociation to subsequent cognitive stages. If this were the case, then decision-making processes should diverge for identity matches and mismatches. This implies that any strategy in which a single counter serves as a sameness and difference measure is unlikely to adequately capture the cognitive decision-making processes underpinning face matching. It follows that more than one decision-making mechanism must exist, separately serving match and mismatch decisions. One possible implementation of this is a race model

(Pike, 1973; Townsend & Ashby, 1983), in which separate counters accumulate information about similarities and differences in parallel, with the counter that reaches a decision threshold first determining the overall identification.

3.3.4.2 Reduction Strategy

An accumulation process may be inappropriate in cases where a single or only a few high-probability perceptual similarities or differences determine the overall matching decision. Reverting to the face pair in Figure 3.3, many of the compared features in a pair of faces can reflect different identities, but this information might be superseded by a shared distinctive feature, which is unlikely to present by coincidence, to indicate an identity match. In turn, it is possible that two faces share many similarities, but an overall mismatch can be deduced from the detection of a high-probability difference that strongly suggests the faces are *not* the same person. Under such circumstances, a reductionism strategy might be exercised, in which the simple accumulation of information is superseded by high probabilities associated with specific features.

3.3.4.3 Match versus Mismatch Decisions

It is also possible that some decision-making strategies are more likely to be associated with either match or mismatch outcomes. One source of evidence for this idea comes from the Matching Familiar Figures Test (MFFT), in which observers have to detect the counterpart of a line-drawn target object in an array of six highly similar objects (see Figure 3.4). In this test, the match in the array is similar to the target in all respects, whereas non-target objects differ by specific features. Thus, matches are defined by accumulation and mismatches by reductionism in this object perception test.

Performance on the MFFT correlates with face-matching accuracy, which suggests that some similar processes are recruited by both tasks (Burton et al., 2010; Megreya & Burton, 2006). If this is the case, then an accumulation strategy might be more likely to apply to facial identity matches by virtue of the fact that 'sameness' of some facial aspects is not an unequivocal indicator of shared identity. Two faces can share similarities in the appearance of the eye regions, for example, but still depict different people. Thus, sameness conclusions may be warranted only if substantiated by accumulation of evidence from other face regions. A single distinctive difference between faces, on the other hand, might be sufficient to support mismatch decisions even in the context of many similarities, pointing to the relative benefits of a reduction strategy for this type of face pairing. These proposals are offered tentatively to stimulate discussion about the dissociation between match and mismatch accuracy in face identification. The example in Figure 3.3 indicates, for example, that a reductionism strategy may be available also for identity matches. It seems also plausible that observers can combine different decisional styles, such as checking counting solutions with reductionism strategies. If accumulation and reductionism strategies are applied to face matching, then they are unlikely to divide match and mismatch processing completely.

Finally, it is also possible that observers can adjust their decision style to specific situations, depending on whether match or mismatch identification errors may be

Figure 3.4 An illustration of the type of stimulus arrays employed in the Matching Familiar Figures Test showing identification by features.

most costly. At passport control, for example, identification of mismatches may have priority over match classification, in order to detect people travelling under false identity (see Stevens, this volume). Under such circumstances, adaptation of a decisional process that reduces the possibility that mismatches are missed could be advantageous even if this reduces the accuracy of match identification. Experimental manipulations of the prevalence of matches and mismatches indicate that observers can exhibit such flexibility by aligning the outcome of their face-matching decisions with the most frequently occurring stimulus type. These effects seem to occur without changes in sensitivity to the perceptual characteristics of faces, pointing to a locus at decisional stages (Papesh & Goldinger, 2014; Papesh et al., 2018).

3.3.4.4 Individual Differences
It seems likely that decision-making processes, like other processes involved in face matching, are also susceptible to individual differences. The accumulation of

information, for example, requires higher-order executive skills to retain, monitor, co-ordinate, and combine multiple sources of information from different features (Gopher, 1996; Mitchell et al., 2016; Rapcsak & Edmonds, 2011). Similarly, the capacity to logic-ally reason through this information, to consider data that may seem contradictory (e.g., some features indicating 'same' but others indicating that 'different' identities are paired), and to weigh up the associated probabilities appear crucial for a reductionism strategy. As with other processes discussed here, these ideas remain to be tested in the domain of unfamiliar face matching.

In summary, theories of face matching must incorporate decision-making processes in which information from across the faces under comparison is integrated to reach an overall identity match or mismatch decision. At present, the processing frameworks that may be applied to combine information to this end are largely unstudied in the face domain. Such processes could reflect mechanisms that count similarities and dif-ferences between faces, or strategies that supersede the accumulation of information when particular features provide exceptionally strong identity information. It is also possible that some decision-making strategies are more likely to be associated either with match or mismatch outcomes, providing a possible explanation for the dissoci-ation in performance for these different types of face pairings.

3.4 The Context

In psychological studies and applied settings, a range of observer groups are required to make facial comparisons, typically in contexts that differ in many ways. The ma-jority of participants in laboratory experiments, for example, are untrained 'lay' ob-servers comprising students taking part for financial reimbursement or course credit. Consequently, these participants may be motivated less by their face-matching per-formance in these experiments than professionals who are expected to perform well in similar tasks as part of their occupation (see Bobak, Dowsett, et al., 2016; Moore & Johnston, 2013; Susa et al., 2019). In turn, professional staff may have undergone selec-tion and training procedures for relevant roles on face matching, and also present with extensive on-the-job experience. Based on this, superior identification performance to lay participants should be expected in these observers even under controlled experi-mental conditions, but it is not always found (e.g., Papesh, 2018; Phillips et al., 2018; Towler et al., 2019; White, Kemp, Jenkins, Matheson, et al., 2014; White et al., 2015). Findings such as these can raise alarm by indicating that some personnel selection and training programmes for occupations that involve face matching do not work (Towler et al., 2019), but they may also indicate that some laboratory tests of face matching only provide limited transfer to operational deployment (Bruce et al., 2018; Moreton et al., 2019; Ramon et al., 2019).

Many key differences also exist across occupations involving face matching and which are typically captured poorly by psychological experimentation in this field. Identifications by forensic facial examiners in police investigations, for example, typically reflect a slow, detailed, and rule-based process that can take days to complete, and which must be documented throughout. In contrast, person identification at passport control is a high-volume process, in which individual cases must be processed quickly. In this setting, the process by which these high-volume facial comparisons are administered is typically not supervised directly and unrecorded. Consequently, the extent to which these professionals adhere to identification protocols is not known and may be determined entirely by the individual operator. Other factors might also present in this setting, such as a traveller's body language and their manner of social interaction during identification. Psychological experiments on face matching are usually nested somewhere in between these applied scenarios by requiring classification of an intermediate number of identities, which are typically rather homogenous by displaying faces from a similar ethnic background and age range (see, e.g., Burton et al., 2010; Fysh & Bindemann, 2018). In addition, accuracy is self-paced but decisions seldom take longer than a few seconds in these low-stake laboratory environments (e.g., Alenezi et al., 2015; Bindemann et al., 2016; Fysh & Bindemann, 2018; Özbek & Bindemann, 2011).

Despite these differences, a few factors present in occupational scenarios that have been explored in laboratory research already. This research underlines that context is likely to induce important differences in the manner in which faces are processed across occupational settings. Passport officers, for example, must identify faces alongside other biographical information provided by photo-identity documents, and they frequently work at night because these roles operate routinely across different daytime shifts. In laboratory experiments, these contextual factors can influence face matching in distinct ways. Lack of sleep, for example, primarily seems to impair the classification of identity matches (Beattie et al., 2016; Experiment 2), whereas embedding faces in photo-identity documents reduces the accuracy for mismatches (McCaffery & Burton, 2016). Such findings emphasize that differences in context are likely to be important for theorizing about face matching. They also highlight that heterogeneity exists in facial comparison occupations in terms of personnel selection, training, working conditions, and procedures. Thus, whereas forensic facial examiners in the police, passport officers, and other professionals are generally all required to compare faces to perform an identification, they may—and often must—solve the task in very different ways.

An analogue scenario exists in psychological experimentation, where a variety of tasks, paradigms, and stimulus sets are employed to study face matching. Variation within participants' performance can be considerable across seemingly comparable tasks and correlations can be moderate (Fysh & Bindemann, 2018; Kokje et al., 2018; Noyes et al., 2018). Even among observers who are thought to be exceptionally good at identifying faces, such as super-recognizers, such variation can be found across stimulus sets and paradigms (see, e.g., Bate et al., 2018; Bate et al., 2019; Bobak et al., 2016b). This indicates that caution must be exercised to directly equate performance on any given face-matching task with a person's ability to match faces (see Bate, Mestry, & Portch, this volume), or the cognitive processes that are applied. In turn, theory development in this field will be limited if concerned with specific tasks, but is served better by focusing on understanding the different ways in which the cognitive system might perform these tasks (Bruce et al., 2018; Logie, 2018). In doing so, scientific theorizing should help to shed light on the perceptual and cognitive mechanisms that govern face matching in laboratory experiments *and* applied settings, and across different occupational contexts.

3.5 Conclusions

Despite its applied importance and the substantial research effort in psychological science, a cognitive theory to explain how human observers perform the identity matching of unfamiliar faces still does not exist. The aim of this chapter is to aid the development of such a theory by outlining issues of importance. The *face* provides the obvious starting point upon which identity matching must be built. This process must be based on detecting visual similarities and differences between faces under comparison, but is complicated by within-person variability in facial appearance as well as a processing dissociation in the classification of identity matches and mismatches. The nature of a face pairing is not known on first presentation, which implies that some similar processes must apply to matches and mismatches during the initial stages of perception. On the other hand, the dissociation in the classification of these stimulus types indicates that face matching is not a unitary process, but must provide more than one route to identification.

If the face provides the data input for comparison, it is the *observer* who performs the task. The perceptual and cognitive mechanisms that observers bring to bear on face matching are likely to reflect a multi-faceted process involving attention, perception, evaluation, and decision stages. These stages need not proceed in a strictly serial manner. During evaluation and decision-making processes, for example, observers might recheck visual aspects of faces that have already been viewed. Each of these stages may also be susceptible to distinct sources of individual differences, adding further complexity to the face-matching process.

Finally, facial comparisons are performed across a range of experimental and occupational *contexts*, but how this links to the perceptual and cognitive mechanisms governing the task is not clear. Theory development that equates face matching with specific stimulus sets and paradigms is likely to limit understanding of the complexity of this process. Focusing such development on the different ways in which face matching can be conducted will instead increase longevity and generalizability of theorizing across different research and occupational settings.

References

Abudarham, N. & Yovel, G. (2016). Reverse engineering the face space: Discovering the critical features for face identification. *Journal of Vision, 16*(3), 40. doi:10.1167/16.3.40

Alenezi, H. M. & Bindemann, M. (2013). The effect of feedback on face-matching accuracy. *Applied Cognitive Psychology, 27*, 735–753. doi:10.1002/acp2968

Alenezi, H. M., Bindemann, M., Fysh, M. C., & Johnston R. A. (2015). Face matching in a long task: Enforced rest breaks and desk-switching cannot maintain identification accuracy. *PeerJ, 3*, e1184. doi:10.7717/peerj.1184

Andrews, S., Jenkins, R., Cursiter, H., & Burton, A. M. (2015). Telling faces together: Learning new faces through exposure to multiple instances. *Quarterly Journal of Experimental Psychology, 68*, 2041–2050. doi:10.1080/17470218.2014.1003949

Balas, B. & Saville, A. (2015). N170 face specificity and face memory depend on hometown size. *Neuropsychologia, 69*, 211–217. doi:10.1016/j.neuropsychologia.2015.02.005

Balas, B. & Saville, A. (2017). Hometown size affects the processing of naturalistic face variability. *Vision Research, 141*, 228–236. doi:10.1016/j.visres.2016.12.005

Bate, S., Frowd, C., Bennetts, R., Hasshim, N., Murray, E., Bobak, A. K., et al. (2018). Applied screening tests for the detection of superior face recognition. *Cognitive Research: Principles and Implications, 3*, 22. doi:10.1186/s41235-018-0116-5

Bate, S., Frowd, C., Bennetts, R., Hasshim, N., Portch, E., Murray, E., et al. (2019). The consistency of superior face recognition skills in police officers. *Applied Cognitive Psychology, 33*, 828–842. doi:10.1002/acp.3525

Beattie, L., Walsh, D., McLaren, J., Biello, S. M., & White, D. (2016). Perceptual impairment in face identification with poor sleep. *Royal Society Open Science, 3*(10), 160321. doi:10.1098/rsos.160321

Bindemann, M., Attard, J., & Johnston, R. A. (2014). Perceived ability and actual recognition accuracy for unfamiliar and famous faces. *Cogent Psychology, 1*, 986903. doi:10.1080/23311908.2014.986903

Bindemann, M., Attard, J., Leach, A., & Johnston, R. A. (2013). The effect of image pixelation on unfamiliar-face matching. *Applied Cognitive Psychology, 27*, 707–717. doi:10.1002/acp2970

Bindemann, M., Avetisyan, M., & Blackwell, K. (2010). Finding needles in haystacks: Identity mismatch frequency and facial identity verification. *Journal of Experimental Psychology: Applied, 16*, 378–386. doi:10.1037/a0021893

Bindemann, M., Avetisyan, M., & Rakow, T. (2012). Who can recognize unfamiliar faces? Individual differences and observer consistency in person identification. *Journal of Experimental Psychology: Applied, 18*, 277–291. doi:10.1037/a0029635

Bindemann, M., Fysh, M. C., Cross, K., & Watts, R. (2016). Matching faces against the clock. *i-Perception, 7*(5), 2041669516672219. doi:10.1177/2041669516672219

Bobak, A. K., Dowsett, A. J., & Bate, S. (2016). Solving the border control problem: Evidence of enhanced face matching in individuals with extraordinary face recognition skills. *PLoS ONE, 11*(2), e0148148. doi:10.1371/journal.pone.0148148

Bobak, A. K., Hancock, P. J. B., & Bate, S. (2016). Super-recognisers in action: Evidence from face-matching and face memory tasks. *Applied Cognitive Psychology, 30*, 81–91. doi:10.1002/acp.3170

Bobak, A. K., Mileva, V. R., & Hancock, P. J. B. (2018). Facing the facts: Naive participants have only moderate insight into their face recognition and face perception abilities. *Quarterly Journal of Experimental Psychology, 72*, 872–881. doi:10.1177/1747021818776145

Bobak, A., Pampoulov, P., & Bate, S. (2016). Detecting superior face recognition skills in a large sample of young British adults. *Frontiers in Psychology, 7*, 1–11. doi:10.3389/fpsyg.2016.01378

Brigham, J. C., Van Verst, M., & Bothwell, R. K. (1982). Accuracy of eyewitness identification in a field setting. *Journal of Personality and Social Psychology, 42*, 673–681. doi:10.1037/0022-3514.42.4.673

Bruce, V., Bindemann, M., & Lander, K. (2018). Individual differences in face cognition: A commentary on Logie. *Journal of Applied Research in Memory and Cognition, 7*, 487–492.

Bruce, V., Henderson, Z., Greenwood, K., Hancock, P. J. B., Burton, A. M., & Miller, P. (1999). Verification of face identities from images captured on video. *Journal of Experimental Psychology: Applied, 5*, 339–360. doi:10.1037/1076-898X.5.4.339

Burton, A. M. (2013). Why has research in face recognition progressed so slowly? The importance of variability. *Quarterly Journal of Experimental Psychology, 66*, 1467–1485. doi:10.1080/17470218.2013.800125

Burton, A. M., Jenkins, R., Hancock, P. J. B., & White, D. (2005). Robust representations for face recognition: The power of averages. *Cognitive Psychology, 51*, 256–284. doi:10.1016/j.cogpsych.2005.06.003

Burton, A. M., Jenkins, R., & Schweinberger, S. R. (2011). Mental representations of familiar faces. *British Journal of Psychology, 102*, 943–958. doi:10.1111/j.2044-8295.2011.02039.x

Burton, A. M., Kramer, R. S., Ritchie, K. L., & Jenkins, R. (2016). Identity from variation: Representations of faces derived from multiple instances. *Cognitive Science, 40*, 202–223. doi:10.1111/cogs.12231

Burton, A. M., White, D., & McNeill, A. (2010). The Glasgow Face Matching Test. *Behavior Research Methods, 42*, 286–291. doi:10.3758/BRM.42.1.286

Busey, T. A. & Loftus, G. R. (2007). Cognitive science and the law. *Trends in Cognitive Sciences, 11*, 111–117. doi:10.1016/j.tics.2006.12.004

Busey, T. A. & Parada, F. J. (2010). The nature of expertise in fingerprint examiners. *Psychonomic Bulletin & Review, 17*, 155–160. doi:10.3758/PBR.17.2.155

Chiroro, P. & Valentine, T. (1995). An investigation of the contact hypothesis of the own-race bias in face recognition. *Quarterly Journal of Experimental Psychology, 48A*, 879–894. doi:10.1080/14640749508401421

Cross, J. F., Cross, J., & Daly, J. (1971). Sex, race, age and beauty as factors in recognition of faces. *Perception and Psychophysics, 10*, 393–396. doi:10.3758/BF03210319

Davis, J. P. & Valentine, T. (2009). CCTV on trial: Matching video images with the defendant in the dock. *Applied Cognitive Psychology, 23*, 482–505. doi:10.1002/acp.1490

Estudillo, A. J. & Bindemann, M. (2014). Generalization across view in face memory and face matching. *i-Perception, 5*, 589–601. doi:10.1068/i0669

Findlay, J. M. (2004). Eye scanning and visual search. In J. M. Henderson & F. Ferreira (eds), *The interface of language, vision, and action: Eye movements and the visual world* (pp. 134–159). New York: Psychology Press.

Fysh, M. C. & Bindemann, M. (2017a). Forensic face matching: A review. In M. Bindemann & A. M. Megreya (eds), *Face processing: Systems, disorders and cultural differences* (pp. 1–20). New York: Nova Science Publishers.

Fysh, M. C. & Bindemann, M. (2017b). Effects of time pressure and time passage on face matching accuracy. *Royal Society Open Science, 4*(6), 170249. doi:10.1098/rsos.170249

Fysh, M. C. & Bindemann, M. (2018). The Kent Face Matching Test. *British Journal of Psychology, 109*, 219–231. doi:10.1111/bjop.12260

Gentry, N. W. & Bindemann, M. (2019). Examples improve facial identity comparison. *Journal of Applied Research in Memory and Cognition, 8*, 376–385. doi: 10.1016/j.jarmac.2019.06.002

Glanzer, M. & Adams, J. K. (1985). The mirror effect in recognition memory. *Memory & Cognition, 13*, 8–20.

Glanzer, M., Adams, J. K., Iverson, G. J., & Kim, K. (1993). The regularities of recognition memory. *Psychological Review, 100*, 546–567.

Godoy, A., Ishii, M., Byrne, P. J., Boahene, K. D., Encarnacion, C. O., & Ishii, L. E. (2011). The straight truth: Measuring observer attention to the crooked nose. *The Laryngoscope, 121*, 937–941. doi:10.1002/lary.21733

Gopher, D. (1996). Attention control: Explorations of the work of an executive controller. *Cognitive Brain Research, 5*, 23–38.

Harrison, V. & Hole, G. J. (2009). Evidence for a contact-based explanation of the own-age bias in face recognition. *Psychonomic Bulletin & Review, 16*, 264–269. doi:10.3758/PBR.16.2.264

Henderson, J. M. (2003). Human gaze control during real-world scene perception. *Trends in Cognitive Sciences, 7*, 498–504. doi:10.1016/j.tics.2003.09.006

Henderson, J. M. (2007). Regarding scenes. *Current Directions in Psychological Science, 16*, 219–222. doi:10.1111/j.1467-8721.2007.00507.x

Henderson, J. M., Williams, C. C., & Falk, R. J. (2005). Eye movements are functional during face learning. *Memory & Cognition, 33*, 98–106. doi:10.3758/bf03195300

Hills, P. J. (2012). A developmental study of the own-age face recognition bias in children. *Developmental Psychology, 48*, 499–508. doi:10.1037/a0026524

Hills, P. J., Cooper, R. E., & Pake, J. M. (2013). Removing the own-race bias in face recognition by attentional shift using fixation crosses to diagnostic features: An eye-tracking study. *Visual Cognition, 21*, 876–898. doi:10.1080/13506285.2013.834016

Hills, P. J. & Pake, J. M. (2013). Eye-tracking the own-race bias in face recognition: Revealing the perceptual and socio-cognitive mechanisms. *Cognition, 129,* 586–597. doi:10.1016/j.cognition.2013.08.012

Ishii, L., Carey, J., Byrne, P., Zee, D. S., & Ishii, M. (2009). Measuring attentional bias to peripheral facial deformities. *The Laryngoscope, 119,* 459–465. doi:10.1002/lary.20132

Jenkins, R. & Burton, A. M. (2011). Stable face representations. *Philosophical Transactions of the Royal Society B: Biological Sciences, 366,* 1671–1683. doi:10.1098/rstb.2010.0379

Jenkins, R., White, D., Van Montfort, X., & Burton, A. M. (2011). Variability in photos of the same face. *Cognition, 121,* 313–323. doi:10.1016/j.cognition.2011.08.001

Kokje, E., Bindemann, M., & Megreya, A. M. (2018). Cross-race correlations in the abilities to match unfamiliar faces. *Acta Psychologica, 185,* 13–21. doi:10.1016/j.actpsy.2018.01.006

Lander, K., Bruce, V., & Bindemann, M. (2018). Use-inspired basic research on individual differences in face identification: Implications for criminal investigation and security. *Cognitive Research: Principles and Implications, 3,* 26. doi:10.1186/s41235-018-0115-6

Logie, R. (2018). Human cognition: Common principles and individual variation. *Journal of Applied Research in Memory and Cognition, 7,* 471–486. doi:10.1016/j.jarmac.2018.08.001

Luck, S. J. & Vecera, S. P. (2002). Attention. In H. Pashler & S. Yantis (eds), *Steven's handbook of experimental psychology: Sensation and perception* (pp. 235–286). New York: John Wiley & Sons.

Malcolm, G. L., Lanyon, L. J., Fugard, A. J. B., & Barton, J. J. S. (2008). Scan patterns during the processing of facial expression versus identity: An exploration of task-driven and stimulus-driven effects. *Journal of Vision, 8*(8), 2. doi:10.1167/8.8.2

Maurer, D., Le Grand, R., & Mondloch, C. J. (2002). The many faces of configural processing. *Trends in Cognitive Sciences, 6,* 255–260. doi: 10.1016/S1364-6613(02)01903-4

McCaffery, J. M. & Burton, A. M. (2016). Passport checks: Interactions between matching faces and biographical details. *Applied Cognitive Psychology, 30,* 925–933. doi:10.1002/acp.3281

Megreya, A. M. & Bindemann, M. (2018). Feature instructions improve face-matching accuracy. *PLoS ONE, 13*(3), e0193455. doi:10.1371/journal.pone.0193455

Megreya, A. M. & Burton, A. M. (2006). Unfamiliar faces are not faces: Evidence from a matching task. *Memory & Cognition, 34,* 865–876. doi:10.3758/BF03193433

Megreya, A. M. & Burton, A. M. (2007). Hits and false positives in face matching: A familiarity-based dissociation. *Perception and Psychophysics, 69,* 1175–1184. doi:10.3758/BF03193954

Megreya, A. M. & Burton, A. M. (2008). Matching faces to photographs: Poor performance in eye-witness memory (without the memory). *Journal of Experimental Psychology: Applied, 14,* 364–372. doi:10.1037/a0013464

Megreya, A. M., Sandford, A., & Burton, A. M. (2013). Matching face images taken on the same day or months apart: The limitations of photo ID. *Applied Cognitive Psychology, 27,* 700–706. doi:10.1002/acp.2965

Mehoudar, E., Arizpe, J., Baker, C. I., & Yovel, G. (2014). Faces in the eye of the beholder: Unique and stable eye scanning patterns of individual observers. *Journal of Vision, 14*(7), 6. doi:10.1167/14.7.6

Meyer-Marcotty, P., Gerdes, A. B., Stellzig-Eisenhauer, A., & Alpers, G. W. (2010). Visual face perception of adults with unilateral cleft lip and palate in comparison to controls: An eye-tracking study. *The Cleft Palate-Craniofacial Journal, 48,* 210–216. doi:10.1597/08-244

Miellet, S., Caldara, R., & Schyns, P. G. (2011). Local Jekyll and global Hyde. *Psychological Science, 22,* 1518–1526. doi:10.1177/0956797611424290

Mitchell, M. B., Shirk, S. D., McLaren, D. G., Dodd, J. S., Ezzati, A., Ally, B. A., et al. (2016). Recognition of faces and names: Multimodal physiological correlates of memory and executive function. *Brain Imaging and Behavior, 10,* 408–423. doi:10.1007/s11682-015-9420-6

Moore, R. M. & Johnston, R. A. (2013). Motivational incentives improve unfamiliar face matching accuracy. *Applied Cognitive Psychology, 27,* 754–760. doi:10.1002/acp.2964

Moreton, R., Castro Martinez, S., Appleby, N., Eklof, F., Leitet, E., Brorsson Läthén, K., et al. (2018). *Best practice manual for facial image comparison.* ENFSI-BPM-DI-01 (vs.01). Available at: http://enfsi.eu/wp-content/uploads/2017/06/ENFSI-BPM-DI-01.pdf (accessed 8 April 2020).

Moreton, R., Pike, G., & Havard, C. (2019). A task- and role-based perspective on super-recognizers: Commentary on 'super-recognizers: From the laboratory to the world and back again'. *British Journal of Psychology, 110*, 486–488. doi:10.1111/bjop.12394

Noyes, E., Hill, M. Q., & O'Toole, A. J. (2018). Face recognition ability does not predict person identification performance: Using individual data in the interpretation of group results. *Cognitive Research: Principles and Implications, 3*, 23. doi:10.1186/s41235-018-0117-4

Noyes, E. & Jenkins, R. (2017). Camera-to-subject distance affects face configuration and perceived identity. *Cognition, 165*, 97–104. doi:10.1016/j.cognition.2017.05.012

Özbek, M. & Bindemann, M. (2011). Exploring the time course of face matching: Temporal constraints impair unfamiliar face identification under temporally unconstrained viewing. *Vision Research, 51*, 2145–2155. doi:10.1016/j.visres.2011.08.009

Palermo, R., Rossion, B., Rhodes, G., Laguesse, R., Tez, T., Hall, B., et al. (2017). Do people have insight into their face recognition abilities? *Quarterly Journal of Experimental Psychology, 70*, 218–233. doi:10.1080/17470218.2016.1161058

Papesh, M. H. (2018). Photo-ID verification remains challenging despite years of practice. *Cognitive Research: Principles and Implications, 3*, 19. doi:10.1186/s41235-018-0110-y

Papesh, M. H. & Goldinger, S. D. (2014). Infrequent identity mismatches are frequently undetected. *Attention, Perception & Psychophysics, 76*, 1335–1349. doi:10.3758/s13414-014-0630-6

Papesh, M. H., Heisick, L. L., & Warner, K. A. (2018). The persistent low-prevalence effect in unfamiliar face-matching: The roles of feedback and criterion shifting. *Journal of Experimental Psychology: Applied, 24*, 416–430. doi:10.1037/xap0000156

Peterson, M. F. & Eckstein, M. P. (2013). Individual differences in eye movements during face identification reflect observer-specific optimal points of fixation. *Psychological Science, 24*, 1216–1225. doi:10.1177/0956797612471684

Phillips, P. J., Yates, A. N., Hu, Y., Hahn, C. A., Noyes, E., Jackson, K., et al. (2018). Face recognition accuracy of forensic examiners, superrecognizers, and face recognition algorithms. *Proceedings of the National Academy of Sciences, 115*, 6171–6176. doi:10.1073/pnas.1721355115

Pike, R. (1973). Response latency models for signal detection. *Psychological Review, 80*, 53–68.

Posner, M. I. & Mitchell, R. F. (1967). Chronometric analysis of classification. *Psychological Review, 74*:5, 392–409. doi.org/10.1037/h0024913

Ramon, M., Bobak, A. K., & White, D. (2019). Super-recognizers: From the lab to the world and back again. *British Journal of Psychology, 110*, 461–479. doi:10.1111/bjop.12368

Rapcsak, S. Z. & Edmonds, E. C. (2011). The executive control of face memory. *Behavioural Neurology, 24*, 285–298. doi:10.1155/2011/692460

Ratcliff, R. & Smith, P. L. (2004). A comparison of sequential sampling models for two-choice reaction time. *Psychological Review, 111*, 333–367. doi:10.1037/0033-295X.111.2.333

Ratcliff, R., Smith P. L., Brown, S. D., & McKoon, G. (2016). Diffusion decision model: Current issues and history. *Trends in Cognitive Sciences, 20*, 260–280. doi:10.1016/j.tics.2016.01.007

Rezlescu, C., Susilo, T., Wilmer, J. B., & Caramazza, A. (2017). The inversion, part-whole, and composite effects reflect distinct perceptual mechanisms with varied relationships to face recognition. *Journal of Experimental Psychology: Human Perception and Performance, 43*, 1961–1973. doi: 10.1037/xhp0000400

Rhodes, M. G. & Anastasi, J. S. (2012). The own-age bias in face recognition: A meta-analytic and theoretical review. *Psychological Bulletin, 138*, 146–174. doi:10.1037/a0025750

Richler, J. J. & Gauthier, I. (2014). A meta-analysis and review of holistic face processing. *Psychological Bulletin, 140*, 1281–1302. doi:10.1037/a0037004

Ritchie, K. L., Smith, F. G., Jenkins, R., Bindemann, M., White, D., & Burton, A. M. (2015). Viewers base estimates of face matching accuracy on their own familiarity: Explaining the photo-ID paradox. *Cognition, 141*, 161–169. doi:10.1016/j.cognition.2015.05.002

Ritz-Timme, S., Gabriel, P., Obertovà, Z., Boguslawski, M., Mayer, F., Drabik, A., et al. (2011). A new atlas for the evaluation of facial features: Advantages, limits, and applicability. *International Journal of Legal Medicine, 125*, 301–306. doi:10.1007/s00414-010-0446-4

Robertson, D. J., Kramer, R. S. S., & Burton, A. M. (2017). Fraudulent ID using face morphs: Experiments on human and automatic recognition. *PLoS ONE, 12*(3), e0173319. doi:10.1371/journal. pone.0173319

Robertson, D. J., Noyes, E., Dowsett, A. J., Jenkins, R., & Burton, A. M. (2016). Face recognition by Metropolitan Police super-recognisers. *PLoS ONE, 11*(2), e0150036. doi:10.1371/journal. pone.0150036

Rossion, B. (2014). Understanding individual face discrimination by means of fast periodic visual stimulation. *Experimental Brain Research, 232*, 1599–1621. doi:10.1007/s00221-014-3934-9

Sauerland, M., Sagana, A., Siegmann, K., Heiligers, D., Merckelbach, H., & Jenkins, R. (2016). These two are different. Yes, they're the same: Choice blindness for facial identity. *Consciousness and Cognition, 40*, 93–104. doi:10.1016/j.concog.2016.01.003

Sunday, M. A., Dodd, M. D., Tomarken, A. J., & Gauthier, I. (2018). How faces (and cars) may become special. *Vision Research, 157*, 202–212. doi:10.1016/j.visres.2017.12.007

Susa, K. J., Gause, C. A., & Dessenberger, S. J. (2019). Matching faces to ID photos: The influence of motivation on cross-race identification. *Applied Psychology in Criminal Justice, 15*, 86–96.

Towler, A., Kemp, R. I., Burton, A. M., Dunn, J. D., Wayne, T., Moreton, R., et al. (2019). Do professional facial image comparison training courses work? *PLoS ONE, 14*(2), e0211037. doi:10.1371/journal.pone.0211037

Towler, A., White, D., & Kemp, R. I. (2014). Evaluating training methods for facial image comparison: The face shape strategy does not work. *Perception, 43*, 214–218. doi:10.1068/p7676

Towler, A., White, D., & Kemp, R. I. (2017). Evaluating the feature comparison strategy for forensic face identification. *Journal of Experimental Psychology: Applied, 23*, 47–58. doi:10.1037/xap0000108

Townsend, J. T. & Ashby, F. G. (1983). *Stochastic modeling of elementary psychological processes.* New York: Cambridge University Press.

Verhallen, R. J., Bosten, J. M., Goodbourn, P. T., Lawrance-Owen, A. J., Bargary, J., & Mollon, J. D. (2017). General and specific factors in the processing of faces. *Vision Research, 141*, 217–227. doi:10.1016/j.visres.2016.12.014

Voss, A., Nagler, M., & Lerche, V. (2013). Diffusion models in experimental psychology: A practical introduction. *Experimental Psychology, 60*, 384–402. doi:10.1027/1618-3169/a000218

White, D., Dunn, J. D., Schmid, A. C., & Kemp, R. I. (2015). Error rates in users of automatic face recognition software. *PLoS ONE, 10*(10), e0139827. doi:10.1371/journal.pone.0139827

White, D., Kemp, R. I., Jenkins, R., & Burton, A. M. (2014). Feedback training for facial image comparison. *Psychonomic Bulletin & Review, 21*, 100–106. doi:10.3758/s13423-013-0475-3

White, D., Kemp, R. I., Jenkins, R., Matheson, M., & Burton, A. M. (2014). Passport officers' errors in face matching. *PLoS ONE, 9*(8), e103510. doi:10.1371/journal.pone.0103510

Wirth, B. E. & Carbon, C. C. (2017). An easy game for frauds? Effects of professional experience and time pressure on passport-matching performance. *Journal of Experimental Psychology: Applied, 23*, 138–157. doi:10.1037/xap0000114

Xu, B., Liu-Shuang, J., Rossion, B., & Tanaka, J. (2017). Individual differences in face identity processing with fast periodic visual stimulation. *Journal of Cognitive Neuroscience, 29*, 1368–1377. doi:10.1162/jocn_a_01126

Yan, X., Liu-Shuang, J., & Rossion, B. (2019). Effect of face-related task on rapid individual face discrimination. *Neuropsychologia, 129*, 236–245. doi:10.1016/j.neuropsychologia.2019.04.002

4

Understanding Professional Expertise in Unfamiliar Face Matching

David White, Alice Towler, and Richard I. Kemp

4.1 Introduction

Deciding whether images of unfamiliar faces are of the same person or different people has been studied extensively in laboratory research since the early 1990s. Yet it is only very recently that researchers have begun to test the accuracy of professional experts on this task. The task is shown in Figure 4.1, and on first inspection it appears straightforward. We routinely identify faces in our everyday lives, so the task is superficially familiar and the format of the task appears quite simple. It requires comparing images presented at the same time, and so does not rely on memory, giving the impression that this is an easy task.

The most important insight from laboratory studies of novice participants is that this initial impression is misguided. Unfamiliar face matching is substantially more difficult than it initially appears. When novice participants are given unlimited time to complete these tasks, error rates in pairwise face-matching tasks range from around 20% with high-quality standardized images (e.g., Bruce et al., 2001; Burton et al., 2010) to 30% or 40% in more challenging tests where images are captured in unconstrained environmental conditions (e.g., Davis & Valentine, 2009; Henderson et al., 2001; Phillips, Yates, et al., 2018). These high error rates are observed even when participants are matching images to people standing directly in front of them (Davis & Valentine, 2009), as is the case when checking photo ID documents (Kemp et al., 1997). Error rates are also higher when participants work under time pressure (Fysh & Bindemann, 2017), experience anxiety (Attwood et al., 2013) or lack sleep (Beattie et al., 2016).

Errors in face matching are not only of academic interest to cognitive psychologists. When these errors are made outside the lab, they can have serious consequences. Face-matching decisions are performed by many thousands of public and private sector staff across the world each day, such as passport officers, police officers, bank clerks, surveillance system operators, security personnel, and retail workers. Identity verification decisions in these professional settings often require staff to compare two or more images of unfamiliar faces and decide whether they show the same person or different people: For example when passport officers compare a traveller to their passport image, or when police officers compare closed-circuit television (CCTV) evidence to mugshot images. As a result, the security of important identity management

David White, Alice Towler, and Richard I. Kemp, *Understanding Professional Expertise in Unfamiliar Face Matching* In: *Forensic Face Matching*. Edited by: Markus Bindemann, Oxford University Press (2021). © Oxford University Press. DOI: 10.1093/oso/9780198837749.003.0004.

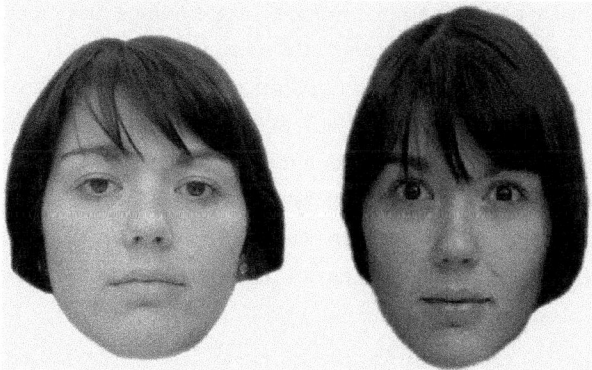

Figure 4.1 An example item from the Glasgow Face Matching Test.

Note: This task requires participants to decide whether pairs of images show the same face or different faces. Despite the images being taken on the same day, with neutral expression, standardised pose and lighting conditions, novice participants make 20% errors on this task. The correct answer is that these images are of the same person.

Source: Adapted from Burton et al. (2010) 'The Glasgow Face Matching Test' *Behavior Research Methods, 42*, 286–291, Figure 1. https://doi.org/10.3758/BRM.42.1.286 © 2010, Springer Nature.

systems underpinning financial transactions, interactions with government, criminal investigations, and legal processes all rely on the accuracy of unfamiliar face-matching decisions.

Knowing whether the staff involved in these decisions are susceptible to the high levels of error observed in novices is therefore a critical question with immediate relevance to society. In professional settings, the task experimental psychologists refer to as 'unfamiliar face matching'[1] is most commonly known as 'facial image comparison', or simply 'facial comparison'. Despite the importance of this task and the substantial literature examining novice accuracy in laboratory studies, it is only within the past decade that researchers have begun to assess the accuracy of professional populations. The purpose of this chapter is to review this emerging literature.

4.2 Professional Expertise in Unfamiliar Face Matching

Many people are required to be experts in unfamiliar face matching as a consequence of their position, professional training, or experience. For instance, we require that border control officers can accurately decide whether the person at a border crossing is the individual shown in their ID document. More specific requirements can also be imposed

---

[1] This term may be underspecified (see Stacchi et al., 2019). Variants include tasks that require perceptually matching the identity of images of faces presented simultaneously, without the requirement that these images are committed to memory, and other 'sequential' versions that require holding an image in memory for a short duration. In this chapter, we focus on a narrow definition of the task whereby images are presented simultaneously to the viewer, and so test perceptual discrimination ability with no requirement to store the face in memory (see Figure 4.1).

by legal requirements—for example, in rules or guidelines that judges use to evaluate the admissibility and weight of expert evidence (see Edmond & Wortley, 2016). We have argued elsewhere that a person's position, qualifications, professional experience, or training are not sufficient to qualify them as an expert in facial image comparison. Rather, a person's expertise in this task should be established on the basis of proven and sustained levels of accuracy in face matching (e.g., Towler et al., 2018). This is consistent with the study of expertise more broadly, where a standard condition of being classified as an expert is 'consistent superior performance on a specified set of representative tasks for a domain' (Ericsson & Lehmann, 1996).

The focus of this chapter is therefore on whether professional groups outperform novices on representative tasks in their domain. As researchers interested in expertise in unfamiliar face matching, we are in an enviable position compared with many others working in the broader field of professional expertise (e.g., Anders et al., 2006), because it is relatively straightforward for us to define the *representative task*. Despite diversity in their job descriptions and roles, an important part of the professional duties performed by all professional staff reviewed in this chapter is captured by the task illustrated in Figure 4.1. The simplicity of this task, and its relative uniformity across a wide range of important applied contexts make it ideally suited to studying expert performance. In addition, the close correspondence between existing laboratory tests and tasks performed in the real world has enabled researchers working in this area to transition quickly from laboratory to field-based studies.

In addition to the clear practical importance, understanding professional expertise in unfamiliar face matching is also of theoretical interest because it can potentially inform broader conceptual understanding of perceptual expertise. Notably, prominent theoretical accounts in the field of face perception have argued that people *in general* are 'face experts' (e.g., Carey, 1992; Diamond & Carey, 1986). According to this definition, perceptual expertise in face identification is acquired in the normal course of our everyday experience, as a consequence of the fundamental importance of accurate face perception in social interactions with other people. However, as Young and Burton (2018) have recently argued, processing the identity of unfamiliar faces is an important exception. For the average person, performing unfamiliar face-matching tasks is error-prone and effortful—and so their performance does not satisfy recognized definitions of expertise, which emphasize accuracy and the presence of automatic cognitive processing (e.g., Ericsson & Lehmann, 1996; Shiffrin & Schneider, 1977). Instead, people in general are experts at recognizing the *familiar* faces of people they know—a task they perform routinely in daily life—but not *unfamiliar* face identification, a task that most people are rarely required to perform.

If the average person is not expert in unfamiliar face matching, and does not perform the task regularly, this raises the important question of whether expertise can be *acquired*. A large body of research shows that familiar face recognition and unfamiliar face matching rely on qualitatively different perceptual and cognitive processes (e.g., Bonner et al., 2003; Clutterbuck & Johnston, 2002; Megreya & Burton, 2006, 2007). Given these distinct processes, it is possible that performance is supported by qualitatively different learning trajectories. Face *recognition* is a task that everyone performs many times each day, and the learning curve that drives our expertise in this task is believed to asymptote around 30 years of age (Germine et al., 2011). However, it is not known whether a separate trajectory of learning can lead to improved accuracy in unfamiliar face matching in the special case where people are required to perform the task in their daily work.

Psychological theories of expert performance predict that deliberate and prolonged practice leads to improvements in performance (Ericsson et al., 1993). In the remainder of this chapter, we evaluate support for this prediction in the task of unfamiliar face matching by reviewing studies that have compared performance of professionals—engaged in the task as part of their employment—to that of novices.

First, we describe the types of professional groups engaged in unfamiliar face matching that have been tested. These practitioners come from diverse backgrounds, are exposed to different types of training and work experiences, and perform a range of different facial comparison tasks in a wide variety of environments (Heyer et al., 2011). Second, we present results from a recent meta-analysis of the studies reviewed in this chapter. This shows large variability in the standardized effect size comparing novice and expert performance across these studies, which appears to be attributable to the relative specialization of professional groups. Third, we examine the individual studies in more detail to assess the factors that appear to promote superior accuracy in specialist groups and the nature of the learning that might produce expert performance. Based on this detailed review, we propose that a combination of factors contribute to the higher accuracy of specialist groups.

We conclude that expertise in unfamiliar face matching can be acquired both *developmentally* and *professionally*. In our final section, we formalize these different types of expertise within a dual-route framework whereby two independent domains of expertise underpin an individual's accuracy in facial image comparison—one based on natural ability and rooted in the core face recognition system, and another that is acquired through professional experience and training in unfamiliar face matching, and is supported by more general perceptual and cognitive mechanisms.

4.3 Subtypes of Professional Groups

There are three broad categorizations of professional roles that require people to perform unfamiliar face matching in their work. Following from recent tests involving diverse groups of face identification practitioners (Phillips, Yates, et al., 2018), we use the terms 'facial reviewer', 'facial examiner' and 'police super-recognizer' to capture the three types of professional experts who have been tested. We use these categories to organize the meta-analysis and literature review below, and provide further details of these roles in the following sections.

This classification is consistent with the internationally recognized standards documents produced by the Facial Identification Scientific Working Group (FISWG, 2010).

These are an authoritative reference for face identification practitioners worldwide. According to the FISWG classification, there are two broad types of personnel who perform unfamiliar face matching in their daily work. First, *facial reviewers*, who process substantial volumes of face identification decisions and typically make these decisions quickly and alongside other administrative checks, such as checking that a traveller has a valid visa or has completed paperwork correctly. Examples include border control officers (e.g., Wirth & Carbon, 2017) and government identity resolution staff (e.g., Heyer et al., 2018). These professionals typically receive only basic training and do not receive mentorship on face matching. Second, *facial examiners*, who perform more rigorous comparison of facial images, may spend hours or days on each comparison, receive more extensive training and mentorship, and typically communicate their conclusions in formal reports. These individuals are often responsible for producing written reports that might be used in legal proceedings (e.g., Norell et al., 2015; Phillips, Yates, et al., 2018).

We also include a third, and relatively new class of face identification, professional *police super-recognizers*. These staff have been selected on the basis of their high performance in face-identification tasks to be part of specialist face-identification teams to support criminal investigations (Davis et al., 2016; Robertson et al., 2016). There are relatively few studies of police super-recognizers, but there is a broader research literature examining non-professional populations who achieve high levels of accuracy on face-identification tests (see Noyes et al., 2017; Ramon et al., 2019, for reviews). In general, natural variability in face-identification ability in the general population is known to be relatively stable over repeated testing (Balsdon et al., 2018; Wilmer et al., 2010; see Wilmer, 2017, for a review; cf. Ramon et al., 2019). This finding has important implications for the selection and recruitment of individuals for professional roles. However, given the narrow focus of this chapter on performance of professional staff who perform unfamiliar face matching in daily work, we do not include studies of super-recognizers from the general population in our meta-analysis.

4.4 Meta-Analysis of Comparisons Between Professionals and Novices

We recently conducted a literature search to identify studies that compared professional experts and novice participants in unfamiliar face-matching accuracy (White, 2020). Criteria for inclusion were that the professional groups performed face matching as part of their daily work, and at least one unfamiliar face-matching task was used to compare their accuracy to a comparison non-expert group. This meant excluding previous tests that either tested professional staff using memory-based face-identification tests (e.g., Burton et al., 1999; Davis et al., 2016, Cambridge Face Memory Test [CFMT]) or did not include a novice comparison group (e.g., Kemp et al., 1997; White, Kemp, Jenkins, Matheson, et al., 2014, photo-to-person test).

Although there was some variation in unfamiliar face-matching tests used to compare novices to professionals across studies—for example, in image quality or presentation format—they all shared the requirement that participants compared images of unfamiliar faces, presented simultaneously, and had to decide whether they showed the same person or different people. To ensure that the studies used tasks that were representative of real-world tasks, we also removed tests from analysis that (i) used test images that were digitally manipulated (e.g., Wirth & Carbon, 2017: 'paraphernalia', 'distinctive feature', and 'hairstyle conditions'); (ii) involved other non-representative experimental manipulations (e.g., White, Phillips, et al., 2015: inverted and 2-second conditions); or (iii) showed clear evidence of ceiling effects (Towler et al., 2019: Experiment 2, high resolution-to-high resolution test).

We identified a total of 12 publications containing professional versus novice comparisons. Many of these either contained multiple tests fitting our definition of unfamiliar face matching (e.g., Robertson et al., 2016; White, Kemp, Jenkins, Matheson, et al., 2014) or multiple professional groups (e.g., Phillips, Yates, et al., 2018; White, Phillips, et al., 2015), giving a total of 29 comparisons that met our inclusion criteria. Over 1,600 practitioners have been tested since 2013—a remarkable achievement given that our review did not uncover any published tests prior to this date. We find this especially encouraging because it suggests that professional organizations are beginning to recognize and address the problem identified by psychologists in the late 1990s—namely, that novices perform badly at unfamiliar face-identification tasks (Bruce et al., 1999; Kemp et al., 1997).

Effect sizes between professional and novice groups are shown in Figure 4.2, categorized by the three types of professional groups described earlier. Positive effect sizes signify superior performance of professionals compared to novices, with statistically significant comparisons indicated by confidence intervals that do not include zero. Visual inspection of Figure 4.2 shows clear differences between the effects observed in the three professional groups. While facial examiners and super-recognizers consistently achieve higher accuracy than novices, facial reviewers generally have the same level of accuracy as novices (Mean Cohen's D facial reviewers = 0.34; facial examiners = 1.43; police super-recognizers = 1.66). In terms of aggregate accuracy differences, reviewers scored 1.5 percentage points higher than novice comparison groups, with examiners scoring 13 and super-recognizers 14 percentage points higher.

This meta-analysis indicates that the different practitioner groups have different levels of expertise. It is likely that the factors contributing to accuracy also vary across these professional groups. Police super-recognizers are explicitly selected on the basis of their ability, whereas other groups are not. Differences between reviewer and examiner groups, on the other hand, may be due to differences in working practice in these roles. While both these groups perform face-matching tasks regularly, there are important differences in the training and professional mentorship they receive, and the time available to undertake the respective tasks. In the following sections, we examine the studies included in this meta-analysis in greater detail, in order to

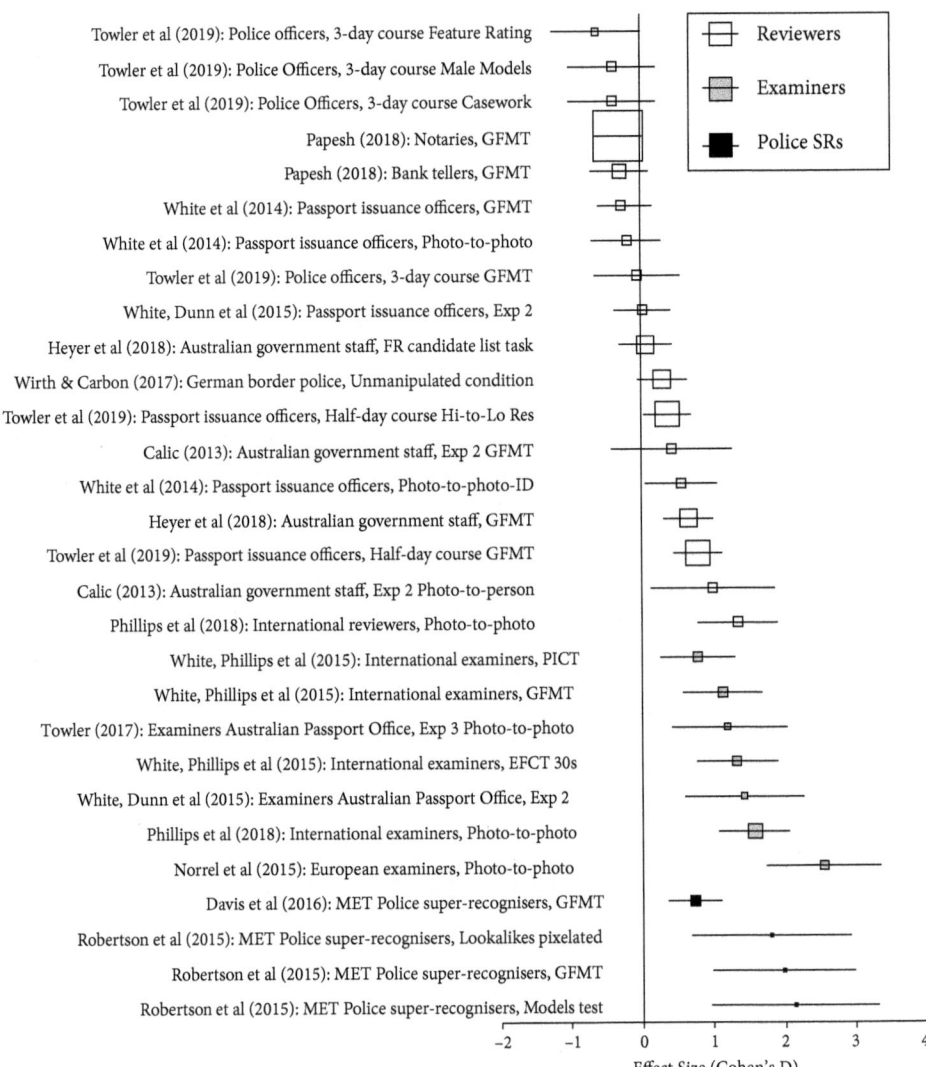

Figure 4.2 Effect sizes for 29 novice vs. professional comparisons in unfamiliar face matching tasks taken from 12 peer-reviewed scientific papers

Note: A positive effect size indicates that the professional cohort outperformed novices, 95% confidence intervals that do not include zero indicate the comparison was statistically significant and the sample size is represented by the size of the marker. Details of the three types of expert and the tasks they perform are provided in the main text. For further details of individual tests please refer to White (2020).

Source: Data from White, D. (2020) 'Do professional groups outperform novices in unfamiliar face matching tasks?' A meta-analysis. *PsyArXiv*.

understand the conditions that lead to higher accuracy in some professional groups and not others. First, we review tests of facial reviewers, where evidence for expert performance is limited, before examining studies of the more specialist groups— facial examiners and police super-recognizers—where evidence points to superior accuracy.

4.5 Facial Reviewers

A variety of facial reviewer cohorts have been compared to novices, including UK police officers (Towler et al., 2019), US bank tellers (Papesh, 2018), US notaries (Papesh, 2018), Australian passport-issuance officers (Towler et al., 2019; White, Dunn, et al., 2015; White, Kemp, Jenkins, Matheson, et al., 2014), Australian government staff (Calic, 2013; Heyer et al., 2018), German border control officers (Wirth & Carbon, 2017), and international cohorts of police and government staff (Phillips, Yates, et al., 2018). All these groups performed unfamiliar face matching in their daily work, and their decisions played a critical part of processes designed to protect against identity fraud and other criminal activity. Nevertheless, visual inspection of Figure 4.2 shows that the majority of these groups did not perform significantly better than the novices, with almost half showing numerically *lower* performance than that of people who do not perform the task regularly.

Across 18 tests, the aggregate percentage point advantage of reviewers over novice comparison groups was 1.6%. Just 6 of the 18 tests showed significant differences whereby reviewers outperformed novices. Effect sizes in tests of facial reviewers were generally small but show a large amount of variability across tests, ranging from 6% *less* accurate (Cohen's D = −0.61) to 17% more accurate (Cohen's D = 1.35). Because of this substantial variability, we first consider studies that did not find significant differences between novices and reviewers, before considering those reporting significant differences.

4.5.1 Non-Significant Differences Between Facial Reviewers and Novices

In total, 12 of 18 tests showed no difference between professional and novice groups. These null results include tests of police officers, bank tellers, notaries, and passport officers—all staff whom the public rely on to make accurate face-matching decisions. Starting with studies showing weakest evidence of expert performance, police officers tested by Towler and colleagues (2019) had been working in roles that required them to make facial image comparison decisions for an average of one and a half years, but only 17% of these staff had received training. This study was designed as an evaluation of a professional training course, and so novice and professional groups performed tests before and after training to assess whether training improved accuracy (the test reported some limited evidence of improvement, see Towler et al., 2019 for details). For the purpose of our meta-analysis, we analysed scores from the four unfamiliar face-matching tests taken before training. Officers performed the Glasgow Face Matching Test (GFMT) and an additional three face-matching tests, shown in Figure 4.3. Across all the four tests, there were no significant differences between police officers and

(A) (B) (C)

Figure 4.3 Police officers tested by Towler et al. (2019) completed four pairwise unfamiliar face matching tasks: the Good, Bad and Ugly test (A), Male Models test (B), Casework test (C); and the Glasgow Face Matching Test (see Figure 4.1).

Source: Adapted from Towler et al. (2019) 'Do professional facial image comparison training courses work?' *PLoS ONE, 14*(2), e0211037, Figure 2. https://doi.org/10.1371/journal.pone.0211037 © 2019 Towler et al.

university students, and police were in fact *less* accurate than novice participants, as indicated by the negative effect size for these contrasts.

Bank tellers and notaries tested by Papesh (2018)—who also showed negative effect sizes in comparison to novices—had many years' experience verifying identity by checking photo ID to protect against identity fraud in financial and legal transactions. Despite the importance of these decisions, they made an average of 25% errors in the photo-to-photo ID matching task shown in Figure 4.4A. Similarly, passport-issuance officers tested by White, Kemp, Jenkins, Matheson, et al. (2014) and White, Dunn, et al. (2015) were responsible for ensuring that the image of the passport applicant matched their previous passport application, and had an average of eight and a half years' experience in this role. When asked to decide whether pairs of images, like those shown in Figure 4.4B, were of the same person or different people, these staff made 20% errors on average—again, no better than university students.

In the three tests comparing the accuracy of passport officers to that of novices in White, Kemp, Jenkins, Matheson, et al. (2014), one test did show significantly higher accuracy compared to novices (photo-to-photo ID task, see Figure 4.4B). It is perhaps tempting to attribute this to the photo ID checking task being more reflective of a passport officer's daily work than the other tests, which used images that were not scanned from current photo ID cards. However, photo ID checking is not in fact the face-matching task performed most regularly by these passport-issuance staff. Instead, the most common task they perform is shown in Figure 4.5, where they must decide whether the person at the top appears anywhere in the gallery of faces below that have been returned by face-recognition software. When White, Dunn, et al. (2015) tested their cohort on this precise task, they found that passport-issuance officers made errors on 50% of trials—the same as a comparison group of university students. This suggests that their superior performance on the photo ID checking test was not simply due to the type of imagery being more familiar to them.

The task shown in Figure 4.5 is an increasingly common task in a variety of professional settings, whereby face-recognition software is used to search for a face in a large database of facial images. The Australian Passport Office, for example, use face-recognition technology to protect against identity fraud when issuing passports. When

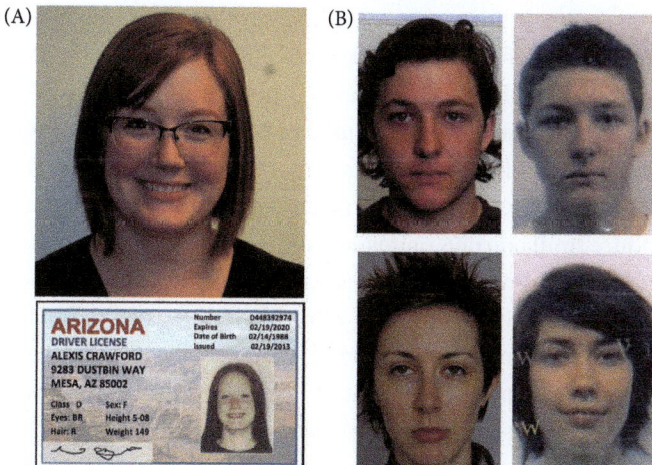

Figure 4.4 (A) Photo-ID matching task used by Papesh (2018) to test bank tellers and notaries. (B) Photo-to-photo-ID matching test used by White et al. (2014) to test passport issuance officers.

Source: (A) Adapted from Papesh (2018) 'Photo ID verification remains challenging despite years of practice' *Cognitive Research: Principles and Implications, 3*, 19, Figure 1. https://doi.org/10.1186/s41235-018-0110-y © 2018 Papesh.

(B) Adapted from White et al. (2014) 'Passport officers' errors in face matching' *PLoS ONE, 9*(8), e103510, Figure 2. https://doi.org/10.1371/journal.pone.0103510 © 2014 White et al.

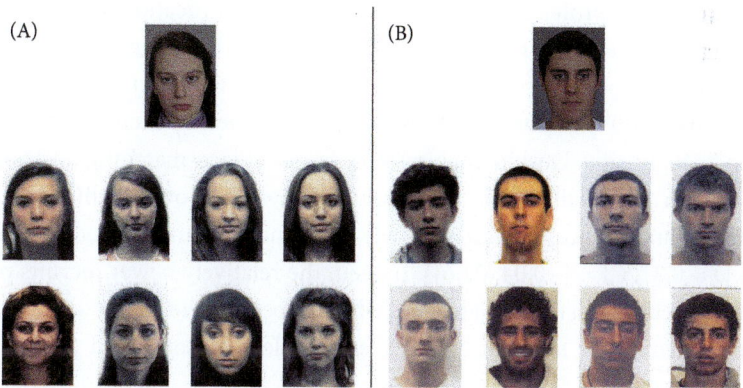

Figure 4.5 Example items from the face recognition software 'candidate list' task used by White et al. (2015) to test passport issuance officers.

Note: White et al. (2015) found that facial reviewers who perform this task as part of their daily work made errors on 1 in every 2 decisions, and mistakenly selected the wrong face as matching the target 40% of the time. These types of false identifications could have serious consequences, especially in the context of law enforcement where this could result in wrongful conviction and imprisonment. The correct answer for A is top row, second from the left. The correct answer for B is target absent.

Source: Reproduced from White et al. (2015) 'Error rates in users of automatic face recognition software' *PLoS ONE, 10*(10), e0139827, Figure 1. https://doi.org/10.1371/journal.pone.0139827 © 2015 White et al.

Australian citizens apply for a passport, their application image is used to search all other passport images. If a matching face is found under a different name, this may signal a fraudulent application. Critically, these types of 'one-to-many' database searches return a 'candidate list' of potential matching faces that a human practitioner must then review to decide if the target face is present (White, Dunn, et al., 2015; White & Kemp, 2016). Face recognition systems used in criminal investigation and live surveillance produce similar arrays of images (see Noyes & Hill, this volume).

Heyer et al. (2018) also tested a professional cohort using a candidate list task generated using face-recognition software. While the task was substantially easier overall than in White, Dunn, et al. (2015),[2] overall accuracy of staff from the Australian government and police did not exceed that of novices. However, this professional group was recruited from a range of Australian government departments. These staff included passport-issuance officers who compare passport images with the support of face-recognition software (as in White, Dunn, et al., 2015; White, Kemp, Jenkins, Matheson, et al., 2014), visa-processing officers who compare applicants to passport images, and forensic artists who produce likenesses of suspects. As a result, there was substantial variability in the precise roles performed across these departments, and also the proportion of time staff devoted to unfamiliar face-matching tasks in their work. When the researchers split this professional cohort by the average number of facial comparison decisions made in their daily work, they found that staff who made more than 50 decisions per day outperformed novices on the 'candidate list' task.

Heyer et al.'s (2018) result may suggest that the number of decisions made by professionals each day is a key factor in the development of expertise. However, while this association appears to exist for the specific cohort they tested, it does not appear to be true in general. For example, German border control officers tested by Wirth and Carbon (2017) were professionals for whom 'person identification during immigration was one of the core tasks (if not the most frequent task) the participating police officers performed on their job'. Wirth and Carbon's (2017) task was carefully constructed to be representative of the passport-checking duties performed by their professional group, as shown in Figure 4.6. Despite making very frequent face-matching decisions on this precise task in their daily work, their results showed no overall difference between professionals and novices (Mean accuracy difference for unmodified images = 3.8%, Cohen's D = 0.31, CI = [−0.04, 0.66]). Indeed, the relatively newer recruits performed significantly better than novices and staff who had been in the job for longer, suggesting that experience in the task does not necessarily lead to improved accuracy. This is

---

[2] Heyer et al.'s (2018) task was easier than White, Dunn, et al.'s (2015) because they constructed their task using images from a publicly available database of high-quality images (Phillips et al., 1998), whereby image capture conditions were under experimental control and images of the same person were taken on the same camera at roughly the same time. In contrast, White, Dunn, et al. (2015) used real passport images whereby matching images were taken many years apart and in more diverse image capture conditions. Another important difference was that Heyer et al.'s (2018) candidate lists were constructed using the top matches from a database of 1,000 faces, while White, Dunn, et al. (2015) selected foil images from a dataset of over a million images. This meant that the non-matching 'foil' faces in White and colleagues' study were likely to be much more similar in appearance to the target face than in Heyer et al.'s study.

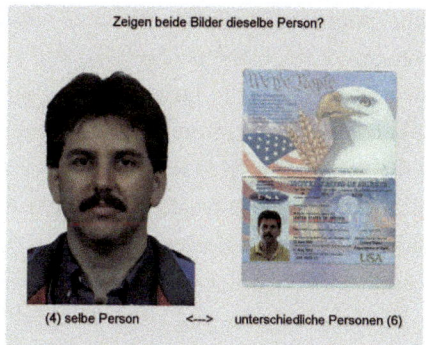

Figure 4.6 Passport-to-photo matching task used by Wirth and Carbon (2017) to test German border security officers.

Note: The image on the left shows a participant performing the task, with examples of the images used in the test shown on the right.

Source: Reproduced from Wirth & Carbon (2017) 'An easy game for frauds? Effects of professional experience and time pressure on passport-matching performance' *Journal of Experimental Psychology: Applied, 23*, 138–157, Figure 2. https://doi:10.1037/xap0000114 Copyright © 2017, American Psychological Association.

consistent with both White, Kemp, Jenkins, Matheson, et al. (2014) and Papesh (2018) who also found that more professional experience did not predict higher accuracy in their cohorts.

Overall, the 12 tests showing non-significant differences between the face-matching accuracy of facial reviewers and novices appear to confirm that simply performing the task of unfamiliar face matching in daily work is not sufficient to produce expertise. Next, we consider the tests of professional groups that do show significant differences, in order to better understand which factors may give rise to expert performance.

4.5.2 Significant Differences Between Facial Reviewers and Novices

Across eighteen tests of facial reviewers, six groups showed significantly greater accuracy in reveiewers compared to novices. For three of these groups, superior accuracy was found in one test (Calic, 2013, Experiment 2; Heyer et al., 2018, GFMT; White, Kemp, Jenkins, Matheson, et al., 2014, photo-to-photo ID) while equivalent accuracy to novices was found in the other tests of the same group (Calic, 2013, GFMT; Heyer et al., 2018, FR candidate list; White, Kemp, Jenkins, Matheson, et al., 2014, GFMT, photo-to-photo). Moreover, where there were significant differences between groups in these studies, effect sizes were relatively small. Given Ericsson and Lehmann's (1996) definition of expertise, which we adopt here, states that a key criteria is 'consistent performance across a set of representative tasks', the inconsistent performance of these groups means that they do not meet this criteria.

The remaining three tests appear to show more compelling evidence of superior performance. Two of these tests were carried out on the same cohort of 204 passport-issuance officers working for the Australian Passport Office (Towler et al., 2019,

Experiment 2). They outperformed students on both the GFMT (Mean accuracy difference = 9.3%, Cohen's D = 0.79) and a bespoke test that required comparing faces in low-quality images to faces in high-quality images (Mean accuracy difference = 4.2%, Cohen's D = 0.38). Interestingly, the passport officers tested by White, Kemp, Jenkins, Matheson, et al. (2014) were a subset of the larger sample tested by Towler et al. (2019). Because the officers tested by White, Kemp, Jenkins, Matheson, et al. (2014) were recruited from a single regional office, they may not have been representative of the overall ability of officers in the organization.

The final test showing a significant difference between facial reviewers and novices was conducted by Phillips, Yates, et al. (2018). Facial reviewers in this test—police and government employees primarily from the USA—were asked to complete a very challenging pairwise unfamiliar face-matching task consisting of 20 image pairs (see Figure 4.6). These reviewers were substantially more accurate than university students on this task (Mean accuracy difference = 17.5%, Cohen's D = 1.35), but facial reviewers had a window of up to three months to complete these face-matching decisions, whereas the student comparison group completed them in a single experimental session. This may well have contributed to their higher accuracy, but the very large effect size—in comparison to the effects of providing novices with additional time in previous tests (e.g., White, Phillips, et al., 2015; cf., Özbek & Bindemann, 2011)—suggests that at least some of the effect can be attributed to the superior ability of this group. Nevertheless, given that details of their professional history, training, and experience were unavailable—and that only a single test was used to verify their expertise—future research is necessary to determine the causes of their superior accuracy.

Overall, the evidence reviewed above provides very little support for *professionally acquired* expertise among facial reviewers. Importantly, however, these professional groups did not receive any extensive training, feedback, or mentorship in unfamiliar face-matching tasks. All these factors have been shown to play some role in the development of expertise in other fields (Ericsson et al., 1993), and so we next consider more specialist professional groups who do benefit from some of these learning opportunities.

4.6 Facial Examiners

Facial examiners are a relatively homogenous group compared to facial reviewers. While they are employed by a variety of organizations, including government departments, police, and private forensic service providers, they tend to perform a similar role in these professional settings. Typically, they are responsible for writing reports that provide a detailed and balanced assessment of the image comparison evidence. A key requirement of their role is to provide an estimate of the likelihood that two images are of the same individual or two different individuals, using a 'conclusion scale' to provide justification for this conclusion and potentially to defend it in court (see Towler et al., 2018).

Facial examiners typically receive facial comparison decisions that have been escalated to them via some initial screening process. This screening is typically performed by the facial reviewers described above. For example, in a law enforcement context, the examiners might receive potential matches that have been uncovered via police investigation and perhaps by investigators using facial recognition software (see Klontz & Jain, 2013). At border control, examiners may be asked to compare an image of a traveller captured by an automated border gate to their passport image, when primary line officers are unable to reach a decision.

All seven comparisons between facial examiners and novices showed large effect sizes, with examiners outperforming novices. The aggregate percentage point advantage of examiners over novice comparison groups was 13%, with six of seven tests reporting a Cohen's D greater than 1 and one of these greater than 2 (Norrell et al., 2015, at 2.55). They attained high levels of accuracy despite making decisions more quickly than they would normally be expected to in their daily work (e.g., 30 seconds in White, Phillips, et al., 2015; 18 seconds in White, Dunn, et al., 2015). Importantly, in all tests— except for one (Phillips, Yates, et al., 2018)—examiners also attained these high levels of accuracy in experimental conditions that did not permit use of digital tools or reference material that might be used in normal working practice. This suggests that the source of their expertise was in their perceptual and cognitive processing, rather than their ability to use specialist tools or decision-making support.

As further evidence of their expertise, when groups of facial examiners have been tested on multiple tests, they have shown consistently superior performance across these tests. Facial examiners in the Australian Passport Office showed superior performance in two separate studies conducted years apart (Towler et al., 2017; White, Phillips, et al., 2015), and the international group of examiners tested by White, Phillips, et al. (2015) showed superior accuracy across three representative tests performed in a single experimental session. Interestingly, the only test reporting an effect size of less than 1 (White, Phillips, et al., 2015, Person Identification Test, Mean accuracy difference = 7.7%, Cohen's D = 0.79), included body and clothing information, and a subset of test items that were specifically selected because they did not include identifying information in the face (Figure 4.7B; see Rice et al., 2013, for details). Figure 4.7 shows examples of the different types of test items employed in the different tests of examiners.

The consistent superior accuracy of facial examiners compared to novices satisfies the criteria of expertise we adopted at the beginning of this chapter (Ericsson & Lehmann, 1996). There are many potential sources of learning above and beyond those available to facial reviewers, which may explain examiners' expertise. First, the training that facial examiners receive is much more detailed (see Towler, Kemp, & White, this volume; see also Towler et al., 2019). Second, most facial examiners work in small teams with many opportunities for mentorship and feedback on their performance. Both performing face-matching tasks collaboratively with high performers (Dowsett & Burton, 2015) and receiving feedback on the accuracy of decisions (Papesh et al., 2018; White, Kemp, Jenkins, & Burton, 2014; cf., Alenezi & Bindemann, 2013) have been shown to

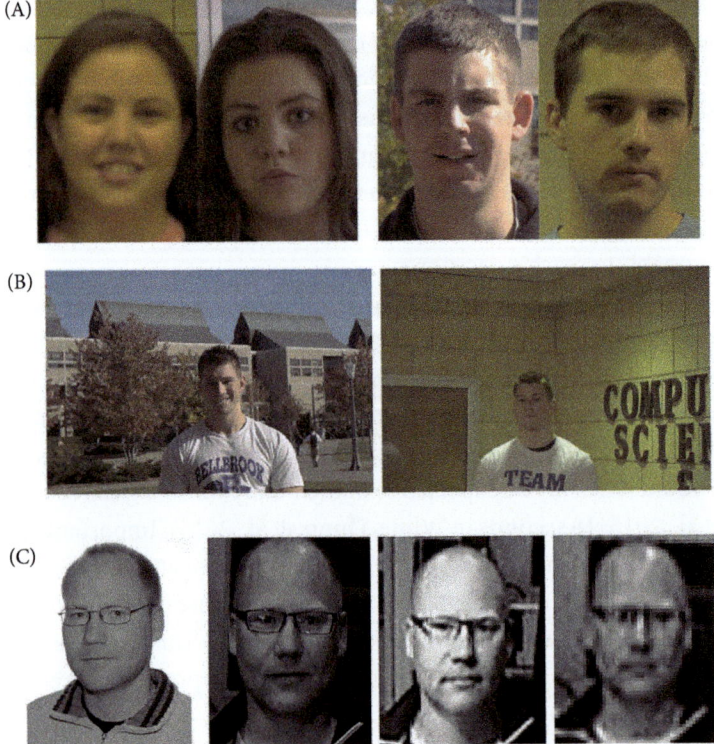

Figure 4.7 Pairwise unfamiliar face matching tasks used to test facial examiners.

Note: (A) Example image pairs used to test examiners in White, Phillips, et al. (2015), Towler et al. (2017) and Phillip, Yates, et al. (2018). The left pair are of the same person and the right pair are of different people. (B) Image pair from the Person Identification Challenge Test used in White, Phillips, et al. (2015). These images are of the same person. (C) An example of reference image (left) and three images of varying quality (right) used to create image pairs of varying quality in Norell et al. (2015).

Sources: (A) Reproduced from Phillips et al. (2018) 'Face recognition accuracy of forensic examiners, superrecognizers, and face recognition algorithms' *PNAS, 115,* 6171–6176, Figure 1. https://doi.org/10.1073/pnas.1721355115 © 2018 National Academy of Sciences of the United States of America.

(B) Adapted from White et al. (2015) 'Perceptual expertise in forensic facial image comparison' *Proceedings of the Royal Society B: Biological Sciences, 282*(1814), 20151292, Figure 1. https://doi.org/10.1098/rspb.2015.1292 © 2015 The Authors.

(C) Adapted from Norell et al. (2015) 'The effect of image quality and forensic expertise in facial image comparisons' *Journal of Forensic Sciences, 60,* 331–340, Figure 1. https://doi.org/10.1111/1556-4029.12660 © 2014 American Academy of Forensic Sciences.

improve novice performance in laboratory studies. It is possible, therefore, that these factors enable effective learning in facial examiners.

However, it is important to clarify that the superior performance demonstrated by facial examiners is in fact *acquired on the job*, rather than arising in some other way. For example, it could be that increased motivation among professional groups contributed to their superior accuracy (Moore & Johnston, 2013; see Noyes et al., 2017). We see two main reasons to doubt this possibility. First, facial examiners have outperformed motivated groups of professional staff who lacked specialist experience in face identification (Phillips, Yates, et al., 2018; White, Phillips, et al., 2015). Second, it is presumably the case that all professional staff required to perform face-identification tasks as part of their job description are motivated to perform well in these tests. However, as we have seen, this motivation does not translate into improved accuracy among facial reviewers. This is despite clear evidence of increased motivation relative to novice comparison groups. For example, passport-issuance officers spent twice as long comparing images than students in White, Kemp, Jenkins, Matheson, et al. (2014), but did not achieve superior accuracy.

Another possible explanation for the superior accuracy of professional groups is that there may have been some element of selection for their role. It is now very well established that, as a consequence of the natural development of perceptual and cognitive systems, people vary in their ability to identify faces (see Wilmer, 2017, for a review). In the next section, we review studies of police super-recognizers—groups who have been selected on the basis of their performance in face-identification tests to perform specialist roles. Facial examiners who have been tested were not explicitly selected in this way. However, there may be more subtle sources of selection bias—for example, a tendency for people with higher levels of natural ability in face identification to gravitate towards these professional roles (e.g., Roy, 1951). This could either be self-selection of the participants themselves—for example, based on the intuition that they are 'good with faces'—or on the basis of their performance in their professional role, where they are believed to have made identification decisions correctly in the past.

However, there is also reason to doubt this explanation. If selection alone were sufficient to explain the high performance of facial examiners, then facial examiners would be predicted to perform like high-performing novices. On the contrary, evidence suggests that examiners and novices perform the task in qualitatively different ways (Towler et al., 2017; White, Phillips, et al., 2015). Two important qualitative differences were identified by White, Phillips, et al. (2015). The first was that examiners only outperformed novices when given a long time to study the images (30 seconds), and not when images were presented for short durations (2 seconds). Novices were relatively unaffected by short study durations (see also Özbek & Bindemann, 2011), suggesting that the examiners extract the necessary information for their decisions relatively slowly. The second difference was that examiners were relatively unimpaired by turning the images upside down. This 'face inversion effect' is thought to index the extent to which people engage in 'holistic' processing of faces (Maurer et al., 2002)—that is, the tendency to process identity information 'at a glance' via a single percept in which individual facial features are integrated. Importantly, the face inversion effect is larger in high-performing novices—'super-recognizers' (Bobak, Bennetts, et al., 2016)—and parallel evidence from eye-tracking studies also points to enhanced holistic processing in this group (Bobak et al., 2017).

These qualitative differences suggest that facial examiners are not simply high-performing novices, but instead that their expertise is acquired via professional experience and training. More specifically, their expertise appears to be related to a strategic shift in the way the task is performed—from a holistic analysis to a more piecemeal and analytic process of feature comparison. This is consistent with the training that these professional staff receive (see Heyer et al., 2011; Prince, 2012; Towler et al., 2019; see also Towler, Kemp, & White, this volume), which prescribes a careful feature-by-feature approach to comparison.

Other evidence of strategic differences in examiners' performance of the task is provided by analysis of the way that they use the response scale relative to novices. Norell et al. (2015) tested the performance of 17 facial examiners from the European Network of Forensic Science Institutes, finding that the accuracy of the examiners was substantially better than that of novices (Mean accuracy difference = 12.9%, Cohen's D = 2.55). Participants in this study made their responses on a 9-point conclusion scale that was chosen to reflect the response scales used by these practitioners in their daily work. Response options ranged from 'extremely strong support that the images are the same person' to 'extremely strong support that the images are of different people'. Their analysis showed that, relative to novices, examiners were far more sensitive to the quality of images being compared when choosing the appropriate point on the response scale. When image quality was low, examiners tended to use midpoints in the scale reflecting low confidence in their decision. When image quality was high, examiners were more likely to use the end points of the scale. However, university students did not show this same systematic pattern, suggesting that an essential part of the expertise of this group was in assessing the quality of the image evidence and incorporating this assessment into their response (see also Phillips, Yates, et al., 2018; Towler et al., 2018).

It could be argued that all the learning described above is non-perceptual. Differences in the use of the response scale are likely to reflect a greater understanding of how to use response scales effectively, and what the various response options mean within the context of the examiners' profession. So this may reflect a change in the way observations are converted to decisions, rather than reflecting a change in perceptual representations underlying the decisions.[3] Similarly, strategic changes such as a greater emphasis on features might alter the way that visual information is sampled, but this change could be procedural and rule-based in origin with training, for example, changing the way that examiners deploy their attention. Therefore, increasing focus on facial features may be argued to reflect changes in cognitive control mechanisms, and not necessarily changes in perceptual representations (see Pylyshyn, 1999).

Notwithstanding the plausibility of this argument, there is preliminary evidence that these strategic changes are indeed accompanied by perceptual learning. Towler et al. (2017) asked facial examiners to rate the similarity of certain facial features, and then examined the extent to which these feature ratings were diagnostic of whether the features were from the same face or different faces. The diagnosticity of examiners' feature ratings was far greater than novices' ratings for the same features. This appears to show greater perceptual sensitivity to diagnostic information contained at the level of individual features. In addition, examiners and novices differed with regard to which

---

[3] On the other hand, perceptual learning may support the assessment of image quality. Norell et al.'s (2015) finding that examiners are more sensitive to the quality of images may suggest they are more skilled at identifying image artefacts, such as lens flare, blurring, or overexposure. Such perceptual expertise would support the ability to moderate the strength of the conclusions drawn from the image evidence.

feature ratings were most diagnostic. For examiners, similarity ratings to ears and facial marks (scars and blemishes) were ranked as being among the most diagnostic, but novices' ratings to these features were not especially diagnostic. These observations raise the possibility that the strategic focus on facial features leads to the development of greater perceptual sensitivity to feature-level details that carry identity information. It also may lead to the discovery of features that novices do not regularly attend to in great detail when identifying faces in their daily lives—such as the ears or facial marks—but that are nevertheless very useful for identification when comparing images of unfamiliar faces.

4.7 Police Super-Recognizers

In contrast to facial examiners, police super-recognizers are professionals who have been explicitly selected on the basis of their performance on face identity-processing tasks. A substantial body of evidence now shows that there is large variation in the general population between individuals' ability in face-matching tasks, and that this variability is relatively stable over repeated testing (Balsdon et al., 2018; Wilmer et al., 2010; see Wilmer, 2017 for a review; cf. Ramon et al., 2019). Indeed, while we have focused entirely on group differences reported in the studies described above, all these studies also show large variability in the performance of individual staff, with some performing near perfectly and others as if they were randomly guessing (e.g., see White, Kemp, Jenkins, Matheson, et al., 2014). Recruiting and selecting practitioners on the basis of their face-matching ability is therefore a promising way to improve the accuracy of face-identity decisions made in professional settings (Bobak, Dowsett, et al., 2016; White, Kemp, Jenkins, Matheson, et al., 2014).

Both studies that have tested police super-recognizers recruited participants from the London Metropolitan Police Service (Davis et al., 2016; Robertson et al., 2016). In the study by Davis et al. (2016), 36 participants were tested on the GFMT and group performance was above novice accuracy (Mean accuracy difference = 5.3%, Cohen's D = 0.74). In the study by Robertson et al. (2016), four participants were tested and the effect size for this group was substantially higher on the GFMT (Mean accuracy difference = 14.5%, Cohen's D = 1.98) and other matching tests (male models test: Mean accuracy difference = 16.7%, Cohen's D = 2.14; celebrity look-alikes test: Mean accuracy difference = 14.5%, Cohen's D = 1.80).

Although both these studies test police super-recognizers from the same organization, there are striking differences in the size of the professional groups in these studies and also the effect sizes that are reported. This is likely to be caused by the progressive specialization of the super-recognizer unit in the London Metropolitan Police Service in the years since it was established. Robertson et al. (2016) tested a subset of participants from Davis et al.'s (2016) study who had been selected on the basis of their on-the-job performance and standardized tests of face identification ability (see Davis, 2019). This selection process is likely to explain the high levels of accuracy shown by the group tested by Robertson et al. (2016), although the precise details of this process are not known.

Given uncertainty regarding how these police super-recognizers were selected, it is important to consider that other factors may have contributed to their higher accuracy in the task. On-the-job experience, mentorship, feedback, training, and increased motivation may also contribute to the higher accuracy of these professionals and, because very few details relating to their professional history are available, it is not possible to rule these out. As we have discussed in previous sections, this is a general problem when aiming to establish the basis of expertise in professional groups. In many cases, there are a number of potential contributors to higher performance that are outside the experimenters' control. To address this problem, it may be necessary to conduct longitudinal tests that track changes in an individual's performance over time, and to conduct studies that enable researchers to report details of the training, experience, and selection criteria used in organizations with more precision.

A final and important point relating to police super-recognizers is that the identity-processing tasks these individuals perform are more diverse than those undertaken by the other professional groups in this chapter. While the primary task performed by other groups included in this review was unfamiliar face matching, super-recognizers are typically asked to perform tasks that require memory—for example, reviewing CCTV recordings and verifying whether the people in the videos are familiar to them or have appeared in other video sequences they have watched. A full discussion of the diverse set of skills and abilities that are potentially sought for CCTV-monitoring tasks is beyond the scope of the chapter. However, it has been argued elsewhere that this diversity poses substantial challenges when designing standardized methods for selecting and training appropriate professionals (see Ramon et al., 2019, and associated commentaries).

Because we have only focused on unfamiliar face matching, the understanding of expertise proposed in this chapter is unlikely to generalize to the full range of face-identification tasks that are performed in professional settings (e.g., face-in-crowd search, see Davis et al., 2018). Indeed, as we outline below, our assumption is that expert performance on face *memory* tasks is unlikely to be acquired through professional experience, as appears to be the case for unfamiliar face matching. An implication of this is that different people are likely to be better suited to different expert face-identification roles. For example, the slow, analytic approach of facial examiners (see White, Phillips, et al., 2015) is not likely to be suited to live CCTV surveillance, where the requirements may be to quickly recognize faces of known suspects from poor-quality imagery.

4.8 Can Expertise in Unfamiliar Face Matching be Acquired? A Dual-Route Hypothesis

In reviewing studies of professional face-matching performance, our aim was to provide some insight into the factors that might underlie superior performance in expert groups. Given that accuracy of facial reviewers does not differ reliably from that of novices, it appears that simply performing the task regularly in daily work is not sufficient to produce higher levels of performance. It is, however, very clear that two groups of professionals—facial examiners and police super-recognizers—meet our definition of expertise by showing consistently higher accuracy than novices on tasks that are representative of their daily work. Moreover, effect sizes for comparisons between novices and these groups are large.

Importantly, these groups appear to achieve high levels of accuracy for different reasons. Police super-recognizers are selected on the basis of their accuracy on tests of face-identification ability, and so it is perhaps unsurprising that they outperform novices. Facial examiners, on the other hand, do not appear to have been selected systematically. The critical distinction between these groups appears to be *how* expertise is acquired. In the case of super-recognizers, their superior ability appears to be predominantly acquired prior to their deployment as face identification specialists—either congenitally or by the requirement to identify people during the course of their normal development. Conversely, facial examiners appear to acquire their expertise through their professional training and experience.

In our other chapter in this volume (Towler, Kemp, & White) we have proposed that these two routes to expertise map to distinct cognitive pathways. Expertise acquired through development exploits processes that have developed for the purpose of recognizing faces—the 'core' face identity-processing system described by Bruce and Young (1986). Professionally acquired expertise appears to exploit the alternative 'directed visual processing' route proposed in this model (see also Brunsdon et al., 2006). This is consistent with the view that recognition memory and unfamiliar face matching are reliant on different processes, with the latter having a greater focus on piecemeal analysis of facial features (Megreya & Burton, 2006, 2007). It is also consistent with the view that holistic and featural processing can offer parallel routes to face identification (Bartlett et al., 2003; Brunsdon et al., 2006; Farah, 1991; cf. Sergent, 1984).

This account can explain why facial examiners do not meet some criteria that have been proposed as hallmarks of expert performance. Specifically, influential theories propose that, with practice, cognitive processing becomes increasingly automatic and reliant on intuition (e.g., Chase & Simon, 1973; Kahneman, 2011; Kahneman & Klein, 2009). Yet, facial examiners appear to be an exception to this rule. As White, Phillips, et al. (2015) show, their expertise is characterized by slow, analytic, and controlled analysis of facial features. Super-recognizers, on the other hand, appear to rely on the fast, relatively intuitive mechanisms that enable them to recognize faces in daily life: They maintain high levels of accuracy when given relatively little time to study images (Russell et al., 2009), and they appear to engage in more holistic processing than participants with normal face-identification ability (Bobak, Bennetts, et al., 2016; Bobak et al., 2017; Russell et al., 2009).

We assume that super-recognizers' expertise is embodied in the core face recognition system and has been acquired through a combination of genetic (e.g., Wilmer et al., 2010) and environmental factors (Germine et al., 2011). Importantly, this expertise has been acquired for the purpose of recognition *memory* tasks that we typically perform in daily life when recognizing family, friends, and other acquaintances—and, because it is essential to normal social functioning and survival, it has been subject to evolutionary pressure throughout human history. This necessity means that face-recognition memory is overlearned, leading to asymptotic performance that is not amenable to further training. This is consistent with the finding that face-memory ability in normal participants does not improve beyond around 30 years of age (Germine et al., 2011; Susilo et al., 2013; see also Yovel et al., 2012).

On the other hand, facial examiners engage more general visual and top-down control mechanisms—which are not part of this core face-recognition system—when performing the task of unfamiliar face matching. This perspective has guided our research into the expertise that can be acquired via this route, and the mechanisms responsible for this learning (Towler et al., 2017; Towler, Kemp, & White, this volume). We reason that gains in accuracy in unfamiliar face-matching tasks are more likely to be found via this controlled processing route through extensive practice in analytic, feature-by-feature comparison. This view is influenced by work showing that unfamiliar face matching recruits domain-general feature-based processing (Megreya & Burton, 2006), and that the development of visual expertise is associated with changes in frontal lobe activation in areas associated with top-down attention control (see, for example, Martens et al., 2018).

The greater reliance of facial examiners on facial features, and other strategic differences, suggests that such training plays some role in the development of their expertise. Paradoxically, however, it does not appear that professional training courses have an immediate impact on accuracy, because tests conducted immediately before and after training sessions show no change in accuracy (Phillips, Heyer, et al., 2018; Towler et al., 2019). To account for this apparent discrepancy, we have argued elsewhere (Towler et al., 2019) that professionally acquired expertise is most likely to be developed through the subsequent application of the visual analysis protocols that are learned during training. By this view, the development of expertise occurs 'on the job' via *deliberate practice* of strategies prescribed in training courses.

The view that deliberate practice is essential to improvements in accuracy is consistent with the broader psychological literature on expertise. Deliberate practice is typically supervised by an instructor, and characterized by the delivery of immediate and informative feedback on the repeated performance of the same task (Ericsson et al., 1993). By this view, training does play an initial role in the development of expertise, by introducing practitioners to a new approach to the task that reorients their perceptual processing towards facial features, and discourages reliance on automatic and holistic processing. Subsequently, deliberate practice over an extended period of time enables them to discover which features are most useful for the purpose of identification, and to develop perceptual expertise in discriminating these features. It appears likely that effective mentorship and feedback are critical components of this learning process, given that laboratory studies have shown these to improve accuracy (Dowsett & Burton, 2015; White, Kemp, Jenkins, & Burton, 2014).

An important aspect of our hypothesis is that facial examiners learn to *override* the instinctive, automatic processing that enables us to recognize familiar faces in daily life. This leads us to propose that training in forensic facial comparison is akin to perceptual *unlearning*, as described in an influential study by Shiffrin and Schneider (1977). In their study, when participants were trained to find a set of letter targets among another set of letter distractors, their decisions became increasingly fast and automatic over training, reflective of perceptual learning of the target set. However, when experimenters then switched the target and distractor sets, participants' performance was impaired relative to initial performance at the start of training, an effect attributed to the fact that attention is captured by the original set of letter targets that are now being used as distractors. Importantly, in this study, it took a very long period of learning to overcome this impairment (2,100 trials), a process that the authors refer to as *perceptual unlearning*. We propose that an analogous process occurs in facial examiners when they begin to perform unfamiliar face-matching tasks: They must *unlearn* processes that support recognition memory, in order to discover features in the images that provide important cues to identity.

4.9 Conclusions

In this chapter, we have reviewed the literature to determine whether professional groups outperform novices on unfamiliar face-matching tasks. Over a third of comparisons between professional groups and novices show non-significant differences, confirming that mere practice is insufficient to develop expertise in unfamiliar face matching. Facial reviewers do not reliably outperform novices, but facial examiners and police super-recognizers do.

Greater opportunities for close mentorship and deliberate practice may partly explain why some groups show higher accuracy, and this appears to be associated with the relative specialization of these groups. We have identified a number of potential sources of learning—strategic, decisional, and perceptual—that may drive improvements in accuracy in specialist groups. It is not possible, based on the available evidence, to make strong conclusions about the mechanisms that are involved in this learning. However, it appears likely that learning in each of these domains contributes to expert performance in facial examiners. More speculatively, this task-specific learning may rest on examiners' ability to inhibit, or *unlearn*, more reflexive processes that support our common ability to recognize faces in daily life. Importantly, this is precisely the opposite trajectory to that typically emphasized to account for perceptual learning, whereby processing is argued to become more automatic, and less analytic, with practice (e.g., Kundel et al., 2007; Thompson & Tangen, 2014).

In future, longitudinal testing of specialist professional groups may be necessary to confirm that deliberate practice is effective in improving performance, and to provide greater insight into this learning trajectory. Combined with carefully designed experimental work, this approach can help delineate the learning mechanisms and knowledge outcomes that underpin professionally acquired expertise in this important task.

Preparation of this chapter was supported by an Australian Research Council Linkage Project grant to White and Kemp (LP160101523), and an Australian Research Council Discovery Project grant to White (DP190100957). The authors thank Megan Papesh, Rebecca Heyer, Josh Davis, and Fredrick Eckloff for providing additional information about the studies reviewed in this chapter, Gary Edmond for providing comments on an early version of the manuscript, and Janice Yung for her support with finalizing the manuscript.

References

Alenezi, H. M. & Bindemann, M. (2013). The effect of feedback on face-matching accuracy. *Applied Cognitive Psychology, 27*, 735–753. doi:10.1002/acp.2968

Anders, K. E., Charness, N., & Feltovich, P. (2006). *Cambridge handbook of expertise and expert performance*. New York: Cambridge University Press.

Attwood, A. S., Penton-Voak, I. S., Burton, A. M., & Munafò, M. R. (2013). Acute anxiety impairs accuracy in identifying photographed faces. *Psychological Science, 24*, 1591–1594. doi:10.1177/0956797612474021

Balsdon, T., Summersby, S., Kemp, R. I., & White, D. (2018). Improving face identification with specialist teams. *Cognitive Research: Principles and Implications, 3*, 25. doi:10.1186/s41235-018-0114-7

Bartlett, J. C., Searcy, J. H., & Abdi, H. (2003). What are the routes to face recognition? In M. Peterson & G. Rhodes (eds), *Perception of faces, objects, and scenes: Analytic and holistic processes* (pp. 21–52). Oxford: Oxford University Press.

Beattie, L., Walsh, D., McLaren, J., Biello, S. M., & White, D. (2016). Perceptual impairment in face identification with poor sleep. *Royal Society Open Science, 3*(10), 160321. doi:10.1098/rsos.160321

Bobak, A. K., Bennetts, R. J., Parris, B. A., Jansari, A., & Bate, S. (2016). An in-depth cognitive examination of individuals with superior face recognition skills. *Cortex, 82*, 48–62. doi:10.1016/j.cortex.2016.05.003

Bobak, A. K., Dowsett, A. J., & Bate, S. (2016). Solving the border control problem: Evidence of enhanced face matching in individuals with extraordinary face recognition skills. *PLoS ONE, 11*(2), e0148148. doi:10.1371/journal.pone.0148148

Bobak, A. K., Parris, B. A., Gregory, N. J., Bennetts, R. J., & Bate, S. (2017). Eye-movement strategies in developmental prosopagnosia and 'super' face recognition. *Quarterly Journal of Experimental Psychology, 70*, 201–217. doi:10.1080/17470218.2016.1161059

Bonner, L., Burton, A. M., & Bruce, V. (2003). Getting to know you: How we learn new faces. *Visual Cognition, 10*, 527–536. doi:10.1080/13506280244000168

Bruce, V., Henderson, Z., Greenwood, K., Hancock, P. J. B., Burton, A. M., & Miller, P. (1999). Verification of face identities from images captured on video. *Journal of Experimental Psychology: Applied, 5*, 339–360. doi:10.1037/1076-898X.5.4.339

Bruce, V., Henderson, Z., Newman, C., & Burton, A. M. (2001). Matching identities of familiar and unfamiliar faces caught on CCTV images. *Journal of Experimental Psychology: Applied, 7*, 207–218. doi:10.1037/1076-898X.7.3.207

Bruce, V. & Young, A. (1986). Understanding face recognition. *British Journal of Psychology, 77*, 305–327. doi:10.1111/j.2044-8295.1986.tb02199.x

Brunsdon, R., Coltheart, M., Nickels, L., & Joy, P. (2006). Developmental prosopagnosia: A case analysis and treatment study. *Cognitive Neuropsychology, 23*, 822–840. doi:10.1080/02643290500441841

Burton, A. M., White, D., & McNeill, A. (2010). The Glasgow Face Matching Test. *Behavior Research Methods, 42*, 286–291. doi:10.3758/BRM.42.1.286

Burton, A. M., Wilson, S., Cowan, M., & Bruce, V. (1999). Face recognition in poor-quality video: Evidence from security surveillance. *Psychological Science, 10*, 243–248. doi:10.1111/1467-9280.00144

Calic, D. (2013). *From the laboratory to the real world: Evaluating the impact of impostors, expertise and individual differences on human face matching performance* (Doctoral dissertation). Available at: https://hekyll.services.adelaide.edu.au/dspace/bitstream/2440/91444/3/02whole.pdf (accessed 12 April 2020).

Carey, S. (1992). Becoming a face expert. *Philosophical Transactions of the Royal Society of London. Series B: Biological Sciences, 335*, 95–103.

Chase, W. G. & Simon, H. A. (1973). Perception in chess. *Cognitive Psychology, 4*, 55–81. doi:10.1016/0010-0285(73)90004-2

Clutterbuck, R. & Johnston, R. A. (2002). Exploring levels of face familiarity by using an indirect face-matching measure. *Perception, 31*, 985–994. doi:10.1068/p3335

Davis, J. P. (2019). The worldwide public impact of identifying super-recognisers for police and business. *The Cognitive Psychology Bulletin, 4*, 17–22.

Davis, J. P., Forrest, C., Treml, F., & Jansari, A. (2018). Identification from CCTV: Assessing police super-recogniser ability to spot faces in a crowd and susceptibility to change blindness. *Applied Cognitive Psychology, 32*, 337–353. doi:10.1002/acp.3405

Davis, J. P., Lander, K., Evans, R., & Jansari, A. (2016). Investigating predictors of superior face recognition ability in police super-recognisers. *Applied Cognitive Psychology, 30*, 827–840. doi:10.1002/acp.3260

Davis, J. P. & Valentine, T. (2009). CCTV on trial: Matching video images with the defendant in the dock. *Applied Cognitive Psychology, 23*, 482–505. doi:10.1002/acp.1490

Diamond, R. & Carey, S. (1986). Why faces are and are not special: An effect of expertise. *Journal of Experimental Psychology: General, 115*, 107–117. doi:10.1037/0096-3445.115.2.107

Dowsett, A. J. & Burton, A. M. (2015). Unfamiliar face matching: Pairs out-perform individuals and provide a route to training. *British Journal of Psychology, 106*, 433–445. doi:10.1111/bjop.12103

Edmond, G. & Wortley, N. (2016). Interpreting image evidence: Facial mapping, police familiars and super-recognisers in England and Australia. *Journal of International and Comparative Law, 3*, 1–50.

Ericsson, K. A., Krampe, R. T., & Tesch-Römer, C. (1993). The role of deliberate practice in the acquisition of expert performance. *Psychological Review, 100*, 363–406. doi:10.1037/0033-295X.100.3.363

Ericsson, K. A. & Lehmann, A. C. (1996). Expert and exceptional performance: Evidence of maximal adaptation to task constraints. *Annual Review of Psychology, 47*, 273–305. doi:10.1146/annurev.psych.47.1.273

Facial Identification Scientific Working Group (FISWG) (2010). *Guidelines and recommendations for facial comparison training to competency.* Available at: https://fiswg.org/FISWG_Training_Guidelines_Recommendations_v1.1_2010_11_18.pdf (accessed 12 April 2020).

Farah, M. J. (1991). Patterns of co-occurrence among the associative agnosias: Implications for visual object representation. *Cognitive Neuropsychology, 8*, 1–19. doi:10.1080/02643299108253364

Fysh, M. C. & Bindemann, M. (2017). Effects of time pressure and time passage on face-matching accuracy. *Royal Society Open Science, 4*(6), 170249. doi:10.1098/rsos.170249

Germine, L. T., Duchaine, B., & Nakayama, K. (2011). Where cognitive development and aging meet: Face learning ability peaks after age 30. *Cognition, 118*, 201–210. doi:10.1016/j.cognition.2010.11.002

Henderson, Z., Bruce, V., & Burton, A. M. (2001). Matching the faces of robbers captured on video. *Applied Cognitive Psychology, 15*, 445–464. doi:10.1002/acp.718

Heyer, R., MacLeod, V., Carter, L., Semmler, C., & Ma-Wyatt, A. (2011). Profiling the facial identification practitioner in Australia: Report on the human operator capability project survey. Report for the Department of Prime Minister and Cabinet: Grant PR09-0078. Available at: https://www.researchgate.net/publication/318206064_Profiling_the_Facial_Comparison_Practitioner_in_Australia (accessed 12 April 2020).

Heyer, R., Semmler, C., & Hendrickson, A. T. (2018). Humans and algorithms for facial recognition: The effects of candidate list length and experience on performance. *Journal of Applied Research in Memory and Cognition, 7*, 597–609. doi:10.1016/j.jarmac.2018.06.002

Kahneman, D. (2011). *Thinking, fast and slow*. New York: Farrar, Straus and Giroux.

Kahneman, D. & Klein, G. (2009). Conditions for intuitive expertise: A failure to disagree. *American Psychologist, 64*, 515–526. doi:10.1037/a0016755

Kemp, R., Towell, N., & Pike, G. (1997). When seeing should not be believing: Photographs, credit cards and fraud. *Applied Cognitive Psychology, 11*, 211–222. doi:10.1002/(SICI)1099-0720(199706)11:3<211::AID-ACP430>3.0.CO;2-O

Klontz, J. C. & Jain, A. K. (2013). *A case study on unconstrained facial recognition using the Boston Marathon bombings suspects*. Michigan State University, technical report, 119–20. Available at: http://biometrics.cse.msu.edu/Publications/Face/KlontzJain_CaseStudyUnconstrainedFacialRecognition_BostonMarathonBombimgSuspects.pdf (accessed 12 April 2020).

Kundel, H. L., Nodine, C. F., Conant, E. F., & Weinstein, S. P. (2007). Holistic component of image perception in mammogram interpretation: Gaze-tracking study. *Radiology, 242*, 396–402. doi:10.1148/radiol.2422051997

Martens, F., Bulthé, J., van Vliet, C., & de Beeck, H. O. (2018). Domain-general and domain-specific neural changes underlying visual expertise. *NeuroImage, 169*, 80–93. doi:10.1016/j.neuroimage.2017.12.013

Maurer, D., Le Grand, R., & Mondloch, C. J. (2002). The many faces of configural processing. *Trends in Cognitive Sciences, 6*, 255–260. doi:10.1016/S1364-6613(02)01903-4

Megreya, A. M. & Burton, A. M. (2006). Unfamiliar faces are not faces: Evidence from a matching task. *Memory & Cognition, 34*, 865–876. doi:10.3758/BF03193433

Megreya, A. M. & Burton, A. M. (2007). Hits and false positives in face matching: A familiarity-based dissociation. *Perception & Psychophysics, 69*, 1175–1184. doi:10.3758/BF03193954

Moore, R. M. & Johnston, R. A. (2013). Motivational incentives improve unfamiliar face matching accuracy. *Applied Cognitive Psychology, 27*, 754–760. doi:10.1002/acp.2964

Norell, K., Läthén, K. B., Bergström, P., Rice, A., Natu, V., & O'Toole, A. (2015). The effect of image quality and forensic expertise in facial image comparisons. *Journal of Forensic Sciences, 60*, 331–340. doi:10.1111/1556-4029.12660

Noyes, E., Phillips, P. J., & O'Toole, A. J. (2017). What is a super-recogniser? In M. Bindemann & A. M. Megreya (eds), *Face processing: Systems, disorders and cultural differences* (pp. 173–201). New York: Nova Science Publishers.

Özbek, M. & Bindemann, M. (2011). Exploring the time course of face matching: Temporal constraints impair unfamiliar face identification under temporally unconstrained viewing. *Vision Research, 51*, 2145–2155. doi:10.1016/j.visres.2011.08.009

Papesh, M. H. (2018). Photo ID verification remains challenging despite years of practice. *Cognitive Research: Principles and Implications, 3*, 19. doi:10.1186/s41235-018-0110-y

Papesh, M. H., Heisick, L. L., & Warner, K. A. (2018). The persistent low-prevalence effect in unfamiliar face-matching: The roles of feedback and criterion shifting. *Journal of Experimental Psychology: Applied, 24*, 416–430. doi:10.1037/xap0000156

Phillips, P. J., Heyer, R., & Michalski, D. (2018). Effectiveness of a facial forensic training course. *Journal of Vision, 18*(10), 560. Poster presented at the Vision Sciences Society Eighteenth Annual Meeting.

Phillips, P. J., Wechsler, H., Huang, J., & Rauss, P. J. (1998). The FERET database and evaluation procedure for face-recognition algorithms. *Image Vision Computing, 16*, 295–306. doi:10.1016/S0262-8856(97)00070-X

Phillips, P. J., Yates, A. N., Hu, Y., Hahn, C. A., Noyes, E., Jackson, K., et al. (2018). Face recognition accuracy of forensic examiners, superrecognizers, and face recognition algorithms. *Proceedings of the National Academy of Sciences, 115*, 6171–6176. doi:10.1073/pnas.1721355115

Prince, J. P. (2012). Report on emerging use of facial recognition systems and facial image comparison procedures. Available at: https://www.churchilltrust.com.au/media/fellows/2012_Prince_Jason.pdf (accessed 12 April 2020).

Pylyshyn, Z. (1999). Is vision continuous with cognition? The case for cognitive impenetrability of visual perception. *Behavioral and Brain Sciences, 22*, 341–365. doi:10.1017/S0140525X99002022

Ramon, M., Bobak, A. K., & White, D. (2019). Super-recognizers: From the lab to the world and back again. *British Journal of Psychology, 110*, 461–479. doi:10.1111/bjop.12368

Rice, A., Phillips, P. J., Natu, V., An, X., & O'Toole, A. J. (2013). Unaware person recognition from the body when face identification fails. *Psychological Science, 24*, 2235–2243. doi:10.1177/0956797613492986

Robertson, D. J., Noyes, E., Dowsett, A. J., Jenkins, R., & Burton, A. M. (2016). Face recognition by Metropolitan Police super-recognisers. *PLoS ONE, 11*(2), e0150036. doi:10.1371/journal.pone.0150036

Roy, A. D. (1951). Some thoughts on the distribution of earnings. *Oxford Economic Papers, 3*, 135–146.

Russell, R., Duchaine, B., & Nakayama, K. (2009). Super-recognizers: People with extraordinary face recognition ability. *Psychonomic Bulletin & Review, 16*, 252–257. doi:10.3758/PBR.16.2.252

Sergent, J. (1984). An investigation into component and configural processes underlying face perception. *British Journal of Psychology, 75*, 221–242. doi:10.1111/j.2044-8295.1984.tb01895.x

Shiffrin, R. M. & Schneider, W. (1977). Controlled and automatic human information processing: II. Perceptual learning, automatic attending and a general theory. *Psychological Review, 84*, 127–190. doi:10.1037/0033-295X.84.2.127

Stacchi, L., Huguenin-Elie, E., Caldara, R., & Ramon, M. (2019). Normative data for two tests of face matching under ecological conditions. doi:10.31234/osf.io/swjrq

Susilo, T., Germine, L., & Duchaine, B. (2013). Face recognition ability matures late: Evidence from individual differences in young adults. *Journal of Experimental Psychology: Human Perception and Performance, 39*, 1212–1217. doi:10.1037/a0033469

Thompson, M. B. & Tangen, J. M. (2014). The nature of expertise in fingerprint matching: Experts can do a lot with a little. *PLoS ONE, 9*(12), e114759. doi:10.1371/journal.pone.0114759

Towler, A., Kemp, R. I., Burton, A. M., Dunn, J. D., Wayne, T., Moreton, R., et al. (2019). Do professional facial image comparison training courses work? *PLoS ONE, 14*(2), e0211037. doi:10.1371/journal.pone.0211037

Towler, A., White, D., Ballantyne, K., Searston, R. A., Martire, K. A., & Kemp, R. I. (2018). Are forensic scientists experts? *Journal of Applied Research in Memory and Cognition, 7*, 199–208. doi:10.1016/j.jarmac.2018.03.010

Towler, A., White, D., & Kemp, R. I. (2017). Evaluating the feature comparison strategy for forensic face identification. *Journal of Experimental Psychology: Applied, 23*, 47–58. doi:10.1037/xap0000108

White, D. (2020). Do professional groups outperform novices in unfamiliar face matching tasks? A meta-analysis. *PsyArXiv*.

White, D., Dunn, J. D., Schmid, A. C., & Kemp, R. I. (2015). Error rates in users of automatic face recognition software. *PLoS ONE, 10*(10), e0139827. doi:10.1371/journal.pone.0139827

White, D. & Kemp, R. (2016). Studying human performance to improve accuracy of biometric facial recognition. *Keesing Journal of Documents & Identity, Annual Report Identity Management, 2016–2017*. Available at: https://www.linkedin.com/pulse/studying-human-performance-improve-accuracy-biometric-david-white (accessed 12 April 2020).

White, D., Kemp, R. I., Jenkins, R., & Burton, A. M. (2014). Feedback training for facial image comparison. *Psychonomic Bulletin & Review, 21*, 100–106. doi:10.3758/s13423-013-0475-3

White, D., Kemp, R. I., Jenkins, R., Matheson, M., & Burton, A. M. (2014). Passport officers' errors in face matching. *PLoS ONE, 9*(8), e103510. doi:10.1371/journal.pone.0103510

White, D., Phillips, P. J., Hahn, C. A., Hill, M., & O'Toole, A. J. (2015). Perceptual expertise in forensic facial image comparison. *Proceedings of the Royal Society B: Biological Sciences, 282*(1814), 20151292. doi:10.1098/rspb.2015.1292

Wilmer, J. B. (2017). Individual differences in face recognition: A decade of discovery. *Current Directions in Psychological Science, 26*, 225–230. doi:10.1177/0963721417710693

Wilmer, J. B., Germine, L., Chabris, C. F., Chatterjee, G., Williams, M., Loken, E., et al. (2010). Human face recognition ability is specific and highly heritable. *Proceedings of the National Academy of sciences, 107*, 5238–5241. doi:10.1073/pnas.0913053107

Wirth, B. E. & Carbon, C. C. (2017). An easy game for frauds? Effects of professional experience and time pressure on passport-matching performance. *Journal of Experimental Psychology: Applied, 23,* 138–157. doi:10.1037/xap0000114

Young, A. W. & Burton, A. M. (2018). Are we face experts? *Trends in Cognitive Sciences, 22,* 100–110. doi:10.1016/j.tics.2017.11.007

Yovel, G., Halsband, K., Pelleg, M., Farkash, N., Gal, B., & Goshen-Gottstein, Y. (2012). Can massive but passive exposure to faces contribute to face recognition abilities? *Journal of Experimental Psychology: Human Perception and Performance, 38,* 285–289. doi:10.1037/a0027077

5

Can Face Identification Ability Be Trained?

Evidence for Two Routes to Expertise

Alice Towler, Richard I. Kemp, and David White

5.1 Introduction

Establishing someone's identity is central to many of the security procedures we rely on to maintain law and order, and protect national security. One of the most common methods of verifying identity is to compare images of a person's face—for example, when border control agents compare a traveller's face to their passport photo, or when forensic practitioners decide if the person captured committing a crime on closed-circuit television (CCTV) matches a police mugshot. Because these identification decisions play an important role in society, it is equally important that people make them accurately.

It is therefore surprising, and somewhat concerning, that many facial image comparison practitioners make a high proportion of errors on these tasks (see White, Towler, & Kemp, this volume). For example, White, Kemp, Jenkins, Matheson, et al. (2014) showed that passport-issuance officers made 20% errors on the Glasgow Face Matching Test—a deceptively difficult test, which requires participants to decide if two simultaneously presented photographs taken on the same day under studio conditions are of the same person or different people. Research has also revealed large individual differences in practitioners' ability to perform unfamiliar face-matching tasks. Some practitioners perform close to chance, while others achieve 100% accuracy (e.g., White, Kemp, Jenkins, Matheson, et al., 2014; Wirth & Carbon, 2017).

Mitigating the risks associated with practitioners' identification errors is a priority for government and forensic organizations, particularly in the wake of highly critical authoritative reports criticizing the lack of scientific validation and reliability in the forensic sciences (see National Research Council, 2009; PCAST, 2016). A potential response to these reports is to rely more heavily on automated facial recognition technology, which has improved steadily in recent years (see Grother & Ngan, 2014; Grother et al., 2018, 2019) and is now widely used at national borders and in police investigations (see Noyes & Hill, this volume).

However, it is important to appreciate that humans remain a critical component of face recognition systems, and will do so for the foreseeable future (see Towler et al., 2017). Indeed, many uses of face recognition software have actually *increased* the need for human processing. For example, when using a query image to search a large

Alice Towler, Richard I. Kemp, and David White, *Can Face Identification Ability Be Trained?* In: *Forensic Face Matching.* Edited by: Markus Bindemann, Oxford University Press (2021). © Oxford University Press. DOI: 10.1093/oso/9780198837749.003.0005.

database of faces, as is the case when using this technology in police investigations, it is the responsibility of investigators to examine the array of possible matches returned by the software and decide if it contains the suspect. Professional staff who use this technology in their daily work are extremely prone to error, identifying the wrong face in the array on 40% of trials (White, Dunn, et al., 2015).

To mitigate these risks, professional organizations typically provide practitioners with training to equip them with the skills necessary to make accurate identification decisions. But, how effective is this training? And, is it even possible to train face identification ability? To answer these questions, we first review the literature on professional training for facial image comparison practitioners. This uncovers a long history of training practitioners to adopt a systematic feature-by-feature comparison strategy, and evidence that modern professional training courses do not improve accuracy, despite adhering to international best practice guidelines (see Towler et al., 2019).

The question of whether it is possible to train face identification is also important outside professional settings. It is important clinically, where researchers have attempted to remediate impaired familiar face recognition ability in people with prosopagnosia. It is also of basic interest in understanding perceptual expertise, and researchers have addressed this by asking whether perceptual learning can transfer from the specific faces studied in training to improve ability to identify faces in general.

Evidence from these three strands of investigation suggests that face identification ability may be *untrainable*. However, in a final section, we review evidence from a specialist group of forensic practitioners known as 'facial examiners', who show consistently higher accuracy than novices. Their superior accuracy appears to be driven by qualitative differences in the way they approach the task, which they derive from training. To reconcile these findings, we argue that examiners' expertise reveals an alternate route to training face identification ability, which bypasses the 'core' face recognition system. We discuss the implications of this alternate route for the future of facial image comparison training.

5.2 Professional Face Matching Training

Professional face-matching training dates back to the late nineteenth century. French criminologist Alphonse Bertillon is thought to have become frustrated by the police's inability to discriminate first-time offenders from reoffenders, so he invented the Bertillon system of identification or 'Bertillonage' (Bertillon, 1896). Bertillon's system involved recording anthropometric measurements of a person's height, arm span, torso length, head length, head width, right ear, left foot, left middle finger, and cubit (the distance between the elbow and tip of the middle finger; see Figure 5.1). These measurements were recorded on identity cards alongside front-facing and profile photographs, and other information such as eye, skin, and hair colour, and scars (see Figure 5.2).

RELEVÉ

DU

SIGNALEMENT ANTHROPOMÉTRIQUE

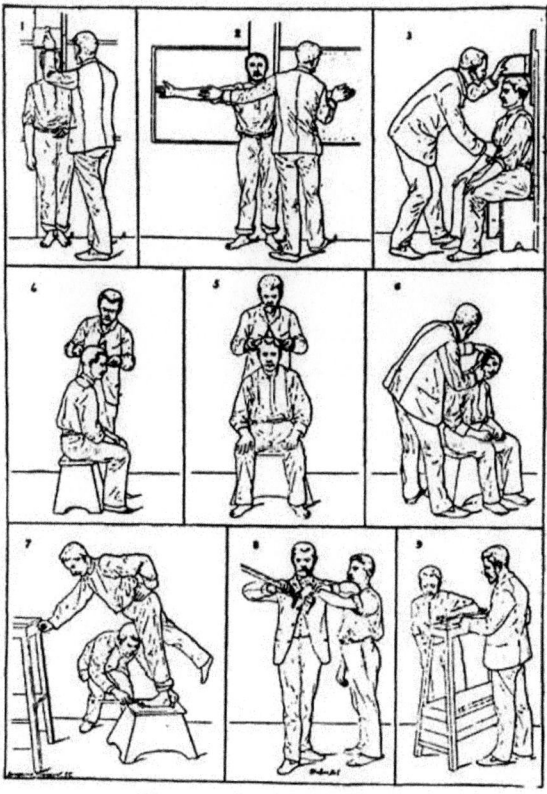

1. Taille. — 2. Envergure. — 3. Buste. ––
4. Longueur de la tête. — 5. Largeur de la tête. — 6. Oreille droite. —
7. Pied gauche. — 8. Médius gauche. — 9. Coudée gauche.

Figure 5.1 A summary of the anthropometric measurements in Bertillon's system of identification.

Source: © The Wende Museum of the Cold War.

The information recorded on these identity cards was thought to be individuating, such that comparison to other cards would permit officers to identify people already in the system. Bertillon also invented a complicated filing system that allowed officers to easily locate relevant identity cards among hundreds of thousands of cards (U.S. National Library of Medicine, 2014). Bertillon taught his identification system to law enforcement officers throughout France and it quickly spread to other European countries, the Americas, and Asia (Piazza, 2016). Bertillon's teaching style was eccentric, making use of large posters that illustrated the possible variants of each facial feature, photographs of corpses, skeletons, and wax figures (see Figure 5.3).

There are also documented examples of face identification training from the 1960s. Stasi passport inspectors responsible for passport control at Checkpoint Charlie, a

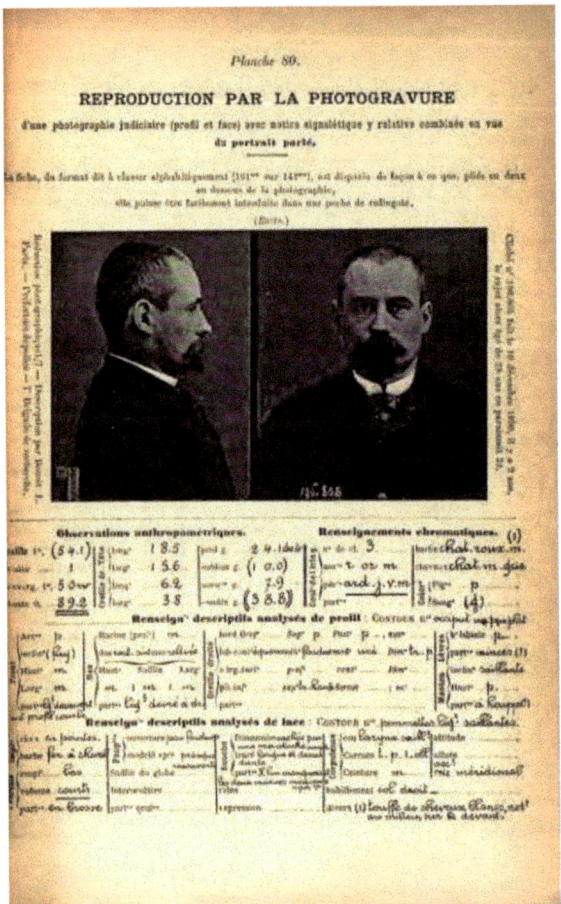

Figure 5.2 A Bertillon identity card.
Source: © The Wende Museum of the Cold War.

key crossing point from West to East Berlin, were trained using booklets containing the various types of noses, mouths, ears, eyes, hairlines, and even moustaches (see Figure 5.4A; Drost, 2016). Inspectors were required to learn each of the feature variants—for example, pointed, straight, triangular, quadrangular, elliptical noses—so that they could recognize and classify the facial features of people attempting to cross the border. The reasoning behind this strategy was that the officers could detect imposters if the facial feature classifications in the passport photograph did not match those of the traveller standing before them.[1] There is also evidence that inspectors were taught to break facial features down into their sub-components for more detailed comparison (see Figure 5.4B).

In 1964, the newly appointed head of the passport division at Checkpoint Charlie concluded that laborious comparison of each facial feature was poorly suited to

---

[1] See Towler et al. (2014) for an evaluation of this type of facial feature classification strategy.

Figure 5.3 Training to use the Bertillion system of identification in France.
Source: © The Wende Museum of the Cold War.

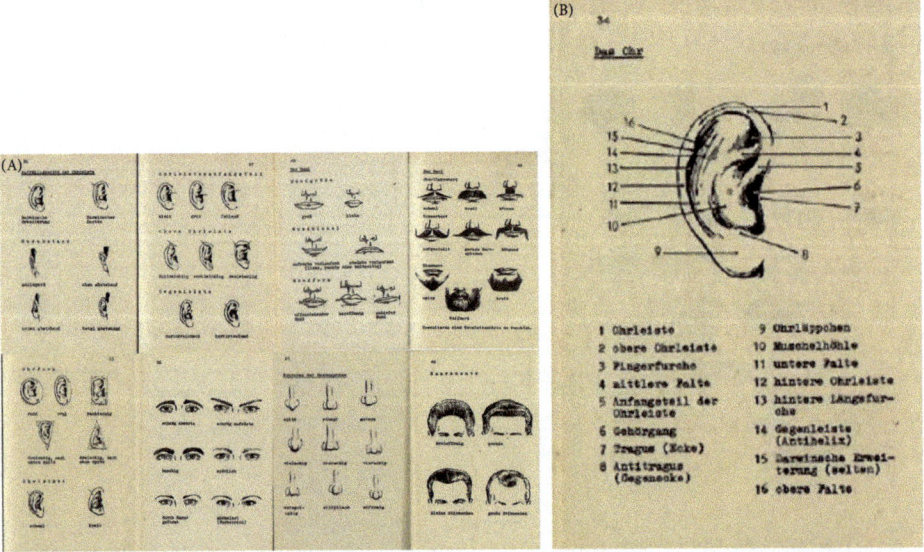

Figure 5.4 Face identification training materials provided to Stasi passport inspectors at Checkpoint Charlie. Inspectors were taught to (A) classify facial features, and (B) break them down into their sub-components for more detailed comparison.
Source: © The Wende Museum of the Cold War.

passport control, where inspectors only had a few moments to determine if the traveller held a valid passport. He was also coming under increasing pressure to eliminate errors—the Stasi would regularly send informants to the border holding fraudulent passports to test passport inspectors.

The head of the passport division believed that face identification was an intuitive skill, and that the officers needed to be trained to develop an expert gaze or '*wichtig schauen*' (Drost, 2016). He began secretly taking photographs of travellers and their passports, and used these to create flashcards so that his officers could practise making face-matching decisions and receive feedback on their accuracy (see Figure 5.5A). He also interviewed his staff to find out which facial features they were using to make identifications. They reported that they tended to focus on the eyes, nose, and mouth, but that they would first attempt to get an overall impression of the face. He incorporated this information into training for new recruits, creating training materials to encourage them to divide the face into three horizontal sections and compare the similarity of each section in turn (see Figure 5.5B).

We recently reviewed 11 training courses provided to practitioners working in national security, police, intelligence, passport issuance, immigration, and border control around the world (see Towler et al., 2019). We found that professional face-matching training had changed surprisingly little since these earlier attempts (see content summary in Figure 5.6). Modern training remains focused on the detailed analysis of facial features, rather than the face as a whole (see Towler et al., 2019). Training courses teach trainees about the anatomy of facial features and the sub-parts of each feature (e.g.,

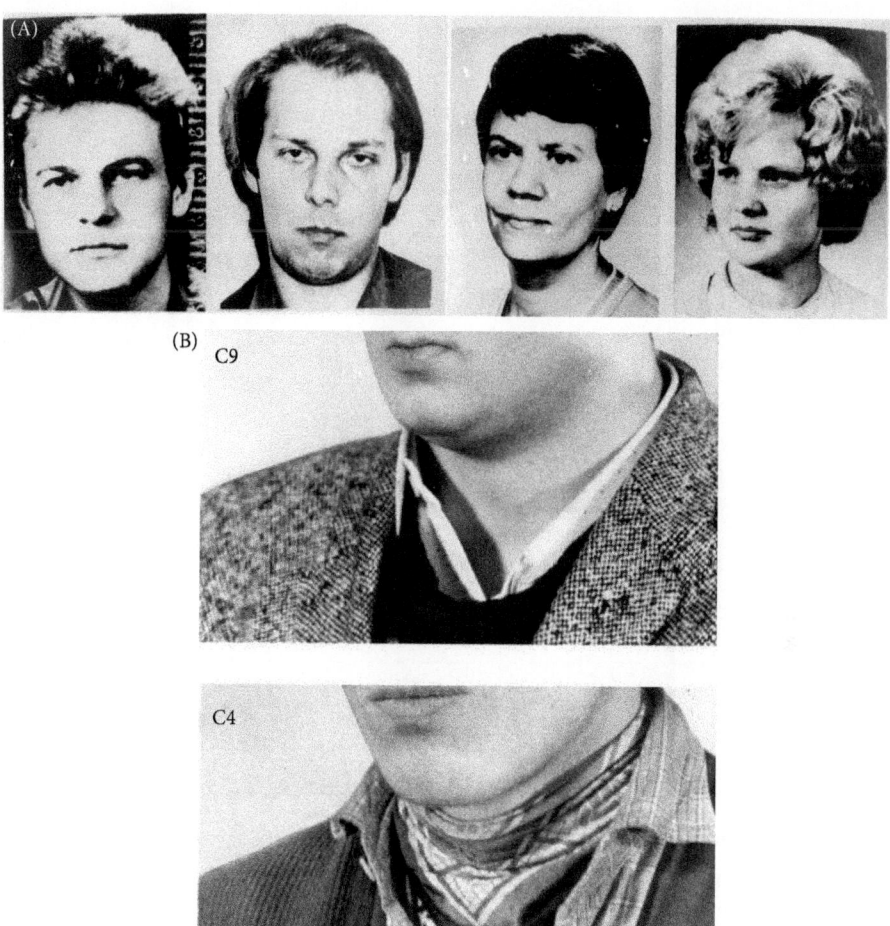

Figure 5.5 Flashcards developed by the head of the passport division at Checkpoint Charlie.

Note: (A) Passport inspectors would decide whether the faces showed the same person or different people and receive feedback on the accuracy of their decisions. (B) Passport officers used these flashcards to practice dividing faces into sections, and comparing the similarity of each section in turn. The correct answers for these image pairs are unknown.

Source: © The Wende Museum of the Cold War.

the tragus, helix, antihelix, and lobe of the ear), sharing striking similarities with the Stasi training material in Figure 5.4. Modern professional training actively discourages trainees from examining the face holistically, and instead encourages them to break each face down into its sub-features and systematically compare the similarities and differences between them. Some training courses are run online, but most are still run face to face and include practical exercises and feedback (see Towler et al., 2019). Once again, these modern training practices share striking similarities to the Stasi training (see Figure 5.5).

Modern training courses adhere to international best practice guidelines set out by the Facial Identification Scientific Working Group (FISWG; see Facial Identification

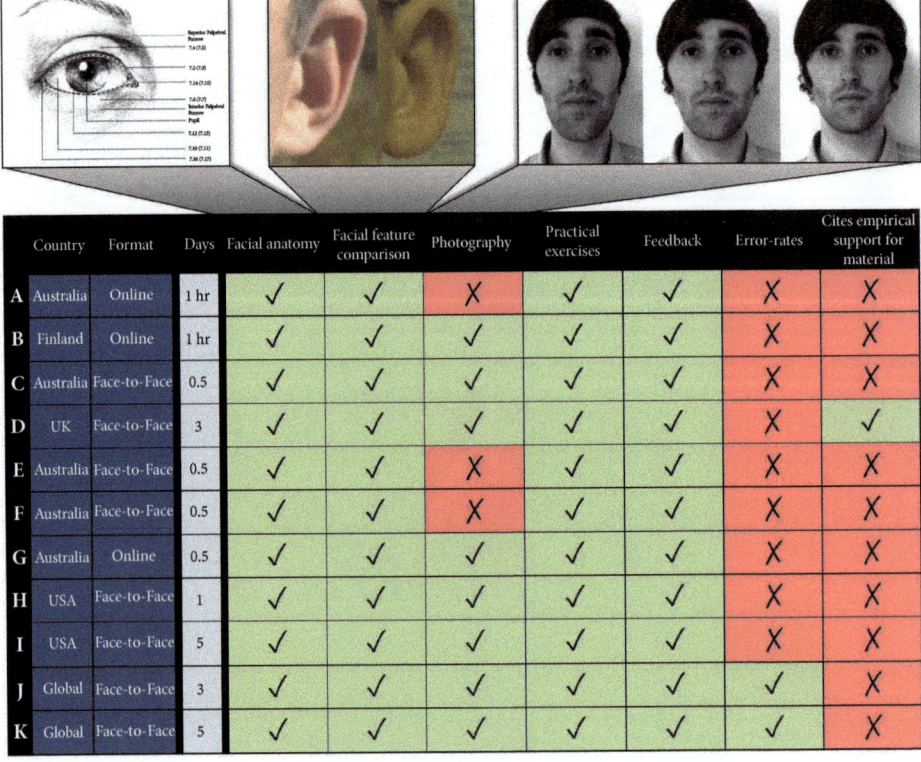

	Country	Format	Days	Facial anatomy	Facial feature comparison	Photography	Practical exercises	Feedback	Error-rates	Cites empirical support for material
A	Australia	Online	1 hr	✓	✓	X	✓	✓	X	X
B	Finland	Online	1 hr	✓	✓	✓	✓	✓	X	X
C	Australia	Face-to-Face	0.5	✓	✓	✓	✓	✓	X	X
D	UK	Face-to-Face	3	✓	✓	✓	✓	✓	X	✓
E	Australia	Face-to-Face	0.5	✓	✓	X	✓	✓	X	X
F	Australia	Face-to-Face	0.5	✓	✓	X	✓	✓	X	X
G	Australia	Online	0.5	✓	✓	✓	✓	✓	X	X
H	USA	Face-to-Face	1	✓	✓	✓	✓	✓	X	X
I	USA	Face-to-Face	5	✓	✓	✓	✓	✓	X	X
J	Global	Face-to-Face	3	✓	✓	✓	✓	✓	✓	X
K	Global	Face-to-Face	5	✓	✓	✓	✓	✓	✓	X

Figure 5.6 Summary of current professional facial image comparison training course content from around the world.

Note: Modern training courses typically teach practitioners facial anatomy and encourage feature-by-feature comparison.

Source: Reproduced from Towler et al. (2019) 'Do professional facial image comparison training courses work?' *PLoS ONE, 14*(2), e0211037, Figure 1. https://doi.org/10.1371/journal.pone.0211037 © 2019 Towler et al. Reprinted under CC BY licence.

Scientific Working Group, 2011; Towler et al., 2019). But do these professional training courses actually improve the face-matching accuracy of trainees? To address this question, we evaluated the effectiveness of four representative professional training courses (Courses A–D in Figure 5.6) by testing novices and genuine trainees immediately before and after completing a training course (see Towler et al., 2019). We found strong evidence that short online courses and a half-day face-to-face course do not improve face-matching accuracy (see also Woodhead et al., 1979).

We also tested an intensive three-day face-to-face course run by the Metropolitan Police Service in London. In this case, we found some evidence of improvement. Trainees improved by 6% on the standard lab-based Glasgow Face Matching Test (GFMT), but not on a test designed to be representative of the police casework for which the training was designed. Further, we found no evidence that training produced qualitative markers of expertise in facial image comparison (see Towler et al.,

2019). Therefore, evidence from evaluation tests indicates that professional training courses do not provide a satisfactory solution to improving face-matching accuracy in practitioners.

5.3 Psychological Approaches to Training

Practitioners' attempts to develop effective training courses in face-matching appear to have been largely unsuccessful. But have psychologists fared better? Psychologists have been investigating how to train face identification ability for many years, and in contrast to professional training—which is based on precedent, practical experience, and practitioners' intuition—have typically taken a theory-driven approach, based on scientific understanding of face processing and familiar face recognition (e.g., DeGutis et al., 2007; Powell et al., 2008; White, Kemp, Jenkins, & Burton, 2014). The short answer is no.

5.3.1 Improving Familiar Face Recognition in Prosopagnosia Patients

Psychologists first became interested in face identification training as a means of treating patients with prosopagnosia (see Beyn & Knyazeva, 1962). Prosopagnosia is a condition characterized by a profound deficit in face recognition, which can leave patients unable to recognize their family, friends, colleagues, and sometimes even themselves (see Behrmann et al., 2010). Some patients acquire prosopagnosia after suffering a brain injury (known as 'acquired prosopagnosia'), whereas others simply fail to develop normal face-processing skills despite otherwise normal perceptual, cognitive, and neurological functioning (known as 'developmental' or 'congenital' prosopagnosia). Because of prosopagnosia's profound effects on patients' day-to-day social functioning and mental health (see Yardley et al., 2008), psychologists have sought to improve their ability to learn and recognize familiar faces (see Bate & Bennetts, 2014; DeGutis et al., 2014, for reviews).

5.3.1.1 Remedial Holistic Processing Training

One theory-driven approach to improving the face recognition abilities of people with prosopagnosia is to remediate their normal holistic face-processing mechanisms. Normal face processing is thought to rely on holistic processes, whereby faces are encoded as unified wholes rather than as a collection of parts (see Tanaka & Farah, 1993; Young et al., 1987). Similarly, familiar face recognition is thought to rely on stored identity representations that encode holistic properties of faces (see Bruce & Young, 1986). Because prosopagnosia patients have significant impairment in holistic face processing and difficulties building robust holistic face representations (see Avidan et al., 2011;

Bukach et al., 2006; Busigny et al., 2010; Farah et al., 1998; Levine & Calvanio, 1989; Palermo et al., 2011; Ramon et al., 2010), this approach is neatly aligned with theoretical understanding of normal cognitive functioning in face recognition.

Attempts to train holistic face processing in patients with acquired prosopagnosia have, however, been unsuccessful. In an early attempt, Ellis and Young (1988) aimed to improve face processing in eight-year-old acquired prosopagnosia patient KD using four different training tasks, including simultaneous matching of familiar and unfamiliar faces with feedback, and learning face–name associations. After 18 months of daily training, KD showed no evidence of improvement on any of the four tasks.

More recently, DeGutis et al. (2013) used a procedure designed by DeGutis et al. (2007) to train 46-year-old acquired prosopagnosia patient CC to integrate configural face information. CC categorized computer-generated faces as belonging to either category 1: Faces with higher eyebrows and lower mouths, or category 2: Faces with relatively lower eyebrows and higher mouths compared to category 1. DeGutis and colleagues reasoned that these categorizations would be slow and effortful at first but that, with practice, CC might learn to integrate the feature spacings simultaneously, increasing her sensitivity to the configuration of internal facial features—a skill thought to be critical to holistic processing (see Piepers & Robbins, 2012). CC showed some evidence of improvement on the categorization task, but this did not generalize to novel faces—which is of course a critical requirement if the training is to be beneficial in helping patients learn to recognize new people.

Researchers have noted that it may not be possible to recover normal face recognition functioning in patients with acquired prosopagnosia because the neural mechanisms supporting face recognition have been irreversibly damaged (see DeGutis et al., 2014). Patients with developmental prosopagnosia, however, have underdeveloped but intact neural mechanisms that may be more amenable to training.

With this in mind, DeGutis et al. (2007) attempted to improve holistic face processing in 48-year-old developmental prosopagnosia patient MZ using the feature-spacing categorization procedure described above. At the start of training, MZ took nearly 13 seconds to categorize each face as belonging to category 1 or 2. After 4,000 trials of daily training over one week, and another 12,000 trials of daily training over three months, MZ's accuracy and reaction time on the feature-spacing categorization task were similar to 10 control participants. She also performed within the normal range on standardized tests of face recognition, including the Cambridge Face Memory Test (see Duchaine & Nakayama, 2006), and showed a greater N170 (a robust neural marker of brain responses) to faces than objects, which had not been the case prior to training. However, the longevity of these training effects is unclear. MZ reported that the improvements she experienced in day-to-day life disappeared one month after the first week of training and, while they re-emerged during the second training period, it is not clear whether these later improvements were longer lasting.

Other attempts to train holistic processing in developmental prosopagnosia patients have been less successful. DeGutis et al. (2014) administered the feature-spacing categorization training to a group of 24 developmental prosopagnosia patients. They observed improvements to holistic face processing on front-view face perception tasks, but not on tasks that required face discrimination from different viewpoints. Dalrymple et al. (2012) also report an unsuccessful attempt by DeGutis and colleagues to train 12-year-old TM to discriminate between photographs of his mother and other women using feedback.

In summary, the evidence indicates that it may be possible to improve holistic processing in developmental prosopagnosia patients to some extent. However, these effects are inconsistent and do not necessarily produce reliable, lasting improvements that support face recognition. Further, given that positive results are more likely to be published compared to null results, it is possible that other unsuccessful training has been carried out but not published.

5.3.1.2 Feature-Based Compensatory Strategy Training

While prosopagnosia patients' normal face recognition systems are impaired, there is evidence that featural face processing is spared in these patients. For example, patient KD was severely impaired in recognizing faces, but was able to accurately discriminate between pairs of isolated facial features. However, when those features were embedded in the context of the whole face, she was no longer able to discriminate between them (Ellis & Young, 1988). This suggests that some people with prosopagnosia can access identity information contained in individual facial features, but that viewing features in the context of a whole face disrupts their ability to do so. Other research suggests that this disruption can be overcome when performing unfamiliar face-matching tasks, because people with both acquired (e.g., Benton & Van Allen, 1972) and developmental prosopagnosia (Duchaine & Nakayama, 2004; White et al., 2017) can achieve normal scores on standardized tests of unfamiliar face-matching—consistent with the idea that unfamiliar face-matching tasks can be performed using a piecemeal process of feature comparison (Megreya & Burton, 2006).

Because of this, some researchers have proposed an alternative approach to training prosopagnosia patients: Teaching them to take advantage of the feature-based processing that appears to be left at their disposal. Indeed, many prosopagnosia patients report using compensatory strategies to recognize familiar people, such as relying on distinguishing facial features, blemishes, idiosyncratic face movements, voice, hairstyle, glasses, clothing, and jewellery (Adams et al., 2019). Deliberate attempts to train these compensatory strategies may therefore provide an alternate means of improving face recognition accuracy. Unlike holistic processing training, compensatory strategy training *can* improve face recognition accuracy for patients with both acquired and developmental prosopagnosia.

In acquired prosopagnosia, training patients to pay attention to facial features (Beyn & Knyazeva, 1962), or to discriminate and describe the facial features of familiar people (Mayer & Rossion, 2007) led to reports of improved face recognition in day-to-day life. Powell et al. (2008) attempted to train acquired prosopagnosia patient WJ to learn faces using three different procedures: Caricaturing (where faces were digitally caricatured to be more distinctive), semantic associations (e.g., 'This is Anita the policewoman whose camera was stolen from a fashion show yesterday.'), and feature-based descriptions (e.g., 'This is Victoria. She has large eyes and freckles.'). Only feature-based descriptions produced an improvement on a subsequent recognition test, increasing accuracy from 70% to 95% after training. However, we note that WJ's performance prior to training was quite high, indicating that perhaps he was not overly impaired on this particular task to begin with.

In developmental prosopagnosia, Brunsdon et al. (2006) taught eight-year-old AL to recognize 17 familiar faces by memorizing their age and gender, and three distinctive facial features for each person, such as eyebrow shape, wrinkles, and face shape. They found improved recognition of new images of the familiar faces, and anecdotal reports of a reduction in AL's tendency to misidentify unfamiliar people as family members, and to confuse family members in daily life. Schmalzl et al. (2008) used the same distinctive feature training for four-year-old K, and they also found improved recognition of new instances of the trained identities, and eye-movement patterns that were more similar to people with no face recognition deficits (i.e., focused on internal rather than external features).

Feature-based compensatory strategies essentially bypass the core face recognition system, but nevertheless appear to be the most promising approach to training prosopagnosia patients. This is an intriguing finding in the context of the broader familiar face recognition literature, where performance is typically impaired when observers are forced to adopt a piecemeal feature-processing strategy (see Coin & Tiberghien, 1997; McKone & Yovel, 2009). It is therefore remarkable that this type of training allows prosopagnosia patients to reliably recognize familiar faces at all. Importantly, it points to the possibility that, through training, we can learn to reliably recognize faces using processes *outside* the core face recognition system (see also Bruce & Young, 1986; Brunsdon et al., 2006).

This is an important insight that can potentially provide a route to professional training, and so we return to this in greater detail later. Importantly, however, training interventions for people with prosopagnosia have understandably focused on improving their ability to recognize *familiar* faces, to facilitate their day-to-day functioning. In forensic settings, face identifications almost exclusively involve *unfamiliar* people, which is a qualitatively different cognitive task to familiar face recognition (Megreya & Burton, 2006). Familiar face recognition is based on *memory* and relies on activation of stored identity representations, whereas unfamiliar face identification relies on *pictorial matching* processes, where face images are simultaneously compared to determine whether they show the same person or different people.

5.3.2 Improving Unfamiliar Face-Matching Accuracy in the General Population

A number of studies have aimed to improve unfamiliar face-matching accuracy in the general population. This interest has not necessarily been fuelled by the applied importance of the task, as is the case for professional training, but rather because unfamiliar face-matching poses an intriguing theoretical problem. We can recognize familiar faces almost perfectly, we easily learn and become familiar with new people, and any unfamiliar face has the potential to become familiar. Perfect unfamiliar face-matching accuracy is therefore tantalizingly just out of reach: If we can make an unfamiliar face familiar, we can solve the problem of unfamiliar face-matching. As a result, training to improve unfamiliar face-matching has mostly focused on re-creating or emulating some of the processes involved in learning and recognizing familiar faces.

5.3.2.1 Fast-Tracking the Creation of Stable Face Representations

Familiar face recognition is thought to rely on stable face representations that are abstracted from multiple encounters with a face, and which allow us to recognize faces even in unusual views (e.g., a friend wearing a Halloween costume). If it is possible to fast-track the formation of these representations, at least partially, they should support face-matching and improve accuracy. Consistent with this, learning an identity from multiple images leads to improved accuracy on both memory (Murphy et al., 2015) and matching tasks (Andrews et al., 2015; Ritchie & Burton, 2016). Even just providing multiple images to compare to another image during a matching task improves accuracy (Dowsett et al., 2015; Matthews & Mondloch, 2018; Menon et al., 2015; White, Burton, Jenkins, et al., 2014; but see Kramer & Reynolds, 2018; Ritchie et al., 2019). The accuracy benefits associated with using multiple images of an identity tend to be around 10%.

However, as we might expect, the benefit of providing multiple images is identity specific. Multiple images do not confer improvements that generalize to new, unfamiliar identities (Dowsett et al., 2015; Matthews & Mondloch, 2018). And so while it is possible to train people to identify a particular unfamiliar person more accurately via multiple images, this type of training has utility only for a limited set of applied cases, such as those where multiple images of the offender are available for comparison to the suspect. Providing multiple images does not lead to generalized improvements in a person's ability to identify new unfamiliar faces.

5.3.2.2 Collaborative Decision Making

Because we tend to learn people's faces by interacting with them in a social context, some studies have attempted to recreate this aspect of familiarization. Bruce et al. (2001) asked pairs of participants to watch short videos and discuss the actors' faces as they watched. In a subsequent recognition test, participants decided whether the actors appeared in eight-person arrays. Participants who discussed the faces with their partner were 10% more accurate than those who had watched the videos alone.

Dowsett and Burton (2015) asked pairs of participants to complete a 1:1 face-matching task by working together and discussing the images. They found that face-matching decisions made in pairs were more accurate than those made individually (see also Jeckeln et al., 2018). They also investigated whether this benefit would generalize to new unfamiliar identities that had not been discussed, and found that, after working with a partner, the lower-ability person in the pair subsequently showed significant improvements when working alone on a face-matching task that contained new unfamiliar identities.

Dowsett and Burton (2015) argued that the discussion must have revealed information that was useful during the paired face-matching task, and which could also be usefully applied to future comparisons. They suggested that the discussion may have alerted the low performer to the value of facial features they would have neglected otherwise, or taught them a more effective comparison strategy. It is unclear exactly what was learned during the discussions, but this study demonstrates that collaborative decision making can improve the face-matching accuracy of low performers.

5.3.2.3 Feedback

In our day-to-day encounters with faces, we receive feedback about the accuracy of our identification decisions. When we greet a friend we recognize at a café, we get immediate feedback that we have correctly recognized them. We may also receive immediate feedback if we fail to recognize an acquaintance or mistake a stranger for someone we know. Errors of this kind are particularly unpleasant and damaging to interpersonal relationships, so we are likely to be sensitive to feedback to help us avoid such situations in the future. In professional settings, practitioners rarely receive feedback about the accuracy of their decisions. If they do, it tends to be the subjective opinion of a more senior practitioner or the verdict of a court case, often months or years after the identification decision was made. Feedback training may therefore improve unfamiliar face identification accuracy.

White, Kemp, Jenkins, and Burton (2014) gave participants trial-by-trial feedback on the GFMT, such as, 'You answered correctly: These images are of the same person.' They found that accuracy increased by 10% over the course of the training, and that the benefits transferred to a subsequent test containing new identities, even though feedback was no longer provided. However, as was the case in Dowsett and Burton's (2015) paired decision-making study, the benefit of feedback training was specific to low-performing participants.

Further, feedback training does not always improve accuracy. Alenezi and Bindemann (2013) found that, instead of improving accuracy, feedback served to merely maintain baseline performance, counteracting a decline in performance observed in participants who did not receive feedback. However, feedback in this study was provided after the images were removed, whereas feedback in White, Kemp, Jenkins, and Burton (2014) was delivered while the faces remained onscreen, which may have helped maximize its benefit.

Alenezi and Bindemann's (2013) finding that feedback prevented a decline in performance suggests that the benefits of feedback may be driven by attentional mechanisms rather than increased perceptual sensitivity to identity information in faces. However, this explanation does not hold true for White, Kemp, Jenkins, and Burton's

(2014) study, where feedback training increased sensitivity to task-relevant information and did not change participants' response criterion (cf., Papesh et al., 2018). Further research is necessary to resolve these mixed findings. Until then, the benefits of feedback training, and the mechanisms driving those benefits, remain unclear.

5.4 The Training Paradox

For face-matching training to be useful in forensic settings, training benefits must generalize to previously unseen identities. A review of the literature on professional training, remedial and compensatory strategy interventions for prosopagnosia patients, and lab-based experiments on the general population reveals only *two* studies employing two different training approaches that have shown training effects that generalize to new unfamiliar faces (see Dowsett & Burton, 2015; White, Kemp, Jenkins, and Burton, 2014). Even so, these procedures only improve the accuracy of people who were initially poor at the task and have not been demonstrated to have consistent effects over repeated tests.

These underwhelming effects of face identification training might lead us to conclude that face identification *cannot be trained*. Indeed, some psychologists have recommended that training for unfamiliar face-matching accuracy be abandoned in favour of recruiting 'super-recognizers'—people who are naturally talented at face recognition—for facial image comparison roles (e.g., see Bobak, Dowsett, et al., 2016; Noyes et al., 2017; Ramon et al., 2019; Robertson et al., 2016).

However, there is one specialist group of facial image comparison practitioners whose performance indicates that face-matching ability *can* be trained. Facial examiners conduct slow, systematic analysis of facial features in order to reach face-matching decisions, and this process can take several hours or days to complete. They are often referred challenging cases by less specialized practitioners, and can be called upon to provide expert identification evidence in court. While individual performance varies, as a group, facial examiners consistently outperform novices, sometimes by as much as 25% (see Phillips et al., 2018; Towler, White, & Kemp, 2017; White, Phillips, et al., 2015; White, Towler, & Kemp, this volume). This observation gives rise to the *training paradox*: How do facial examiners acquire their expertise, if not through training?

We have discussed potential alternative contributions to the superior performance of facial examiners in another chapter in this volume (White, Towler, & Kemp). There, we conclude that other factors, summarized below, cannot entirely account for examiners' superior performance. First, it is unlikely that examiners' expertise developed as a consequence of performing identification tasks in their daily work because length of employment does not predict face-matching accuracy (White, Dunn, et al., 2015; White, Kemp, Jenkins, Matheson, et al., 2014; Wirth & Carbon, 2017). Second, motivation cannot explain examiners' expertise because they outperform other similarly motivated practitioner groups (Phillips et al., 2018; White, Phillips, et al., 2015). Finally, it is possible that facial examiners are naturally better at face-matching, and that they simply choose the profession because they have a talent for it. However, this possibility is inconsistent with evidence that facial examiners perform face-matching tasks in a *qualitatively* different manner from that of untrained participants.

For example, White, Phillips, et al. (2015) compared facial examiners to untrained student novices on a 1:1 face identification task. When given just two seconds to view the images, there was no evidence of examiners' expertise—both groups performed equally well (see Figure 5.7). Critically, however, when given 30 seconds to view the images, examiners outperformed novices by nearly 10%. Examiners benefitted more from the additional time than students, indicating that their expertise lies in slow, careful analysis of faces.

In Towler, White, et al. (2017), we showed that the slow, systematic, feature-based comparison strategy used by facial examiners produces higher face-matching accuracy than just making 'gut instinct' decisions. Importantly, facial examiners are experts at using this strategy. Not only do examiners outperform novices when using a feature-by-feature comparison strategy, but they extract more diagnostic identity information from facial features. We calculated the extent to which examiners' similarity ratings for each facial feature predicted the ground truth, and found that examiners' feature similarity ratings were far more diagnostic of identity than those of novices (Cohen's D = 1.44; see Towler, White, et al., 2017). Underlying examiners' expertise is therefore an enhanced ability to extract identity information from facial features.

Comparison between examiners and super-recognizers provides further evidence that examiners' expertise is acquired through training and not just a consequence of

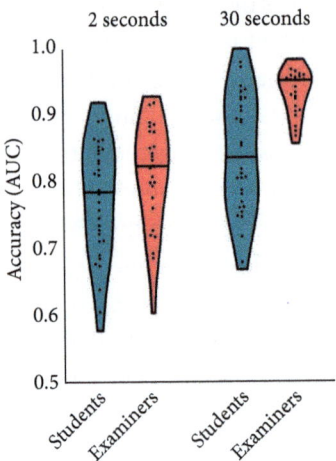

Figure 5.7 Performance data from White, Phillips, et al. (2015) of untrained students and facial examiners performing a 1:1 face identification task after seeing the face images for 2 seconds vs. 30 seconds.

Note: Examiners' expertise is apparent when the images were visible for 30 seconds but not 2 seconds, indicating that their expertise lies in slow, careful analysis of faces.

Source: Data from White et al. (2015) 'Perceptual expertise in forensic facial image comparison' *Proceedings of the Royal Society of London B: Biological Sciences*, 282, 1814–1822. https:// doi.org/ 10.1098/rspb.2015.1292. Figure produced by David White.

naturally occurring superior performance. Super-recognizers are born with natural expertise in face identification and, because they show quantitative differences in performance to novices, they are thought to represent the very top end of the normal distribution of face-recognition ability rather than a distinct group (see Noyes et al., 2017). Super-recognizers experience larger face inversion effects than novices (Bennetts et al., 2017; Bobak, Bennetts, et al., 2016; Russell et al., 2009), whereas facial examiners experience smaller or no inversion effects compared to novices (Towler, White, et al., 2017; White, Phillips, et al., 2015). Inversion is thought to disrupt normal holistic face-recognition processes, leaving observers to rely on piecemeal, feature-based processes (see McKone & Yovel, 2009; Rossion, 2008; Yin, 1969). The finding that examiners' performance is resistant to inversion therefore suggests that, unlike super-recognizers, their expertise does not rely on normal face-recognition processes, but instead relies on piecemeal feature-based processes.

Examiners achieve very high levels of accuracy using a different strategy to novices and super-recognizers. These findings provide strong evidence that it is possible to learn skills that improve face-matching ability, indicating that this ability can be trained. However, these findings also reinforce the training paradox. Examiners are experts at identifying faces because of their reliance on slow, systematic facial feature comparison. Professional training courses encourage practitioners to use a feature-by-feature comparison strategy, and yet, the evidence indicates that professional training courses do not work (see Towler et al., 2019). How, then, do examiners learn their skills?

In Towler et al. (2019), we argued that examiners probably learn their skills through extensive on-the-job practice and mentoring from other examiners, and this is certainly consistent with anecdotal reports by examiners. For example, it may not be enough to simply tell trainees to conduct feature-by-feature comparison, as is typical in professional training courses (see Towler et al., 2019). Inhibiting natural holistic face processing in favour of piecemeal analysis of facial features would likely require extensive practice. Further, working alongside another examiner, learning about the strategies they use and receiving their feedback (e.g., 'Yes, the noses do look similar, but notice the subtle differences in nostril shape') could help refine examiners' ability to search for and extract useful identity information from facial features.

Evidence for learning via this kind of mechanism comes from the Metropolitan Police Service's three day professional training course we evaluated in Towler et al. (2019). This is the only training course we tested that showed any evidence of improving matching accuracy. Unlike the other courses, a considerable proportion of this course involved group discussion of facial features, which may have conferred some small immediate benefit. Further, on-the-job training may serve as a more elaborate and information-rich version of the paired decision-making task (Dowsett & Burton, 2015) and feedback training (Alenezi & Bindemann, 2013; White, Kemp, Jenkins, & Burton, 2014) reported in the psychology literature as providing some benefit. Further research is necessary to understand exactly how examiners acquire their feature-based expertise on the job but, for now, it appears that they develop their expertise through professional training.

5.5 Two Routes to Face Identification Expertise

Given the evidence reviewed above, it appears that facial examiners derive at least part of their expertise in facial image comparison from extensive on-the-job training in feature comparison. This is in contrast to unsuccessful attempts to train face recognition through perceptual tasks that involve holistic perceptual processing. For instance, there is almost no evidence that remedial holistic training for prosopagnosia patients can rehabilitate normal face recognition functioning (see Bate & Bennetts, 2014; DeGutis, Chiu, et al., 2014). Similarly, the evidence for improving face-matching ability in the general population using procedures inspired by the processes supporting familiar face recognition have had limited success in producing generalized improvements in accuracy (see Bate & Bennetts, 2014; DeGutis, Chiu, et al., 2014). These findings indicate that the core face recognition system—responsible for recognizing faces in daily life—is not amenable to training. This conclusion is consistent with evidence that our face-recognition abilities are largely predetermined by genetics (Shakeshaft & Plomin, 2015; Wilmer et al., 2010), and that performance in challenging face-memory tasks reaches asymptote in adulthood (Germine et al., 2011).

In contrast, training methods that promote feature-based strategies have had much more success. The most promising approach for training prosopagnosia patients to recognize familiar faces is to teach them compensatory strategies, such as relying on distinctive facial features, voice, and hairstyle (Brunsdon et al., 2006; Schmalzl et al., 2008). It also seems that the most reliable way to improve face-matching accuracy in the general population is to adopt the feature-based comparison strategy used by facial examiners (Towler, White, et al., 2017).

To account for these findings, we propose that there are *two routes to expertise in face identification*. One route is the core face-recognition system that supports familiar face recognition by matching visual input to stored holistic face representations. Our skill at employing this route appears to be acquired through normal development and resistant to training. The other route is feature-based and draws on piecemeal, feature-by-feature matching processes that bypass the core face recognition system and is better suited to unfamiliar face-matching tasks. Importantly, the feature-based mechanisms driving performance in this route appear to be trainable.

We are not the first to argue that there are two separable routes involved in face identification. In her seminal work explaining patterns of co-occurrence in associative agnosias, Farah (1991) argued that face, word, and object recognition rely on two levels of perceptual processing: One where 'complex parts' are recognized as a single unified object, and another where 'numerous parts' are decomposed further into multiple elementary parts. Further, Bartlett et al. (2003) conducted a thorough literature review and concluded that face recognition involves two distinct but complementary routes: A fast, holistic processing route and a slow, feature-based processing route.

Bruce and Young's (1986) functional model of face recognition also distinguishes between two separable routes involved in face identification. The 'core' face recognition system, built to recognize familiar faces, proceeds along the right-hand route high-lighted in blue in Figure 5.8. The structural properties of the face are encoded and these in turn activate face recognition units (cognitive face representations), which allow us to recognize familiar faces quickly and with almost perfect accuracy. However, the model also describes 'directed visual processing', the left-hand route highlighted in red in Figure 5.8, which allows us to selectively and strategically attend to aspects of the face to encode particular information (e.g., to carefully search for distinctive features in order to remember someone's face in the future). Bruce and Young (1986) suggested that this type of processing may play a particularly important role in unfamiliar face-matching. In support of this, Megreya and Burton (2006) demonstrated that familiar face recognition and unfamiliar face-matching recruit qualitatively different cognitive mechanisms. Unlike familiar faces, unfamiliar faces are matched more like objects than faces, recruiting piecemeal, feature-based processing.

While there has been compelling evidence for two routes to face identification for some time, featural face processing has historically been associated with poorer performance compared to holistic face processing (e.g., see Tanaka & Farah, 1993; Yin,

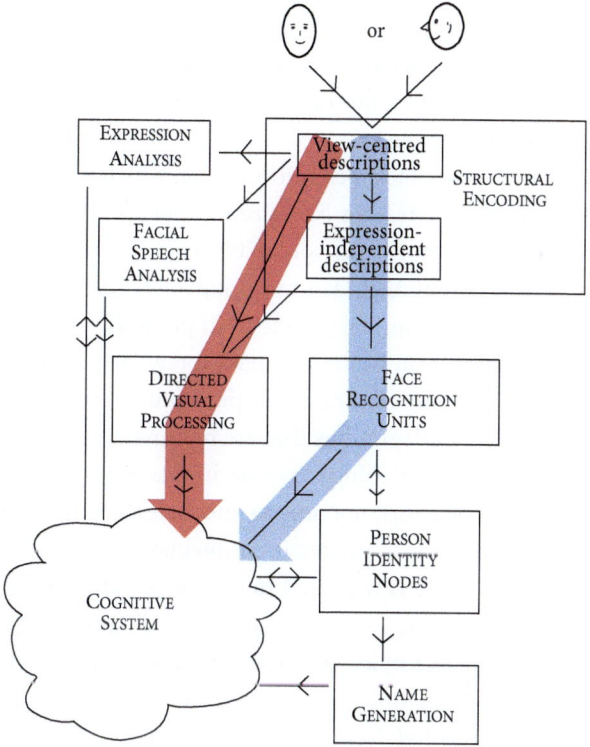

Figure 5.8 Bruce and Young's (1986) functional model of face recognition.

Note: The two routes to face identification are overlayed—the blue right-hand route is the core face recognition system that allows us to recognise familiar faces, the red left-hand route is a feature-based alternative that permits reliable face-matching decisions in facial examiners, and familiar face recognition in prosopagnosia patients.

Source: Adapted from Bruce & Young (1986) 'Understanding face recognition' *British Journal of Psychology, 77,* 305–327, Figure 1. https://doi.org/10.1111/j.2044-8295.1986.tb02199.x © 1986, The British Psychological Society.

1969). This probably reflects the fact that research has paid much more attention to face *recognition* memory than to perceptual matching tasks. As it turns out, this route can be especially useful in face-matching tasks. It appears that facial examiners are able to achieve very high levels of performance by deliberately employing a feature-by-feature comparison strategy, and directing their attention to specific facial features in order to detect and analyse similarities and differences between faces (Phillips et al., 2018; Towler, White, et al., 2017; White, Phillips, et al., 2015). This feature-based face processing strategy does not align with the holistic processes we typically think of as 'normal' face recognition, and yet, they use this strategy to achieve very high levels of accuracy in face-matching tasks. We therefore argue that both routes can lead to expert-level face identification performance.

Acquiring expertise in each route appears to require quite different experiences. Expertise in the core face recognition route likely develops naturally as a consequence of needing to recognize familiar faces in our daily lives. Because of this, most of us would already be considered experts in this route (see Young & Burton, 2018), the exception of course being prosopagnosia patients. Interestingly, super-recognizers appear to be 'super-experts' at using this route because they seem to use it for unfamiliar face identification tasks, not just familiar face recognition. Their unfamiliar face identification performance mirrors many of the characteristics of familiar face recognition—quick, automatic, and highly accurate. This may indicate that super-recognizers are particularly skilled at extracting stable identity representations, which benefit accuracy in both memory and matching tasks.

Unlike expertise in the core face recognition route, which appears to develop naturally, acquiring expertise in the feature-based route appears to require deliberate effort. Prior to the invention of photography some 200 years ago, unfamiliar face-matching was not performed *at all*. Unfamiliar face-matching only exists because of our modern-day customs of identifying unfamiliar people from photo ID and CCTV footage. Even so, only a very small proportion of the population regularly undertake this task. It is therefore unsurprising that our cognitive and perceptual systems have not developed the necessary feature-based adaptations that are required to perform unfamiliar face-matching tasks accurately. Developing expertise in this feature-based route is likely to involve significant cognitive effort, not only to fine-tune the skill itself, but also to learn to override automatic holistic face-processing strategies.

We propose that each route is recruited to varying extents for familiar face recognition and unfamiliar face-matching tasks, and depending on the person making the identification decision. For example, while the core face recognition route is best suited for recognizing familiar faces, this system is not necessarily an option for prosopagnosia patients, so they can switch to the feature-based route to use compensatory strategies to recognize familiar faces with reasonable success. Similarly, facial examiners report forming an intuitive initial impression of a facial comparison, but then deliberately switch to engaging a slower, feature-by-feature comparison strategy in order to reach their final identification decision.

Without some level of awareness of the most useful strategies for the particular face identification task at hand, people are likely to recruit these two routes in suboptimal ways. For example, a novice may attempt to make an unfamiliar face-matching decision by garnering a holistic overall impression of each face, rather than taking a feature-by-feature approach. To illustrate why the holistic approach can lead to inaccurate decisions, consider the faces in Figure 5.9. Do they show the same person or different people? At first glance, the faces appear very dissimilar suggesting that they are two different people. However, upon closer inspection of the facial features—particularly the ears, eyelids, freckle to the left of the mouth, and the sideburn-cheek contours—we can see striking similarities that point to the correct answer: The photos are of the same person. Relying on an initial holistic impression of the faces would mean that informative cues to identity such as these would be missed. Recruiting the core face recognition system for an unfamiliar face-matching task, rather than the feature-based route, could therefore contribute to poor performance on unfamiliar face-matching tasks (see Towler, White et al., 2017). Training people to use the feature-based route for

Figure 5.9 Do these faces show the same person or different people? Your initial impression may be that these faces look very different and thus show different people. Upon closer inspection of the facial features however—particularly the ears, eyelids, freckle to the left of the mouth, and the sideburn-cheek contours—we see striking similarities that indicate these photos are actually of the same person, which is the correct answer.

Source: Phillips et al. (2012) 'The good, the bad, and the ugly face challenge problem' *Image and Vision Computing,* 30, 177–185. https:// doi.org/ 10.1016/j.imavis.2012.01.004 Copyright © 2012 Elsevier B.V.

unfamiliar face-matching tasks, rather than the core face recognition system, may help boost face-matching accuracy.

5.6 Conclusion

We have argued that there are two routes to expertise in face identification. One route is our core face recognition system, which is built to recognize familiar faces using quick, intuitive, holistic judgements. The second route is feature-based, and suited to performing unfamiliar face-matching tasks using a slow, feature-by-feature comparison strategy. Importantly, it appears that only the feature-based route can be trained. Expertise in the core face recognition system is largely resistant to training.

Training to improve unfamiliar face-matching ability in facial image comparison practitioners should therefore focus on improving their ability to extract identity information from facial features, rather than attempt to train the processes that support familiar face recognition. For now, it seems the only way to train this feature-based route is to undergo the extensive on-the-job training experienced by facial examiners. However, this type of training is extremely time and resource intensive. We therefore encourage practitioners and academics to work together to identify efficient evidence-based training methods to replace current training practices.

References

Adams, A., Hills, P. J., Bennetts, R. J., & Bate, S. (2019). Coping strategies for developmental prosopagnosia. *Neuropsychological Rehabilitation*, 4, 1–20. doi:10.1080/09602011.2019.1623824

Alenezi, H. M. & Bindemann, M. (2013). The effect of feedback on face-matching accuracy. *Applied Cognitive Psychology*, 27, 735–753. doi:10.1002/acp.2968

Andrews, S., Jenkins, R., Cursiter, H., & Burton, A. M. (2015). Telling faces together: Learning new faces through exposure to multiple instances. *Quarterly Journal of Experimental Psychology*, 68, 2041–2050. doi:10.1080/17470218.2014.1003949

Avidan, G., Tanzer, M., & Behrmann, M. (2011). Impaired holistic processing in congenital prosopagnosia. *Neuropsychologica*, 49, 2541–2552. doi:10.1016/j.neuropsychologia.2011.05.002

Bartlett, J. C., Searcy, J. H., & Abdi, H. (2003). What are the routes to face recognition? In M. Peterson & G. Rhodes (eds), *Perception of faces, objects, and scenes: Analytic and holistic processes* (pp. 21–52). Oxford: Oxford University Press.

Bate, S. & Bennetts, R. J. (2014). The rehabilitation of face recognition impairments: A critical review and future directions. *Frontiers in Human Neuroscience*, 8:491, 1–17. doi:10.3389/fnhum.2014.00491

Behrmann, M., Avidan, G., Thomas, C., & Humphreys, K. (2010). Congenital and acquired prosopagnosia: Flip sides of the same coin? In I. Gauthier, M. Tarr, & D. Bub (eds), *Perceptual expertise: Bridging brain and behavior*. Oxford Scholarship Online.

Bennetts, R. J., Mole, J., & Bate, S. (2017). Super-recognition in development: A case study of an adolescent with extraordinary face recognition skills. *Cognitive Neuropsychology*, 34, 357–376. doi:10.1080/02643294.2017.1402755

Benton, A. L. & Van Allen, M. W. (1972). Prosopagnosia and facial discrimination. *Journal of the Neurological Sciences, 15,* 167–172. doi:10.1016/0022-510X(72)90004-4

Bertillon, A. (1896). *The Bertillon system of identification.* Chicago: Werner Company.

Beyn, E. S. & Knyazeva, G. R. (1962). The problem of prosopagnosia. *Journal of Neurology, Neurosurgery, and Psychiatry, 25,* 154–158. doi:10.1136/jnnp.25.2.154

Bobak, A. K., Bennetts, R. J., Parris, B. A., Jansari, A., & Bate, S. (2016). An in-depth cognitive examination of individuals with superior face recognition skills. *Cortex, 82,* 48–62. doi:10.1016/j.cortex.2016.05.003

Bobak, A. K., Dowsett, A. J., & Bate, S. (2016). Solving the border control problem: Evidence of enhanced face matching in individuals with extraordinary face recognition skills. *PLoS ONE, 11*(2), e0148148. doi:10.1371/journal.pone.0148148

Bruce, V., Henderson, Z., Newman, C., & Burton, A. M. (2001). Matching identities of familiar and unfamiliar faces caught on CCTV images. *Journal of Experimental Psychology: Applied, 7,* 207–218. doi:10.1037/1076-898X.7.3.207

Bruce, V. & Young, A. W. (1986). Understanding face recognition. *British Journal of Psychology, 77,* 305–327. doi:10.1111/j.2044-8295.1986.tb02199.x

Brunsdon, R., Coltheart, M., Nickels, L., & Joy, P. (2006). Developmental prosopagnosia: A case analysis and treatment study. *Cognitive Neuropsychology, 23,* 822–840. doi:10.1080/02643290500441841

Bukach, C. M., Bub, D. N., Gauthier, I., & Tarr, M. J. (2006). Perceptual expertise effects are not all or none: Spatially limited perceptual expertise for faces in a case of prosopagnosia. *Journal of Cognitive Neuroscience, 18,* 48–63. doi:10.1162/089892906775250094

Busigny, T., Joubert, S., Felican, O., Ceccaldi, M., & Rossion, B. (2010). Holistic perception of the individual face is specific and necessary: Evidence from an extensive case study of acquired prosopagnosia. *Neuropsychologica, 48,* 4057–4092. doi:10.1016/j.neuropsychologia.2010.09.017

Coin, C. & Tiberghien, G. (1997). Encoding activity and face recognition. *Memory, 5,* 545–568. doi:10.1080/741941479

Dalrymple, K. A., Corrow, S., Yonas, A., & Duchaine, B. (2012). Developmental prosopagnosia in childhood. *Cognitive Neuropsychology, 29,* 393–418. doi:10.1080/02643294.2012.722547

DeGutis, J. M., Bentin, S., Robertson, L. C., & D'Esposito, M. (2007). Functional plasticity in ventral temporal cortex following cognitive rehabilitation of a congenital prosopagnosic. *Journal of Cognitive Neuroscience, 19,* 1790–1802. doi:10.1162/jocn.2007.19.11.1790

DeGutis, J. M., Chiu, C., Grosso, M. E., & Cohan, S. (2014). Face processing improvements in prosopagnosia: Successes and failures over the last 50 years. *Frontiers in Human Neuroscience, 8:561,* 1–14. doi:10.3389/fnhum.2014.00561

DeGutis, J. M., Cohan, S., Kahn, D., Aguirre, G., & Nakayama, K. (2013). Facial expression training improves emotion recognition and changes in neural tuning in a patient with acquired emotion recognition deficits and prosopagnosia. *Journal of Vision, 13:9,* 993. doi:10.1167/13.9.993

DeGutis, J. M., Cohan, S., & Nakayama, K. (2014). Holistic face training enhances face processing in developmental prosopagnosia. *Brain, 137,* 1781–1798. doi:10.1093/brain/awu062

Dowsett, A. J. & Burton, A. M. (2015). Unfamiliar face matching: Pairs out-perform individuals and provide a route to training. *British Journal of Psychology, 106,* 433–445. doi:10.1111/bjop.12103

Dowsett, A. J., Sandford, A., & Burton, A. M. (2015). Face learning with multiple images leads to fast acquisition of familiarity for specific individuals. *Quarterly Journal of Experimental Psychology, 69,* 1–10. doi:10.1080/17470218.2015.1017513

Drost, M. (2016). The unique method for face recognition of the Stasis. *Volkskrant.*

Duchaine, B. C. & Nakayama, K. (2004). Developmental prosopagnosia and the Benton Facial Recognition Test. *Neurology, 62,* 1219–1220. doi:10.1212/01.wnl.0000118297.03161.b3

Duchaine, B. C. & Nakayama, K. (2006). The Cambridge Face Memory Test: Results for neurologically intact individuals and an investigation of its validity using inverted face stimuli and prosopagnosic participants. *Neuropsychologia, 44,* 576–585. doi:10.1016/j.neuropsychologia.2005.07.001

Ellis, H. D. & Young, A. W. (1988). Training in face-processing skills for a child with acquired prosopagnosia. *Developmental Neuropsychology, 4,* 283–294. doi:10.1080/87565648809540412

Facial Identification Scientific Working Group (FISWG) (2011). Guidelines and recommendations for facial comparison training to competency (Version 1.1). Available at: https://fiswg.org/FISWG_Training_Guidelines_Recommendations_v1.1_2010_11_18.pdf (accessed 13 April 2020).

Farah, M. J. (1991). Patterns of co-occurrence among the associative agnosias: Implications for visual object representation. *Cognitive Neuropsychology, 8*, 1–19. doi:10.1080/02643299108253364

Farah, M. J., Wilson, K. D., Drain, M., & Tanaka, J. W. (1998). What is 'special' about face perception? *Psychological Review, 105*, 482–498. doi:10.1037/0033-295x.105.3.482

Germine, L. T., Duchaine, B., & Nakayama, K. (2011). Where cognitive development and aging meet: Face learning ability peaks after age 30. *Cognition, 118*, 201–210. doi:10.1016/j.cognition.2010.11.002

Grother, P. & Ngan, M. (2014). *Face Recognition Vendor Test (FRVT)*. Information Access Division, National Institute of Standards and Technology. Available at: https://nvlpubs.nist.gov/nistpubs/ir/2014/NIST.IR.8009.pdf (accessed 15 April 2020).

Grother, P., Ngan, M., & Hanaoka, K. (2018). Ongoing Face Recognition Vendor Test (FRVT) Part 1: Verification. Information Access Division, National Institute of Standards and Technology. Available at: https://www.nist.gov/system/files/documents/2018/02/15/frvt_report_2018_02_15.pdf (accessed 5 May 2020).

Grother, P., Ngan, M., & Hanaoka, K. (2019). Ongoing Face Recognition Vendor Test (FRVT) Part 1: Verification. Information Access Division, National Institute of Standards and Technology. Available at: https://www.nist.gov/system/files/documents/2019/07/31/frvt_report_2019_07_31.pdf (accessed 5 May 2020).

Jeckeln, G., Hahn, C. A., Noyes, E., Cavazos, J. G., & O'Toole, A. J. (2018). Wisdom of the social versus non-social crowd in face identification. *British Journal of Psychology, 109*, 724–735. doi:10.1111/bjop.12291

Kramer, R. S. S. & Reynolds, M. G. (2018). Unfamiliar face matching with frontal and profile views. *Perception, 47*, 1–18. doi:10.1177/0301006618756809

Levine, D. N. & Calvanio, R. (1989). Prosopagnosia: A defect in visual configural processing. *Brain and Cognition, 10*, 149–170. doi:10.1016/0278-2626(89)90051-1

Matthews, C. M. & Mondloch, C. J. (2018). Finding an unfamiliar face in a line-up: Viewing multiple images of the target is beneficial on target-present trials but costly on target-absent trials. *British Journal of Psychology, 109*, 1–18. doi:10.1111/bjop.12301

Mayer, E. & Rossion, B. (2007). Prosopagnosia. In J. Bogousslavsky & O. Godefroy (eds), *The behavioral and cognitive neurology of stroke* (pp. 315–334). Cambridge: Cambridge University Press.

McKone, E. & Yovel, G. (2009). Why does picture-plane inversion sometimes dissociate perception of features and spacing in faces, and sometimes not? Toward a new theory of holistic processing. *Psychonomic Bulletin and Review, 16*, 778–797. doi:10.3758/PBR.16.5.778

Megreya, A. M. & Burton, A. M. (2006). Unfamiliar faces are not faces: Evidence from a matching task. *Memory and Cognition, 34*, 865–876. doi:10.3758/bf03193433

Menon, N., White, D., & Kemp, R. I. (2015). Variation in photos of the same face drives improvements in identity verification. *Perception, 44*, 1332–1341. doi:10.1177/0301006615599902

Murphy, J., Ipser, A., Gaigg, S., & Cook, R. (2015). Exemplar variance supports robust learning of facial identity. *Journal of Experimental Psychology: Human Perception and Performance, 41*, 577–584. doi:10.1037/xhp0000049

National Research Council (2009). *Strengthening forensic science in the United States: A path forward.* Available at: https://www.nap.edu/catalog/12589/strengthening-forensic-science-in-the-united-states-a-path-forward (accessed 15 April 2020).

Noyes, E., Phillips, P. J., & O'Toole, A. J. (2017). What is a super-recogniser? In M. Bindemann & A. M. Megreya (eds), *Face processing: Systems, disorders and cultural differences* (pp. 173–201). New York: Nova Science Publishers.

Palermo, R., Willis, M. L., Rivolta, D., McKone, E., Wilson, C. E., & Calder, A. J. (2011). Impaired holistic coding of facial expression and facial identity in congenital prosopagnosia. *Neuropsychologia, 49*(5), 1226–1235

Papesh, M. H., Heisick, L. L., & Warner, K. A. (2018). The persistent low-prevalence effect in unfamiliar face-matching: The roles of feedback and criterion shifting. *Journal of Experimental Psychology: Applied, 24*, 416–430. doi:10.1037/xap0000156

PCAST (President's Council of Advisors on Science and Technology) (2016). *Forensic science in criminal courts: Ensuring scientific validity of feature-comparison methods.* (September). Available at: https://obamawhitehouse.archives.gov/sites/default/files/microsites/ostp/PCAST/pcast_forensic_science_report_final.pdf (accessed 15 April 2020).

Phillips, P. J., Yates, A. N., Hu, Y., Hahn, C. A., Noyes, E., Jackson, K., et al. (2018). Face recognition accuracy of forensic examiners, superrecognizers, and face recognition algorithms. *Proceedings of the National Academy of Sciences, 115*, 6171–6176. doi:10.1073/pnas.1721355115

Piazza, P. (2016). Alphonse Bertillon and the identification of persons (1880–1914). *Suspects, Defendants, Guilty.* Available at: https://criminocorpus.org/en/exhibitions/suspects-defendants-guilty/alphonse-bertillon-and-identification-persons-1880-1914/ (accessed 13 April 2020).

Piepers, D. W. & Robbins, R. A. (2012). A review and clarification of the terms 'holistic', 'configural', and 'relational' in the face perception literature. *Frontiers in Psychology, 3*:559, 1–11. doi:10.3389/fpsyg.2012.00559

Powell, J., Letson, S., Davidoff, J., Valentine, T., & Greenwood, R. (2008). Enhancement of face recognition learning in patients with brain injury using three cognitive training procedures. *Neuropsychological Rehabilitation, 18*, 182–203. doi:10.1080/09602010701419485

Ramon, M., Bobak, A. K., & White, D. (2019). Super-recognizers: From the lab to the world and back again. *British Journal of Psychology, 110*, 461–479. doi:10.1111/bjop.12368

Ramon, M., Busigny, T., & Rossion, B. (2010). Impaired holistic processing of unfamiliar individual faces in acquired prosopagnosia. *Neuropsychologica, 48*, 933–944. doi:10.1016/j.neuropsychologia.2009.11.014

Ritchie, K. L. & Burton, A. M. (2016). Learning faces from variability. *Quarterly Journal of Experimental Psychology, 70*, 1–9. doi:10.1080/17470218.2015.1136656

Ritchie, K. L., Mireku, M. O., & Kramer, R. S. S. (2019). Face averages and multiple images in a live matching task. *British Journal of Psychology*, 1–11. doi:10.1111/bjop.12388

Robertson, D. J., Noyes, E., Dowsett, A. J., Jenkins, R., & Burton, A. M. (2016). Face recognition by Metropolitan Police super-recognisers. *PLoS ONE, 11*(2), e0150036. doi:10.1371/journal.pone.0150036

Rossion, B. (2008). Picture-plane inversion leads to qualitative changes of face perception. *Acta Psychologica, 128*, 274–289. doi:10.1016/j.actpsy.2008.02.003

Russell, R., Duchaine, B., & Nakayama, K. (2009). Super-recognizers: People with extraordinary face recognition ability. *Psychonomic Bulletin and Review, 16*, 252–257. doi:10.3758/PBR.16.2.252

Schmalzl, L., Palermo, R., Green, M., Brunsdon, R., & Coltheart, M. (2008). Training of familiar face recognition and visual scan paths for faces in a child with congenital prosopagnosia. *Cognitive Neuropsychology, 25*, 704–729. doi:10.1080/02643290802299350

Shakeshaft, N. G. & Plomin, R. (2015). Genetic specificity of face recognition. *Proceedings of the National Academy of Sciences, 112*, 12887–12892. doi:10.1073/pnas.1421881112

Tanaka, J. W. & Farah, M. J. (1993). Parts and wholes in face recognition. *Quarterly Journal of Experimental Psychology Section A: Human Experimental Psychology, 46*, 225–245. doi:10.1080/14640749308401045

Towler, A., Kemp, R. I., Burton, A. M., Dunn, J. D., Wayne, T., Moreton, R., et al. (2019). Do professional facial image comparison training courses work? *PLoS ONE, 14*(2), e0211037. doi:10.1371/journal.pone.0211037

Towler, A., Kemp, R. I., & White, D. (2017). Unfamiliar face matching systems in applied settings. In M. Bindemann & A. M. Megreya (eds), *Face processing: Systems, disorders and cultural differences* (pp. 21–40). New York: Nova Science Publishers.

Towler, A., White, D., & Kemp, R. I. (2014). Evaluating training methods for facial image comparison: The face shape strategy does not work. *Perception, 43*, 214–218. doi:10.1068/p7676

Towler, A., White, D., & Kemp, R. I. (2017). Evaluating the feature comparison strategy for forensic face identification. *Journal of Experimental Psychology: Applied, 23*, 47–58. doi:10.1037/xap0000108

U.S. National Library of Medicine (2014). The Bertillon system. *Visible proofs: Forensic views of the body.* Available at: https://www.nlm.nih.gov/exhibition/visibleproofs/galleries/technologies/bertillon.html (accessed 13 April 2020).

White, D., Burton, A. M., Jenkins, R., & Kemp, R. I. (2014). Redesigning photo-ID to improve unfamiliar face matching performance. *Journal of Experimental Psychology: Applied*, *20*, 166–173. doi:10.1037/xap0000009

White, D., Dunn, J. D., Schmid, A. C., & Kemp, R. I. (2015). Error rates in users of automatic face recognition software. *PLoS ONE*, *10*(10), e0139827. doi:10.1371/journal.pone.0139827

White, D., Kemp, R. I., Jenkins, R., & Burton, A. M. (2014). Feedback training for facial image comparison. *Psychonomic Bulletin and Review*, *21*, 100–106. doi:10.3758/s13423-013-0475-3

White, D., Kemp, R. I., Jenkins, R., Matheson, M., & Burton, A. M. (2014). Passport officers' errors in face matching. *PLoS ONE*, *9*(8), e103510. doi:10.1371/journal.pone.0103510

White, D., Phillips, P. J., Hahn, C. A., Hill, M., & O'Toole, A. J. (2015). Perceptual expertise in forensic facial image comparison. *Proceedings of the Royal Society of London B: Biological Sciences*, *282*(1814), 20151292. doi:10.1098/rspb.2015.1292

White, D., Rivolta, D., Burton, A. M., Al-Janabi, S., & Palermo, R. (2017). Face matching impairment in developmental prosopagnosia. *Quarterly Journal of Experimental Psychology*, *70*, 287–297. doi:10.1080/17470218.2016.1173076

Wilmer, J. B., Germine, L., Chabris, C. F., Chatterjee, G., Williams, M., Loken, E., et al. (2010). Human face recognition ability is specific and highly heritable. *Proceedings of the National Academy of Sciences*, *107*, 5238–5241. doi:10.1073/pnas.0913053107

Wirth, B. E. & Carbon, C. C. (2017). An easy game for frauds? Effects of professional experience and time pressure on passport-matching performance. *Journal of Experimental Psychology: Applied*, *23*, 138–157. doi:10.1037/xap0000114

Woodhead, M. M., Baddeley, A. D., & Simmonds, D. C. V. (1979). On training people to recognize faces. *Ergonomics*, *22*, 333–343. doi:10.1080/00140137908924617

Yardley, L., McDermott, L., Pisarski, S., Duchaine, B., & Nakayama, K. (2008). Psychosocial consequences of developmental prosopagnosia: A problem of recognition. *Journal of Psychosomatic Research*, *65*, 445–451. doi:10.1016/j.jpsychores.2008.03.013

Yin, R. K. (1969). Looking at upside-down faces. *Journal of Experimental Psychology*, *81*, 141–145. doi:10.1037/h0027474

Young, A. W. & Burton, A. M. (2018). Are we face experts? *Trends in Cognitive Sciences*, *22*, 100–110. doi:10.1016/j.tics.2017.11.007

Young, A. W., Hellawell, D. J., & Hay, D. C. (1987). Configurational information in face perception. *Perception*, *16*, 747–759. doi:10.1068/p160747

6

Individual Differences Between Observers in Face Matching

Sarah Bate, Natalie Mestry, and Emma Portch

6.1 Face Processing: An Individual Differences Approach

Face identification is a great challenge for the visual system: human faces consist of a number of component features that can all differ in their size, shape, and positioning. While it has long been known that some people are clinically poor at this task (i.e., those who lose the ability to recognize faces following brain damage—a condition known as 'prosopagnosia'; e.g., Wigan, 1844), it has only recently been acknowledged that the face recognition ability of typical perceivers varies greatly, and that this variation represents meaningful data rather than uninformative noise (Wilmer, 2017). In fact, the full range of adult abilities has been revealed by the existence of 'super-recognizers' (Russell et al., 2009), who have an extraordinary ability to recognize faces. These realizations initiated a new innovative individual differences approach to the study of adult face recognition that has transformed the field, integrating the rigour of traditional experimental psychology with a psychometric approach, in which the reliability and validity of face recognition measures were further scrutinized. Although this approach has expanded the field's methodological and statistical skill set, encouraging a fine-grained analysis of the extent to which individuals, rather than groups, differ in their face recognition skills, this work and the strength of its theoretical implications are still in their infancy. In particular, it is unclear how individual differences translate across different aspects of face processing, where standardized tests, with confirmed reliability, validity, and sensitivity have not yet been implemented.

This is a pertinent issue for the field of forensic face matching, where research findings have the potential to have an impact on policy in policing and security settings. Many forensic tasks require an employee to match two or more simultaneously presented unfamiliar faces according to identity, such as person-to-passport matching or the comparison of faces captured in closed-circuit television (CCTV) images (see Fysh, this volume). Even under optimal conditions, this task can be notoriously difficult, and performance is easily disrupted by changes in personal appearance, viewpoint, or lighting (see Hancock et al., 2000). Identifying individuals who are proficient at face matching, and resilient to its obstacles, is therefore a key issue of theoretical and practical importance. Yet, rapid progression on this issue is currently hindered by a number of factors.

Sarah Bate, Natalie Mestry, and Emma Portch, *Individual Differences Between Observers in Face Matching* In: *Forensic Face Matching*. Edited by: Markus Bindemann, Oxford University Press (2021). © Oxford University Press.
DOI: 10.1093/oso/9780198837749.003.0006.

First, standardized tests of face matching have not yet been developed, and researchers seldom report how reliable and valid their tests are for measuring the construct of interest. This makes it unclear whether variance in face-matching performance represents noise resulting from the task itself (e.g., poor reliability or test–retest effects) or genuine individual differences in ability (Young & Noyes, 2019). This issue is further complicated by a potential lack of congruency between real-world and laboratory face-matching tasks (Bate et al., 2018, 2019b; Ramon et al., 2019), whereby the former often allows extra-facial cues to *person* identity that are not captured in existing face-matching tasks, such as body shape, gait, and facial motion (Bate et al., 2019c). Furthermore, because dominant tests of face *memory* are available, individual differences in face *matching* are often only explored as a secondary variable. That is, because face memory is used as the sole entry criteria in many psychological studies, it is unclear whether key individual differences in face matching are being missed, precluding investigation of whether face memory and face matching are interrelated or separable abilities.

In light of these issues, this chapter reviews the available evidence supporting individual differences in face matching. First, individual differences within typical, or average, perceivers are considered, alongside the psychometric properties of currently available face-matching tasks. Second, the potential underpinnings of these individual differences are discussed, in context with current findings related to the distribution(s) of face-processing skills. Finally, as applied tasks could benefit from the identification of individuals who are particularly proficient at face matching, the skills of super-recognizers are evaluated. The extent and limitations of their ability are considered, alongside practical issues in identifying and mobilizing the most proficient face matchers.

6.2 Individual Differences in Face Matching: A Psychometric History

Before reviewing evidence of individual differences in forensic face matching, it is important to consider where this process fits within traditional and contemporary theoretical models of face processing. Face-matching tasks typically involve the comparison of two or more simultaneously presented faces—a perceptual process that places no demands on memory. Instead, two facial images are viewed at the same time, and a perceiver decides whether or not the two images depict the same identity. As no demands are placed on memory, the perceiver does not need prior experience with the face(s) to complete this task. Early theoretical models (e.g., Bruce & Young, 1986) posited functional independence between the *perception* and *memory* of *familiar* faces, influenced by evidence of sequential processing in typical observers (Liu et al., 2002; Young et al., 1985) and patterns of deficits in neurological cases of prosopagnosia (Bate & Bennetts, 2015; Malone et al., 1982). That is, while many individuals presented with impairments in all aspects of face processing, those of others were restricted to face memory (Tranel et al., 1988). This early implementation of the individual differences approach prompted hypotheses of distinct subtypes of prosopagnosia (De Renzi et al., 1991) and the need for standardized tests of face perception to assist with differential diagnosis.

The first dominant test of face perception was the Benton Facial Recognition Test (BFRT: Benton et al., 1983), which required participants to select a target identity from simultaneously presented arrays containing three or six uncropped faces. All images were captured using the same camera, but viewpoint varied within each array. While the BFRT has frequently been used to assess the face-matching skills of impaired versus typical perceivers (e.g., Duchaine & Nakayama, 2004; Nunn et al., 2001), and occasionally within the typical population (Palermo et al., 2017; Schretlen et al., 2001), its validity has been called into question. Duchaine and Weidenfeld (2003) found that even participants with prosopagnosia can successfully complete the task by using extra-facial information, such as the target's hairstyle and clothing, and/or pictorial cues, such as differences in background colour and lighting, to assist identity matching. Furthermore, because this task was developed to detect impaired face perception, it is unsurprising that it does not have the sensitivity or ecological validity to tap individual differences on more applied tasks within the typical population.

The Cambridge Face Perception Test (CFPT: Duchaine et al., 2007) is now more commonly used to assess the face-perception skills of people with prosopagnosia. In this task, participants are required to sort six test images in order of their similarity to a target face. Each test image represents a 'morph', or computer-generated amalgamation, of the target face and a discrete unfamiliar non-target identity; test images are morphed on a progressive basis such that the contribution made by the target face is reduced in steady increments until the test image represents 28% of the target identity and 72% of the non-target identity. While the CFPT is sometimes used to tap individual differences in the typical population (Hildebrandt et al., 2010; Rezlescu et al., 2017), its psychometric properties indicate that it is not suitable for this purpose. The task attracts a wide range of scores that may result from the complex task instructions rather than genuine individual differences in face-perception ability. Furthermore, because of wide variation in test scores, it is often difficult to identify 'average' performance levels in this task, which has implications for statistical separation of typical from atypical performers. In addition, the artificial adjustments applied to the facial images distance the paradigm from real-world forensic face-matching challenges.

While the cognitive neuropsychological literature has thus far failed to provide standardized psychometric tests that are capable of capturing variability in real-world face perception, investigations have been more fruitful in the field of forensic psychology. Early forensic face-matching tasks established the extreme difficulty of the process in typical perceivers (e.g., Bruce et al., 1999, 2001; Clutterbuck & Johnston, 2002; Kemp et al., 1997; Megreya & Burton, 2008), mostly via a group means approach. While there were some indications of individual variation in performance, the tasks were often developed for the scientific paper in hand, with little to no consideration of whether they were valid and reliable measures of the construct of interest.

Awareness of the serious error-prone nature of face matching, together with a new-found acknowledgement of individual differences even in the performance of relevant 'professionals' (e.g., Burton et al., 1999; Kemp et al., 1997), initiated the need for standardized tests of face matching. This movement occurred alongside critical theoretical developments that segregated familiar from unfamiliar face processing. For instance, a seminal study reported that adults can easily group together images of the same *familiar* identity, or person, even when captured weeks or months apart. In contrast, people who were *unfamiliar* with the same identity or person falsely perceived the images to represent different individuals (Jenkins et al., 2011). This finding raised a key difference between familiar and unfamiliar face recognition, suggesting that an inability to account for within-person variation in appearance across images may underpin the large error rates in unfamiliar face-matching tasks (Burton et al., 2005; Jenkins & Burton, 2008). In response, a new wave of face-matching tests has embraced image variability as a key aspect of the task, in relation to both photograph quality and natural time-related changes in a person's appearance. This move stands in direct contrast to the face-perception tasks offered by the cognitive neuropsychological approach, which traditionally eliminated such variation by heavily cropping facial images to remove any extraneous cues to identity, such as hairstyle, clothing, and accessories.

The first standardized face-matching task to embrace image variability was the Glasgow Face Matching Test (GFMT: Burton et al., 2010, see Figure 6.1). In this task, participants are shown pairs of simultaneously presented faces and asked to judge whether their identity is the same or different, with no time limit imposed on responses. For matched trials, the two images of the same individual are captured only minutes apart, displaying the entire face in good lighting conditions. However, one image is captured by a photographic camera, whereas the other is a still image extracted from a video. While this test employs optimal matching conditions with good-quality images, evidence suggests there is nevertheless substantial variation in the performance of typical perceivers. For instance, the original paper reports scores that range from 62% to 100% correct in 300 typical participants ($M = 89.9$; $SD = 7.3$). Other normative data show that average performance on the GFMT is around 80% to 90%, with individual accuracy ranging from near-chance to perfect (Fysh & Bindemann, 2018; Megreya et al., 2011a; White et al., 2013). Demonstrating good internal reliability, Burton and colleagues found strong positive correlations when participant's performance on the first and last set of trials were compared (.81), and many further studies have used the GFMT to measure individual differences in face-matching performance in both typical civilian participants and those employed in forensic settings (e.g., Robertson et al., 2016; White et al., 2014, 2015b).

While the GFMT has been well-received by the field, the drive to detect the most proficient face matchers has recently been informed by statistical principles used within cognitive neuropsychology. In the same way that single-case statistics have been used to determine significantly impaired performance in people with prosopagnosia, the forensic face-matching field has recently used the same principles to identify people with

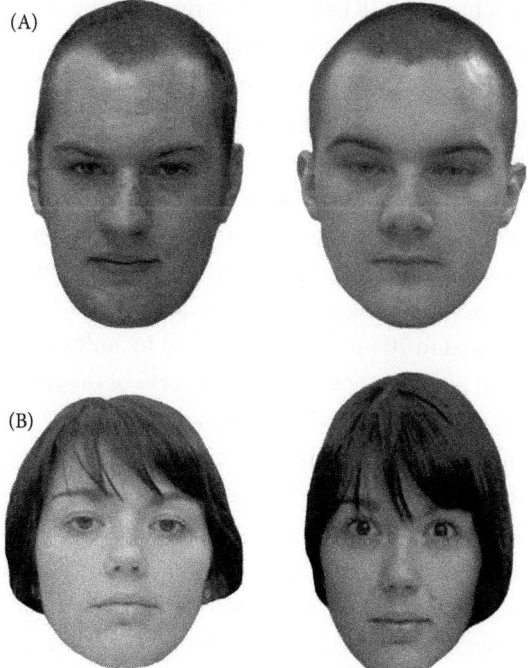

Figure 6.1 Example pairs from the Glasgow Face Matching Test. Pair A represents a mismatching pair of identities, and pair B match in identity.

Source: Reproduced from Burton et al. (2010) 'The Glasgow Face Matching Test' *Behavior Research Methods, 42,* 286–291, Figure 1. https://doi.org/10.3758/BRM.42.1.286 Copyright © 2010, Springer Nature.

superior skills. Here, instead of comparing the average performance levels of one group of participants (controls) to another (i.e., a group-means approach), proficiency is determined by assessing whether a particular individual has exceeded the control mean by two standard deviations. This approach is difficult to implement for the GFMT where average performance for a control sample is typically 89.9% accurate, meaning that two standard deviations cannot be cleared before reaching perfect or 'ceiling' performance levels (i.e., 100% accurate). Thus, in recent years, more challenging standardized face-matching tasks have been developed, encompassing more extreme image variability into their design.

For instance, the Models Face Matching Test (MFMT: Dowsett & Burton, 2015) is similar in design to the GFMT, but consists of more challenging facial stimuli. The task uses the faces of models, with each image captured from a different photoshoot and displaying larger variations in appearance across multiple images of the same identity. In the MFMT, participants view pairs of facial images and make 'same' or 'different' identity decisions for each trial. As in the GFMT, this test uses percentage accuracy measures of performance, and does not impose time restrictions on responses. While this test is clearly more difficult than the GFMT (mean performance is 72.2%), it has not been fully validated, and unfortunately the authors do not hold the copyright to the component images.

The Kent Face Matching Test (KFMT; Fysh & Bindemann, 2018) was also developed as a more challenging face-matching task that depicts ecologically valid forensic face-matching scenarios. The short version of the task contains 20 match and 20 mismatch trials, whereby one image is captured at least three months after the second image, which was taken from student identification cards. Overall accuracy on the short form of the KFMT has been reported to be 66%, with a range of 40% to 88%, revealing large individual differences in performance. The test–retest reliability of the short form of the KFMT is high, evidenced by strong positive correlations between two separate sessions for overall accuracy as well as both match and mismatch trials. A longer version of the task with 200 match and 20 mismatch trials also includes identity pairs of different ethnic origins. Overall performance on this long form of the KFMT has been reported to be 70%, with 78% on match and 64% on mismatch trials.

In sum, the forensic face-matching literature has embraced the value of an individual differences approach in the past decade, and the few publicly available standardized tests have been designed to ensure that they are of sufficient difficulty to statistically differentiate 'typical' from 'atypical' face perceivers (i.e., those who fall at either end of the face recognition continuum). However, other important psychometric principles (e.g., reliability) are not always reported, and some tests have not been appropriately validated. This is a fundamental issue when assessing the consistency of performance across multiple attempts at the same and different face-matching tasks.

6.3 The Consistency of Individual Differences in Face Matching

The issue of consistency in face-matching performance is vital for personnel selection: Rather than reflecting true ability, isolated high scores may be artificial artefacts that result from use of an insufficiently difficult or unreliable task, or may have occurred by chance. These issues can be overcome by assessing performance on multiple attempts at the same and different tests. For instance, Bindemann et al. (2012) assessed individual differences in face-matching skills on image pairs extracted from the Glasgow Unfamiliar Face Database (Burton et al., 2010). In two studies, individual differences in performance were observed both when comparing across different performers, as expected, and also within the same performers, when participants completed the exact same task across consecutive days. Specifically, while an individual participant could perform with similar overall accuracy levels when they completed the same test administered across three days, their responses to the exact same pairings could often differ. In a five-day study, participants encountered new face pairs on each day: When ceiling performers were removed from the dataset, the separate measures of accuracy and consistency did not correlate across observers. While this study indicates that performance can vary from day to day, other work suggests that matching performance can vary between blocks (Alenezi et al., 2015) and even between trials that involve the same identity (Bindemann & Sandford, 2011; Russ et al., 2018).

It is also important to note that face-matching paradigms incorporate both trials that require the verification of identity and those that involve the detection of mismatches in identity. Very high scores on standardized tests will invariably reflect a high ability to perform both types of task, but some evidence suggests that they tap different processes. It might be assumed that individuals who are best able to correctly respond 'match' to a matched pairing will also be best able to correctly respond 'mismatch' to a mismatched pairing or, in other words, show the highest sensitivity to variations in identity. However, evidence suggests that there is no correlation between a participant's provision of both types of correct response across different types of matching task (Megreya & Burton, 2007). Furthermore, across own- and other-race faces, Kokje et al. (2018) found no correlation between match and mismatch performance in either a one-to-one matching task or a one-to-many matching task. Importantly, these inconsistencies in performance appear to dissipate across repeated testing with the same images, suggesting that they result from a lack of familiarity with the target stimuli.

In sum, the findings reviewed above suggest that the ability to match an unfamiliar face is unrelated to the ability to reject a comparison between two different identities, and screening for face-matching ability should independently assess consistency of performance in both types of trial. These recommendations reflect gold standard psychometric protocols in other aspects of cognitive assessment, and are required for the reliable implementation of face-matching screening procedures in occupational settings. This is an important issue because increasing evidence suggests that individual differences in face-matching skills prevail even in those employed in relevant occupations, and the ability is remarkably resilient to improvement.

6.4 Individual Differences in Occupational Settings

Some work has examined the face-matching abilities of employees who work within relevant settings, often using new tests that attempt to reproduce the real-world task at hand, rather than employing psychometric standard tests of face-matching ability. This is clearly an issue that the field sorely needs to address: While ecological validity and understanding of the specific task at hand is critical, laboratory replications of that task nevertheless need to be validated. These requirements have not yet been simultaneously implemented within the forensic face-matching literature, where standardized tasks (e.g., the GFMT) do not tightly replicate real-world tasks, and more direct replications have not been standardized.

Nevertheless, there is some evidence to suggest that, while forensic facial examiners (professionals who compare images of faces to provide identification evidence to police investigations and in criminal trials) as a group are better at face matching than other security professionals, they do not consistently outperform members of the general public who have little experience performing these tasks (e.g., White et al., 2015a, 2015b; see White, Towler, & Kemp, this volume). Other work indicates no differences in face-matching ability between lay perceivers and employees who are required to regularly carry out person-to-identity document comparisons. For instance, Papesh (2018) found that professionals whose jobs frequently require such judgements (i.e., professional notaries and bank tellers) are no better than inexperienced student controls at face matching. Furthermore, neither the frequency with which each individual performed face-matching tasks at work, nor number of years' experience, predicted performance. White et al. (2014) also found no differences in performance on a passport-matching task when comparing groups of border officers to controls, and the officers' performance was not related to the length of their operational experience. Burton et al. (1999) obtained similar findings when comparing the performance of police officers and controls in a matching task that utilized CCTV images. However, Bate and Dudfield (2019) present evidence that length of on-the-job training might be related to target-absent matching performance (i.e., the ability to make correct rejections) in police officers, although self-ratings of ability showed that officers were unaware of this skill.

Perhaps more critically, the individual differences approach has revealed a wide range of ability even within groups of apparently high-performing individuals. That is, even when a group of professionals have been found to outperform people from the typical population, there is considerable variability in the performance of individual employees. For instance, White et al. (2015) found that the average performance of a group of highly trained and experienced facial examiners (passport control examiners) was approximately 20% greater than the average score of a group of students. Yet, inspection of individual data points indicates that the difference between the best- and worst-performing facial examiner was at least 15%. Likewise, Phillips et al. (2018) reported the distribution of performance within groups of face specialists (facial examiners, facial reviewers, and super-recognizers). At least one participant in all groups performed below the median score of a group of students, with considerable individual differences in the overall performance distributions (see Figure 6.2).

Notably, other very recent evidence suggests that it is remarkably difficult to improve face-matching skills via formal training (see Towler, Kemp, & White, this volume). Towler et al. (2019) found that the face-matching skills of police and passport control officers did not improve after they attended a professional training course, despite their belief that they had become better at the task. Together with other evidence of limited gains in face matching following more informal training strategies (e.g., Alenezi & Bindemann, 2013; Towler et al., 2014), these findings suggest that face-matching ability is either remarkably resilient to change, or that current training attempts do not adequately target the relevant mechanisms. Indeed, the limited gains in the forensic face-matching literature stand in some contrast to the relatively more successful attempt to improve face recognition in prosopagnosia (Davies-Thompson et al., 2017; DeGutis et al., 2014; but, for a more considered discussion, see Bate & Bennetts, 2014)—where theoretical understanding of the processes involved in face memory is arguably more sophisticated. As such, advances in our theoretical understanding of the processes underpinning face matching are clearly required for successful training programmes to be developed, and to garner a full understanding of why individual differences occur.

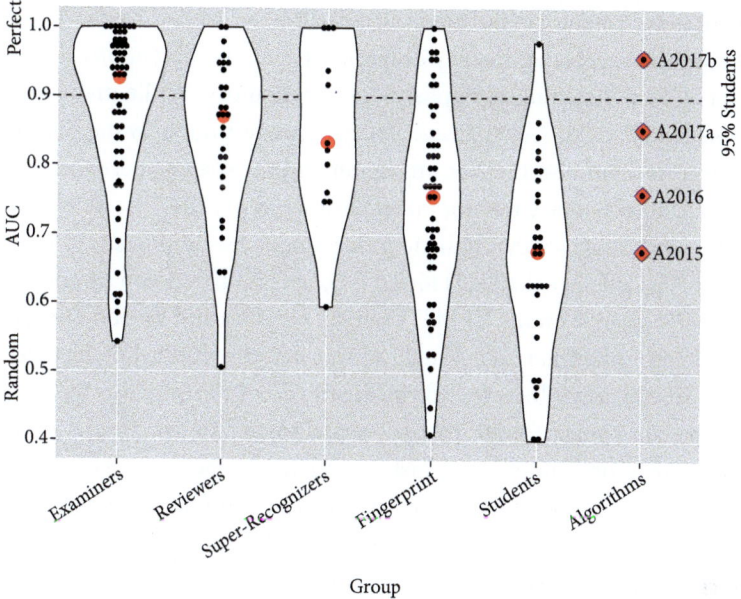

Figure 6.2 Figure showing human and machine accuracy with black dots representing individuals and red dots representing the median for each group. The dashed line represents the accuracy of a 95th percentile student.

Source: Reproduced from Phillips et al. (2018) 'Face recognition accuracy of forensic examiners, superrecognizers, and face recognition algorithms' *PNAS*, *115*, 6171–6176, Figure 2. https://doi.org/10.1073/pnas.1721355115 © 2018 National Academy of Sciences of the United States of America.

6.5 Why Are Some People Better at Face Matching than Others?

While there is increasing evidence to support individual differences in face matching, the underpinnings of these effects are unclear. The broader face recognition literature has recently seen a flurry of correlational studies that attempt to relate unfamiliar face-memory skills to a variety of cognitive and personality variables (e.g., Bate et al., 2010; Li et al., 2010; Megreya & Bindemann, 2013), yet much less work has considered the underpinnings of face matching. This is an important issue because at least some of the processes that underpin face matching are likely to be very different from those involved in face memory.

Most of the work that has been offered to date focuses on the processing strategies that are employed in face matching. Early hypotheses suggested that unfamiliar face-matching skills do not draw on the face-processing system at all, and are more analogous to object perception. For instance, Megreya and Burton (2006) demonstrated moderate correlations between unfamiliar face matching and other tasks of visual cognition, with the strongest relationship observed with performance on an inverted version of the same task (a manipulation that is thought to tap the processing strategies that underpin object as opposed to face recognition [Yin, 1969]). Pertinently, performance on the GFMT has also been shown to correlate more strongly with object matching than face memory (Burton et al., 2010).

Other studies suggest that the key difference is in the different processing strategies demanded by face matching as opposed to face memory. While many authors advocate the use of holistic processing (the ability to process not only the size and shape of the facial features, but also their arrangement and the spacing between them: Maurer et al., 2002) for tasks of face memory (see Rezlescu et al., 2017, for an in-depth discussion), other work suggests that holistic processing is less important to face matching. For instance, Verhallen et al. (2017) found no correlation between a holistic processing index and performance on the GFMT, whereas Megreya and Burton (2006) found that performance on unfamiliar face matching was better predicted by feature-by-feature processing—the strategy believed to underpin object recognition. In support of this assertion, the latter study found that face-matching ability was moderately associated with performance on a number of tasks unrelated to face processing—for example, visual short-term memory for simple line drawings of objects, perceptual matching of variants of the same object, and matching of letters, digits, and objects in a time-constrained perceptual speed task. Finally, performance on the 'local' or featural condition of the Navon task has also been found to correlate with face-matching performance (McCaffery et al., 2018).

However, other work has indicated a stronger overlap between face perception and both familiar and unfamiliar face memory, suggesting a more general 'face' factor that is employed in all face-processing tasks (Verhallen et al., 2017). In support, McCaffery et al. (2018) reported associations between the GFMT, the Cambridge Face Memory Test (CFMT: Duchaine & Nakayama, 2006), and a famous face recognition test, 'Before They Were Famous', and concurred that this general face factor may account for approximately 25% of performance across tasks. Notably, Bowles et al. (2009) also report an association between the CFMT and CFPT, and Davis et al. (2016) note a relationship between the GFMT and a memory array task. In addition, Fysh (2018) reported a correlation between face matching and face memory, but warned that the association was less clear when data were considered on a case-by-case (i.e., individual differences) basis.

There are also some indications that other factors can have subtle influences on face-matching performance. While gender differences are small in comparison to other measures (Fysh & Bindemann, 2017), an age-related decline has been observed. For instance, Megreya and Bindemann (2015) report a developmental improvement in face matching until adulthood, with a decline in older age (see also Schretlen et al., 2001). Hildebrandt et al. (2010) used a battery of 15 tasks to demonstrate differing onsets of age-related decrements in different aspects of face processing, and showed that face perception began to decline at a much later age (after the age of 60 years) than face memory (before the age of 50 years).

Individual differences in face-matching performance may also be linked to some personality characteristics. Megreya and Bindemann (2013) provided evidence that individual differences in performance on a 1-in-10 matching task could be linked to anxiety. In this task, participants must decide whether a target face, extracted from video footage and positioned at a 30-degree angle, matches a member of a simultaneously presented 10-person line-up (target absent line-ups are displayed on 50% of trials). The authors reported a negative correlation between correct identifications and emotional stability and tension in female participants, perhaps reflecting levels of neuroticism. It has also been shown that acute state anxiety, induced by inhaling 7.5% CO_2, leads to a reduction in the number of correct match responses given to matched pairings in the GFMT, but no decrease in the number of incorrect match responses given to mismatched pairings (Attwood et al., 2013).

In sum, there are some suggestions that face-matching tasks employ distinct processing strategies to those used in tasks of face memory, despite some overlap between the two processes. While future work needs to uncover these strategies, Bruce et al. (2018) note their automaticity and resilience to change. It is therefore possible that there is some innate or biological predisposition for such skills (for evidence supporting a genetic link to face memory, see Wilmer et al., 2010; Zhu et al., 2010), and it is pertinent that a genetic association has been observed for perceptual performance on the Mooney Face Test (a holistic processing task where participants detect faces within ambiguous images comprised of black and white shaded areas; Verhallen et al., 2014). At the same time, it is also likely that there is some heterogeneity in the face-matching techniques employed by top-end performers, and different factors promote performance in different individuals.

Importantly, this is where the individual differences approach comes back into play. While correlational studies within the typical population can reveal modest relationships between different factors, it is not possible to reveal causal direction. Instead, in-depth case-by-case consideration of the individuals at the very top of the spectrum may be more fruitful. Such an approach can inform whether the most successful face matchers are merely using an extension of the techniques used by typical individuals, or whether they employ a qualitatively different method of performance. Elucidation of the nature and range of the face-matching continuum, and its overlap with the face-memory continuum, is required in order to answer this question.

6.6 Super-Recognizers: Qualitatively or Quantitatively Different Face Matchers?

The past decade has seen a flurry of interest in people with exceptional face recognition skills. These individuals were first identified by Russell et al. (2009), who used group-based statistics to indicate superior face-perception and face-memory skills in four cases. Differences were observed on three tests: An extended form of the Cambridge Face Memory Test (CFMT+), the CFPT, and a Before They Were Famous Test. Subsequently, a number of papers have adopted the CFMT+ to demonstrate superior face recognition skills in larger group studies and on a range of tasks, including forensic face matching (e.g., Bobak et al., 2016c; Robertson et al., 2016).

However, there is appreciable variability in the way that researchers identify super-recognizers. While some base their recruitment criteria on self-reported abilities, others consider on-the-job performance. Furthermore, many researchers consider how an individual performs on tests of face memory and matching. However, few of these tests have undergone rigorous validation to determine how well they measure the ability of interest, and where statistical cut-offs should be imposed to separate exceptional from average performers. As such, no formal definition of super-recognition has yet been agreed, and it is very difficult to elucidate whether investigations are truly considering top performers. This issue raises a critical question, probing whether super-recognizers are qualitatively or merely quantitatively different from the rest of the population (Bate & Tree, 2017; Bobak et al., 2017; Young & Noyes, 2019). A quantitative outcome would imply that screening studies should rank perceivers in terms of their ability, acknowledging that any statistical cut-offs are merely functional and arbitrary. Alternatively, findings of a qualitative difference in processing strategy and/or a biological underpinning would allow imposition of a formal cut-off, and consequently a stronger definition of super-recognition.

Currently, few studies have addressed this issue. Bobak et al. (2017) presented eye-tracking evidence to suggest that super-recognizers use an exaggerated information-extraction strategy (focusing on the nose) to that used by typical perceivers, and Tardif et al. (2019) found that information extracted from the eyes and mouth in a famous face identification task strongly correlates with face recognition skills across all abilities. While this evidence implies a common spectrum for both face memory and face perception (correlations were observed with both the CFMT and CFPT in the latter study), it is unknown whether the same finding extends to face matching. Indeed, the CFPT lacks sensitivity at the top end (see earlier) and the extent of the overlap between different aspects of face processing is not only questioned by findings from typical perceivers, but also by more recent evidence that not all super-recognizers excel at forensic face-matching tasks.

6.7 Are Super-Recognizers also Super-Matchers?

Various models of face processing suggest that earlier perceptual processes, involved in face matching, are a necessary precursor for successful recognition of facial identity (e.g., Bruce & Young, 1986). As such, it is expected that exceptional ability in tests of unfamiliar face memory should be underpinned by successful early perceptual analysis, and individuals who excel in one task (unfamiliar face memory) should also excel in the other (unfamiliar face matching). However, findings from people with prosopagnosia suggest that proficient face-perception skills alone are not sufficient. While most patients show severe impairment in tests of unfamiliar face memory, only some show impaired performance on tests of face perception, with others performing comparably to controls (e.g., Bate & Bennetts, 2015; Dalrymple et al., 2014). In support of previous suggestions in this chapter, these dissociations indicate that face-matching and memory tasks tap at least partially different components of face recognition (e.g., Megreya & Burton, 2006), or rely to a different extent on holistic processing (Burton et al., 2010; Verhallen et al., 2017)—a mechanism linked to the deficits displayed by people with prosopagnosia (e.g., DeGutis et al., 2014).

Bate et al. (2018) raise the possibility of an alternative argument, suggesting that dissociations in performance may arise as face-memory and matching tasks vary in difficulty. Common tests of unfamiliar face memory, such as the CFMT+, expose participants to the same unfamiliar face multiple times during encoding and testing phases. This is unlike the situation posed in simultaneous face-matching tasks, where participants have limited, single exposure to a target face. Repeated exposure likely builds a more stable representation of the face, facilitating performance in memory but not matching tasks. This may account for the greater individual differences found in tests of matching compared with memory (e.g., Bindemann et al., 2012).

Various researchers have examined whether super-recognizers show consistently exceptional performance across tests of unfamiliar face memory and face matching, using the two standard deviation cut-off discussed above. While the CFMT+ is typically used to assess face memory and is appropriately calibrated for this protocol, ceiling effects have frequently been observed on tests of face perception (e.g., Bobak et al., 2016d). These differences in test calibration, together with a lack of validation data, make it difficult to draw firm conclusions across findings.

With this caveat in mind, some studies have provided evidence that the skills of only some super-recognizers extend to face matching. Davis et al. (2016) experienced similar difficulties when using the GFMT to assess performance consistency. Their sample comprised 10 civilian super-recognizers, who had achieved at least 88.2% on the CFMT+, as well as 36 police 'identifiers' from the Metropolitan Police Service. Although it is unclear whether police identifiers had been screened using the CFMT+, officers were sampled based on the number of suspect identifications they had made within a 12-month period. At a group level, super-recognizers and police identifiers displayed similar accuracy rates and both groups significantly outperformed controls. However, single-case statistics revealed no significant differences in matching sensitivity between each super-recognizer or identifier and the control mean. Davis et al. (2016) attributed these null effects to data overlap, finding evidence of ceiling performance in seven participants (three super-recognizers and four police identifiers), and control performance that was higher than the average usually obtained for this test. Low task difficulty may have contributed towards overlaps in the data. However, it is also possible that the authors sampled super-recognizers of lower ability than those used in past work. These lower-ability levels may also account for the further inconsistencies that Davis et al. (2016) noted; specifically, that the two highest performers on the CFMT+ performed relatively poorly on the GFMT, and also on the other face-memory tasks within the battery (the delayed 1-in-10 task [Bruce et al., 1999] and a different, untitled, famous face recognition test, which sampled blurred and pixelated adult celebrity identities [Lander et al., 2001]).

Bobak et al. (2016a) compared super-recognizer performance across the CFMT+ and a sequential matching task, in which an unfamiliar probe face was briefly shown before being replaced by a target face, which remained on the screen until a response was made. All six super-recognizers reached statistically significant cut-offs on the CFMT+. While group-level analyses revealed that all super-recognizers also outperformed controls on the sequential face-matching task, single-case comparisons were only significant for two individuals.

Further studies have explored consistency in performance using larger testing batteries that comprise ecologically valid tests of both unfamiliar face memory and matching. Bobak et al. (2016c) compared the performance of seven super-recognizers across two moderately correlated tests of face memory (the CFMT+ and an ecologically valid test that posed static images at encoding, and short, dynamic video clips at test), and the 1-in-10 simultaneous face-matching task (Bruce et al., 1999). Unsurprisingly, group-level statistics revealed that super-recognizers outperformed typical perceivers on all three tasks. However, while all super-recognizers reached required cut-offs on the CFMT+, only four individuals showed significantly higher sensitivity scores on the face-matching task when single-case statistics were applied, and only one on the extremely difficult test of face memory. More importantly, while correlational analyses revealed a strong, positive relationship between face matching and memory performance (particularly on the CFMT+), a number of interesting discrepancies were noted. First, the two super-recognizers recording the lowest scores on the CFMT+, and barely reaching cut-off, were among the strongest performers on both the ecologically valid tests of face memory and matching, outperforming those who had recorded the highest scores on the CFMT+. Second, the highest scorer on the CFMT+ did not significantly outperform typical perceivers on either of the other tasks.

The findings of Bobak et al. (2016c) speak to the heterogeneity of super-recognizer performance both across tests that tap the same (face memory) and different (face memory and matching) components of face recognition. This dissociation was further explored in a large-scale investigation using 200 self-sampled participants, 89 of whom met the cut-off on the CFMT+ (Bate et al., 2018). Alongside the CFMT+, participants were required to complete further, ecologically valid tests of face memory (the Models Memory Test: MMT) and face matching (the Pairs Matching Test: PMT). Similar to the MFMT (Dowsett & Burton, 2015), each new test sampled non-occluded whole-face colour photographs, taken from online modelling profiles. In the matching task, participants decided whether two simultaneously presented photographs depicted the same person or two different people; in matched pairs, the individual's appearance was subject to real-world variation in lighting, picture quality, and passage of time, enhancing task difficulty. Ninety-three participants reached the statistical cut-off on the PMT, and fairly strong correlations were found between performance in the face-memory and matching tasks. However, while 78 participants showed exceptional performance on the PMT and one test of face memory (either the CFMT+ or MMT), only 37 participants reached cut-off on all three tasks (although notably most participants performed between 1 and 1.5 standard deviations above the control mean in all tests, see Figure 6.3).

Bate et al.'s (2018) findings again indicate heterogeneity in performance, but also reveal a new facet: 18 participants only exhibited exceptional performance on the PMT and not on either test of memory, with a reversed trend noted in 13 participants. Evidence for the former was most compelling, with three participants demonstrating

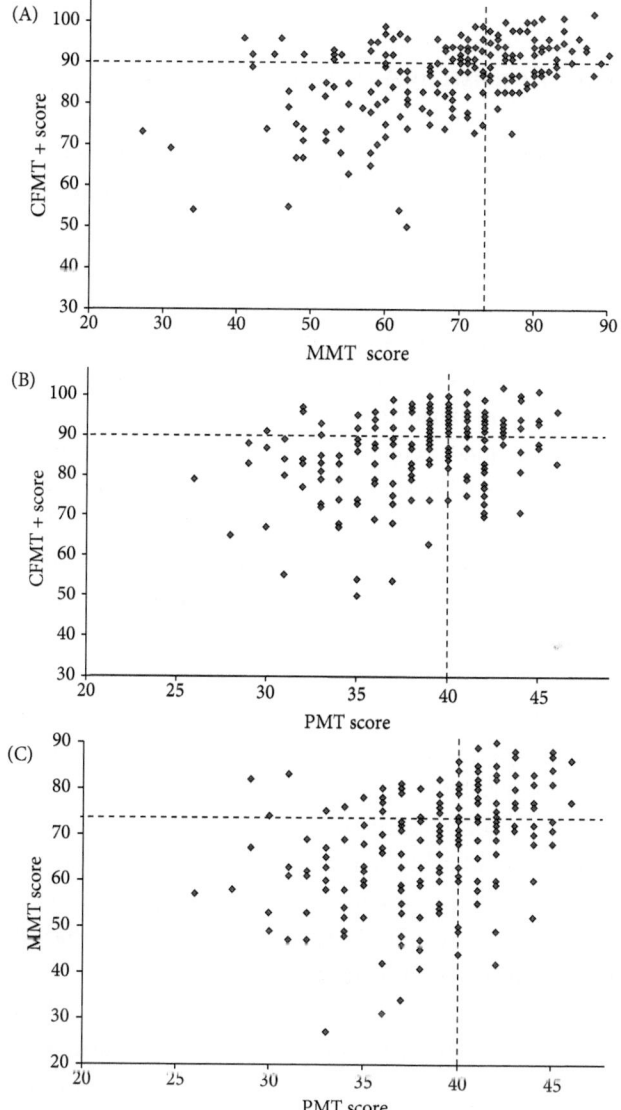

Figure 6.3 The correlation between the experimental group's performance on (A) the CFMT+ and the MMT, (B) the CFMT+ and the PMT, and (C) the MMT and the PMT. Dashed lines represent the cut-offs for superior performance on each test.

Source: Reproduced from Bate et al. (2018) 'Applied screening tests for the detection of superior face recognition' *Cognitive Research: Principles and Implications*, 3, 22, Figure 8. https://doi.org/10.1186/s41235-018-0116-5 © 2018 The Authors.

very large deviations from control means in their respective PMT and CFMT+ scores. As such, Bate et al.'s (2018) findings are suggestive of the existence of a small group of 'super-matchers': Individuals who are unlikely to be sampled when standard memory assessments form the basis of super-recognizer identification. However, as consistency of face-matching performance has also been found to be unstable in typical participants (Bindemann et al., 2012), it is necessary to substantiate these findings across repetitive testing.

6.8 How Consistent Are Superior Face-Matching Skills?

Some attempts have been made to examine the question of consistency in superior face-matching performance, assessing stability in scores across different tasks. For example, Bobak et al. (2016b) compared super-recognizer performance across the GFMT (Burton et al., 2010) and the more ecologically valid and difficult MFMT (Dowsett & Burton, 2015). Group-level statistics for the GFMT were inconsistent, dependent on whether match or mismatch trials were sampled, and whether standard or motivated controls formed the comparison group (motivated controls received additional financial inducements for good performance). When single-case statistics were applied, only three of the seven super-recognizers outperformed control participants. In contrast, group-level statistics were significant for MFMT performance and, while only four super-recognizers outperformed motivated controls, six surpassed the standard control group. At first glance, these findings appear to suggest that super-recognizers demonstrate inconsistent performance across these strongly correlated tasks of face matching, although, as noted above, calibration issues with the GFMT limit the sensitivity of comparisons in top performers.

To address these concerns, Bate et al. (2019b) compared consistency of performance across three equally calibrated versions of the PMT, in which different ecologically valid manipulations of variability were applied to image pairs (pose, and the addition of glasses and facial hair). Thirty police officers were sampled, each of whom had passed a liberal cut-off of 1.5 standard deviations on the CFMT+. Overall, only five officers significantly outperformed control participants on all three versions of the PMT, demonstrating consistently exceptional performance, with a further 24 surpassing control performance on at least one task (see Figure 6.4).

Bate et al.'s (2019b) results also revealed interesting inconsistencies in target-present and target-absent face-matching performance. These performance inconsistencies have implications for operational tailoring because, while the ability to accurately assess whether two photographs match or mismatch in identity is practically important, the consequences of each type of response may vary across occupational settings (e.g., mismatching identity documents are more likely in immigration versus passport control settings; Devue, 2019). When task performance was pooled, Bate et al. (2019b) found that super-recognizers differed in the relative proportion of accurate match and mismatch decisions they made. However, these dissociable patterns were also observed

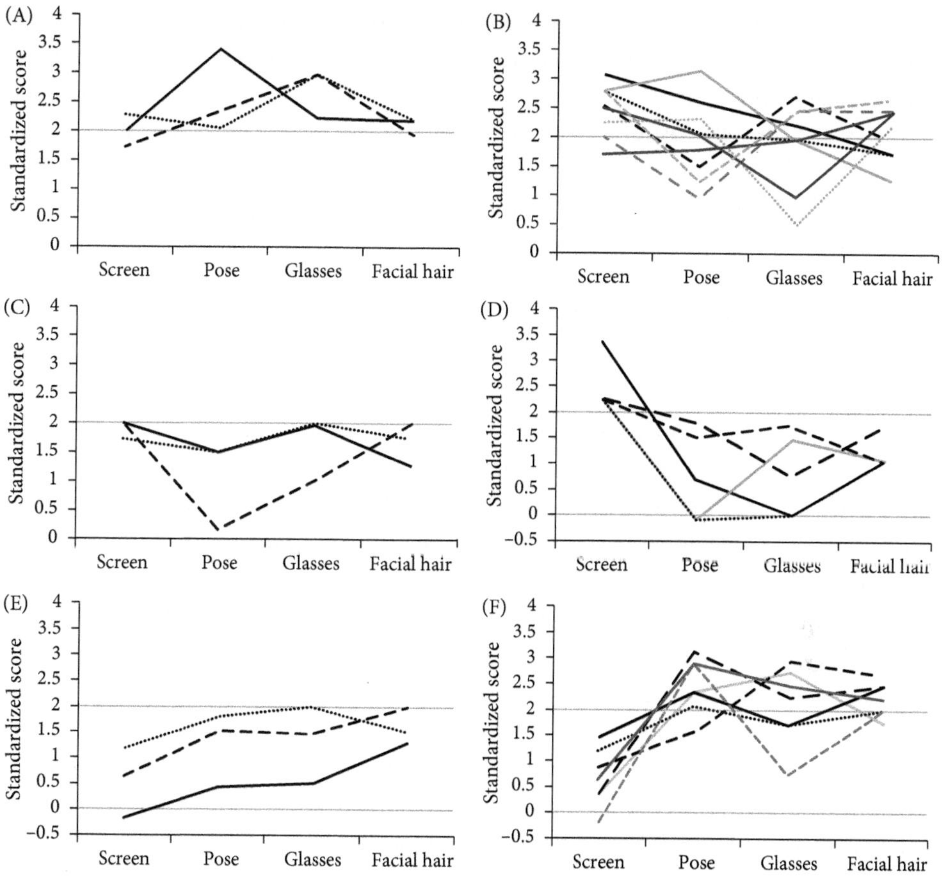

Figure 6.4 Consistency of officers' performance on the PMT at screening and in the three new blocks. Figures demonstrate those who outperformed controls at screening (according to the liberal 1.5 SD cut-off), then by the more conservative 1.96 SD cut-off on (A) all three blocks, (B) any two blocks, (C) any one block, and (D) no further block; and those who did not pass the initial screening criterion but outperformed controls on (E) only one or no block, or (F) on any two or three blocks.

Source: Reproduced from Bate et al. (2019) 'The consistency of superior face recognition skills in police officers' *Applied Cognitive Psychology*, 33, 828–842, Figure 6. https://doi.org/10.1002/acp.3525 © 2019 John Wiley & Sons Ltd.

within individuals across the three tasks. These findings speak to further heterogeneity within the super-recognizer population: While all likely exceed control performance in both target-absent and target-present trials at the group level, showing little evidence of response bias (see also Bate et al., 2018; Bobak et al., 2016c; Davis et al., 2016), exceptional performance may be limited to one or other type of trial. Indeed, these inconsistencies would mirror unfamiliar face-matching performance in the typical population (e.g., Megreya & Burton, 2007) and find support in the findings of Devue et al. (2019), who reported that super-recognizers were relatively better at correctly assessing that two faces were mismatching, as opposed to matching, in identity.

Bate et al. (2018, 2019b) offer two further pieces of evidence. First, two factor analyses revealed that target-present performance in both ecologically valid tests of face memory and matching load separately to target-absent performance in those same tests. Second, when Bate et al. (2018) created two separate indices for target-present and target-absent performance by pooling data across both face-memory and matching tasks, they found differences in the numbers of super-recognizers who outperformed controls on each index. While 103 individuals showed significantly higher indices of target-present performance, only nine showed the same advantage for target-absent performance, with just five exhibiting superior performance across both indices.

Noyes et al. (2018) explored a different angle, examining whether exceptional performance in face matching would translate to other instances of person perception. This is an important question because extra-facial information is often available in forensically relevant tasks, such as matching instances of an individual across static and dynamic CCTV captures (Bate et al., 2019c). The authors used performance on the GFMT to identify a sample of super-recognizers, comparing accuracy here to another difficult instance of face matching (the Expertise in Facial Comparison Test, White et al., 2015b) and tasks of body and biological motion matching (Baragchizadeh & O'Toole, 2017; O'Toole et al., 2005). Despite possible limitations when using the GFMT for sample selection, only limited relationships were found between performance across the various matching tasks, with only 4 of 14 super-recognizers showing significantly higher performance than controls across the board. These findings likely suggest that the super-recognizer advantage does not translate to wider instances of person perception, and that there may be at least some limitations to their skills.

6.9 Are there Further Limitations in the Face-Matching Skills of Super-Recognizers?

Much work within the face-matching literature suggests that typical perceivers are subject to a range of biases that influence performance accuracy. For instance, Megreya et al. (2011b) investigated other-race biases in a 1-in-10 simultaneous matching task, sampling British and Egyptian faces. Both English and Egyptian participants were better at matching own-race compared with other-race faces, and these effects disappeared when faces were inverted. However, interesting disparities in error rates suggest that the two groups of participants may have been using different response criteria. While UK participants were equally likely to identify own- and other-race targets from target-present arrays, they were more likely to incorrectly identify other-race foils when the target face was absent from the array. The Egyptian participants showed an opposite trend, performing similarly in target-absent arrays that displayed own- and other-race faces, but struggling to correctly identify an other-race target from target-present arrays.

Similar own-ethnicity biases have recently been reported in super-recognizers. Bate et al. (2019a) compared performance across two versions of the PMT (Bate et al., 2018), one that utilized unfamiliar Caucasian faces and, the other, East Asian faces. They sampled eight Caucasian super-recognizers and groups of Caucasian and Asian typical perceivers. First, it was noted that both Caucasian super-recognizers and Caucasian typical perceivers exhibited the other-race effect to a similar magnitude, performing significantly better on the Caucasian versus East Asian versions of the PMT. Second, group-level analyses revealed that Caucasian super-recognizers significantly outperformed Caucasian typical perceivers on the East Asian version of the task, with single-case comparisons revealing that all super-recognizers recorded scores that were at least 1.2 standard deviations above the control mean. However, no super-recognizer significantly outperformed East Asian typical perceivers (see Figure 6.5). This finding suggests that super-recognizers may be more useful than their own-ethnicity counterparts when matching faces of other races, but even typical native perceivers will likely outperform other-race super-recognizers on the same task. Indeed, when they extended their comparisons to include Black and Arab versions of the PMT, Bate et al. (2019a) found only weak correlations between Caucasian super-recognizer performance in own-race versus other-race matching and memory tasks. More specifically, top performers in own-race tasks did not always show superior performance in other-race tasks, and some super-recognizers displayed better performance in other-race than own-race tasks.

Recent research also examines whether the own-age bias, frequently found in face-memory paradigms (e.g., Chance et al., 1986; Rhodes & Anastasi, 2012), extends to instances of simultaneous face matching. Here, participants are poorer at recognizing or matching faces that belong to a different age group from their own, perhaps because

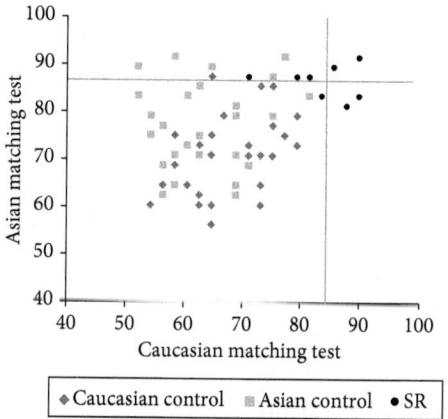

Figure 6.5 The overall percentage correct scores for super-recognisers in relation to control participants on the Caucasian and East-Asian matching tests. Lines represent the cut-offs from Caucasian norming data (no super-recogniser exceeded the cut-off from the Asian norming data on the Asian matching test).

Source: Reproduced from Bate et al. (2019) 'The limits of super recognition: An other-ethnicity effect in individuals with extraordinary face recognition skills' *Journal of Experimental Psychology: Human Perception and Performance*, 45, 363–377, Figure 2c. https://doi.org/10.1037/xhp0000607 Copyright © 2019 American Psychological Association.

other-age faces are subjectively judged to look 'more alike' (e.g., Harrison & Hole, 2009). White et al. (2015b) used a 1-in-8 simultaneous array task in which the target could vary in age by up to six years. Although age disparities reduced performance in all trials, participants were poorer at matching child (aged between 6 and 13 years) compared with adult targets. Using a simultaneous paired matching task, Kramer et al. (2018) found that participants performed less accurately when presented with pairs that comprised two infant faces (Experiment 1), or one infant and one child face (Experiments 2 and 3), in comparison to two adult faces. Evidence of an own-age bias was present even when no attempts were made to enhance difficulty.

Recently, Belanova et al. (2018) explored whether the own-age bias was present in a group of super-recognizers. They compared performance across sequential matching tasks in which unfamiliar adult and child faces were shown very briefly, and separated by a short inter-stimulus interval. Short presentation durations were used to mitigate the influence of memory, although arguably this reduces the generalizability of find-ings to applied security settings, where a simultaneous format is commonly used (e.g., passport control). Mirroring two important aspects of Bate et al.'s (2019a) findings, this study first showed an own-age bias of similar magnitude in both super-recognizers and typical perceivers, with each group recording higher performance in the adult versus infant face-matching task. Second, super-recognizers performed better than typical perceivers on both face-matching tasks. Belanova et al. (2018) also asked their participants to complete inverted versions of both tasks. Interestingly, while controls showed clear inversion effects on both tasks, super-recognizers only showed inversion effects for adult faces. Assuming that enhanced holistic processing is key to the super-recognizer advantage in face memory (e.g., Bobak et al., 2016a), this finding may sug-gest that super-recognizers strategically deploy these techniques only to stimuli with which they have perceptual expertise.

Taken together, the findings of Bate et al. (2019a) and Belanova et al. (2018) show that, while super-recognizers outperform typical perceivers when asked to match stimuli with which they have less experience, they still exhibit common perceptual biases. Perhaps, within this 'context', super-recognizers struggle to employ the strat-egies that usually underpin their superior ability. It remains unclear whether the nature of the stimuli, or the task itself (face matching), provides a greater contextual barrier because both may reduce holistic processing (e.g., Megreya & Burton, 2006; Papesh & Goldinger, 2009). Thus, it is imperative that the underpinnings of super-recognition, together with the limitations of the ability, are uncovered in order for these individuals to be most effectively used in occupational settings.

6.10 The Future of Super-Recognizers

The criminal justice system routinely accepts expert testimony from forensic face examiners, a subset of rigorously trained individuals who have been shown to outper-form controls on facial image comparison (e.g., White et al., 2015a). Yet, as discussed above, there are nevertheless vast individual differences in the face recognition skills of these individuals. Furthermore, given the ineffectiveness of current training procedures (e.g., Alenezi & Bindemann, 2013; Towler et al., 2014, 2019), the deployment of known super-recognizers in forensic settings is an attractive option. Yet, the above evidence suggests that only a minority of individuals display consistently superior face recognition performance that also extends to face matching, and even these individuals are subject to limitations in their ability. As such, very few 'consistent' super-recognizers may exist and, while their deployment would likely result in practical gains, screening may necessarily become a rigorous and time-consuming process.

This issue is further complicated by evidence suggesting that different individuals may be suited to different aspects of face processing, and by extension, to different operational tasks. An alternative approach is to assess whether super-recognizers meet a 'lower bar', by consistently outperforming control participants across different tests of face matching. If so, these individuals may provide a useful operational alternative to forensic face examiners, whose accuracy often depends on painstaking and time-consuming facial image comparison: A procedure unsuited for some 'real-time' operational tasks, such as surveying crowds for known offenders (Robertson et al., 2016).

Extrapolating from the evidence reviewed in previous sections, it is clear that super-recognizers frequently do meet this practically important 'lower bar' in face-matching tasks. This conclusion is possible because the statistical criterion for defining 'excellence' (a criterion used in our previous assessment of super-recognizer consistency across face-memory and matching tasks) is based upon the respective average performance levels of controls. Thus, the same data can inform both 'within-group' and 'between-groups' comparisons. Within this previous work, single-case statistics revealed that super-recognizers did not always significantly outperform controls on tests of face matching (Bate et al., 2018; Bobak et al., 2016b, 2016c; Davis et al., 2016). However, even where these comparisons were non-significant, researchers frequently noted that super-recognizers outperformed controls by 1–1.5 standard deviations (e.g., Bate et al., 2018, 2019b). Furthermore, in cases where face-matching tasks were of sufficient difficulty, researchers frequently found significant group-level differences between super-recognizers and control participants (Bate et al., 2018; Bobak et al., 2016a, 2016b). Thus, while many super-recognizers do not consistently perform 'exceptionally' in tasks of face matching, it could be claimed that some do appear to possess a more general natural skill set that frequently sets them apart from typical perceivers. While their facilitated performance may not significantly differ from typical perceivers, the discrepancy in performance between these individuals and true super-recognizers may be quantitatively negligible. Thus, it may be irrelevant from a practical perspective as to whether an operator is genuinely a super-recognizer or someone who simply possesses higher than average face-processing skills—a viewpoint that would be bolstered by theoretical findings of a common face-matching spectrum.

Some forensic agencies have already attempted to make use of individuals who possess these natural skills (e.g., the Metropolitan Police Service). Indeed, some empirical work samples police super-recognizers, using annual on-the-job identification statistics as sole or supplementary inclusion criteria (e.g., Davis et al., 2016, 2018; Robertson et al., 2016). In one such investigation, Robertson et al. (2016) compared the performance of four super-recognizers (sampled from the New Scotland Yard Central Forensic Image Unit) to controls across three tests of simultaneous face matching. At a group level, super-recognizers significantly outperformed control participants on the GFMT (Burton et al., 2010), MFMT (Dowsett & Burton, 2015), and the pixelated look-alike test, which assesses the ability to match heavily distorted examples of celebrity images (i.e. a familiar-identity matching task). Although the authors did not report single-case statistics, some interesting performance discrepancies are shown (see Figure 6.6). There were substantial overlaps in control and super-recognizer performance in the GFMT and pixelated look-alike test; 42 (of 198) and 7 (of 30) control participants respectively equalled or exceeded the lowest-scoring super-recognizer in each test. However, in the more difficult MFMT, all super-recognizers surpassed the control mean by one standard deviation, and while three controls (from a sample of 54) equalled or surpassed the performance of the top-performing super-recognizer, accuracy in the remaining sample fell short of the tightly clustered super-recognizer group.

On the other hand, despite apparent 'successful' deployment of super-recognizers in forensic settings, recent reviews suggest that applied interest may outstrip current theoretical understanding, creating a dangerous gap that ultimately limits our ability to predict how accurately super-recognizers will perform in such settings (Ramon et al., 2019). In order to close this gap, and ultimately increase confidence in operational

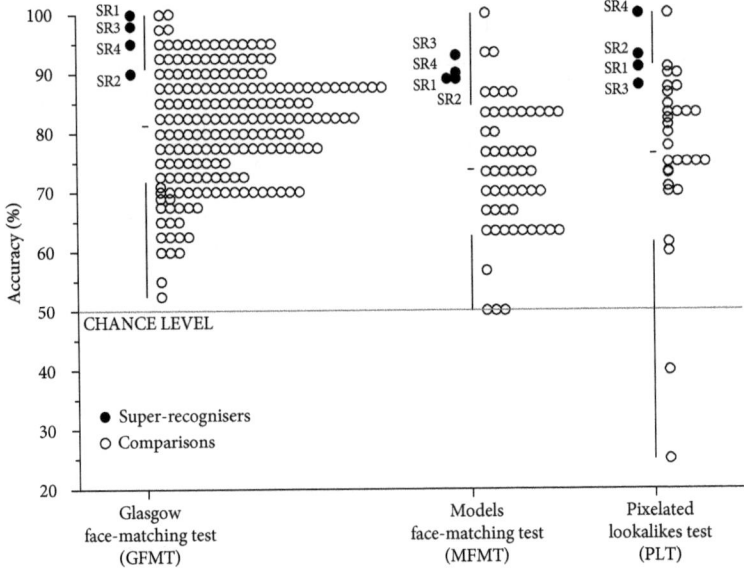

Figure 6.6 Figure showing accuracy of super-recognisers and controls on the Glasgow Face Matching Test, Models face-matching test and pixelated lookalikes test. Grey line indicates chance level performance.

Source: Reproduced from Robertson et al. (2016) 'Face recognition by Metropolitan Police super-recognisers' *PLoS ONE*, 11(2), e0150036, Figure 2. https://doi.org/10.1371/journal.pone.0150036 © 2016 Robertson et al.

generalizability, academics must design screening and selection measures that appropriately mimic operational roles. Notably, the academic community has made several worthwhile attempts in recent years, such as replacing tightly controlled facial stimuli (as found in the CFMT+) with more ecologically valid representations that vary in naturalistic ways (e.g., Bate et al., 2018, 2019b), and that include extra-facial information (Noyes et al., 2018).

A study by Davis et al. (2018) is a key example. These authors created a simultaneous matching task in which participants attempted to match a target across a variable number of naturalistic photographs (as might be provided by relatives during a missing person investigation) and crowd footage, filmed using existing CCTV units in London. Both target-present and target-absent footage were provided, and the authors found that Metropolitan Police super-recognizers and a wider pool of cross-London super-recognizer officers demonstrated higher-task sensitivity than control participants. Interestingly, Davis et al. (2018) also found that performance on this new task was poorly predicted by conventional and artificial screening tests, such as the CFMT+ and the GFMT. This finding raises a critical caveat in the application of existing super-recognizer research to the real world, suggesting that current screening tests may not tap the same skill set that is required in forensic face-matching settings. Per task, these skills are likely to be complex and numerous (Bate et al., 2019c; Moreton et al., 2019). For example, successfully matching an individual across two instances of CCTV crowd footage involves visual search, discrimination of unfamiliar identities, image stabilization across variability in appearance and image quality, and the consideration of extra-facial cues. In addition, more intrinsic applied factors may influence individual differences in performance, such as time pressure, task repetition, and relative proportions of target-present and absent trials (e.g., Devue, 2019; Robertson & Bindemann, 2019).

Ramon et al. (2019) therefore advocate for a collaborative and continuous feedback loop between academics and practitioners: An agenda that is, and should continue to be, raised at existing interdisciplinary forums (e.g., the NIST Face Identification Subcommittee; Ramon et al., 2019; and the Facial Identification Scientific Working Group; Moreton et al., 2019), and would benefit from the involvement of further agencies, such as Border Control, the Home Office, the Passport Office and the Ministry of Justice (Robertson & Bindemann, 2019). Clearly, alongside the acknowledgement that the current conceptualization and entry criteria for super-recognizers may not identify the best individuals for specific real-world tasks, this work needs to proceed with careful development and psychometric validation of new assessment tools that reflect real-world face-matching scenarios.

In sum, while it is clear that not all super-recognizers will excel at every individual face-matching task, it needs to be established whether more liberal inclusion criteria will reliably identify those who perform 'well enough' on most tasks (for attempts to create more general indices of performance see Bate et al., 2018, 2019b), or whether a more thorough task-based screening procedure for each individual deployment opportunity is warranted. Admittedly, the latter will certainly demand more time and resources, and possibly will only result in slight improvements in performance outcome. While future work will no doubt address these issues, in the meantime it is perhaps necessary for both academics and practitioners to return to the start of the super-recognizer journey. The super-recognizers first identified by Russell et al. (2009) were presented as a theoretical supplement to the cognitive neuropsychological literature on prosopagnosia, adopting the field's tightly controlled dominant task of face memory. Thus, not only is the current terminology inappropriately informal for forensic professional and legal settings, but the existing approach most likely fails to translate to the forensic face-matching field and the true skill set that is required for its real-world tasks (Bate et al., 2019c). Indeed, if the forensic face-matching field were to start from the beginning in identifying superior performers, it would no doubt have followed a rather different pathway.

6.11 Conclusion

This chapter has reviewed the evidence for individual differences in forensic face-matching tasks. Remarkably few appropriately calibrated and well-validated tasks are available, although it is clear that people differ wildly in their ability to complete such tasks. The reasons for this are unknown, and cannot be reliably explored until a wider range of psychometric-standard tasks are developed. This is also necessary for exploration of the relative overlap between different aspects of face processing, and the continua that they occupy. The individual differences approach has been shown to be theoretically and practically powerful in other domains, and no doubt has the potential to have great impact in the field of forensic face matching. Yet, as recent discussion has identified, the use of super-recognizers in forensic settings has preceded the necessary theoretical and scientific advances, leaving the field in an uncomfortable state of disarray. Collaborative work between academics and practitioners can readdress this balance, merging experimental rigour with ecological validity and psychometric excellence. However, the outcome is likely to initiate rather a different view of 'super-recognition' to that currently adhered to in forensic settings.

References

Alenezi, H. M. & Bindemann, M. (2013). The effect of feedback on face-matching accuracy. *Applied Cognitive Psychology*, 27, 735–753. doi:10.1002/acp2968

Alenezi, H. M., Bindemann, M., Fysh, M. C., & Johnston, R. A. (2015). Face matching in a long task: Enforced rest breaks and desk-switching cannot maintain identification accuracy. *PeerJ*, 3, e1184. doi:10.7717/peerj.1184

Attwood, A. S., Penton-Voak, I. S., Burton, A. M., & Munafò, M. R. (2013). Acute anxiety impairs accuracy in identifying photographed faces. *Psychological Science*, 24, 1591–1594. doi:10.1177/0956797612474021

Baragchizadeh, A. & O'Toole, A. (2017). Identity matching of unfamiliar people from point-light biological motion. *Journal of Vision, 17*(10), 62. doi:10.1167/17.10.62

Bate, S. & Bennetts, R. J. (2014). The rehabilitation of face recognition impairments: A critical review and future directions. *Frontiers in Human Neuroscience, 8*, 1–30. doi:10.3389/fnhum.2014.00491

Bate, S. & Bennetts, R. J. (2015). The independence of expression and identity in face-processing: Evidence from neuropsychological case studies. *Frontiers in Psychology, 6*, 1–7. doi:10.3389/fpsyg.2015.00770

Bate, S., Bennetts, R., Hasshim, N., Portch, E., Murray, E., Burns, E., et al. (2019a). The limits of super recognition: An other-ethnicity effect in individuals with extraordinary face recognition skills. *Journal of Experimental Psychology: Human Perception and Performance, 45*, 363–377. doi:10.1037/xhp0000607

Bate, S. & Dudfield, G. (2019). Subjective assessment for super recognition: An evaluation of self-report methods in civilian and police participants. *PeerJ, 7*, e6330. doi:10.7717/peerj.6330

Bate, S., Frowd, C., Bennetts, R., Hasshim, N., Murray, E., Bobak, A. K., et al. (2018). Applied screening tests for the detection of superior face recognition. *Cognitive Research: Principles and Implications, 3*, 22. doi:10.1186/s41235-018-0116-5

Bate, S., Frowd, C., Bennetts, R., Hasshim, N., Portch, E., Murray, E., et al. (2019b). The consistency of superior face recognition skills in police officers. *Applied Cognitive Psychology, 33*, 828–842. doi:10.1002/acp.3525

Bate, S., Parris, B., Haslam, C., & Kay, J. (2010). Socio-emotional functioning and face recognition ability in the normal population. *Personality and Individual Differences, 48*, 239–242. doi:10.1016/j.paid.2009.10.005

Bate, S., Portch, E., Mestry, N., & Bennetts, R. J. (2019c). Redefining super recognition in the real world: Skilled face or person identity recognizers? *British Journal of Psychology, 110*, 480–482. doi:10.1111/bjop.12392.

Bate, S. & Tree, J. J. (2017). The definition and diagnosis of developmental prosopagnosia. *Quarterly Journal of Experimental Psychology, 70*, 193–200. doi:10.1080/17470218.2016.1195414

Belanova, E., Davis, J., & Thompson, T. (2018). Cognitive and neural markers for super-recognisers' face processing superiority and enhanced cross-age effect. *Cortex, 108*, 92–111. doi:10.1016/j.cortex.2018.07.008

Benton, A. L., Sivan, A. B., Hamsher, K., Varney, N. R., & Spreen, O. (1983). *Contribution to neuropsychological assessment.* New York: Oxford University Press.

Bindemann, M., Avetisyan, M., & Rakow, T. (2012). Who can recognize unfamiliar faces? Individual differences and observer consistency in person identification. *Journal of Experimental Psychology: Applied, 18*, 277–291. doi:10.1037/a0029635

Bindemann, M. & Sandford, A. (2011). Me, myself, and I: Different recognition rates for three photo-IDs of the same person. *Perception, 40*, 625–627. doi:10.1068/p7008

Bobak, A. K., Bennetts, R. J., Parris, B. A., Jansari, A., & Bate, S. (2016a). An in-depth cognitive examination of individuals with superior face recognition skills. *Cortex, 82*, 48–62. doi:10.1016/j.cortex.2016.05.003

Bobak, A. K., Dowsett, A. J., & Bate, S. (2016b). Solving the border control problem: Evidence of enhanced face matching in individuals with extraordinary face recognition skills. *PLoS ONE, 11*(2), e0148148. doi:10.1371/journal.pone.0148148

Bobak, A. K., Hancock, P. J. B., & Bate, S. (2016c). Super-recognisers in action: Evidence from face-matching and face memory tasks. *Applied Cognitive Psychology, 30*, 81–91. doi:10.1002/acp.3170

Bobak, A. K, Pampoulov, P., & Bate, S. (2016d). Detecting superior face recognition skills in a large sample of young British adults. *Frontiers in Psychology, 7*, 1–11. doi:10.3389/fpsyg.2016.01378

Bobak, A. K., Parris, B. A., Gregory, N. J., Bennetts, R. J., & Bate, S. (2017). Eye-movement strategies in developmental prosopagnosia and 'super' face recognition. *Quarterly Journal of Experimental Psychology, 70*, 201–217. doi:10.1080/17470218.2016.1161059

Bowles, D. C., McKone, E., Dawel, A., Duchaine, B., Palermo, R., Schmalzl, L., et al. (2009). Diagnosing prosopagnosia: Effects of ageing, sex, and participant-stimulus ethnic match on the Cambridge Face Memory Test and Cambridge Face Perception Test. *Cognitive Neuropsychology, 26*, 423–455. doi:10.1080/02643290903343149

Bruce, V., Bindemann, M., & Lander, K. (2018). Individual differences in face perception and person recognition. *Cognitive Research: Principles and Implications*, 3, 18. doi:10.1186/s41235-018-0109-4

Bruce, V., Henderson, Z., Greenwood, K., Hancock, P. J. B., Burton, A. M., & Miller, P. (1999). Verification of face identities from images captured on video. *Journal of Experimental Psychology: Applied*, 5, 339–360. doi:10.1037/1076-898X.5.4.339

Bruce, V., Henderson, Z., Newman, C., & Burton, A. M. (2001). Matching identities of familiar and unfamiliar faces caught on CCTV images. *Journal of Experimental Psychology: Applied*, 7, 207–218. doi:10.1037/1076-898X.7.3.207

Bruce, V. & Young, A. W. (1986). Understanding face recognition. *British Journal of Psychology*, 77, 305–327. doi:10.1111/j.2044-8295.1986.tb02199.x

Burton, A. M., Jenkins, R., Hancock, P. J. B., & White, D. (2005). Robust representations for face recognition: The power of averages. *Cognitive Psychology*, 51, 256–284. doi:10.1016/j.cogpsych.2005.06.003

Burton, A. M., White, D., & McNeill, A. (2010). The Glasgow Face Matching Test. *Behavior Research Methods*, 42, 286–291. doi:10.3758/BRM.42.1.286

Burton, A. M., Wilson, S., Cowan, M., & Bruce, V. (1999). Face recognition in poor-quality video: Evidence from security surveillance. *Psychological Science*, 10, 243–248. doi:10.1111/1467-9280.00144

Chance, J. E., Goldstein, A. G., & Andersen, B. (1986). Recognition memory for infant faces: An analog of the other-race effect. *Bulletin of the Psychonomic Society*, 24, 257–260. doi:10.3758/BF0333013

Clutterbuck, R. & Johnston, R. A. (2002). Exploring levels of face familiarity by using an indirect face-matching measure. *Perception*, 31, 985–994. doi:10.1068/p3335

Dalrymple, K. A., Garrido, L., & Duchaine, B. (2014). Dissociation between face perception and face memory in adults, but not children, with developmental prosopagnosia. *Developmental Cognitive Neuroscience*, 10, 10–20. doi:10.1016/j.dcn.2014.07.003

Davies-Thompson, J., Fletcher, K., Hills, C., Pancaroglu, R., Corrow, S. L., & Barton, J. J. S. (2017). Perceptual learning of faces: A rehabilitative study of acquired prosopagnosia. *Journal of Cognitive Neuroscience*, 29, 573–591. doi:10.1162/jocn_a_01063

Davis, J. P., Forrest, C., Treml, F., & Jansari, A. (2018). Identification from CCTV: Assessing police super-recogniser ability to spot faces in a crowd and susceptibility to change blindness. *Applied Cognitive Psychology*, 32, 337–353. doi:10.1002/acp.3405

Davis, J. P., Lander, K., Evans, R., & Jansari, A. (2016). Investigating predictors of superior face recognition ability in police super-recognisers. *Applied Cognitive Psychology*, 30, 827–840. doi:10.1002/acp.3260

De Renzi, E., Faglioni, P., Grossi, D., & Nichelli, P. (1991). Apperceptive and associative forms of prosopagnosia. *Cortex*, 27, 213–221. doi:10.1016/s0010-9452(13)80125-6

DeGutis, J., Cohan, S., & Nakayama, K. (2014). Holistic face training enhances face processing in developmental prosopagnosia. *Brain*, 137, 1781–1798. doi:10.1093/brain/awu062

Devue, C. (2019). Breaking face processing tasks apart to improve their predictive value in the real world: A comment on Ramon, Bobak, and White (2019). *British Journal of Psychology*, 110, 483–485. doi:10.1111/bjop.12391

Devue, C., Wride, A., & Grimshaw, G. M. (2019). New insights on real-world human face recognition. *Journal of Experimental Psychology: General*, 148, 994–1007. doi:10.1037/xge0000493

Dowsett, A. J. & Burton, A. M. (2015). Unfamiliar face matching: Pairs out-perform individuals and provide a route to training. *British Journal of Psychology*, 106, 433–445. doi:10.1111/bjop.12103

Duchaine, B., Germine, L., & Nakayama, K. 2007. Family resemblance: Ten family members with prosopagnosia and within-class object agnosia. *Cognitive Neuropsychology*, 24, 419–430. doi:10.1080/02643290701380491

Duchaine, B. C. & Nakayama, K. (2004). Developmental prosopagnosia and the Benton Facial Recognition test. *Neurology*, 62, 1219–1220. doi:10.1212/01.wnl.0000118297.03161.b3

Duchaine, B. C. & Nakayama, K. (2006). The Cambridge Face Memory Test: Results for neurologically intact individuals and an investigation of its validity using inverted face stimuli and prosopagnosic participants. *Neuropsychologia*, 44, 576–585. doi:10.1016/j.neuropsychologia.2005.07.001

Duchaine, B. C. & Weidenfeld, A. (2003). An evaluation of two commonly used tests of unfamiliar face recognition. *Neuropsychologia, 41*, 713–720. doi:10.1016/s0028-3932(02)00222-1

Fysh, M. C. (2018). Individual differences in the detection, matching and memory of faces. *Cognitive Research: Principles and Implications, 3*, 20. doi:10.1186/s41235-018-0111-x

Fysh, M. C. & Bindemann, M. (2017). Forensic face matching: A review. In M. Bindemann & A. M. Megreya (eds), *Face processing: Systems, disorders and cultural differences* (pp. 203–222). New York: Nova Science Publishers.

Fysh, M. C. & Bindemann, M. (2018). The Kent Face Matching Test. *British Journal of Psychology, 109*, 219–231. doi:10.1111/bjop.12260

Hancock, P. J., Bruce, V., & Burton, A. M. (2000). Recognition of unfamiliar faces. *Trends in Cognitive Sciences, 4*, 330–337. doi:10.1016/S1364-6613(00)01519-9

Harrison, V. & Hole, G. J. (2009). Evidence for a contact-based explanation of the own-age bias in face recognition. *Psychonomic Bulletin and Review, 16*, 264–269. doi:10.3758/PBR.16.2.264

Hildebrandt, A., Sommer, W., Herzmann, G., & Wilhelm, O. (2010). Structural invariance and age-related performance differences in face cognition. *Psychology and Aging, 25*, 794–810. doi:10.1037/a0019774

Jenkins, R. & Burton, A. M. (2008). 100% accuracy in automatic face recognition. *Science, 319*, 435. doi:10.1126/science.1149656

Jenkins, R., White, D., Van Montfort, X., & Burton, A. M. (2011). Variability in photos of the same face. *Cognition, 121*, 313–323. doi:10.1016/j.cognition.2011.08.001

Kemp, R., Towell, N., & Pike, G. (1997). When seeing should not be believing: Photographs, credit cards and fraud. *Applied Cognitive Psychology, 11*, 211–222. doi:10.1002/(SICI)1099-0720(199706)11:3<211::AID-ACP430>3.0.CO;2-O

Kokje, E., Bindemann, M., & Megreya, A. M. (2018). Cross-race correlations in the abilities to match unfamiliar faces. *Acta Psychologica, 185*, 13–21. doi:10.1016/j.actpsy.2018.01.006

Kramer, R. S., Mulgrew, J., & Reynolds, M. G. (2018). Unfamiliar face matching with photographs of infants and children. *PeerJ, 6*, e5010. doi:10.7717/peerj.5010

Lander, K., Bruce, V., & Hill, H. (2001). Evaluating the effectiveness of pixelation and blurring on masking the identity of familiar faces. *Applied Cognitive Psychology, 15*, 101–116. doi:10.1002/1099-0720(200101/02)15:1<101::AID-ACP697>3.0.CO;2-7

Li, J., Tian, M., Fang, H., Xu, M., Li, H., & Liu, J. (2010). Extraversion predicts individual differences in face recognition. *Communicative and Integrative Biology, 3*, 295–298. doi:10.4161/cib.3.4.12093

Liu, J., Harris, A., & Kanwisher, N. (2002). Stages of processing in face perception: An MEG study. *Nature Neuroscience, 5*, 910–916. doi:10.1038/nn909

Malone, D. R., Morris, H. H., Kay, M. C., & Levin, H. S. (1982). Prosopagnosia: A double dissociation between the recognition of familiar and unfamiliar faces. *Journal of Neurology, Neurosurgery & Psychiatry, 45*, 820–822. doi:10.1136/jnnp.45.9.820

Maurer, D., Le Grand, R., & Mondloch, C. J. (2002). The many faces of configural processing. *Trends in Cognitive Sciences, 6*, 255–260. doi:10.1016/S1364-6613(02)01903-4

McCaffery, J. M., Robertson, D. J., Young, A. W., & Burton, A. M. (2018). Individual differences in face identity processing. *Cognitive Research: Principles and Implications, 3*, 21. doi:10.1186/s41235-018-0112-9

Megreya, A. M. & Bindemann, M. (2013). Individual differences in personality and face identification. *Journal of Cognitive Psychology, 25*, 30–37. doi:10.1080/20445911.2012.739153

Megreya, A. M. & Bindemann, M. (2015). Developmental improvement and age-related decline in unfamiliar face matching. *Perception, 44*, 5–22. doi:10.1068/p7825

Megreya, A. M., Bindemann, M., & Havard, C. (2011a). Sex differences in unfamiliar face identification: Evidence from matching tasks. *Acta Psychologica, 137*, 83–89. doi:10.1016/j.actpsy.2011.03.003

Megreya, A. M. & Burton, A. M. (2006). Unfamiliar faces are not faces: Evidence from a matching task. *Memory and Cognition, 34*, 865–876. doi:10.3758/bf03193433

Megreya, A. M. & Burton, A. M. (2007). Hits and false positives in face matching: A familiarity-based dissociation. *Perception & Psychophysics, 69*, 1175–1184. doi:10.3758/BF03193954

Megreya, A. M. & Burton, A. M. (2008). Matching faces to photographs: Poor performance in eye-witness memory (without the memory). *Journal of Experimental Psychology: Applied, 14*, 364–372. doi:10.1037/a0013464

Megreya, A. M., White, D., & Burton, A. M. (2011b). The other-race effect does not rely on memory: Evidence from a matching task. *Quarterly Journal of Experimental Psychology, 64*, 1473–1483. doi:10.1080/17470218.2011.575228

Moreton, R., Pike, G., & Havard, C. (2019). A task- and role-based perspective on super-recognizers: Commentary on 'Super-recognizers: From the laboratory to the world and back again'. *British Journal of Psychology, 110*, 486–488. doi:10.1111/bjop.12394

Noyes, E., Hill, M. Q., & O'Toole, A. J. (2018). Face recognition ability does not predict person iden-tification performance: Using individual data in the interpretation of group results. *Cognitive Research: Principles and Implications, 3*, 23. doi:10.1186/s41235-018-0117-4

Nunn, J. A., Postma, P., & Pearson, R. (2001). Developmental prosopagnosia: Should it be taken at face value? *Neurocase, 7*, 15–27. doi:10.1093/neucas/7.1.15

O'Toole, A. J., Harms, J., Snow, S. L., Hurst, D. R., Pappas, M. R., Ayyad, J. H., et al. (2005). A video data-base of moving faces and people. *IEEE Transactions on Pattern Analysis and Machine Intelligence, 27*, 812–816. doi:10.1109/TPAMI.2005.90

Palermo, R., Rossion, B., Rhodes, G., Laguesse, R., Tez, T., Hall, B., et al. (2017). Do people have in-sight into their face recognition abilities? *Quarterly Journal of Experimental Psychology, 70*, 218–233. doi:10.1080/17470218.2016.1161058

Papesh, M. H. (2018). Photo-ID verification remains challenging despite years of practice. *Cognitive Research: Principles and Implications, 3*, 19. doi:10.1186/s41235-018-0110-y

Papesh, M. H. & Goldinger, S. D. (2009). Deficits in other-race face recognition: No evidence for encoding-based effects. *Canadian Journal of Experimental Psychology, 63*, 253–262. doi:10.1037/a0015802

Phillips, P. J., Yates, A. N., Hu, Y., Hahn, C. A., Noyes, E., Jackson, K., et al. (2018). Face recognition ac-curacy of forensic examiners, superrecognizers, and face recognition algorithms. *Proceedings of the National Academy of Sciences, 115*, 6171–6176. doi:10.1073/pnas.1721355115

Ramon, M., Bobak, A. K., & White, D. (2019). Super-recognizers: From the lab to the world and back again. *British Journal of Psychology, 110*, 461–479. doi:10.1111/bjop.12368

Rezlescu, C., Susilo, T., Wilmer, J. B., & Caramazza, A. (2017). The inversion, part-whole, and com-posite effects reflect distinct perceptual mechanisms with varied relationships to face recogni-tion. *Journal of Experimental Psychology: Human Perception and Performance, 43*, 1961–1973. doi:10.1037/xhp0000400

Rhodes, M. G. & Anastasi, J. S. (2012). The own-age bias in face recognition: A meta-analytic and the-oretical review. *Psychological Bulletin, 138*, 146–174. doi:10.1037/a0025750

Robertson, D. J. & Bindemann, M. (2019). Consolidation, wider reflection, and policy: Response to 'Super-recognisers: From the lab to the world and back again'. *British Journal of Psychology, 110*, 489–491. doi:10.1111/bjop.12393

Robertson, D. J., Noyes, E., Dowsett, A. J., Jenkins, R., & Burton, A. M. (2016). Face recognition by Metropolitan Police super-recognisers. *PLoS ONE, 11*(2), e0150036. doi:10.1371/journal.pone.0150036

Russ, A. J., Sauerland, M., Lee, C. E., & Bindemann, M. (2018). Individual differences in eyewitness accuracy across multiple lineups of faces. *Cognitive Research: Principles and Implications, 3*, 30. doi:10.1186/s41235-018-0121-8

Russell, R., Duchaine, B., & Nakayama, K. (2009). Super-recognizers: People with extraordinary face recognition ability. *Psychonomic Bulletin & Review, 16*, 252–257. doi:10.3758/PBR.16.2.252

Schretlen, D. J., Pearlson, G. D., Anthony, J. C., & Yates, K. O. (2001). Determinants of Benton Facial Recognition Test performance in normal adults. *Neuropsychology, 15*, 405–410. doi:10.1037//0894-4105.15.3.405

Tardif, J., Duchesne, X. M., Cohan, S., Royer, J., Blais, C., Fiset, D., et al. (2019). Use of face informa-tion varies systematically from developmental prosopagnosics to super-recognizers. *Psychological Science, 30*, 300–308. doi:10.1177/0956797618811338

Towler, A., Kemp, R. I., Burton, A. M., Dunn, J. D., Wayne, T., Moreton, R., et al. (2019). Do professional facial image comparison training courses work? *PLoS ONE, 14*(2), e0211037. doi:10.1371/journal.pone.0211037

Towler, A., White, D., & Kemp, R. I. (2014). Evaluating training methods for facial image comparison: The face shape strategy does not work. *Perception, 43*, 214–218. doi:10.1068/p7676

Tranel, D., Damasio, A. R., & Damasio, H. (1988). Intact recognition of facial expression, gender, and age in patients with impaired recognition of face identity. *Neurology, 38*, 690–696. doi:10.1212/wnl.38.5.690

Verhallen, R. J., Bosten, J. M., Goodbourn, P. T., Bargary, G., Lawrance-Owen, A. J., & Mollon, J. D. (2014). An online version of the Mooney Face Test: Phenotypic and genetic associations. *Neuropsychologia, 63*, 19–25. doi:10.1016/j.neuropsychologia.2014.08.011

Verhallen, R. J., Bosten, J. M., Goodbourn, P. T., Lawrance-Owen, A. J., Bargary, J. & Mollon, J. D. (2017). General and specific factors in the processing of faces. *Vision Research, 141*, 217–227. doi:10.1016/j.visres.2016.12.014

White, D., Burton, A. M., Kemp, R. I., & Jenkins, R. (2013). Crowd effects in unfamiliar face matching. *Applied Cognitive Psychology, 27*, 769–777. doi:10.1002/acp.2971

White, D., Dunn, J. D., Schmid, A. C., & Kemp, R. I. (2015a). Error rates in users of automatic face recognition software. *PLoS ONE, 10*(10), e0139827. doi:10.1371/journal.pone.0139827

White, D., Kemp, R. I., Jenkins, R., Matheson, M., & Burton, A. M. (2014). Passport officers' errors in face matching. *PLoS ONE, 9*(8), e103510. doi:10.1371/journal.pone.0103510

White, D., Phillips, P. J., Hahn, C. A., Hill, M., & O'Toole, A. J. (2015b). Perceptual expertise in forensic facial image comparison. *Proceedings of the Royal Society B: Biological Sciences, 282*(1814), 20151292. doi:10.1098/rspb.2015.1292

Wigan, A. L. (1844). Duality of the mind. *The Lancet, 43*, 451. doi:10.1016/S0140-6736(02)75299-9

Wilmer, J. B. (2017). Individual differences in face recognition: A decade of discovery. *Current Directions in Psychological Science, 26*, 225–230. doi:10.1177/0963721417710693

Wilmer, J. B., Germine, L., Chabris, C. F., Chatterjee, G., Williams, M., Loken, E., et al. (2010). Human face recognition ability is specific and highly heritable. *Proceedings of the National Academy of Sciences, 107*, 5238–5241. doi:10.1073/pnas.0913053107

Yin, R. K. (1969). Looking at upside-down faces. *Journal of Experimental Psychology, 81*, 141–145. doi:10.1037/h0027474

Young, A. W., Hay, D. C., & Ellis, A. W. (1985). The faces that launched a thousand slips: Everyday difficulties and errors in recognizing people. *British Journal of Psychology, 76*, 495–523. doi:10.1111/j.2044-8295.1985.tb01972.x

Young, A. W. & Noyes, E. (2019). We need to talk about super-recognizers: Invited commentary on: Ramon, M., Bobak, A. K., & White, D. 'Super-recognizers: From the lab to the world and back again'. *British Journal of Psychology, 110*, 492–494. doi:10.1111/bjop.12395

Zhu, Q., Song, Y., Hu, S., Li, X., Tian, M., Zhen, Z., et al. (2010). Heritability of the specific cognitive ability of face perception. *Current Biology, 20*, 137–142. doi:10.1016/j.cub.2009.11.067

7

Forensic Face Matching

Procedures and Application

Reuben Moreton

7.1 Introduction

Face images provide vital evidence in criminal investigations, such as matching closed-circuit television (CCTV) images of an offender to mugshots of a suspect in a murder investigation, identifying victims in child sexual abuse imagery, or linking multiple burglaries committed by the same perpetrator. Each of these scenarios is an example of applied face matching, the process of comparing two or more faces that are unfamiliar to the observer, in order to establish whether the faces are of the same individual. A related but distinct process is the recognition of familiar faces, which is also commonly used in police investigations and as evidence in the UK courts; for clarity, this will be referred to as 'familiar recognition'. The term 'face identification' will be used when referring in general terms to the various processes used to determine who someone is based on their face.

Face matching is used in a range of different policing and criminal justice applications, which may not always result in an output that can be presented as admissible evidence in the courtroom. These applications include gathering intelligence about particular individuals to provide substantive lines of enquiry in an investigation, reviewing results from automated face-recognition systems, or controlling access at a point of entry, such as at a major event, or to a restricted area. In the UK, when used as evidence in the courtroom, face matching is classed as a type of opinion-based evidence rather than evidence of fact. This means that the evidence is derived from the subjective opinion of the person presenting it, rather than a substantiated fact. Opinion-based evidence is largely inadmissible in court unless presented by an expert witness. In face matching, such experts are known as 'forensic face examiners' who conduct forensic facial comparisons or face examinations (Facial Identification Scientific Working Group, 2019).

Forensic face-matching examinations are universally accepted in UK courts and have been presented as expert evidence for over 25 years (*R v Stockwell*, 1993). This evidence can give substantial weight to a case. For example, in 1999, a defendant was convicted solely on the basis of facial comparison evidence (*R v Hookway*, 1999). Many commercial companies now provide a forensic face-matching service and in 2003 it was estimated in the UK that approximately 600 forensic face examinations were presented in court a year (Bromby & Plews, 2003). However, forensic face matching has been largely self-regulated in the 25 years since its introduction into UK courts. As a

Reuben Moreton, *Forensic Face Matching* In: *Forensic Face Matching*. Edited by: Markus Bindemann, Oxford University Press (2021).
© Oxford University Press. DOI: 10.1093/oso/9780198837749.003.0007.

result, there has often been inconsistency in working practices between different examiners, and little attempt at scientific validation of forensic face-matching procedures and processes (Campbell-Tiech, 2005; Edmond et al., 2009; Mallett & Evison, 2013).

More recently, there have been attempts to standardize forensic face-matching procedures through the work of practitioner-led international working groups such as the Facial Identification Scientific Working Group and the European Network of Forensic Science Institutes. The guidance and best practice documentation of these working groups is freely available online.[1, 2] Several scientific studies have now published data on the accuracy of face examiners and forensic face-matching procedures (Norell et al., 2015; Phillips et al., 2018; Towler et al., 2017; White, Dunn, et al., 2015; White, Phillips, et al., 2015; see White, Towler, & Kemp, this volume). These are significant steps towards understanding how reliable forensic face-matching procedures really are.

This chapter will begin by discussing the various ways facial identification can be presented as evidence in UK courts, including forensic face matching, then move on to discuss the scientific validity of the processes used in forensic matching, and finally present a mock case example demonstrating how face-matching procedures are used in practice.

7.2 Face-Identification Evidence in UK Courts

In the UK criminal justice system, face-matching evidence is classed as a form of opinion-based evidence (note that the courts frequently refer to face-matching evidence as 'facial mapping'). However, opinion is only admissible as evidence if it is given by an individual whom the court recognizes as a suitably qualified expert witness. The law is not prescriptive on what constitutes suitable qualification, but refers in general terms to specialized knowledge based on study, training, and professional experience. The two pieces of UK legislation that govern the admissibility of expert evidence are part 19 of the Criminal Procedure Rules (2015), which governs the contents of expert reports, and division V part 19A of the Criminal Practice Directions (2015), governing the reliability of expert opinion evidence. Two key exceptions to the expert opinion rule specific to face matching and face recognition are as follows:

1. That the jury are entitled to their own opinion when matching face images, in order to fulfil their role as the trier of fact (i.e., to decide whether the defendant is guilty or not guilty).
2. If someone is personally familiar with a person and recognizes them from an image or video, this is also admissible as evidence in the UK even if that person is not deemed an expert witness.

---

[1] https://fiswg.org/documents.html (accessed 3 May 2020).
[2] http://enfsi.eu/documents/best-practice-manuals (accessed 3 May 2020).

7.2.1 Face-Matching by the Jury

In the UK criminal justice system, the jury are entitled by case law to make a comparison of face images of the offender and the defendant. In *R v Dodson & Williams* (1984), two men were captured on CCTV committing an armed robbery. There were no witnesses available who could recognize the defendant from the CCTV. It was therefore deemed permissible to show the CCTV directly to the jury and allow them to make a decision as to whether or not the images depicted the defendants. In such a scenario, a jury member will be even more likely to make an incorrect decision if the images are low quality, such as from a CCTV system (see Fysh, this volume). We also know that people are generally poor at understanding their own face-matching ability (Bindemann et al., 2014). These factors could have profound consequences if jurors were left to compare face imagery unaided in the courtroom, particularly if members of the jury were very poor at face matching and not aware of this fact.

It has been widely evidenced in the scientific literature that people are, on average, surprisingly poor at comparing unfamiliar faces. Even when face images are taken on the same day and under the same conditions, observers only make the correct decision on average 80% of the time (Burton et al., 2010). As quality and capture conditions between the images become more dissimilar (e.g., low resolution, non-matching pose, or obscured features), the chance of someone correctly matching the faces decreases (Fysh & Bindemann, 2018; Kramer et al., 2019). Individual accuracy varies substantially even on the same face-matching test, with some people achieving 100% accuracy and others performing close to chance (Burton et al., 2010). This is further exacerbated by the fact that people are largely unaware of the difficulty of unfamiliar face matching and frequently overestimate their own ability (Bindemann et al., 2014). This variability in accuracy, particularly for low-quality images such as CCTV, is a major issue for criminal investigations that rely on face matching to determine whether a suspect is guilty of committing a crime.

In 2002, the UK Attorney General elaborated on the ruling in *R v Dodson & Williams* that the jury are entitled to make comparisons of *sufficiently clear images* (Attorney General's Reference No. 2, 2002, para. 19):

> Where the photographic image is sufficiently clear, the jury can compare it with the defendant sitting in the dock (*Dodson & Williams*).

In situations where the image is not 'sufficiently clear' the reference states that a suitably qualified 'facial mapping' expert can provide an opinion on the images (*R v Clarke*, 1995; *R v Hookway*, 1999; *R v Stockwell*, 1993):

> A suitably qualified expert with facial mapping skills can give opinion evidence of identification based on a comparison between images from the scene, whether expertly enhanced or not, and a reasonably contemporary photograph of the defendant, provided the images and the photograph are available for the jury (Stockwell [1993] 97 Cr App R 260, Clarke [1995] 2 Cr App R 425 and Hookway [1999] Crim LR 750).

However, the reference does not elaborate on what constitutes a sufficiently clear image, and does not appear to acknowledge that face matching is a challenging, error-prone task even when images are clear and of high quality.

7.2.2 Familiar Recognition

The majority of face identification evidence entering the UK courts actually derives from familiar recognition rather than unfamiliar face matching. It is therefore worthwhile making clear the distinction between face-matching evidence, where the faces are unfamiliar or unknown to the observer, and familiar recognition evidence, where the observer recognizes a person as someone they know. The recognition of a suspect from an image, by someone who knows and is familiar with them, is widely used as evidence in UK police investigations. In 2017, visual recognitions provided primary identification evidence in 1,741 Metropolitan Police Service investigations, greater than that of fingerprint evidence (1,200 investigations).[3] Unlike face-matching evidence, familiar recognition evidence (or visual recognition) does not need to have been carried out by an expert to be admissible in the courtroom. In fact, in the UK, the admissibility of expert face-matching evidence and visual recognition evidence are governed by entirely different laws.

Typically, familiar recognitions are made by police officers who have previously encountered the suspected offenders and therefore have first-hand familiarity. However, any individual, such as an eyewitness to a crime, may make a visual recognition from an image or video, provided that the means by which the recognition was made complies with Code D Section 3 Part (B) of the Police and Criminal Evidence Act (1984) (hereafter referred to as 'PACE Code D' for brevity). PACE Code D includes a series of steps meant to safeguard against visual recognitions being mistaken or made under collusion. These steps include the following requirements (PACE Code D, 1984, para. 3.35):

(a) that the films, photographs and other images are shown on an individual basis;
(b) that any person who views the material;
   (i) is unable to communicate with any other individual to whom the material has been, or is to be, shown;
   (ii) is not reminded of any photograph or description of any individual whose image is shown or given any other indication as to the identity of any such individual;
   (iii) is not be told whether a previous witness has recognised any one (Home Office, 2017)

When recording their recognition, the witness must also include the reason they know the person, the wording used when they recognized them, any expressions of doubt

---

[3] https://www.met.police.uk/SysSiteAssets/foi-media/metropolitan-police/disclosure_2018/october_2018/information-rights-unit---crimes-detected-and-feature-forensic-sanction-detentions-from-2013-to-2017 (accessed 3 May 2020).

and what, if any, specific features triggered the recognition. This information will be used by the court to evaluate the reliability of the evidence. A recognition may only be submitted as evidence if it complies with the requirements of PACE Code D.

Both the familiarity of the subject to the witness and the innate ability of the observer to recognize people they know can affect the reliability of recognition evidence. Recognition ability varies across the population. At the extreme end of the distribution are prosopagnosiacs, individuals with 'face blindness' caused by either a congenital condition or acquired brain injury that prevents that individual from being able to recall faces. However, it should be mentioned that prosopagnosia manifests to different extents in different people and is certainly not a homogenous condition (Bate & Tree, 2017). At the other end of the spectrum are purported 'super-recognizers' (SRs), individuals with extraordinary face-recognition ability first demonstrated by Russell, Duchaine, and Nakayama (2009). Like prosopagnosics, SRs are also not a homogenous group, with SR performance varying on different types of face-recognition and face-matching tasks (Bate et al., 2018; see Bate, Mestry, & Portch, this volume).

It has long been acknowledged by the courts that human recognition is variable, with the 1976 Devlin Committee into visual identification evidence commenting that 'The capacity to memorise a face differs enormously from one man to another, but there is no way of finding out in the witness box how much of it the witness has got; no-one keeps a record of his successes and failures to submit to scrutiny' (Devlin, 1976, para. 4.25). Despite a plethora of recent research into human face recognition, there is limited consensus in the scientific research community on a standard, accurate measure of recognition ability (Ramon et al., 2019a). Given that the leading researchers in the field cannot agree, it looks to be a long time before such a measure could be considered suitably reliable to be used to assess recognition witnesses in court.

7.2.3 Super-Recognizers

There has been much attention in both the scientific literature and the media on the existence of SRs, those with superior, innate face-identification abilities. Some researchers have been quick to point out that SRs may provide a potential solution to the issues of reliability of face-matching evidence (Davis et al., 2016; Edmond & Wortley, 2016). However, based on our current understanding of SR ability, it is something that is innate rather than a skill based on specialist knowledge and training (Noyes et al., 2017). The UK Forensic Science Regulator has clearly stated that the work of SRs in police units does not constitute a 'forensic science' (Forensic Science Regulator, 2018, pp. 19–20):

> 'Super recogniser' is a popular term for an individual who is believed to have above average face processing ability, which may include a greater propensity to remember and recall familiar faces. The Regulator's input was sought on a review of the work of 'super recognisers', following a case that had been discontinued when the 'identification' made by a 'super recogniser' was found to be flawed.

Work undertaken by super recognisers may have investigative value. However, the Regulator does not consider it to be forensic science for the following reasons:

(a) the work is generally carried out within an operational policing unit, with no separation to ensure independence and impartiality;

(b) photographs of known suspects or offenders are studied prior to watching the footage containing unknown individuals, without implementing safeguards against cognitive bias; and

(c) although there is scientific literature to support the fact that some people have a greater propensity to match faces, the 'super recogniser' process of attempting to match faces from photographs against CCTV footage is not based on scientifically validated methodology, nor are error rates known.

There is now a substantial body of research demonstrating the existence of SRs in the general population (Bate et al., 2018; Bobak, Pampoulov, and Bate, 2016; Russell et al., 2009). The benefits of recruiting SRs into operational roles that conduct quick face-matching decisions in high-risk environments (e.g., as a police investigator or border guard) are self-evident (Bobak, Dowsett, et al., 2016), particularly given the limited effectiveness of short professional training courses at improving face-matching accuracy (Towler et al., 2019). However, because face matching by SRs is based on natural ability rather than a demonstrable scientific method, it does not meet current UK admissibility requirements for expert evidence. That is not to say that a SR could not become an expert in forensic face matching, and would likely be a good candidate for the role but, until there is further research and a wider scientific consensus on how superior face-processing ability is measured and defined, caution should be exercised in using SRs in operational situations like forensic face matching (Moreton et al., 2019; Ramon et al., 2019b).

As a counter-argument, SRs as a group have been shown to perform as accurately as forensic face examiners in controlled face-matching tasks, although more likely to make high confidence errors (Phillips et al., 2018). Although SRs are currently excluded from providing expert opinion on face matching, UK courts have readily allowed self-regulated face-matching experts to present compelling evidence derived from methods with little or no scientific validity. Edmond and Wortley (2016) discuss an interesting potential alternative to the current status quo, whereby face-matching evidence from an SR could be presented alongside evidence from a cognitive psychologist as a novel form of expert opinion. Further investigation into the roles and interoperability of SRs and forensic face examiners in the courtroom will be an interesting avenue for future research.

7.2.4 Forensic Face Matching

In order to be admissible as expert evidence, first and foremost, the expert's opinion must provide knowledge and expertise beyond the experience of the jury. According to *R v Turner* (1975), if the judge and jury can form their own opinion unaided, then the knowledge of an expert witness is unnecessary. This raises an interesting question for forensic face matching. Unlike other forensic identification techniques such as DNA profiling, judges and juries are quite capable of proffering an opinion on whether two face images depict the same person although, as discussed previously, they may not necessarily be correct. Therefore, forensic face-matching procedures must provide probative information beyond what the jury can derive on their own. There is no legal requirement for forensic face-matching experts to follow a particular methodology or use a certain technique. In fact, UK courts are quite prepared to accept novel techniques even if they have been largely untested. In the UK, there is no statutory test for the admissibility of forensic expert and scientific procedures. Experts must demonstrate that they comply with the requirements of both common law and legislation, but it is up to the discretion of individual judges to determine whether a certain expert's evidence is admissible and their procedures sufficiently reliable. This approach has been criticized as being too lenient in allowing new and untested forensic techniques into the courtroom, with expert evidence being admitted 'without sufficient regard to whether or not it is sufficiently reliable to be presented to the jury' (Law Commission, 2011, para. 1.8).

Forensic face matching has been largely self-regulated since its initial use in court in 1993, and face examiners were left to their own devices to devise forensic methods and procedures to compare faces. This resulted in a lack of standardization in techniques, with experts borrowing from other scientific fields to develop procedures (Bromby, 2006). These procedures were largely untested on the types of images that examiners were applying them to (often low-resolution CCTV imagery captured under poor lighting conditions). As a result, the error rates of the techniques in a forensic context are unknown (Edmond et al., 2009; Mallett & Evison, 2013). The significance of this point cannot be understated.

The issue of a lack of scientific foundation is not isolated to forensic face matching, having been raised across many forensic pattern and object matching disciplines, such as bitemark comparison (Saks et al., 2016) and handwriting comparison (Sulner, 2017). The much-cited US National Research Council report entitled *Strengthening Forensic Science* (2009) strongly criticized many subjective forensic comparison disciplines as having a dearth of peer-reviewed studies that establish the validity of their methods and procedures. And, five years later, the 'PCAST report' from the President's Council of Advisors on Science and Technology again 'raised the need to evaluate specific forensic methods to determine whether they have been scientifically established to be valid and reliable' (PCAST, 2016: 1). In light of issues specific to the reliability of forensic face-matching evidence in the UK, the Forensic Regulator, in collaboration with the Metropolitan Police Service, Crown Prosecution Service, and National Crime Agency published a guidance document for prosecutors and investigators on how to commission work from reliable forensic face examiners. The guidance document included criteria that the examiner's chosen methodology and procedures must comply with (Forensic Science Regulator, 2016b: 3):

1. The expert has followed an analytical process that has been documented and can be repeated by another suitably qualified expert.
2. The methods and processes used during the comparison process have been validated to such an extent that the limitations are known and that they are suitable for the purpose for which they are used.
3. Simply citing years of experience and stating that the type of evidence has been previously accepted by the courts is insufficient to ensure that the expert is competent and their analysis and conclusions are reliable.

Despite these requirements for demonstrable scientific validity and reliability, there is a long history of face-matching evidence based on procedures demonstrated to have limited scientific basis being admitted in the courtroom. In recent years, practitioner guidance has recommended that such procedures should no longer be used in forensic face matching.

7.3 Face-Matching Procedures

The procedures devised by forensic face examiners to compare faces can be broadly categorized into four types; morphological analysis, facial feature classification, photo anthropometry, and superimposition (Facial Identification Scientific Working Group, 2019). How the procedure is applied in practice may vary between different examiners and be referred to by a different title, but it will follow a similar underlying process. For example, photo anthropometry may be referred to as 'proportional alignment' or superimposition as 'overlaying', but they are in essence the same procedure (European Network of Forensic Science Institutes, 2018). Of the four procedures, only morphological analysis is recommended by the two major practitioner working groups in the field; the European Network of Forensic Science Institutes and the Facial Identification Scientific Working Group (European Network of Forensic Science Institutes, 2018; Facial Identification Scientific Working Group, 2019). Although once used widely by forensic face examiners, the three procedures of photo anthropometry, superimposition, and feature classification have all been found to have significant issues in terms of consistency, accuracy, and validity in published scientific research. The following sections offer an overview of the four forensic face-matching procedures and a critical review of the scientific validity of each.

7.3.1 Photo Anthropometry

Photo anthropometry in the context of forensic face matching is the comparison of facial proportions based on measurements between specific facial landmarks. The facial landmarks are derived from both soft tissue features of the face, such as the endocanthions (En) and ectocanthions (Ec) (inner and outer corners of the eye), and

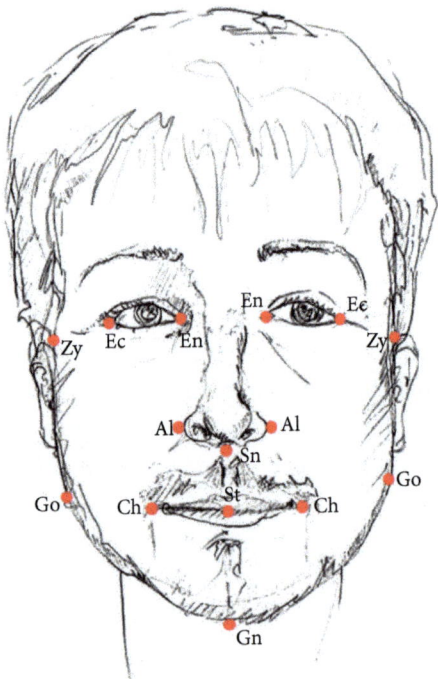

Figure 7.1 Diagram depicting facial landmarks used for photo anthropometry.
Source: Illustration by Jennifer Harris and reproduced with permission.

the bony structures of the skull, such as the zygoma (Zy) and gonions (Gn) (the cheekbones and the angle of the jaw) (Iscan, 1993). When applying photo anthropometry, the face examiner must first plot the location of the landmarks on the image. Figure 7.1 shows an example of some of the facial landmarks used in photo anthropometric comparison.

Once positioned, the landmarks are used to derive the distances between facial features. Facial proportions are then compared between images to determine whether the faces are those of the same person or different people. However, these assessments of similarity and dissimilarity are subjective. Figure 7.2 shows an example of photo anthropometry commonly seen in forensic face-matching reports. The images depict the same individual but note that the facial proportions vary due to differences in pose, distance to camera, and facial expression.

An appealing aspect of photo anthropometry is its apparent objective basis using the measurements and ratios between images, whereas other face-matching procedures, such as morphological analysis, are subjective in nature and based on the knowledge, experience, and interpretation of the observer. However, this apparent objectivity is a fallacy. Locating facial landmarks is often a manual process, therefore open to interpretation by different observers. Photo anthropometry has been applied to high-resolution images in controlled environments and, in these contrived conditions, has shown limited effectiveness in face matching (Yoshino et al., 2000). In forensic casework,

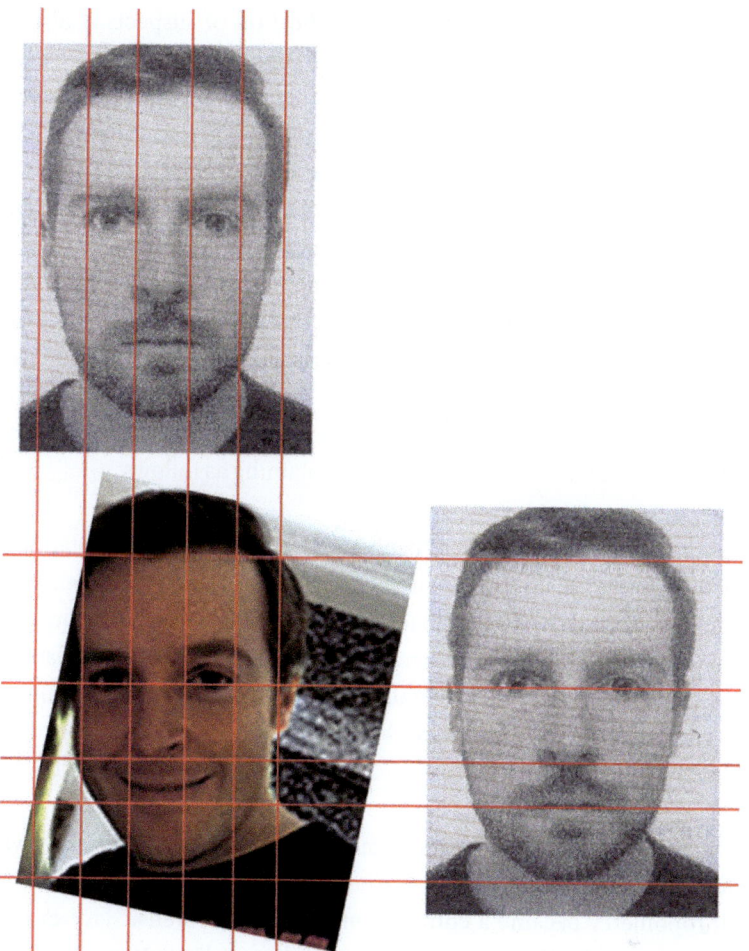

Figure 7.2 An example of photo anthropometry between two images of the same individual.

Note: Lines denote vertical and horizontal proportions for comparison between the two images. Note how proportions vary due to extraneous factors such as pose and expression.

images are unconstrained and often poor quality. Factors such as low-resolution imagery (Moreton & Morley, 2011), variation in camera angle (Kleinberg et al., 2007), and distance of the subject from the camera (Edmond et al., 2009; Noyes & Jenkins, 2017) have all been demonstrated to alter facial proportions in images. Photo anthropometry has now been largely derided by much of the forensic facial comparison community as unreliable (European Network of Forensic Science Institutes, 2018; Facial Identification Scientific Working Group, 2019) but this was not always the case. This shift in perspective was only brought about after many examples of scientific research demonstrating the fundamental flaws in this procedure.

Attempting to infer information about identity from facial measurements is not a new idea. Anthropologists have attempted to use facial proportions to measure latent characteristics of a face, such as age, gender, and ethnicity (Zhuang et al., 2010). The application of facial measurement to the identification of suspects is also not novel. In the late nineteenth century, a Parisian named Alphonse Bertillon created a system for recording facial and bodily measurements to identify recidivists in police custody (Bertillon, 1893). This approach was time-consuming and quickly superseded by the comparison of fingerprint ridge detail (Prabhakar et al., 2004).

An early semi-automated facial recognition system, designed by Woodrow Bledsoe in the 1960s, required human operators to annotate facial landmarks on images. The machine then calculated a set of facial measurements based on the distances between these landmarks. A set of measurements were stored for each face in a database, with the intention that the machine would be able to recall a previously stored face based on a set of measurements from a new image of that face. This approach proved to be time-consuming to process and inaccurate when faces varied in pose, camera, or expression. Bledsoe himself was critical of the technique, explaining as follows:

> This recognition problem is made difficult by the great variability in rotation and tilt, lighting intensity and angle, facial expression, aging, etc. Some other attempts at facial recognition by machine have allowed for little or no variability in these quantities. Yet the method of correlation (or pattern matching) of unprocessed optical data, which is often used by some researchers, is certain to fail in cases where the variability is great. In particular, the correlation is very low between two pictures of the same person with two different head rotations. (Ballantyne, Boyer, & Hines, 1996, pp. 10–11)

Despite the limitations of facial measurements being known 30 years previously, the rise of forensic face matching in the early 1990s saw a resurgence in the technique. Photo anthropometry became a common procedure for forensic face examiners and was readily accepted by the courts despite its inherent limitations. In *R v Hookway* (1999), the first stated case where a defendant was convicted solely on face-matching evidence, discussions of facial proportions feature heavily, with the case summary stating that the expert said 'the proportions of the robber's face were totally consistent with the proportions of the appellant's face, both in relation to frontal and side views'. He (the expert) said the findings were 'very powerful support for the assertion that the offender was the appellant'. Scientific research had raised concerns about the use of facial proportions and measurements by forensic experts three years prior to the Hookway case, highlighting the necessity for an established database of facial proportions within the population (Mardia et al., 1996). Without such a database, how could experts be able to state a level of certainty for the similarity between facial proportions? Such a database was not developed and, as is seen in Hookway, experts were still assigning levels of support to face-matching examinations based on proportions with little or no empirical basis.

Not all experts were unanimous on the use of photo anthropometry and facial proportions, reflecting the fragmented and self-regulatory nature of forensic face matching at the time. In a 2003 case at Winchester Crown Court, four face-matching experts were asked their opinion of photo anthropometry as a comparison technique. Photo anthropometry was 'condemned by two experts as being without scientific foundation and impossible in any event to apply since the angle of the facial or bodily feature could never be aligned exactly between the known and disputed images.' (Campbell-Tiech, 2005: 4). Even the condemnation of the technique by practising experts was insufficient for the courts to deem photo anthropometry unreliable.

In 2007, Kleinberg, Vanezis, and Burton published a research paper with the unequivocal title 'Failure of anthropometry as a facial identification technique using high-quality photographs', concluding that for the landmarks tested in the study, photo anthropometry 'does not generate the consistent results necessary for use in a court of law' (Kleinberg et al., 2007: 779). However, in the 2009 Facial Identification Guidance, issued by the UK National Police Improvement Agency two years after the publication by Kleinberg et al. (2007), facial proportions were still listed as a procedure for forensic face matching (National Police Improvement Agency, 2009). In a research paper published the same year, Wilkinson and Evans (2009) stated that the majority of face-matching experts in the UK used a combination of morphological analysis and photo anthropometry.

Possibly because of the overwhelming scientific evidence that photo anthropometry is unreliable for identification, many forensic face-matching experts stated that the technique would only be used for elimination purposes (i.e., determining that two faces do not show the same person). Research from the Metropolitan Police in 2011 echoed the findings of Kleinberg et al. (2007) as to the inconsistency of photo anthropometric results and went further to conclude that 'photoanthropometric facial comparison, as it is currently practised, is unsuitable for elimination purposes' because of the variability in proportions of the same face caused by changes in pose and camera angle exceeding the variability in facial proportions of different individual's faces (Moreton & Morley, 2011: 1). McNeill et al. (2015) found that simply overlaying a grid of facial proportions on two face images increased the chance that untrained observers would decide that two non-matching faces were the same person, debunking the notion that photo anthropometry and the comparison of facial proportions are an effective elimination tool. McNeill et al. (2015) went as far as referring to the technique and others used by face-matching experts as 'pseudoscience' in the title of their paper.

Guidance from the Facial Identification Scientific Working Group is unambiguous in stating that 'photo anthropometry should NOT be used' for forensic face matching, citing many of the scientific studies above as grounds for this decision (Facial Identification Scientific Working Group, 2019: 7). In 2013, the UK Forensic Science Regulator stated there is 'paucity of scientific underpinning and validation on the analysis of facial characteristics and proportions from photographs using anthropometric landmarks, dimensions and angles' (Forensic Science Regulator, 2013: 3) and the 2018 European Network of Forensic Science Institutes' facial image comparison best practice manual further recommended against the use of measurements and proportions in forensic face matching (European Network of Forensic Science Institutes, 2018).

The use of photo anthropometry has decreased in recent years and internationally forensic face examiners report to no longer use the technique (e.g., Houlton & Steyn,

2018). But, at the time of writing, a simple internet search reveals several UK face-matching experts who do still use the technique, despite there being over 40 years of empirical evidence demonstrating the lack of reliability of photo anthropometry, practitioner guidance stating that it should not be used, and criticism that the technique lacks scientific underpinning by the Forensic Science Regulator.

As can be seen in the case of photo anthropometry, UK courts seldom go so far to exclude a specific technique as unreliable, even with a substantial body of scientific research supporting such a decision. Therefore, the onus is on practitioners and researchers to work together to ensure that forensic procedures, including those used for forensic face matching, have been sufficiently validated and give consistent and reliable results in the courtroom.

7.3.2 Facial Feature Classification

The concept of assigning an individual's features to certain categories in order to identify them is not new, having its roots in late nineteenth-century physical anthropology. Head shape has long been used by anthropologists to determine the 'racial affinity' of humans both living and deceased (Ripley, 1897). Forensic face examiners have taken this concept and developed categories with which to assign different shapes of facial features (Iscan, 1993; Vanezis et al., 1996).

In principle, this sounds like an objective and systematic way of comparing faces, but in practice this is not the case. Facial features are not discrete variables that can be simply assigned to one category or another. There is continuous variability in facial feature shape and form derived from complex genetic, hormonal, and environmental interactions (Claes et al., 2014; Guyuron et al., 2009). Extraneous factors such as image quality, pose, and camera angle may also have an impact on the appearance of facial features (see Fysh, this volume).

Ritz-Timme et al. (2011) evaluated the reproducibility of facial feature categorization between different observers and by the same observer on different days. The categories were devised from a dataset of 900 adult males forming an atlas of 43 different features, with multiple categories of shape and form per feature (Ohlrogge et al., 2008). The list of features used in the atlas is given in Table 7.1. Each feature is then subdivided into discrete categories based upon shape—for example, the nose bridge breadth (frontal) may be classified as 'narrow', 'average', or 'broad'.

Observer consistency was evaluated by two pairs of observers categorizing a subset of images used to develop the atlas. Both the observers in the first pair had received training in human identification from an expert and categorized the facial features of 60 randomly chosen faces from a larger sample of 270 faces. In the second pair, only one observer was trained in face matching from photographs. This pair categorized a different subset of 25 face images. The same images were categorized again one month after the initial study.

Table 7.1 List of features from the facial feature atlas

No.	Feature	No.	Feature
01	Head shape (frontal)	23	Nasal breadth (frontal)
02	Frontal height (frontal)	24	Alar wing length (lateral)
03	Frontal breadth (frontal)	25	Alar wing height (lateral)
04	Frontal hairline (frontal)	26	Nostrils (lateral)
05	Forehead bias (lateral)	27	Philtrum height (frontal)
06	Eyebrow height (frontal)	28	Philtrum depth (frontal)
07	Eyebrow density (frontal)	29	Philtrum shape (frontal)
08	Eyebrow shape (frontal)	30	Upper lip notch (frontal)
09	Mono-brow (frontal)	31	Labial breadth (frontal)
10	Distance upper eyelid-eyebrow (frontal)	32	Orientation of mouth corner (frontal)
11	Upper eyelid (frontal)	33	Chin shape (frontal)
12	Lid axis (frontal)	34	Chin transition (frontal)
13	Lower eyelid fold (frontal)	35	Chin protrusion (lateral)
14	Nasal root (frontal)	36	Chin dimple (frontal)
15	Nose bridge length (frontal)	37	Ear height (lateral)
16	Nose bridge breadth (frontal)	38	Ear breadth (lateral)
17	Nose bridge process (frontal)	39	Ear lobe size (lateral)
18	Nose profile (lateral)	40	Ear lobe attachment (lateral)
19	Inclination of the columella (lateral)	41	Ear protrusion (frontal)
20	Nose tip shape (frontal)	42	Transition head-neck (frontal)
21	Nose tip incisure (frontal)	43	Pronunciation of cheek bones (frontal)
22	**Nose protrusion (lateral)**		

Source: Ohlrogge et al. (2008). 'Anthropological atlas of male facial features'. Frankfurt: Verlag fur Polizeiwissenschaft.

Disagreement between observers was found to occur approximately 40% of the time and disagreements from the same observer categorizing the same images on different days ranged from 19% to 30%. Interestingly, 30% of disagreements were from an observer who had received training in feature classification, meaning that even with training this observer changed their opinion on face categories in almost one third of observations.

More recently, Towler et al. (2014) evaluated observer rating consistency in the categorization of face shape, using categories similar to those shown in Figure 7.3. Inter-observer (different person) consistency in face shape classification was found to be low, with each individual face image being classified, on average, as having three different shapes by different observers. Of most concern, intra-observer agreement was also low, with only 56% of repeat classifications made by the same observers being consistent. Instruction in face shape classification had no impact on accuracy on a laboratory test of face matching (the Glasgow Face Matching Test; see Burton et al., 2010) given after the face shape categorization task.

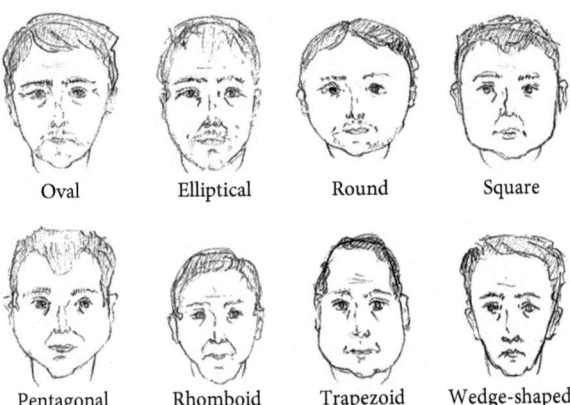

Oval Elliptical Round Square

Pentagonal Rhomboid Trapezoid Wedge-shaped

Figure 7.3 Examples of face shape diagrams similar to those used by Towler, White, & Kemp (2014). Evaluating training methods for facial image comparison: The face shape strategy does not work. *Perception*, 43, 214–218. doi:10.1068/p7676
Source: Illustrations by Jennifer Harris. Reproduced with permission.

Despite earlier studies advocating the use of facial feature categorization (Iscan, 1993; Vanezis et al., 1996), and considerable effort put into developing classification schemes (Ohlrogge et al., 2008; Ohlrogge et al., 2009), research has demonstrated poor consistency in categorizations and no observable benefit in face-matching accuracy from this approach. Facial feature classification has been largely superseded by morphological analysis and is not recommended for use by both the Facial Identification Scientific Working Group (2019) and the European Network of Forensic Science Institutes (2018).

7.3.3 Superimposition

Superimposition is the process of merging two or more face images using various image-processing techniques to create a single composite image. The intention is that the composite image will highlight any apparent similarities or differences between the two faces and assist in determining whether the images depict the same person. Superimposition, in various guises, has been widely used by forensic face-matching experts since the introduction of this type of evidence in UK courts. Vanezis and Brierley (1996) reviewed 46 forensic face-matching cases of superimposition from a two-year period. They found the technique to be useful in some cases but of limited applicability in others due to differences in pose of the subjects and angle of the camera. This study only reviewed past cases and therefore the ground truth of the images used are unknown, which greatly limits the scientific validity of the conclusion. The paper also overlooked a major factor—the impact of superimposition on face-matching decisions made by untrained 'lay' observers, such as a jury.

Superimposition has not only been used by forensic experts but also criminals attempting to commit identity fraud. Face morphing is a risk for identification verification, such as at a border, where criminals will attempt to create morphed face images in passports that bear sufficient resemblance to multiple individuals, thwarting human passport reviewers and automated facial recognition systems. The passport can then be used illegally by two or more different individuals. Robertson et al. (2017) found that, when lay participants were presented with morphed face images, they commonly accepted that the image was of a single face, failing to detect the morph. Even when participants were told that some images were morphs, some still accepted them. The fact that observers can be so easily deceived into thinking a morph of two different faces depicts a single individual is a major concern for forensic use. In a forensic face-matching case, it is likely that the defendant will share some degree of similarity with the offender to end up being arrested for the crime, even if they did not actually commit it. The fact that morphs of two difference faces can appear so convincing is a significant risk when presenting superimposition evidence to a jury, with its potential to mislead an observer into believing two different faces are the same.

The courts have raised issues in the past as to the reliability of the technique (*R v Clarke*, 1995) but not enough to prevent its use in future cases. Strathie et al. (2012) evaluated the impact of presenting a single image formed from two faces on matching accuracy. The technique impaired observer accuracy and introduced a biasing effect, where observers were more likely to respond that a superimposed image was the same individual when the two face halves were from different individuals. A biasing effect and accuracy impairment was also observed by Strathie and McNeill (2016) when the superimposition was performed using 'facial wipes' where a video clip gradually alternates from one face to another, a technique also used by forensic face examiners.

In light of the biasing effect of superimposition and the significant risk this poses in the court room, the European Network of Forensic Science Institutes (2018) recommends the technique not be used in forensic face matching. Confusingly, the Facial Identification Scientific Working Group (2019) acknowledges the limitations of superimposition, including the potential biasing effect, but has not gone as far as stating that it should not be used. Instead, the recommendation is that superimposition should be used only in conjunction with morphological analysis, as a visual aid. But, given that multiple studies have demonstrated the false positive bias caused by superimposition, this recommendation appears counter to the findings of scientific research.

7.3.4 Morphological Analysis

The final comparison procedure used by forensic face-matching experts is morphological analysis, whereby the individual features of the face are systematically analysed and compared. Examiners focus on individual features, such as the nose or ears, and compare the shape and form of these features between face images. If there is sufficient detail, facial feature components are further broken down into sub-components

Table 7.2 Characteristic descriptors of the nose from the facial image comparison feature list for morphological analysis

9 - Nose	
Component Characteristics	**Characteristic Descriptors**
9.1 Nasal outline (profile and front view)	• Overall shape • Length and/or width relative to rest of face • Prominence • Symmetry
9.2 Nasal root (bridge)	• Front view: width, length, shape, depth • Profile view: length, depth, angle
9.3 Nasal body	• Front view: width, length, shape, angle • Profile view: length, angle, contour
9.4 Nasal tip	• Shape (in front and profile view) • Angle (e.g., up, down) • Symmetry
9.5 Nasal base	• Width • Height • Deviation to the right or left
9.6 Nasal base: alae (wings of nose)	• Thickness • Symmetry • Shape
9.7 Nasal base: nostrils (nasal openings)	• Shape and size of opening • Symmetry • Hair
9.8 Nasal base: columella (soft tissue between nostrils)	• Width and length • Relative position • Symmetry

Source: Facial Identification Scientific Working Group (2018). Facial image comparison feature list for morphological analysis. Available at: https://fiswg.org/FISWG_Morph_Analysis_Feature_List_v2.0_20180911.pdf (accessed 3 May 2020).

(also known as 'characteristics descriptors'), such as the shape of the nostrils or the size and adherence of the ear lobes. Fine feature detail, such as wrinkles or facial marks, will also be described and compared. Often a set list of features will be used by the examiner as an aide memoire, such as the *Standard Guide for Facial Image Comparison Feature List for Morphological Analysis E3149–18*, published by the American Society for Testing and Materials (ASTM) in 2018 and based on the earlier feature list of the Facial Identification Scientific Working Group (2018). Table 7.2 gives an example of the characteristic descriptors of the nose from the Facial Identification Scientific Working Group checklist, with a supporting diagram from the document shown in Figure 7.4.

Although morphological analysis is the recommended method for forensic face matching, there has been limited published research validating its use. Towler et al. (2017) found that, when using a simplified list of facial features similar to those given in the ASTM standard guide, untrained students were more accurate at matching the same face but the list gave no discernible benefit for non-matching faces. When trained face examiners were tested using the same list of features, they not only outperformed

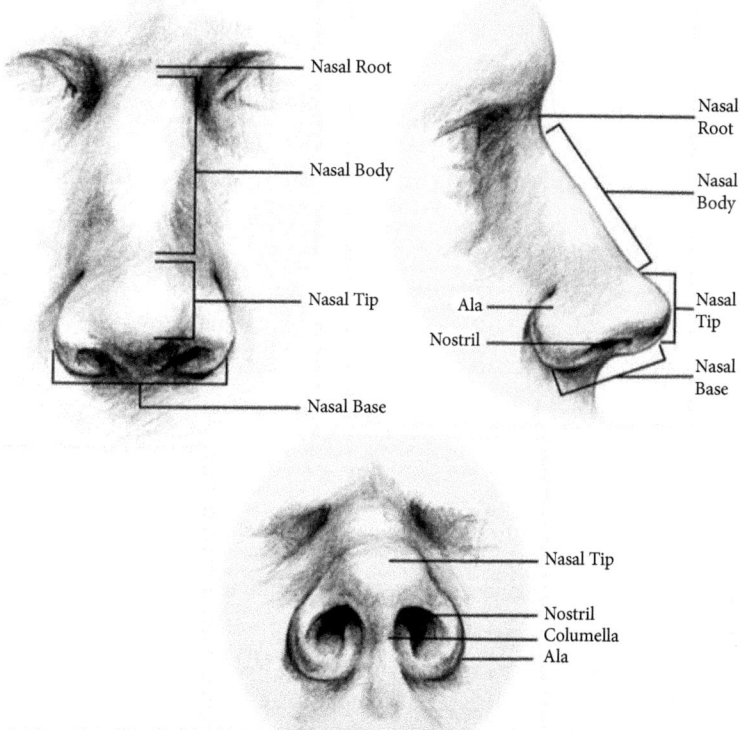

Nasal Root

Nasal Body

Nasal Tip

Nasal Base

Nasal Root

Nasal Body

Ala

Nostril

Nasal Tip

Nasal Base

Nasal Tip

Nostril
Columella
Ala

Figure 7.4 Diagram of the characteristic descriptors of the nose from the facial image comparison feature list for morphological analysis (European Network of Forensic Science Institutes (2018). ENFSI Best practice manual for facial image comparison (vol. 1). Available at: http://enfsi.eu/wp-content/uploads/2017/06/ENFSI-BPM-DI-01.pdf (accessed 28 April 2020). Source: Illustrations by Jane Wankmiller. Reproduced with permission.

untrained participants but their facial feature similarity ratings were more diagnostic of identity than those of novices. This finding implies that examiners with training and experience in morphological analysis have greater understanding of the discriminatory power of different facial features and are more proficient in the procedure. For examiners, the ears and scars and marks were found to be the most diagnostic facial features used, which reinforces anecdotal evidence from examiners that the ears are the most useful features for comparison (Towler et al., 2017) and the fact that scars and facial marks can distinguish between identical twins (Biswas et al., 2011).

A study of forensic facial examiners undertaking quick-decision face-matching tasks showed that, although more accurate than control participants at the group level, the examiners suffered greater impairment to accuracy when the task was constrained to two seconds' duration (White, Phillips, et al., 2015). These findings, and those of Towler et al. (2017), indicate that facial examiners trained in morphological analysis are using a qualitatively different approach to matching faces that is based more on individual feature detail than the face as a whole.

The initial findings of Towler et al. (2017) are promising signs that morphological analysis can give accurate forensic face-matching results when conducted by trained face examiners. But the findings of this one study alone are insufficient to justify the use of a procedure in court. Only seven forensic face examiners from the same agency were tested, analysing images captured in similar conditions. It is currently unknown how applicable morphological analysis is to matching different sources of imagery, such as low-quality CCTV footage to high-quality police mugshots, a common scenario in forensic casework. Examiners must conduct validation studies of their procedures using the types of images they will encounter in casework. Validation studies should investigate the accuracy, precision, range, repeatability, reproducibility, and robustness of the procedure to ensure it meets the requirements of its intended use (European Network of Forensic Science Institutes, 2018).

7.4 Example of a Forensic Morphological Analysis

When used in forensic face-matching casework, a full morphological analysis may take a face examiner hours or even days depending upon the complexity of the material. To give a clearer understanding of how morphological analysis is used in practice, this section will outline an example case based on current practitioner guidance (European Network of Forensic Science Institutes, 2018; Facial Identification Scientific Working Group, 2019) and the author's own experiences working as a forensic face examiner in the UK for seven years from 2011 to 2018.

7.4.1 Case Scenario

Investigators have requested a forensic face examiner team to compare two images and provide an evidential report on whether the images depict the same or different persons. In this simulated case, investigators have recovered an image from social media linked to a potential suspect via intelligence; this is the questioned image. Investigators have access to a known image of the offender from an identity document database; this is the reference image. The investigation team know that there are at least two years' time difference between the questioned and reference images.

7.4.2 Managing Contextual Information

When a forensic face examiner receives a request from an investigator, the request often contains contextual information that is irrelevant to the morphological analysis but could cognitively bias the outcome. Examples of such information include if the suspect has a previous criminal record or other forensic evidence linking them to the offence. Cognitive bias caused by extraneous contextual information is a phenomenon that has been repeatedly demonstrated across a range of forensic disciplines, including fingerprint comparison (Dror et al., 2006) and the interpretation of DNA profiles (Dror & Hampikian, 2011). It is an issue that all forensic examiners should be aware of and take steps to mitigate. One way to mitigate this risk is to give examiners the bare minimum of information required to conduct their analyses and, if further details are needed, to reveal them as required by sequential unmasking (Krane et al., 2008). Forensic face-matching departments should implement a procedure for context management, whereby an individual who will not undertake the examination strips a case of all but the most essential contextual information before it is passed to the examiner (Found & Ganas, 2013). In the current example, such essential information would be the two-year time difference between the questioned image and the reference image.

During the management of contextual information, the propositions for evaluation may also be established. These are the different scenarios against which the examiner must assess the evidential strength of their observations. The propositions must be mutually exclusive (i.e., only one can be true). The aim of having at least two propositions to evaluate the evidence is to help ensure that the findings are balanced and not biased towards one particular outcome (European Network of Forensic Science Institutes, 2015). In this case example, two such propositions may be:

Proposition A: The questioned image and reference image depict the same adult male.

Proposition B: The questioned image and reference image depict different adult males.

7.4.3 Analysis

It is currently recommended that the morphological analysis of faces be conducted within an ACE-V framework (European Network of Forensic Science Institutes, 2018). ACE-V is a linear workflow of four different phases, comprising analysis, comparison, evaluation and verification. ACE-V is used across many forensic pattern matching disciplines to provide robustness and transparency in comparison procedures. In the analysis phase, the examiner analyses the questioned image (Figure 7.5) in isolation of the reference image. The rationale for this procedure is to reduce the risk of confirmation bias, whereby observation of the target or reference image at the same time as the questioned image may alter the examiner's observations (Dror et al., 2011). Throughout the ACE-V process, the examiner will keep thorough contemporaneous notes, including the parameters of the image, any processing steps applied to the image (e.g., resizing, rotating, or brightness adjustments), and their observations of facial feature detail.

During the analysis phase, the examiner will note down the parameters of the image file, such as the file type and resolution of the image, and any conditions in the image that will have an impact on the comparison phase. Examples of such conditions may arise from the file itself (e.g., a low-resolution or heavily compressed image), the subject in the image

Figure 7.5 Questioned image.

(e.g., pose and facial expression), the image capture device (e.g., exposure settings and focal distance), and the environment in which the image was taken (e.g., light source and intensity). The examiner should be competent in understanding how these complex and interacting conditions may impact on the observations made in the comparison phase.

The examiner may also comment on the level of facial detail present in the questioned image using a standardized facial feature checklist (e.g., ASTM, 2018). Facial feature observations include which features are visible and how well resolved they are. For instance, such observations should capture whether only the basic outline of the feature can be discerned, or whether sub-components of the feature are visible. The examiner will also note the presence of fine feature detail, such as scars or facial marks.

In this example, the questioned image (Figure 7.5) is fairly low resolution, causing a loss of facial feature detail, and captured with a non-neutral expression. The examiner will make a note of these factors because they may have an impact upon the subsequent comparison.

7.4.4 Comparison

Once the examiner has completed the analysis of the questioned image, they can then view the reference or target image. An analysis of the reference image may be conducted, making note of the conditions of the image and the visibility of features. In this example, the subject in the reference image is too close to the camera, causing perspective distortion and the apparent enlargement of medial facial features, such as the nose (see Figure 7.6). This type of distortion has been shown to impair face-matching

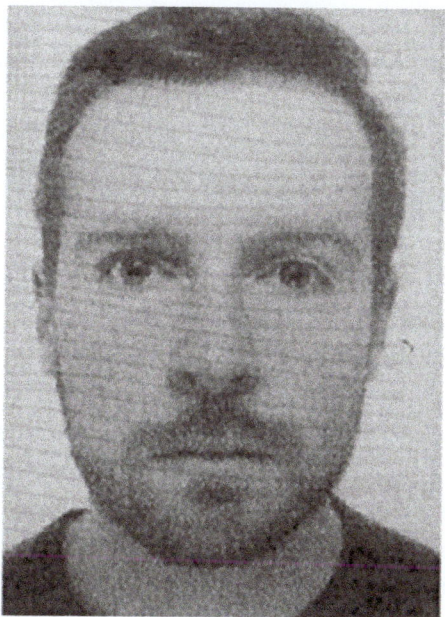

Figure 7.6 Reference image.

accuracy (Noyes & Jenkins, 2017) and is a factor the examiner must consider when comparing facial feature detail.

The examiner will then systematically compare the questioned and reference images on a feature-by-feature basis, noting any apparent similarities or differences in facial feature detail. The examiner may annotate their observations onto the images. In the

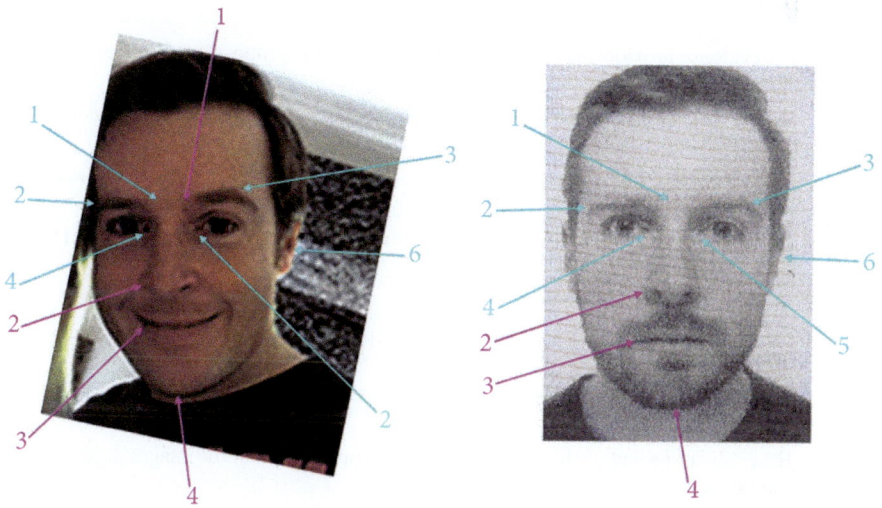

Figure 7.7 Side-by-side comparison of the questioned image and reference image, annotated with similarities (blue arrows) and differences (pink arrows).

example in Figure 7.7, similarities are annotated in blue, such as the shape and curve of the eyebrows (blue arrows 2 and 3), and differences are annotated in pink. The examiner should also note possible explanations for their observations based on the image conditions noted in the analysis phase. For example, the difference in the visibility of a mark by the left eyebrow may be caused by the mark being a transient feature (pink arrow 1), and the difference in the size of the chin may be attributable to perspective distortion in the reference image (pink arrow 4).

7.4.5 Evaluation

During the evaluation phase, the examiner will assess the strength of their observations under the competing propositions established at the start of the examination. This will then be presented as a level of support on a conclusion scale, which represents the strength of the evidence rather than a measure of the examiner's confidence. There is currently no standardized conclusion scale for evidence evaluation in forensic face matching. Table 7.3 shows an example conclusion scale that could be used by forensic face-matching examiners.

Evidence evaluation and conclusion scales are a contested topic across forensic science, with many advocating a logical approach to evaluation based on Bayes theorem over more traditional frequentist approaches or categorical identity judgements (e.g., match or non-match) (Jackson et al., 2006; Meuwly et al., 2015; Redmayne et al., 2011). Such a discussion is beyond the scope of this chapter. Regardless of the conclusion scale

Table 7.3 Example conclusion scale for face-matching examinations

Level	Description
+4	The evidence provides extremely strong support for the proposition that the images depict the same adult male.
+3	The evidence provides strong support for the proposition that the images depict the same adult male.
+2	The evidence provides moderate support for the proposition that the images depict the same adult male.
+1	The evidence provides limited support for the proposition that the images depict the same adult male.
0	The evidence does not support either proposition/The evidence is inconclusive.
−1	The evidence provides limited support for the proposition that the images depict different adult males.
−2	The evidence provides moderate support for the proposition that the images depict different adult males.
−3	The evidence provides strong support for the proposition that the images depict different adult males.
−4	The evidence provides extremely support for the proposition that the images depict different adult males.

and evaluation model in use, the face examiner should consider as a minimum the types of features compared, the level of detail observed for those features, and the impact of conditions in the images on their observations (European Network of Forensic Science Institutes, 2018).

There is no database of facial features available to allow a quantitative, statistical evaluation of face-matching evidence. Evaluations are therefore based on the subjective knowledge and experience of the examiner. Subjective opinions are accepted by UK courts for forensic face matching but juries are advised to treat them with caution. Face examiners must make clear when giving evidence that there is no empirical basis for their conclusion (*R v Atkins & another*, 2009).

7.4.6 Verification

Because morphological analysis is a subjective process and open to interpretation, it is recommended that all examinations are independently verified by another examiner (Facial Identification Scientific Working Group, 2019). During the verification, another face examiner will repeat all or part of the ACE-V process. If the two examiners' findings agree, the conclusion can be given to the investigator. If the examiners do not agree, there will need to be some form of resolution procedure, such as review by a third examiner. Verification may be conducted blind, whereby the second examiner does not know the first examiner's findings, or non-blind whereby the findings are known. To reduce the risk of biasing the second examiner, blind verification is the preferred approach (European Network of Forensic Science Institutes, 2018).

7.5 Discussion

Despite being readily accepted by the courts, the procedures used by forensic face-matching experts have been subject to extensive and justified criticism in the scientific literature and, previously, forensic face examiners made little effort to validate face-matching procedures. In more recent years, international practitioner-led working groups have begun to produce standards, guidelines, and best practice documents to address these criticisms and bring greater accountability and rigour to the field.[4,5,6] In the UK specifically, the Forensic Science Regulator's Codes of Practice and Conduct require forensic examiners to demonstrate that they are both competent as experts to carry out a certain procedure and that the procedure has been validated to the extent

[4] http://www.fiswg.org (accessed 23 April 2020).
[5] http://enfsi.eu/about-enfsi/structure/working-groups/digital-imaging (accessed 23 April 2020).
[6] https://www.nist.gov/topics/organization-scientific-area-committees-forensic-science/facial-identification-subcommittee (accessed 23 April 2020).

that any limitations are known (Forensic Science Regulator, 2016a). The Regulator's Codes cover a range of forensic disciplines, which include forensic face matching. The combination of existing legislative requirements, the work of practitioner working groups, the Forensic Regulator's Codes and empirical research will help to ensure that forensic face-matching procedures are of a sufficiently reliable standard to be used as expert evidence in a court of law, where lifechanging decisions may be made on the basis of that evidence.

There is a consensus among much of the forensic face-examiner community that morphological analysis is the recommended procedure for face matching, with a standardized list of features now available (ASTM, 2018). This move towards standardization is a promising step but further work is required to validate morphological analysis as a reliable procedure across various image types, and to establish known error rates. To establish the error rates of subjective feature comparison methods, such as morphological analysis, the PCAST report advocates 'black-box' testing of examiners undertaking many test comparisons (PCAST, 2016). From these repeated tests, the error rates of a procedure can be calculated, and the validity and reliability of the method established. In 2018, the first large-scale study of forensic face-examiner accuracy was published, testing 57 examiners from five continents. The aim of the study was to be the first to compare the accuracy of trained face examiners against untrained observers and automated facial recognition algorithms on a challenging face-matching task (Phillips et al., 2018). The face examiners were requested to complete the task using their forensic face-matching procedures with no time limit.

As a group. the forensic face examiners were found to outperform both untrained 'lay' participants and fingerprint examiners. However, there was considerable overlap in the range of accuracy for individual participants in all groups, including face examiners and untrained participants. Several face examiners even performed more poorly than the average score of the untrained group. This is highly alarming. That there could be such a range in accuracy for different face examiners using forensic procedures has major ramifications for the use of face-matching evidence in court. The forensic face-matching community must take urgent action to address and produce validated procedures that give consistent results when used by different trained examiners.

Complying with the regulatory requirements of forensic accreditation should eventually lead to validated procedures that can be safely used to provide evidence in the courtroom, but forensic face matching is on a long journey to get there. Greater collaboration between the practitioner and relevant scientific communities will help to make the journey shorter. Cognitive scientists and psychologists have extensive experience in human performance testing for perceptual tasks, and much of this is transferable to the testing and validation of forensic face-matching procedures (for particularly useful examples, see Edmond et al., 2017; Martire & Kemp, 2016). By working together, the forensic face-matching community and researchers can develop suitable tests to validate procedures, quantify error rates, and establish the limitations of forensic face matching. This will lead to safe and reliable forensic evidence in the courtroom, and prevent potential miscarriages of justice that can have catastrophic effects on people's lives.

References

ASTM (American Society for Testing and Materials) (2018). *Standard guide for facial image comparison feature list for morphological analysis E3149-18*. Available at: https://www.astm.org/Standards/E3149.htm (accessed 22 April 2020).

Ballantyne, M., Boyer, R. S., & Hines, L. (1996). Woody Bledsoe—His life and legacy. *AI Magazine, 17*, 7–20. Available at: https://www.aaai.org/ojs/index.php/aimagazine/article/viewFile/1207/1108 (accessed 28 April 2020).

Bate, S., Frowd, C., Bennetts, R., Hasshim, N., Murray, E., Bobak, A. K., et al. (2018). *Applied screening tests for the detection of superior face recognition* (June). Available at: https://doi.org/10.1186/s41235-018-0116-5 (accessed 28 April 2020).

Bate, S. & Tree, J. J. (2017). The definition and diagnosis of developmental prosopagnosia. *Quarterly Journal of Experimental Psychology, 70*, 193–200. doi:10.1080/17470218.2016.1195414

Bertillon, A. (1893). *Identification anthropométrique*. Available at: https://archive.org/details/identificationan00bert/page/n7 (accessed 28 April 2020).

Bindemann, M., Attard, J., & Johnston, R. A. (2014). Perceived ability and actual recognition accuracy for unfamiliar and famous faces. *Cogent Psychology, 1*, 986903. doi:10.1080/23311908.2014.986903 OK

Biswas, S., Bowyer, K. W., & Flynn, P. J. (2011). A study of face recognition of identical twins by humans. *2011 IEEE International Workshop on Information Forensics and Security*, (November). doi:10.1109/WIFS.2011.6123126

Bobak, A. K., Dowsett, A. J., & Bate, S. (2016). Solving the border control problem: Evidence of enhanced face matching in individuals with extraordinary face recognition skills. *PLoS ONE, 11*(2), e0148148. doi:10.1371/journal.pone.0148148

Bobak, A. K., Pampoulov, P., & Bate, S. (2016). Detecting superior face recognition skills in a large sample of young British adults. *Frontiers in Psychology, 7*, 1–11. doi:10.3389/fpsyg.2016.01378

Bromby, M. (2006). CCTV and expert evidence: Addressing the reliability of new sciences. *Archbold News, 9*, 6–9. Available at: https://papers.ssrn.com/sol3/papers.cfm?abstract_id=1551791 (accessed 28 April 2020).

Bromby, M. & Plews, S. (2003). Facing up to change? *E-Law Review, 13*. Available at: http://ssrn.com/abstract=1561606 (accessed 28 April 2020).

Burton, A. M., White, D., & McNeill, A. (2010). The Glasgow Face Matching Test. *Behavior Research Methods, 42*, 286–291. doi:10.3758/BRM.42.1.286

Campbell-Tiech, A. (2005). Stockwell revisited: The unhappy state of facial mapping. *Archbold News, 6*, 4–6.

Claes, P., Liberton, D. K., Daniels, K., Rosana, K. M., Quillen, E. E., Pearson, L. N., et al. (2014). Modeling 3D facial shape from DNA. *PLoS Genetics, 10*(3), e1004224. doi:10.1371/journal.pgen.1004224

Committee on Identifying the Needs of the Forensic Sciences Community, National Research Council (2009). *Strengthening forensic science in the United States: A path forward*. Washington: National Academies Press. Available at: https://www.ncjrs.gov/pdffiles1/nij/grants/228091.pdf (accessed 28 April 2020).

Criminal Practice Directions (2015). London, Ministry of Justice. Available at: https://www.justice.gov.uk/courts/procedure-rules/criminal/docs/2015/crim-practice-directions-V-evidence-2015.pdf (accessed 28 April 2020).

Criminal Procedure Rules (2015). London, Ministry of Justice. Available at: https://www.justice.gov. uk/courts/procedure-rules/criminal/docs/2015/crim-proc-rules-2015-part-19.pdf (accessed 28 April 2020).

Davis, J. P., Lander, K., Evans, R., & Jansari, A. (2016). Investigating predictors of superior face recognition ability in police super-recognisers. *Applied Cognitive Psychology, 30*, 827–840. doi:10.1002/acp.3260

Devlin, L. P. (1976). *Report to the Secretary of State for the Home Department of the Departmental Committee on Evidence of Identification in Criminal Cases.* Available at: https://assets.publishing. service.gov.uk/government/uploads/system/uploads/attachment_data/file/228523/0338.pdf (accessed 28 April 2020).

Dror, I. E., Champod, C., Langenburg, G., Charlton, D., Hunt, H., & Rosenthal, R. (2011). Cognitive issues in fingerprint analysis: Inter- and intra-expert consistency and the effect of a 'target' comparison. *Forensic Science International, 208*, 10–17. doi:10.1016/j.forsciint.2010.10.013

Dror, I. E., Charlton, D., & Péron, A. E. (2006). Contextual information renders experts vulnerable to making erroneous identifications. *Forensic Science International, 156*, 74–78. doi:10.1016/j.forsciint.2005.10.017

Dror, I. E. & Hampikian, G. (2011). Subjectivity and bias in forensic DNA mixture interpretation. *Science and Justice, 51*, 204–208. doi:10.1016/j.scijus.2011.08.004

Edmond, G., Biber, K., Kemp, R., & Porter, G. (2009). Law's looking glass: Expert identification evidence derived from photographic and video images. *Current Issues in Criminal Justice, 20*, 337–377. doi:10.1080/10345329.2009.12035817

Edmond, G., Towler, A., Growns, B., Ribeiro, G., Found, B., White, D., et al. (2017). Thinking forensics: Cognitive science for forensic practitioners. *Science and Justice, 57*, 144–154. doi:10.1016/j.scijus.2016.11.005

Edmond, G. & Wortley, N. (2016). Interpreting image evidence: Facial mapping, police familiars and super recognisers in England and Australia. *Journal of International and Comparative Law, 3*, 473–522.

European Network of Forensic Science Institutes (2015). *ENFSI guideline for evaluative reporting in forensic science: Strengthening the evaluation of forensic results across Europe.* Available at: http://enfsi.eu/wp-content/uploads/2016/09/m1_guideline.pdf (accessed 28 April 2020).

European Network of Forensic Science Institutes (2018). *ENFSI best practice manual for facial image comparison*, vol. 1. Available at: http://enfsi.eu/wp-content/uploads/2017/06/ENFSI-BPM-DI-01.pdf (accessed 28 April 2020).

Facial Identification Scientific Working Group (2018). *Facial image comparison feature list for morphological analysis.* Available at: https://fiswg.org/FISWG_Morph_Analysis_Feature_List_v2.0_20180911.pdf (accessed 3 May 2020).

Facial Identification Scientific Working Group (2019). *Facial comparison overview and methodology guidelines.* Available at: https://fiswg.org/fiswg_facial_comparison_overview_and_methodology_guidelines_V1.0_20191025.pdf (accessed 3 May 2020).

Forensic Science Regulator (2013). *Newsletter 22.* Available at: https://assets.publishing.service.gov. uk/government/uploads/system/uploads/attachment_data/file/268605/FSR_22_1_.pdf (accessed 28 April 2020).

Forensic Science Regulator (2016a). *Codes of Practice and Conduct for forensic science providers and practitioners*, 3. Available at: https://assets.publishing.service.gov.uk/government/uploads/system/uploads/attachment_data/file/499850/2016_2_11_-_The_Codes_of_Practice_and_Conduct_-_Issue_3.pdf (accessed 28 April 2020).

Forensic Science Regulator (2016b). *Forensic image comparison and interpretation evidence: Guidance for prosecutors and investigators*, 2. Available at: https://assets.publishing.service.gov.uk/government/uploads/system/uploads/attachment_data/file/511168/Image_Comparison_and_Interpretation_Guidance_Issue_2.pdf (accessed 28 April 2020).

Forensic Science Regulator (2018). *Annual Report November 2016–November 2017.* Available at: https://assets.publishing.service.gov.uk/government/uploads/system/uploads/attachment_data/file/674761/FSRAnnual_Report_2017_v1_01.pdf (accessed 28 April 2020).

Found, B. & Ganas, J. (2013). The management of domain irrelevant context information in forensic handwriting examination casework. *Science and Justice, 53*, 154–158. doi:10.1016/j.scijus.2012.10.004

Fysh, M. C. & Bindemann, M. (2018). The Kent Face Matching Test. *British Journal of Psychology, 109*, 219–231. doi:10.1111/bjop.12260

Guyuron, B., Rowe, D. J., Weinfeld, A. B., Eshraghi, Y., Fathi, A., & Iamphongsai, S. (2009). Factors contributing to the facial aging of identical twins. *Plastic and Reconstructive Surgery, 123*, 1321–1331. doi:10.1097/PRS.0b013e31819c4d42

Home Office (2017). *Police and Criminal Evidence Act 1984, Code D revised*. Available at: https://assets.publishing.service.gov.uk/government/uploads/system/uploads/attachment_data/file/592562/pace-code-d-2017.pdf (accessed 28 April 2020).

Houlton, T. M. R. & Steyn, M. (2018). Finding Makhubu: A morphological forensic facial comparison. *Forensic Science International, 285*, (February), 13–20. doi.org/10.1016/j.forsciint.2018.01.022

Iscan, M. Y. (1993). Introduction to techniques for photographic comparison: Potential and problems. In M. Y. Iscan & R. P. Helmer (eds), *Forensic analysis of the skull: Craniofacial analysis, reconstruction, and identification* (pp. 57–70). New York: Wiley-Liss.

Jackson, G., Jones, S., Booth, G., Champod, C., & Evett, I. W. (2006). The nature of forensic science opinion—a possible framework to guide thinking and practice in investigation and in court proceedings. *Science & Justice, 46*, 33–44. doi:10.1016/S1355-0306(06)71565-9

Kleinberg, K. F., Vanezis, P., & Burton, A. M. (2007). Failure of anthropometry as a facial identification technique using high-quality photographs. *Journal of Forensic Sciences, 52*, 779–783. doi:10.1111/j.1556-4029.2007.00458.x

Kramer, R. S. S., Mohamed, S., & Hardy, S. C. (2019). Unfamiliar face matching with driving licence and passport photographs. *Perception, 48*, 175–184. doi:10.1177/0301006619826495

Krane, D. E., Ford, S., Gilder, J. R., Inman, K., Jamieson, A., Koppl, R., et al. (2008). Sequential unmasking: A means of minimizing observer effects in forensic DNA interpretation. *Journal of Forensic Sciences, 53*, 1006–1007. doi:10.1111/j.1556-4029.2008.00787.x

Law Commission (2011). *The admissibility of expert evidence in criminal proceedings in England and Wales: A new approach to the determination of evidentiary reliability*. Available at: http://www.lawcom.gov.uk/app/uploads/2015/03/cp190_Expert_Evidence_Consultation.pdf (accessed 28 April 2020).

Mallett, X. & Evison, M. P. (2013). Forensic facial comparison: Issues of admissibility in the development of novel analytical technique. *Journal of Forensic Sciences, 58*, 859–865. doi:10.1111/1556-4029.12127

Mardia, K. V., Coombes, A., Kirkbride, J., Linney, A., & Bowie, J. L. (1996). On statistical problems with face identification from photographs. *Journal of Applied Statistics, 23*, 655–676. doi:10.1080/02664769624008

Martire, K. A. & Kemp, R. I. (2016). Considerations when designing human performance tests in the forensic sciences. *Australian Journal of Forensic Sciences, 50*, 166–182. doi:10.1080/00450618.2016.1229815

McNeill, A., Suchomska, M., & Strathie, A. (2015). Expert facial comparison evidence: Science versus pseudoscience. *Psychology and Law, 5*, 127–140. doi:10.17759/psylaw.2015050411

Meuwly, D., Ramos, D., & Haraksim, R. (2015). A guideline for the validation of likelihood ratio methods used for forensic evidence evaluation. *Forensic Science International, 276*, 142–153. doi:10.1016/j.forsciint.2016.03.048

Moreton, R. & Morley, J. (2011). Investigation into the use of photoanthropometry in facial image comparison. *Forensic Science International, 212*, 231–237. doi:10.1016/j.forsciint.2011.06.023

Moreton, R., Pike, G., & Havard, C. (2019). A task- and role-based perspective on super-recognizers: Commentary on 'Super-recognizers: From the laboratory to the world and back again'. *British Journal of Psychology, 110*, 486–488. doi:10.1111/bjop.12394

National Policing Improvement Agency (2009). *Facial identification guidance*. Available at: http://library.college.police.uk/docs/acpo/facial-identification-guidance-2009.pdf (accessed 28 April 2020).

National Research Council, Committee on Identifying the Needs of the Forensic Sciences Community (2009). *Strengthening forensic science in the United States: A path forward*. Washington: National Academies Press. Available at: https://www.ncjrs.gov/pdffiles1/nij/grants/228091.pdf (accessed 28 April 2020).

Norell, K., Läthén, K. B., Bergström, P., Rice, A., Natu, V., & O'Toole, A. (2015). The effect of image quality and forensic expertise in facial image comparisons. *Journal of Forensic Sciences, 60*, 331–340. doi:10.1111/1556-4029.12660

Noyes, E. & Jenkins, R. (2017). Camera-to-subject distance affects face configuration and perceived identity. *Cognition, 165*, 97–104. doi:10.1016/j.cognition.2017.05.012

Noyes, E., Phillips, P. J., & O'Toole, A. J. (2017). What is a super-recogniser? In M. Bindemann & A. M. Megreya (eds), *Face processing: Systems, disorders and cultural difficulties* (pp. 173–201). New York: Nova Science Publishers.

Ohlrogge, S., Arent, T., Huckenbeck, W., Gabriel, P., & Ritz-Timme, S. (2009). *Anthropological atlas of female facial features*. Frankfurt: Verlag für Polizeiwissenschaft.

Ohlrogge, S., Nohrden, D., Schmitt, R., Drabik, A., Gabriel, P., & Ritz-Timme, S. (2008). *Anthropological atlas of male facial features*. Frankfurt: Verlag für Polizeiwissenschaft.

Phillips, P. J., Yates, A. N., Hu, Y., Hahn, C. A., Noyes, E., Jackson, K., et al. (2018). Face recognition accuracy of forensic examiners, superrecognizers, and face recognition algorithms. *Proceedings of the National Academy of Sciences, 115*, 6171–6176. doi:10.1073/pnas.1721355115

Prabhakar, S., Jain, A., & Ross, A. (2004). An introduction to biometric recognition. *IEEE Transactions on Circuits and Systems for Video Technology, 14*, 4–20. doi:10.1109/TCSVT.2003.818349

PCAST (President's Council of Advisors on Science and Technology) (2016). *Forensic science in criminal courts: Ensuring scientific validity of feature-comparison Methods*. (September), 1–174. Available at: https://obamawhitehouse.archives.gov/sites/default/files/microsites/ostp/PCAST/pcast_forensic_science_report_final.pdf (accessed 28 April 2020).

Ramon, M., Bobak, A. K., & White, D. (2019a). Super-recognizers: From the lab to the world and back again. *British Journal of Psychology, 110*, 461–479. doi:10.1111/bjop.12368

Ramon, M., Bobak, A. K., & White, D. (2019b). Towards a 'manifesto' for super-recognizer research. *British Journal of Psychology, 110*, 495–498. doi:10.1111/bjop.12411

Redmayne, M., Roberts, P., Aitken, C., & Jackson, G. (2011). Forensic science evidence in question. *Criminal Law Review, 5*, 347–356.

Ripley, W. Z. (1897). The shape of the head as a racial trait. *Appletons' Popular Science Monthly, 50*, 577–594.

Ritz-Timme, S., Gabriel, P., Obertová, Z., Boguslawski, M., Mayer, F., Drabik, A., et al. (2011). A new atlas for the evaluation of facial features: Advantages, limits, and applicability. *International Journal of Legal Medicine, 125*, 301–306. doi:10.1007/s00414-010-0446-4

Robertson, D. J., Kramer, R. S. S., & Burton, A. M. (2017). Fraudulent ID using face morphs: Experiments on human and automatic recognition. *PLoS ONE, 12*(3), e0173319. doi:10.1371/journal.pone.0173319

Russell, R., Duchaine, B., & Nakayama, K. (2009). Super-recognizers: People with extraordinary face recognition ability. *Psychonomic Bulletin & Review, 16*, 252–257. doi:10.3758/PBR.16.2.252

Saks, M. J., Albright, T., Bohan, T. L., Bierer, B. E., Bowers, C. M., Bush, M. A., et al. (2016). Forensic bitemark identification: Weak foundations, exaggerated claims. *Journal of Law and the Biosciences, 3*, 538–575. doi:10.1093/jlb/lsw045

Strathie, A. & McNeill, A. (2016). Facial wipes don't wash: Facial image comparison by video superimposition reduces the accuracy of face matching decisions. *Applied Cognitive Psychology, 30*, 504–513. doi:10.1002/acp.3218

Strathie, A., McNeill, A., & White, D. (2012). In the dock: Chimeric image composites reduce identification accuracy. *Applied Cognitive Psychology, 26*, 140–148. doi:10.1002/acp.1806

Sulner, A. (2017). Critical issues affecting the reliability and admissibility of handwriting identification opinion evidence—How they have been addressed (or not) since the 2009 NAS report, and how they should be addressed going forward: A document examiner tells all. *48 Seton Hall L.R. 631* (2018). Available at SSRN: doi.org/10.2139/ssrn.3062250

Towler, A., Kemp, R. I., Burton, A. M., Dunn, J. D., Wayne, T., Moreton, R., et al., (2019). Do professional facial image comparison training courses work? *PLoS ONE, 14*(2), e0211037. doi:10.1371/journal.pone.0211037

Towler, A., White, D., & Kemp, R. I. (2014). Evaluating training methods for facial image comparison: The face shape strategy does not work. *Perception, 43,* 214–218. doi:10.1068/p7676

Towler, A., White, D., & Kemp, R. I. (2017). Evaluating the feature comparison strategy for forensic face identification. *Journal of Experimental Psychology: Applied, 23,* 47–58. doi:10.1037/xap0000108

Vanezis, P. & Brierley, C. (1996). Facial image comparison of crime suspects using video superimposition. *Science & Justice, 36,* 27–34. doi:10.1016/s1355-0306(96)72551-0

Vanezis, P., Lu, D., Cockburn, J., Gonzalez, A., McCombe, G., Trujillo, O., & Vanezis, M. (1996). Morphological classification of facial features in adult Caucasian males based on an assessment of photographs of 50 subjects. *Journal of Forensic Sciences, 41,* 786–791. Available at: http://www.ncbi.nlm.nih.gov/pubmed/8789838 (accessed 28 April 2020).

White, D., Dunn, J. D., Schmid, A. C., & Kemp, R. I. (2015). Error rates in users of automatic face recognition software. *PLoS ONE, 10*(10), e0139827. doi:10.1371/journal.pone.0139827

White, D., Phillips, P. J., Hahn, C. A., Hill, M., & O'Toole, A. J. (2015). Perceptual expertise in forensic facial image comparison. *Proceedings of the Royal Society B: Biological Sciences, 282*(1814), 20151292. doi:10.1098/rspb.2015.1292

Wilkinson, C. & Evans, R. (2009). Are facial image analysis experts any better than the general public at identifying individuals from CCTV images? *Science and Justice, 49,* 191–196. doi:10.1016/j.scijus.2008.10.011

Yoshino, M., Matsuda, H., Kubota, S., Imaizumi, K., & Miyasaka, S. (2000). Computer-assisted facial image identification system using a 3-D physiognomic range finder. *Forensic Science International, 109,* 225–237. doi:10.1016/S0379-0738(00)00149-3

Zhuang, Z., Landsittel, D., Benson, S., Roberge, R., & Shaffer, R. (2010). Facial anthropometric differences among gender, ethnicity, and age groups. *Annals of Occupational Hygiene, 54,* 391–402. doi:1093/annhyg/meq007

Cases

Attorney General's Reference No. 2. of 2002 (2002) EWCA Crim 2373.
R v Atkins (2009) EWCA Crim 1876.
R v Clarke (1995) 2 Cr App R 425.
R v Dodson & Williams (1984) 79 Cr App R 220.
R v Hookway (1999) Crim LR 750.
R v Stockwell (1993) 97 Cr App R 260.
R v Turner (1975) 1 All ER 70.

8

Forensic Face Matching

A Legal Perspective

Andrew Roberts

8.1 Introduction

The subject of this chapter is the way in which the law regulates the use of evidence of forensic face matching in criminal trials. More precisely, it is concerned with the law governing the admissibility and presentation of evidence provided by those who have engaged in some form of forensic face matching, either image-to-image comparison or comparison of an image and a live person. It does not provide a detailed exposition of the law of any one jurisdiction. It deals with broad principles of admissibility, particularly those that are proved to be problematic and controversial. Although there are variations in the form of the applicable law, for the most part, the substantive approach to questions of admissibility and presentation of the kind of evidence that is the concern of this book is broadly consistent across common law jurisdictions.

Although many have suggested that image comparison has become an important and commonly led form of evidence in criminal trials, there appears to be no systematic empirical study of the frequency with which it is relied upon, nor of the kind of cases in which it is used. Although this chapter considers both the admissibility of image-to-image (hereafter referred to as 'forensic image comparison') and image-to-person comparison evidence, it is heavily weighted towards the former (referred to in legal contexts as 'facial-mapping' evidence). There are a number of significant appellate cases that deal with the admissibility of the former, and none of any note with the latter. One reason for this—perhaps the most significant reason—might be that facial-mapping evidence is treated as a form of expert evidence, while identification of persons from a single image has traditionally been considered a task that does not involve (or call for) expertise. As a consequence, evidence of image-to-person comparison is more likely to be excluded than forensic image comparison evidence.

Although routinely received in criminal trials, forensic image comparison evidence is vulnerable to criticism that has been directed at comparison evidence generally in a number of authoritative reports. In a now widely cited passage of its report on the state of forensic sciences in the United States, for example, an interdisciplinary committee of the National Research Council (NRC) concluded that '[w]ith the exception of nuclear DNA analysis ... no forensic method has been rigorously shown to have the capacity to consistently, and with a high degree of certainty, demonstrate a connection

Andrew Roberts, *Forensic Face Matching* In: *Forensic Face Matching*. Edited by: Markus Bindemann, Oxford University Press (2021).
© Oxford University Press. DOI: 10.1093/oso/9780198837749.003.0008.

between evidence and a specific individual or source' (NRC report, 2009: 7). Despite these concerns, the absence of any robust data establishing the scientific validity of forensic face comparison has been met with indifference by the appellate courts. The prevailing view is that any limitations in such evidence can be adequately exposed through cross-examination of the witness who is providing it. The faith that is placed in this process is accompanied by a belief that it will be possible for a jury to determine how much weight ought to be attached to it on the basis of matters revealed in cross-examination and concessions made by the witness regarding the limitations of the evidence.

While the admissibility of forensic image comparison evidence has generated a number of appellate decisions, those dealing with evidence of image-to-person evidence are rare. As previously suggested, this is probably accounted for—at least in part—by the fact that the former is considered expert evidence. Those who provide it are assumed to be able to draw inferences about identity that would be more reliable than any drawn by the jury. In contrast, those who offer evidence based on person-to-image comparison are assumed to be no better placed to draw inferences about identity than would a jury that is provided with the image and able to observe the accused in court. By the end of the chapter, we will be in a position to reflect on whether these assumptions are well grounded.

The chapter has two parts that correspond with the two forms of comparison evidence that provide the subject matter of the book. The first is concerned with the admissibility of forensic image comparison evidence in common law jurisdictions.[1] The second deals with evidence of person-to-image comparison. The broad principles that govern the reception of both forms of evidence will be set out in the course of the first part of the chapter. This exposition will be used to inform consideration of the admissibility of image-to-person comparison in the second part. As a consequence—and in keeping with the volume of case law on each form of evidence—the first part of the chapter will be rather more substantial than the second.

8.2 Image-to-Image Comparison

The starting point for consideration of the admissibility of any form of evidence is the concept of relevance. The requirement of relevance is the foundational condition of admissibility. Evidence will be relevant if it has the capacity to affect rational assessment of some fact, the existence of which is disputed by the parties to the proceeding. The identity of the offender will often be a matter in dispute in a contested criminal trial. It will not always be the case—in some cases, the defendant will concede that they are the person who engaged in the acts that form the basis of the charges, but argue that their actions fall outside the scope of the offence, or they might concede that they committed

---

[1] Although there are fundamental differences in common law and civil law legal systems, the problems associated with forensic science evidence, such as image-to-image comparison evidence, are common to both. See Vuille (2018).

the act but will be able to rely on some defence that is provided by the law. But where the defence is one of mistaken identity, any evidence that might have some bearing on the jury's determination of whether or not the defendant was the person who committed the offence will meet the requirement of relevance. The first question of significance for our purposes is whether the evidence of a witness who has compared an image of the defendant to one of the offender, and offers some assessment of the probability of them being the same person, satisfies the condition of relevance. The routine reception of such evidence in criminal trials suggests that it does. If comparison of the facial features of persons depicted in two images reveals certain similarities, and no dissimilarities, this finding increases the probability that the images are of the same person. This, of course, assumes that the methodology employed is reliable, and the person using it is competent in the use of that method. The principles that regulate the admissibility of expert evidence direct courts' attention to these matters. But, as we now turn to consider the application of those principles to forensic image comparison evidence, I will explain that they overlap with the idea of relevance.

8.2.1   Comparing Faces: A Matter of Opinion

In a criminal trial, there is a general prohibition on evidence of opinion—'the opinion rule'. The expectation is that witnesses called by the parties will give evidence of fact— that is to say, an account of the events that is based on their own direct perception of those events. The line between evidence of fact and opinion is not one that can be drawn with any precision. The latter, according to one Australian court, is 'a conclusion, usually judgmental or debatable, reasoned from facts' (*R. W. Miller v Krupp Australia Pty Ltd*, 1992; *Hodgson v Amcor Ltd*, 2011). Such conclusions might be more or less debatable and the point at which it is appropriate to consider evidence provided by witnesses to be evidence of fact rather than opinion might in some cases be difficult to identify. In *R v Leung and Wong* (1999), the New South Wales Court of Criminal Appeal suggested in respect of eyewitness identification that '[t]he ordinary observer would regard evidence given by a man identifying his wife of thirty years as evidence of fact; but a witness who identifies a suspect in a police lineup would be perceived as giving evidence more closely allied to opinion evidence' (para. 43). Consistent with this view, evidence in the form of a subjective judgment, given by those comparing images of persons with whom they claim no prior familiarity, is properly treated as evidence of opinion. As a consequence, it is subject to the opinion rule.

To understand why, although it constitutes evidence of opinion, forensic image comparison evidence is admissible (and—as we will see later—why evidence of person-to-image comparison will generally be excluded), we need to consider the rationale of the opinion rule. The principal rationale for excluding opinion evidence is that, in offering an opinion about some matter that is disputed by the parties, the witness is engaging in an inquiry that is assigned to the jury. The opinion is superfluous: A duplication of the fact-finder's task. The justification for excluding evidence of opinion could also be explained by reference to the concept of relevance. If the witness is no better placed to draw the inference that is necessarily involved in forming an opinion than the jury, the latter would have no rational grounds for deferring to the witness's opinion on the matter in dispute. Put differently, the opinion offered by the witness cannot rationally affect the jury's assessment of the matter in dispute, and lacking this capacity it would not satisfy the requirement of relevance.

However, the opinions expressed by those who provide facial-mapping evidence are admissible by virtue of a long-standing exception to opinion rule for those who possess skills, experience, and/or knowledge that are not commonly found in the population at large, and which the jury is therefore unlikely to possess. The exception rests on the presumption that if the jury does not have access to this knowledge, skill, and experience, it will not be capable of engaging in the inferential reasoning required to determine the disputed issue, or, if it attempts to do so, its reasoning or evaluation is likely to be flawed. In broad terms, then, the justification for permitting those possessing expertise to give evidence of opinion is that it will assist the jury. This is explicitly acknowledged in the US Federal Rules of Evidence, Rule 702 of which provides that 'a witness who is qualified as an expert ... may testify in the form of an opinion if the expert's scientific, technical, or other specialized knowledge will *help* the trier of fact to understand the evidence or to determine a fact in issue' (emphasis added).

Facial-mapping evidence will meet this broad condition of admissibility if a witness's opinion about the probability of the defendant being the person depicted in the image of the offender is likely to be more accurate or reliable than an opinion formed by a jury that is presented with the two images. There are a number of principles relating to the admissibility of expert evidence that are intended to ensure that such evidence will only be presented to a jury if this broad condition is satisfied. Perhaps the most significant of these concern the reliability of the methods used, and the expertise of those who use them. I will now deal with each of these issues in turn.

8.2.2 Reliability: The Law as Stated

The general position in common law jurisdictions is that a witness who is 'suitably qualified' in forensic image comparison may give expert opinion based on image comparison (*R v Stockwell*, 1993; *R v Clarke*, 1995; *Attorney General's Reference No.2 of 2002*, 2002). However, the reception of such evidence will be consistent with the rationale for permitting experts to offer opinions only if those opinions are the product of sufficiently reliable methods. This position is set out in statements of the law governing the reception of expert evidence in most common law jurisdictions,[2] in more or less explicit terms. The US Federal Rules of Evidence, for example, provide that expert evidence is

---

[2] Except in Australian Uniform Evidence Law jurisdictions in which the issue of reliability is considered to be largely irrelevant to the question of whether image-to-image comparison or any other form of expert evidence should be admitted.

admissible if it is based on 'sufficient facts or data, and is the product of reliable principles and methods that have been reliably applied to the facts' (r.702). This formulation of the rule is distilled from the decision of the US Supreme Court in *Daubert v Merrell Dow Pharmaceuticals Inc.* (1993). In a well-known and frequently cited passage, the Court explained that the Rules require a trial judge to ensure that 'any and all scientific testimony or evidence admitted is not only relevant, but reliable'. Determining the reliability of such evidence, the Court observed, requires consideration of whether it is 'grounded in the methods and procedures of science'. It went on to identify a number of factors that would be relevant to a determination of whether the theory or technique employed by an expert constitutes 'scientific knowledge' and the evidence based on it admissible, namely: (i) whether the theory or technique has been tested, (ii) whether it has been subject to peer review and publication, (iii) the known or potential error rate, (iv) the existence and maintenance of standards controlling the techniques operation, and (v) whether the technique has gained 'general acceptance' in the field.

In England and Wales, the common law is frequently said to incorporate a reliability requirement as a condition of the admissibility of expert evidence. But it is not at all clear what it entails, and the judgments handed down by appellate courts provide little clarification. The following passage found in a relatively short judgment of the South Australian Supreme Court in *R v Bonython* (1984) is often taken by English courts to be an accurate statement of the relevant common law principles:

> ... before admitting the opinion of a witness into evidence as expert testimony, the judge must consider ... whether the subject matter of the opinion forms part of a body of knowledge or experience which is sufficiently organized or recognized to be accepted as a reliable body of knowledge or experience, a special acquaintance with which by the witness would render his opinion of assistance to the court.

Although often recited, there has been no attempt to elucidate the brief reference to reliability (Roberts, 2008). In *R v Dallagher* (2002), it was said that the approach of the English courts is analogous to that established by the US Federal Rules of Evidence and the US Supreme Court's decision in *Daubert*. It has been suggested that a number of relatively recent cases (*R v Reed*, 2009; *R v Broughton*, 2010; *R v Weller*, 2010; *R v C*, 2010; *R v Duglosz*, 2013) in which the Court of Appeal has stated that expert evidence must be 'sufficiently reliable to be admitted' has added little to the 'well-worn' words in *Bonython* (Ward, 2015). To date, the English appellate courts have declined to offer any substantive guidance as to how the reliability of expert evidence ought to be determined.

In its report on expert evidence in criminal proceedings, the UK Law Commission described the common law's approach to the issue of reliability as 'rudimentary' (Law Commission, 2011: para. 3.3), and proposed legislation that, if enacted, would have established a *Daubert*-like reliability test in English law. Although the Government declined to legislate on the grounds of the perceived cost of some of the Commission's proposals (Ministry of Justice, 2013), it suggested that the Criminal Procedural Rules

(2019) be amended 'to provide a stronger indication of the factors that trial judges should consider when assessing expert evidence' (Ministry of Justice, 2013: para. 12).

The Rules, which are supplemented by a set of Criminal Practice Directions (2019), are administrative guidelines that serve a number of competing aims and objectives, among which are efficiency, fairness—and perhaps above all—the conviction of the guilty and acquittal of the innocent (Criminal Procedure Rules, 2019: 1.1). Following the suggestion of the Ministry of Justice, the *Daubert*-like criteria that the Law Commission recommended as a statutory reliability test have been incorporated into the Criminal Practice Directions. Part 19A.5 of the Directions explains that the factors that a trial judge may take into account when determining the reliability of expert scientific opinion include:

(a) the extent and quality of the data on which the expert's opinion is based, and the validity of the methods by which they were obtained;

(b) if the expert's opinion relies on an inference from any findings, whether the opinion properly explains how safe or unsafe the inference is (whether by reference to statistical significance or in other appropriate terms);

(c) if the expert's opinion relies on the results of the use of any method (for instance, a test, measurement or survey), whether the opinion takes proper account of matters, such as the degree of precision or margin of uncertainty, affecting the accuracy or reliability of those results;

(d) the extent to which any material upon which the expert's opinion is based has been reviewed by others with relevant expertise (for instance, in peer-reviewed publications), and the views of those others on that material;

(e) the extent to which the expert's opinion is based on material falling outside the expert's own field of expertise;

(f) the completeness of the information which was available to the expert, and whether the expert took account of all relevant information in arriving at the opinion (including information as to the context of any facts to which the opinion relates);

(g) if there is a range of expert opinion on the matter in question, where in the range the expert's own opinion lies and whether the expert's preference has been properly explained; and

(h) whether the expert's methods followed established practice in the field and, if they did not, whether the reason for the divergence has been properly explained.

The provision of this guidance is a welcome and much-needed development. However, it is a significantly weaker approach to the issue of reliability than that proposed by the Law Commission. The legislation proposed by the Commission would have *required* a trial judge to have regard to the factors set out above in determining whether expert evidence was sufficiently reliable to be admitted at trial. But the Practice Directions do not have this effect. Indeed, they make it clear that the common law—that is to say, the principles set out in judgments handed down by the appellate courts—is the authoritative source of the criteria, by reference to which courts are to determine the admissibility of expert evidence. As we have already noted, the common law offers little in this regard. An observation made in the Practice Directions is that nothing in the common law prevents judges from assessing the reliability according to the criteria set out above, and 'actively encourages' trial judges to do so. But the language of use in the Directions is unambiguously discretionary—*may* take into account, rather than *must* take into account. It is not clear whether they will herald a new approach to the issue of reliability. In *Stephen H v The Queen* (2014), the Court of Appeal suggested that the changes would require 'a new and more rigorous approach on the part of the courts to the handling of expert evidence'. But this was an observation regarding the content of expert reports, rather than the way in which courts would approach questions of reliability in the future.

8.2.3 Reliability: The Law as Applied to Forensic Image Comparison Evidence

Neither the common law requirement that expert evidence be 'sufficiently reliable', nor application of the reliability criteria set out in Rule 702 of the US Federal Rules of Evidence and *Daubert* has led the courts to declare facial-mapping evidence to be generally inadmissible. Such evidence has been admitted in English criminal trials since at least the early 1990s (see, e.g., *R v Stockwell*, 1993; *R v Clarke*, 1995). In the United States, facial-mapping experts have been permitted in some cases to make positive identifications—to assert that the defendant is the person depicted in the image of the offender. But, in others, such witnesses have been permitted to give evidence of similarities in the features of the person or persons depicted in the images, but not their subjective opinion regarding the probability of the defendant being the person seen in the image of the offender—a judicial practice known as 'splitting' (see Edmond et al., 2013; also, on similar restrictions placed on fingerprint experts, see Cole, 2011; Edmond et al., 2013).

The focus of the most notable challenges to the reliability of forensic image comparison evidence has been the claims that are made about the significance of similarities. The leading English case on this issue is *R v Atkins* (2009), in which the witness expressed an opinion about the identity of the person depicted in the image of the offender being the defendant, in the form of a probability estimate using the descriptors in Table 8.1.

The witness's testimony was that the level of support that similarities identified in the images provided to the proposition that they were of the same person was somewhere between the top of Level 3 and Level 4 on this scale. There was no objection to the expert giving evidence of the examination and comparison of the images, or to evidence concerning the similarities that were found. The appellant's challenge to the admissibility of the expert evidence was that the absence of a database meant that there was no objective basis for the opinion regarding levels of support.

Table 8.1 Descriptors of probability estimates concerning similarity between offender and defendant in *R v Atkins* (2009).

Level	Description
0	Lends no support
1	Lends limited support
2	Lends moderate support
3	Lends support
4	Lends strong support
5	Lends powerful support

Source: *R v Atkins* (2009) EWCA Crim 1876.

Those engaged in this form of probabilistic evaluation can, and do, claim that they draw on considerable experience in the field in determining the appropriate point on the scale. However, as counsel for the defendant in *Atkins* suggested, the use of this kind of scale carries the risk that purely subjective evaluation will be invested with spurious scientific authority, and may mislead the jury into attaching more weight to the opinion than it ought to be given. The response of the Court was consistent with the general approach of the English appellate courts—the limitations of the evidence could be explored in cross-examination, and the basis on which the opinion is advanced ought to be made clear to the jury. However, the fact that the jury is aware of these matters does not change a fact that is common to all forms of identification evidence: That where such evidence is based on nothing more than subjective judgment, its reliability cannot be determined effectively at trial. As Edmond et al. (2010) point out, concessions regarding the limitations of expert evidence are no substitute for validating and demonstrating the reliability of the technique. Unless the frequency of a particular type of facial feature, or combination of features, is known, it is difficult to say with any certainty what—if any—significance should be attached to the fact that the defendant and the offender both share those features (Edmond et al., 2010; Roberts, 2015).

The English Court of Appeal has engaged with this problem, albeit fleetingly so. In a passage worthy of close attention, it observed in *R v Gray* (2003) that:

[The expert in the case], like some other facial imaging and mapping experts, said that comparison of the facial characteristics provided "strong support for the identification of the robber as the appellant". No evidence was led of the number of occasions on which any of the six facial characteristics identified by him as "the more unusual and thus individual" were present in the general population, nor as to the frequency of the occurrence in the general population, of combinations of these or any other facial characteristics. [The expert] did not suggest that there was any national database of facial characteristics or any accepted mathematical formula, as in the case of fingerprint comparison, from which conclusions as to the probability of occurrence of particular facial characteristics or combinations of facial characteristics could safely be drawn.

This court is not aware of the existence of any such database or agreed formula. In their absence, any estimate of probabilities and any expression of the degree of support provided by particular facial characteristics or combinations of facial characteristics must be only the subjective opinion of the facial imaging or mapping witness. There is no means of determining objectively whether or not such an opinion is justified. Consequently, unless and until a national database or agreed formula or some other such objective measure is established, this court doubts whether such opinions should ever be expressed by facial imaging or mapping witnesses. The evidence of such witnesses, including opinion evidence, is of course both admissible and frequently of value to demonstrate to a jury with, if necessary, enhancement techniques afforded by specialist equipment, particular facial characteristics or combinations of such characteristics so as to permit the jury to reach its own conclusion ... but on the state of the evidence in this case, and if this court's understanding of the current position is correct in other cases too, such evidence should stop there. (*R v Gray*, 2003: [16])

Although the judgment in Gray addressed widely held concerns about probabilistic opinions offered by those providing forensic image comparison evidence, it was soon marginalized and its significance downplayed. In *R v Gardiner* (2004), a case decided the following year, the Court suggested that the observations made in Gray should be viewed as nothing more than a 'note of caution' regarding new techniques. It explained that there was no rule in the common law that prevented an expert, having identified similarities, from expressing an opinion as to the degree of probability that the images depict one and the same person.

Of course, the issue of reliability does not arise only in relation to probability estimates. Guidance issued in the United Kingdom by the Forensic Science Regulator (2016) identifies a number of factors that might affect the reliability of image comparison and the opinions about the presence of similarities in images. The guidance explains that attempts at identification of persons from images 'can be impacted by numerous factors ... such as: low resolution; poor lighting leading to under- or overexposure of the face; compression, resulting in fine detail being removed in order to save recording space; and non-matching camera angle' (for a review of these factors, see Fysh, this volume). The guidance notes that any of these effects, either individually, or in combination with one another, 'may cause two images of different people to become indistinguishable or introduce differences in appearance between different imagery of the same person (Forensic Science Regulator, 2016: Part 4.2).' These are matters that ought to be central to determination of the admissibility of forensic image comparison evidence. But they are matters that the appellate courts have not yet considered.

8.2.4   Reliability: The Future?

A reading of the leading cases will reveal that, although reliability is said to be a condition that expert evidence must satisfy to be admissible in a criminal trial, there has been little engagement with reliability issues that arise in respect of image comparison evidence. It has been suggested in respect of the law in England and Wales, that the effect of incorporating the Law Commission's *Daubert*-like reliability test in the Criminal Practice Directions might promote more rigorous scrutiny of expert evidence. It may well be doing so but, to date, it seems that no systemic study of the way in which judges are applying the criteria set out in the Directions has been undertaken.

8.2.4.1 Reliability and Validity

It might reasonably be expected that robust and rigorous engagement with the questions relating to reliability, as set out in the Criminal Practice Directions, would cast doubt on the admissibility of forensic image comparison evidence. Take the first of these—the extent and quality of the data on which the expert's opinion is based, and the validity of the methods by which they were obtained. Edmond and colleagues suggest that a challenge that those engaged in facial image comparison have so far failed to meet is 'to produce a credible and reproducible technique for overcoming image distortions' (Edmond et al., 2010: 150; for consideration of these issues, see Edmond et al., 2009). Mallett and Evison (2013) offer the more general observation that 'no attempt has been made to thoroughly test any of the methods using substantial and well-controlled datasets of images varying in quality and in the presence and absence of confounding factors'. If methods have not been tested, this ought to weigh heavily against admitting evidence based on them. But Mallett and Evison's observation points to a problematic issue. If methods have been tested, what form of testing is required, and by whom should it be carried out? An answer to the first question might be found in the report of the US President's Council of Advisors on Science and Technology (the 'PCAST report', 2016). This sets out a clear framework for demonstrating the foundational validity of forensic sciences. A method or technique will be valid in this sense insofar as it has been shown by empirical testing to be '*repeatable, reproducible,* and *accurate* at levels that have been measured and are appropriate to the intended application' (PCAST report, 2016: 47; see also Saks, 2010).

The adoption of reliability criteria to guide decisions about the admissibility of expert evidence generally, and image comparison evidence in particular, is laudable. However, whether they in fact lead to more rigorous evaluation of forensic science evidence is open to doubt. The US Supreme Court's decision in *Daubert v Merrell Dow Pharmaceuticals* (1993) is perhaps the most well-known and widely cited example of such an approach. It is routinely discussed in academic writing on expert evidence, has been referred to frequently by appellate courts in common law jurisdictions (e.g., the United Kingdom Supreme Court in *Kennedy v Cordia Services LLP*, 2016; the High Court of Australia in *Honeysett v The Queen*, 2014; the New Zealand Court of Appeal in *Lundy v R*, 2018; the Supreme Court of Canada in *R v Trochym*, 2007), and provided the basis of the UK Law Commission's recommendations for the incorporation of a reliability test in English law relating to the reception of expert evidence (Law Commission, 2011). But there are good grounds for the view that it has been generally ineffective in keeping unreliable expert evidence out of criminal trials, at least where it is relied upon by the prosecution (see Rozelle, 2007). As is the case with many other forms of forensic science evidence, image comparison evidence was admissible in US proceedings prior to the US Supreme Court's decision in *Daubert* and remains so in its wake, notwithstanding the publication of a number of authoritative reports that cast doubt on the reliability of many of the forensic sciences and various forms of comparison evidence (Campbell Inquiry, 2011; Goudge Inquiry, 2008; NIST report, 2012; NRC report, 2009; see generally Edmond, 2015).

8.2.4.2 Existing Reliability Tests: A Low Threshold

Notwithstanding the intention of *Daubert*, the requirement of reliability appears, in practice, to be a relatively undemanding standard. There have been various suggestions as to why this might be the case. Among the most plausible, is the practice of 'grandfathering', whereby a decision in a previous case, that a particular form of evidence is admissible, provides the justification for its continuing admissibility. This can occur even if the original decision predates the adoption of new criteria for evaluating reliability, and/or despite contemporary concerns about the validity of the methods used or the claims that these are said to support (see Cole, 2004). Further, a decision to admit a particular form of evidence in one legal jurisdiction is often used to support decisions to admit it in others (Edmond et al., 2013). An equally credible explanation is that, in the absence of the knowledge and understanding that is required to evaluate the scientific validity of forensic science evidence (see Gatowski et al., 2001), judges will tend to look for peripheral cues to validity, such as the extent to which the method is accepted within the scientific community (Saks, 2008), although the question of what should constitute the relevant community for such purposes appears far from obvious (Roberts, 2008). If the relevant reference group is those engaged in forensic image comparison, the commonly practised methods may be 'validated' on the basis of nothing more than the fact that they are commonly used, and there is no necessary connection between this fact and the scientific validity of the method concerned.

8.2.4.3 The Limitations of the Trial as a Forensic Process

The failure of the courts to subject image comparison evidence to rigorous scrutiny would not be a significant concern if we could be confident that the criminal trial's forensic processes are capable of consistently exposing unreliable expert evidence. However, the Law Commission observed that '[c]ross-examination, the adduction of contrary expert evidence and judicial guidance at the end of the trial are currently assumed to provide sufficient safeguards in relation to expert evidence, by revealing to the jury factors adversely affecting reliability and weight. However, ... it is doubtful whether these are valid assumptions' (Law Commission, 2011: 1.20, 1.24). Consistent with this view, empirical studies suggest that cross-examination is largely ineffective in exposing both the extent of any limitations in methodology, and inflated opinion offered by expert witnesses (McQuiston-Surrett & Saks, 2009). The reality might be, therefore, that juries from their disadvantaged position can either defer to the opinion of the expert, or reject it on grounds that may not be entirely rational (Allen & Miller, 1993; Edmond & Roberts, 2011).

In England and Wales, experts are required to state the limitations of the evidence that they offer. But expression of such limitations in qualitative terms—pointing out that a conclusion about the probability of the defendant being the person depicted in the image of the offender is subjective, for example—is not particularly helpful to a jury when it comes to the task of determining how much weight ought to be placed on the evidence. The significance of this shortcoming lies in one of the fundamental principles of the criminal justice system—the presumption of innocence. Jackson and Summers (2012) suggest that the presumption provides the foundation for a range of evidentiary mechanisms that ensure the risk of error is distributed in a way that protects individuals against wrongful conviction, of which the standard of proof—beyond reasonable doubt—is taken to be the 'supreme example'. However, its effectiveness in this respect will depend on insistence that the limitations of the evidence on which the prosecution rely be fully exposed, and this requires rigorous evaluation of the scientific basis of the evidence. A jury will be far better placed to consider the probability that the defendant might not be the offender, and whether there is a reasonable doubt about their guilt, if provided with reliable quantitative information about the error rate associated with forensic image comparison, than with nebulous concessions regarding the absence of testing, the subjective nature of the witness's conclusions, and so on.

One way of ensuring that this kind of work is undertaken would be for courts to refuse to admit forensic image comparison evidence, unless the party that seeks to rely on it is also able to provide reliable evidence of scientific validity and error rates. However, from a judicial perspective, this is likely to be seen as a radical response to a problem that can be adequately dealt with by the traditional forensic processes deployed in the criminal trial. It is doubtful that the impetus for remedial work to establish the scientific validity of comparison evidence will be instigated by the courts. In light of which we might ask the question, 'where will it come from?' From the parties themselves, perhaps? As Odgers (2015) points out, the defence generally lacks the resources to challenge the scientific basis of such evidence (see also Roach, 2010). He also dismisses, as unrealistic, suggestions that prosecutors should be responsible for engaging in a thorough review of a field of forensic science before using evidence derived from it (on which, see Edmond, 2013).

It might be that the solution to the problem of ensuring that the limitations of forensic image comparison are known—that is to say, quantified and publicized—lies with the scientific community. Chin et al. (2019), for example, point to what they claim to be a revolution of methodology in the mainstream sciences, prompted by the realization that various findings in the bioscientific literature could not be replicated or reproduced by independent laboratories. They argue that there are pressing reasons for forensic science to adopt the open scientific practices that are said to exemplify this revolution—'the open science movement'. First, misleading results in the forensic sciences might lead to serious injustice. Second, open and transparent knowledge generation is consistent with fundamental legal principles, such as the presumption of innocence and access to justice. Third, 'open science' is a more efficient way of validating forensic sciences. Open science, as the designation suggests, involves making data and research methods freely available on publicly accessible web platforms. It is said that the sharing of this information enables other researchers to replicate and reproduce testing, to identify errors or flaws in studies that are published, and to combine datasets and engage in meta-analysis (Chin et al., 2019).

8.2.5 Expertise

The admissibility of forensic image comparison evidence will depend not only on it being accepted by the courts as a matter about which expert evidence can properly be given—a body of knowledge or experience that is sufficiently organized or recognized to be accepted as reliable. The witness who provides it must also demonstrate that they possess the requisite expertise. This will be a matter for the judge to determine. In practice, if the witness can demonstrate that they have undertaken training and had their work validated, the court is likely to recognize them as someone who is qualified to give expert evidence. However, Edmond and Martire (2017) suggest that, in many cases, expertise is assumed rather than demonstrated, and that experience is routinely accepted as a proxy for demonstrable expertise.

Just as the approach to questions of the foundational reliability of facial image comparison has attracted criticism, so too has the courts' general approach to determining whether a witness possesses the requisite expertise. Neither qualifications, nor experience, are sufficient to establish that a person can do what they claim to be able to do. The authors of the PCAST report observed that 'the only way to establish scientifically that an examiner is capable of applying a foundationally valid method, is through appropriate empirical testing to measure how often the examiner gets the correct answer' (2016: 58). It suggested that tests should reflect as far as possible the conditions in which the subjects usually undertake their task—using images that vary in quality, for example. Importantly, the report proposes that testing be 'blind'—that is to say, samples should be included in the flow of the examiner's casework without their knowledge.

Empirical studies have established that those who engage in forensic face matching possess expertise, outperforming those who are untrained (White et al., 2015; in respect of fingerprint examiners, see Tangen et al., 2011). But for the reasons articulated in the previous sections, what juries (and arguably, the presumption of innocence) require is an indication of how accurate the witness in the case has demonstrated themselves to be in the task of comparing faces (for insight into individual differences in face matching, see Bate, Mestry, & Portch, this volume).

8.3 Image-to-Person Comparison

At the beginning of this chapter, I stated that far more attention would be given to the law relating to the admissibility of image-to-image comparison than that concerning image-to-person comparison. The reason for this is that in most circumstances such evidence will fail to satisfy the first and most fundamental condition of admissibility—relevance.

While there do not appear to be any reported cases in which the admissibility of contemporaneous image-to-person evidence has been considered, those dealing with the admissibility of evidence provided by a person who recognizes a person depicted in an image as someone already known to them, provide a good indication of the approach that courts are likely to take to this form of comparison evidence. In *R v Smith* (2001), the High Court of Australia considered identification evidence provided by two police officers who asserted that the offender, seen in closed-circuit television images recorded during a bank robbery, was the defendant, with whom they had had some dealings in the past. The Court found the evidence to be inadmissible because it failed to meet the requirement of relevance. Although there is a body of empirical research that suggests those who are familiar with a person are more likely to be significantly more accurate in their attempts to match faces than those who are unfamiliar (Megreya & Burton, 2007; Ritchie et al., 2015; Young & Burton, 2017), it took the view that the police officers' previous encounters did not give them any advantage in recognizing the person in the images.[3] The images were available to the jury, and its members had an opportunity to compare the defendant—who was present in court—with the person in the images, and to reach their own conclusions as to whether or not that person was the defendant. The majority of the court suggested that the police officers were in no better position to make a comparison than members of the jury, or indeed any member of the public who might happen to be observing the proceedings:

> The fact that someone else has reached a conclusion about the identity of the accused and the person in the picture does not provide any logical basis for affecting the jury's assessment of the probability of the existence of that fact when the conclusion is based only on material that is not different in any substantial way from what is available to the jury. (*R v Smith*, 2001: para. 11)

If we now consider evidence of image-to-person comparison, there seems to be no justification for departing from the view that such evidence will ordinarily fail to satisfy the requirement of relevance. If we assume that the person to whom the image has been compared is the defendant, the defendant is present in court, and that the image is available to the jury, the witness who proposes to give evidence that the person image is of the defendant, seems no better placed to make this judgment than the jury.

Of course, if the witness does have some advantage over the jury, then evidence of comparison might be admissible. Such circumstances will include those in which the appearance of the defendant has changed substantially in the period between the

---

[3] However, see the dissenting judgment of Kirby J., who concluded that because of the officers' previous opportunities to see the defendant from angles that the jury could not, and to observe a wider and more natural range of facial expressions than were observable in court, they had been able to draw inferences about identity that the jury could not. Consequently, their evidence was relevant.

comparison undertaken by the witness and the subsequent trial. Similarly, if the image that was used to undertake the comparison is no longer available, a witness may well be permitted to give an opinion about identity of the person on the basis of the earlier comparison. But there is a further circumstance in which evidence of image-to-person comparison might be admissible.

There is growing scientific interest in so-called super-recognizers—members of the community who are said to possess extraordinary ability to recognize faces (see Bate, Mestry, & Portch, this volume; White, Towler, & Kemp, this volume). If it could be established on the basis of reliable evaluation that they do in fact possess this aptitude, then they could conceivably be permitted to give evidence of identity based on image-to-person comparison on the basis of demonstrable expertise. As we have seen, for expert evidence to be admissible, it must be established that 'study or experience will give a witness's opinion an authority which the opinion of one not so qualified will lack' and that the witness must be qualified to express the opinion (*R v Luttrell*, 2004). There might be some question as to whether a super-recognizer's ability to identify is something that is acquired through skill or experience. Such persons appear to have an innate ability. A response to this might be that, if their evidence would assist the jury, then it should be admissible. One way of ensuring this would be to take the view that, although super-recognizers might have an innate and extraordinary ability to match faces, this is something that will have been fully developed through their interactions with the world around them. In other words, it is an ability that has been acquired, in part, through experience.

However, it seems that questions regarding the admissibility of image-to-person comparison evidence provided by super-recognizers are unlikely to exercise the courts in the near future. Although used across a range of operational settings, there has been no systematic study of the tasks that persons referred to as super-recognizers undertake, and it is not known if any routinely engage in image-to-person comparison (however, for a summary of key research findings, see Noyes et al., 2017).

Researchers have pointed out that there is no unified definition of a super-recognizer (Moreton et al., 2019), and that no appropriate diagnostic criteria for determining whether someone is, in fact, a super-recognizer have been identified (Ramon et al., 2019a). It has been suggested that, until we have a better scientific understanding of the superior abilities of super-recognizers, and more data on the validity and reliability of their abilities to identify persons, caution should be exercised in deploying them (see Bate, Mestry, & Portch, this volume; Ramon et al., 2019b). The point carries greater force in respect of the question of whether the courts should permit them to give comparison evidence.

8.4 Conclusion

This chapter has considered the admissibility of both forensic image comparison evidence and evidence of image-to-person comparison. While there are a number of significant appellate decisions that deal with the former, there are none that deal with the latter. The most likely explanation for this is that, if adduced, image-to-person comparison is likely to be excluded on grounds of relevance. Forensic image comparison evidence, on the other hand, appears to be routinely admitted in criminal trials, notwithstanding criticism that the scientific validity of the methods that are commonly used has not been established. Although the common law is said to impose a reliability test, it appears to be an undemanding one, the prevailing view of the courts being that the forensic processes of the criminal trial will expose the limitations of such evidence. In England and Wales, incorporation of the reliability criteria for the Law Commission's Draft Bill in the Criminal Practice Directions are seen by some as requiring a new and more rigorous approach to determining the admissibility of expert evidence, or at least providing a new opportunity for the adoption of such an approach. But in other jurisdictions, the existence of similar criteria does not appear to have had the effect that some envisage the Criminal Practice Directions having. The criteria are not definitive of the issue of admissibility, they are merely matters that a trial judge might take into account. Moreover, it is entirely possible—perhaps predictable—that in the absence of any data relating to their validity, the courts will rely on the fact that the expert's methods constitute established practice in the field as the justificatory ground for continuing to admit forensic image comparison evidence. If this transpires, then there appears little incentive for those who practise this form of forensic science to undertake or cooperate with work to determine the validity of their methods, and generate error rates. Such evidence will remain admissible but controversial.

References

Allen, R. J. & Miller, J. S. (1993). The common law theory of experts: Deference or education? *Northwestern University Law Review, 87,* 1131–1147.

Campbell Inquiry (2011). *The Fingerprint Inquiry Report.* Glasgow, APS Group Scotland.

Chin, J., Ribeiro, G., & Rairden, A. (2019). Open forensic science. *Journal of Law and Biosciences, 6,* 255–288. doi:10.1093/jlb/lsz009

Cole, S. (2004). Grandfathering evidence: Fingerprint admissibility rulings from *Jennings* to *Llera Plaza* and back again. *American Criminal Law Review, 41,* 1189–1276.

Cole, S. (2011). Splitting hairs: Evaluating 'split testimony' as an approach to the problem of forensic expert evidence. *Sydney Law Review, 33,* 459–485.

Criminal Practice Directions (2015). London, Ministry of Justice. Available at: https://www.justice.gov.uk/courts/procedure-rules/criminal/docs/2015/criminal-procedure-rules-practice-directions-april-2019.pdf (accessed 25 April 2020).

Criminal Procedure Rules (2015). London, Ministry of Justice. Available at: https://www.justice.gov.uk/courts/procedure-rules/criminal/docs/2015/criminal-procedure-rules-practice-directions-april-2019.pdf (accessed 25 April 2020).

Edmond G. (2013). (Ad)ministering justice: Expert evidence and the professional responsibilities of prosecutors. *University of New South Wales Law Journal, 36,* 921–953.

Edmond, G. (2015). What lawyers should know about the forensic 'sciences'. *Adelaide Law Review, 36,* 33–100.

Edmond, G., Biber, K., Kemp, R., & Porter, G. (2009). Law's looking glass: Expert identification evidence derived from photographic and video images'. *Current Issues in Criminal Justice, 20,* 337–377. doi:10.1080/10345329.2009.12035817

Edmond, G., Cole, S., Cunliffe, E., & Roberts, A. (2013). Admissibility compared: The reception of incriminating expert opinion (i.e. forensic science) evidence in four adversarial jurisdictions. *University of Denver Criminal Law Review, 3*, 31–109.

Edmond, G., Kemp, R., Porter, G., Hamer, D., Burton, A. M., Biber, K., & San Roque, M., 2010. Atkins v The Emperor: The 'cautious' use of unreliable 'expert' opinion. *International Journal of Evidence and Proof, 14*, 146–166. doi:10.1350/ijep.2010.14.2.349

Edmond, G. & Martire, K. (2017). Knowing experts? Section 79, Forensic science evidence and the limits of 'training, study or experience'. In A. Roberts & J. Gans (eds), *Critical perspectives on the uniform evidence law* (pp. 80–103). Sydney: Federation Press.

Edmond, G. & Roberts, A. (2011). Procedural fairness, the criminal trial, and forensic science and medicine. *Sydney Law Review, 33*, 359–394.

Forensic Science Regulator (2016). *Forensic image comparison and interpretation evidence: Guidance for prosecutors and investigators.* Issue 2. Available at: http://www.gov.uk/government/publications/forensic-image-comparison-and-interpretation-evidence-issue-2 (accessed 23 April 2020).

Gatowski, S. I., Dobbin, S. A., Richardson, J. T., Ginsburg, G. P., Melino, M. L., & Dahir, V. (2001). Asking the gatekeepers: A national survey of judges on judging expert evidence in a post-Daubert world. *Law and Human Behavior, 25*, 433–458. doi:10.1023/A:101289903

Goudge Inquiry (2008). *Inquiry into pediatric forensic pathology in Ontario.* Ontario, Ontario Ministry of the Attorney General, Queen's Printer.

Jackson, J. & Summers, S. (2012). *The internationalisation of criminal evidence: Beyond the common law and civil law traditions.* Cambridge: Cambridge University Press.

Law Commission (2011). *Expert evidence in criminal proceedings in England and Wales.* Law Communication No. 325, HC 829. London: The Stationery Office.

Mallett, X. & Evison, M. (2013). Forensic facial comparison: Issues of admissibility in the development of novel analytical technique. *Journal of Forensic Sciences, 58*, 859–865. doi:10.1111/1556-4029.12127

McQuiston-Surrett, D. & Saks, M. (2009). The testimony of forensic identification science: What expert witnesses say and what fact-finders hear. *Law and Human Behavior, 33*, 436–453. doi:10.1007/s10979-008-9169-1

Megreya, A. M. & Burton, A. M. (2007). Hits and false positives in face matching: A familiarity-based dissociation. *Perception & Psychophysics, 69*, 1175–1184. doi:10.3758/BF03193954

Ministry of Justice (2013). The Government's response to the Law Commission report: 'Expert evidence in criminal proceedings in England and Wales'. *Law Com No 325.*

Moreton, R., Pike, G., & Havard, C. (2019). A task- and role-based perspective on super-recognizers: Commentary on 'super-recognizers: From the laboratory to the world and back again'. *British Journal of Psychology, 110*, 486–488. doi:10.1111/bjop.12394

NIST (National Institute of Standards and Technology) report (2012). Expert working group on human factors in latent print analysis. *Latent print examination and human factors: Improving the practice through a systems approach.* US Department of Commerce. Available at: https://nvlpubs.nist.gov/nistpubs/ir/2012/NIST.IR.7842.pdf (accessed 1 May 2020).

Noyes, E., Phillips, P. J., & O'Toole, A. J. (2017). What is a super-recogniser? In M. Bindemann & A. M. Megreya (eds), *Face processing: Systems, disorders and cultural differences* (pp. 173–201). New York: Nova Science Publishers.

NRC (National Research Council) report (2009). *Strengthening forensic science in the united states: A path forward.* Washington D.C.: The National Academies Press.

Odgers, S. (2015). What lawyers should do about forensic science evidence. *Adelaide Law Review, 36*, 147–151.

PCAST report (President's Council of Advisors on Science and Technology) (2016). *Forensic science in criminal courts: Ensuring scientific validity of feature-comparison methods.* (September), 1–174. Available at: https://obamawhitehouse.archives.gov/sites/default/files/microsites/ostp/PCAST/pcast_forensic_science_report_final.pdf (accessed 23 April 2020).

Ramon, M., Bobak, A. K., & White, D. (2019a). Super-recognizers: From the lab to the world and back again. *British Journal of Psychology, 110*, 461–479. doi:10.1111/bjop.12368

Ramon, M., Bobak, A. K., & White, D. (2019b). Towards a 'manifesto' for super-recognizer research. *British Journal of Psychology, 110*, 495–498. doi:10.1111/bjop.12411

Ritchie, K. L., Smith, F. G., Jenkins, R., Bindemann, M., White, D., & Burton A. M. (2015). Viewers base estimates of face matching accuracy on their own familiarity: Explaining the photo-ID paradox. *Cognition, 141*, 161–169. doi:10.1016/j.cognition.2015.05.002

Roach, K. (2010). Wrongful convictions: Adversarial and inquisitorial themes. *North Carolina Journal of International Law and Commercial Regulation, 35*, 387–446.

Roberts, A. (2008). Drawing on expertise: Legal decision-making and the reception of expert evidence. *Criminal Law Review, 6*, 443–462.

Roberts, A. (2015). Eyewitness identification and facial image comparison evidence in common law jurisdictions. In T. Valentine & J. Davis (eds), *Forensic facial identification: Theory and practice of identification from eyewitnesses, composites and CCTV* (pp. 287–321). Chichester: Wiley-Blackwell.

Rozelle, S. D. (2007). Daubert, Schmaubert: Criminal defendants and the short end of the science stick. *Tulsa Law Review, 43*, 597–607.

Saks, M. J. (2008). Explaining the tension between the supreme court's embrace of validity as the touchstone of admissibility of expert testimony and lower courts' (seeming) rejection of the same. *Episteme, 5*, 339–342. doi:10.3366/E1742360008000439

Saks, M. J. (2010). Forensic identification: From faith-based 'science' to a scientific science. *Forensic Science International, 201*, 14–17. doi:10.1016/j.forsciint.2010.03.014

Tangen, J. M., Thompson, M. B., & McCarthy, D. J. (2011). Identifying fingerprint expertise. *Psychological Science, 22*, 995–997. doi:10.1177/0956797611414729

Vuille, J. (2018). Forensic science evidence in non-adversary criminal justice systems. In P. Roberts & M. Stockdale (eds), *Forensic science evidence and expert witness testimony: Reliability through reform* (pp. 354–375). Cheltenham: Edward Elgar.

Ward, T. (2015). A new and more rigorous approach to expert evidence in England and Wales. *International Journal of Evidence and Proof, 19*, 228–245. doi:10.1177/1365712715591471

White, D., Phillips, P. J., Hahn, C. A., Hill, M., & O'Toole, A. J. (2015). Perceptual expertise in forensic facial image comparison. *Proceedings of the Royal Society B: Biological Sciences, 282*(1814), 20151292. doi:10.1098/rspb.2015.1292

Young, A. W. & Burton, A. M. (2017). Recognizing faces. *Current Directions in Psychological Science, 26*, 212–217. doi:10.1177/0963721416688114

Cases

Attorney General's Reference No.2 of 2002 (2002) EWCA Crim 2373.
Daubert v Merrell Dow Pharmaceuticals Inc. (1993) 509 U.S. 579.
Hodgson v Amcor Ltd (2011) VSC 272.
Honeysett v The Queen (2014) HCA 29.
Kennedy v Cordia (Services) LLP (2016) UKSC 6.
Lundy v R (2018) NZCA 410.
R v Atkins (2009) EWCA Crim 1876.
R v Bonython (1984) 38 SASR 45.
R v Broughton (2010) EWCA Crim 549.
R v C (2010) EWCA Crim 2578.
R v Clarke (1995) 2 Cr. App. R. 425.
R v Dallagher (2002) EWCA Crim 1903.
R v Duglosz (2013) EWCA Crim 2.
R v Gardner (2004) EWCA Crim 1639.
R v Gray (2003) EWCA Crim 1001.
R v Leung and Wong (1999) NSWCCA 287.
R v Luttrell (2004) EWCA Crim 1344.
R v Reed (2009) EWCA Crim 2698.

R v Smith (2001) HCA 50.

R v Stockwell (1993) 97 Cr. App. R. 260.

R v Trochym (2007) 1 SCR 239.

R v Weller (2010) EWCA Crim 1085.

R. W. Miller v Krupp Australia Pty Ltd (1992) 34 NSWLR 129.

Stephen H v The Queen (2014) EWCA Crim 1555.

9

Automatic Recognition Systems and Human Computer Interaction in Face Matching

Eilidh Noyes and Matthew Q. Hill

9.1 Introduction

Automated face recognition systems play an important role in security and policing scenarios. They can process a large amount of data at rapid speeds and, unlike humans, are not affected by limiting factors such as fatigue or boredom (Alenezi et al., 2015; Beattie et al., 2016). Their prevalence has increased in recent years, which is a direct reflection on advances in algorithm technology and, consequently, in performance.

At the present time, the role of face recognition algorithms in security and policing scenarios is typically to *assist* humans in the identity verification process. The example that is likely most familiar to readers is the use of electronic e-gates at passport control. E-gates make identifications by comparing a traveller's live image against their passport image (1:1 image matching) for similarity. If a potential mismatch in identity is detected, the traveller is referred to a human operator who will adjudicate the identification.

Human and machine face recognition systems are also used to assist identifications in policing. Computer algorithms aid suspect identification by comparing a target image for similarity against another image, or a database of known offenders. The number of face images present in a comparison database can range from just a few to millions. Thus, algorithms can compare a target image against far more images than possible by human eye alone, and they can process these image similarity computations in fractions of a second. The images of highest similarity are then returned as a 'candidate list', which is subsequently reviewed by a human officer. In addition, when there are many images of multiple people of interest, algorithms can facilitate grouping of identities (clustering). Again, a human review is then required to verify algorithm accuracy.

This chapter is divided into four sections. In Section 9.2, we provide a brief overview of how algorithms work. In Section 9.3, we discuss the role that algorithms play in policing and border control scenarios. In Section 9.4, we review accuracy of automatic face recognition systems and provide comparisons with human performance. Finally, in Section 9.5, we consider the advantages and disadvantages of human and machine interaction.

Eilidh Noyes and Matthew Q. Hill, *Automatic Recognition Systems and Human Computer Interaction in Face Matching* In: *Forensic Face Matching*. Edited by: Markus Bindemann, Oxford University Press (2021). © Oxford University Press.
DOI: 10.1093/oso/9780198837749.003.0009.

9.2 A Basic Overview of the Workings of Algorithms

The design and structure of automatic face recognition systems are fascinatingly complex. However, basic knowledge of algorithm design and the image comparison procedure allows the strengths, limitations, and potential of these systems to be evaluated. The following text provides an overview of algorithm design and the face identification procedure.

9.2.1 How Do Algorithms Determine Identity from Images?

Algorithms perform a series of steps to compute image comparisons. First, they must find the face in the image (face detection). Next, the algorithm must process relevant features of the image (feature extraction), and configure a measure of similarity between images (distance metric learning). A similarity score can then be computed and compared against a decision rule (used to determine whether the images are similar enough to be considered the same identity). There are different ways of extracting features from an image. These will be looked at in more detail below. First, we will consider the comparison metric used by most algorithms, which is an image *similarity* score. A high similarity score for a pair of images indicates that they are likely to be images of the same identity, whereas a low similarity score suggests that the images are of different identities.

This similarity score can be used to aid identification in 1:1 comparison, 1:N comparison, and clustering scenarios:

- 1:1 image matching: The similarity score helps determine whether two specific images are of the same identity or different identities. An example is the passport control e-gate scenario, whereby a passenger's live-capture image is compared against the passport photo.
- 1:N image matching: Similarity scores are obtained for a target image against a database of other images. Typically, a specified number of images of highest similarity to the target are returned as a ranked list. For example, the image of a suspect (captured by closed-circuit television [CCTV]) can be compared against a database of police custody images of known offenders.
- Clustering: A large set of images can be grouped according to similarity scores. A set of rules are used to determine which images in a set are likely to be of the same person, based on their similarity to other images in the set.

But how similar must the images be to be considered the same identity? An operator-defined criterion score determines the level of similarity required to constitute an identity match. In this context, an algorithm can make two types of error—a false acceptance or a false rejection. The criterion score dictates the likelihood of each error type. Therefore, choosing a criterion for an imperfect system requires a trade-off between the two types of error (false accept, false reject).

- False acceptance rate: This is how often an algorithm mistakes two different people as being the same person. For example, a false acceptance will occur when an algorithm accepts an impostor as the rightful owner of a presented identity document.
- False reject rate: This is how often the algorithm fails to match images of the same face. For example, a false reject can occur when the rightful owner of a passport is not successfully matched to their passport image by the algorithm.

This criterion score is based on operational false acceptance rates—the score at which x percentage of non-matched identity pairs will be labelled as a matched identity pair by the network. In practice, the criterion score for a system often depends on its operational usage. A shift in criterion changes the likelihood of a false accept scenario (saying that two people are the same when they are actually different identities—e.g., accepting an imposter as a match to a stolen passport) versus that of a false reject (e.g., saying that a person is not a match to their passport when they actually are). The trade-off must be considered carefully for operational usage (see Figure 9.1). If there is a greater risk associated with accepting two different people as the same identity than there is of rejecting multiple images of a true same identity as a match, then a more conservative criterion should be chosen (lower false accept rate, higher false reject rate). On the other hand, if it is more risky to reject multiple images of the same person, then a more liberal criterion score should be used (higher false accept rate, lower false reject rate).

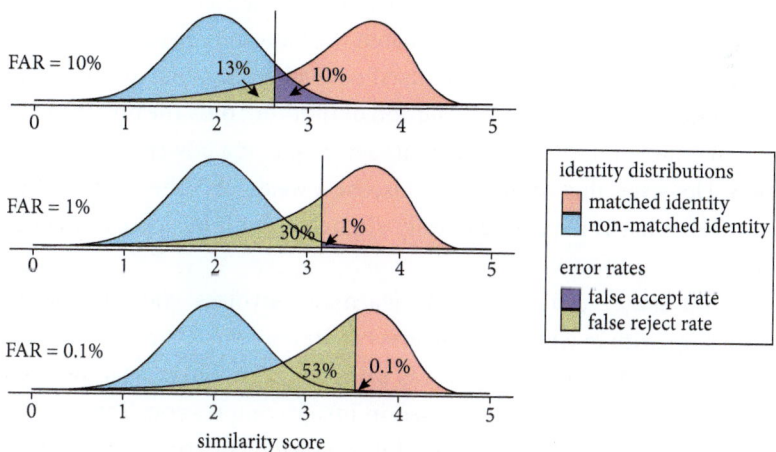

Figure 9.1 Choosing a criterion for an imperfect system requires a trade-off between the two types of error (false accept, false reject).

Note: In this example, setting the criterion to a 10% false accept rate (FAR) results in a false reject rate (FRR) of 13%. A more conservative FAR of 1% results in an FRR of 30%. The FAR of 0.1% that is required by passport systems results here in an FRR of 53%. This is significantly higher than the allowed 5% FRR of passport systems, meaning that this example system would not be accurate enough for their standards.

9.2.2 Algorithm Design

Below we provide an overview of early algorithm designs and more modern designs.

9.2.2.1 Early Algorithm Design

Early algorithms were programmed to compute image similarity scores or identity classifications using hand-coded features (e.g., lines in the image) on a pixel-by-pixel basis. In other words, the coder dictates the image qualities that are compared by the automatic system. To illustrate this process with an oversimplified example, an algorithm might be programmed to compare the location of black pixels in one image with black pixels in a second image. For the purpose of this example, a strong match in black pixel location is indicative of an identity match. In practice, the feature extraction procedures are far more sophisticated.

Early face recognition algorithms generally consisted of two stages of processing: Feature extraction, in which the algorithm processes information in the image deemed useful for the task; and distance metric learning, in which the algorithm tunes up a similarity measure to compare the extracted features of two images. The types of features extracted from an image in the first stage were often carefully designed, and based on well-known principles of cognition or information theory. Many of these techniques employed a process known as 'convolution'. Convolution uses a matrix of numbers called a 'kernel' that describes a pattern to be detected in an image (see Figure 9.2). This kernel is 'convolved' over the image, tiling in steps of n pixels, where n is a parameter chosen by the designer of the algorithm. The output is a matrix of either the same size as the original image, or smaller, depending on parameters including the step size n. The values of the output matrix can be treated as a measure of how well the pixels at a given location in the image match the pattern (i.e., feature) detailed by the kernel. This makes the output matrix itself equivalent to a map of the feature's presence in the image. The fact that convolution outputs not only the presence of a feature, but also a measure of its location in the image, makes it a powerful method of feature extraction. However, this strength can also be a weakness. The method's reliance on location means that it requires carefully aligned stimuli in order to match patterns effectively.

The second stage—distance metric learning—involves choosing or building a measure of similarity in which face images can be compared. An early distance metric used for computer face recognition was principal component analysis (PCA) (Turk & Pentland, 1991), a technique also used in image compression. This method can reduce the size of the face representation while preserving important information, which made it an attractive solution in a time when storage space and processing power were scarce. PCA is an 'unsupervised' learning method, meaning that it is trained without any information about true identity labels. Some other methods use training data labelled with the true identity in order to improve performance (e.g., linear discriminant analysis and support vector machines). These methods are referred to as 'supervised'.

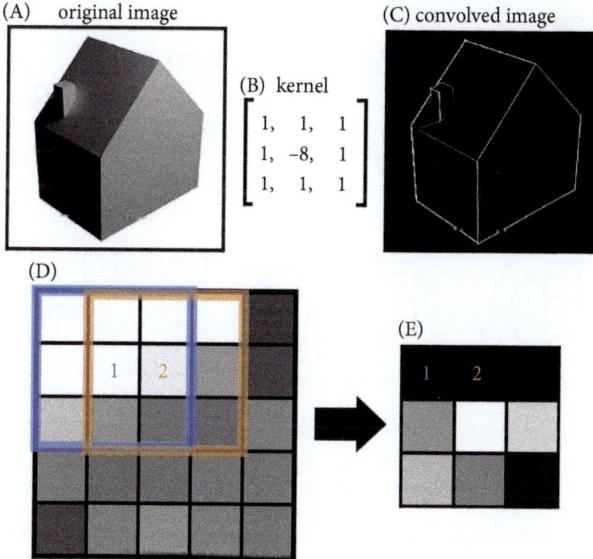

Figure 9.2 The process of convolution.

Note: In this process, (A) an image is taken as input. (B) A matrix of numbers called a 'kernel' defines the feature to be detected. Here, a common edge detection kernel is shown. (C) The final result is an image in which high values (white) represent a close match with the kernel's feature at that location, and low values (black) represent the absence of the feature. (D) To find the feature over the whole image, the kernel is tiled in steps of one or more pixels. The blue box (1) and yellow box (2) show the area covered by the first and second steps, respectively. (E) Each cell in the kernel is multiplied by the value at its overlapping pixel in the image at each location. The multiplied numbers are then summed to give the final result at that location. The blue 1 and yellow 2 show the result of the convolution from the first and second steps, respectively. These pixels are black because the kernel was not a good match with the image at those locations.

Once a distance metric is in place, the operator can obtain similarity scores between sets of images.

9.2.2.2 Deep Convolutional Neural Networks

The current state-of-the-art in face recognition algorithms is defined by deep convolutional neural networks (DCNNs). Consistent with some of their predecessors, these networks use convolution operations to extract features from an image. The main innovations of DCNNs are twofold: 1) They leverage multiple layers of processing (the *depth* in a *deep* neural network); and 2) the (multiple) kernels they use at each layer are not hand-coded but rather learned from training data (Krizhevsky et al., 2012). The depth of these networks allows them to combine simple features from early layers into more complex features at deeper layers. This is similar to how the primate brain processes visual information, and gives DCNNs the ability to process images robustly across significant changes in viewpoint and illumination (Cadieu et al., 2014).

Each layer in a deep network can be thought of as one of many consecutive steps in processing (see Figure 9.3). The first layer of an effective network will capture simple features in the image such as lines, dots, or opposing colours (cf. Zeiler & Fergus, 2014). The second layer's features are created by combining the first layer's features into more

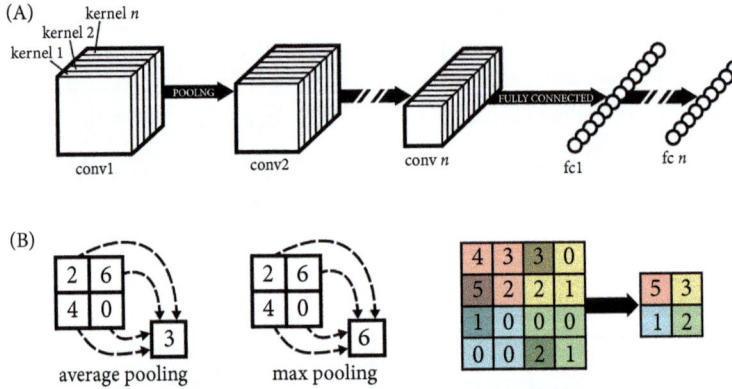

Figure 9.3 The architecture of a deep convolutional neural network (DCNN).

Note: (A) The architecture of a DCNN can take many forms, but the common structure is such that multiple layers of convolution and pooling are followed by one or more 'fully connected' layers. Each convolutional layer utilises multiple kernels (see Figure 9.2) to find features in the image. The image is processed from left to right, whereby 'fc n' produces the final identity representation. (B) Pooling combines the values of neighbouring pixels in order to reduce the size of the representation. This also increases the size of a kernel's receptive window relative to the original image. Average pooling (left) takes a contiguous block of pixels and averages them together. More common in DCNNs is max pooling (middle), which simply chooses the highest value in the block as its output. This allows the strongest signal of a feature within that block to pass through the network. A simple example of max pooling (right) is shown for illustration. Each colour shows a pooling block, with the highest value darkened for emphasis.

complex features. These second-order features might, for example, combine lines at different orientations into corners or curves. Each layer builds its features by combining the features of the previous layer. After one or more layers of convolution, a pooling layer will combine neighbouring pixels in groups of four (i.e., 2×2) or more, depending on the architecture of the network. Pooling reduces the size of a layer while also increasing the receptive window of a feature. This means that a feature in a deeper layer of a DCNN will represent information from a larger section of the original image than an earlier-layer feature. As a consequence of this, the deeper layers of a DCNN are less bound to specific locations in the original image than earlier layers. After multiple layers of convolution and pooling, a DCNN has one or more 'fully connected' layers. As the name suggests, each unit of this type of layer is fully connected to each unit of the previous layer. Here, a unit refers to a simulated neuron, or a node connected to other nodes in the neural network. Unlike convolutional layers, the units of a fully connected layer have no relationship to a location in the original image.

When a face image is input into a face identification DCNN, the output is generally a vector of numbers that acts as an identity descriptor. This is conceptually similar to the identity descriptors derived by traditional approaches, but derived entirely from the training images and identity labels. The angle (or sometimes distance) between two such vectors can be used as a measure of similarity between images. In order for this similarity score to result in a match or non-match decision about the two images, the designer must choose a criterion cut-off score. As described earlier, the criterion is the similarity score above which the images are considered a match, and below which the images are considered a non-match. One method for finding a criterion score is to choose the percentage of false positives an operator is willing to accept, and to find the similarity score that yields the desired percentage using a dataset with ground-truth identity labels.

The complexity of DCNNs makes them incredibly powerful, but it also requires a staggering amount of training data to be effective. For instance, the MegaFace training dataset contains 4.7 million images of 672,000 different identities (Nech & Kemelmacher-Shlizerman, 2017). It is important that a training dataset not only has a large number of images, but also multiple images per identity. The images should also be highly variable in terms of, for example, lighting and viewpoint, so the network can properly learn to recognise a person across these changes. As a consequence of the complexity of the networks and the size of the training data, DCNNs can sometimes take weeks to train even with powerful parallel processing although, once the network is trained, a face can be processed in fractions of a second.

9.3 What Role Can Algorithms Play in Security Scenarios?

9.3.1 Automated Border Control and Secure Authentication (1:1 Matching)

One of the most familiar uses of face recognition for people who travel internationally are Automated Border Control (ABC) e-gates. The traveller presents their passport to the e-gates while their face is also captured by a camera, allowing an image-matching comparison to be computed. E-gates are featured at airports internationally. Best practice guidelines state that 'all ABC systems must be monitored by a human operator' (FRONTEX, 2015).

E-gates generally compute identification quickly, despite several steps involved in the process. The ABC system must first check that the passport chip is genuine and that it is a match to demographic information on the passport. The live-capture image of the holder, as taken by the camera attached to the e-gate, is then compared against the image stored on the passport chip. It is recommended that the captured image should also be compared against the scanned image on the passport to catch instances of passport tampering. Additionally, in an attempt to identify wanted suspects or missing people, these images may be compared against a database (e.g., a watchlist). If there are any inconsistencies in image matches, a flag against a watchlist image, or if the system 'times out', the traveller is referred to a passport officer for adjudication. Otherwise, the e-gate opens to allow the passenger to pass.

According to FRONTEX guidelines, algorithms must operate at a false acceptance rate (FAR) of 0.1% or less (see Figure 9.4). This is equivalent to a scenario whereby someone gets away with using another person's passport (the e-gate opens in error) 1 in 1,000 times. Additionally, the false rejection rate (FRR) should not exceed 5%. This means that only 1 in 20 people will be flagged in error to be processed by a border

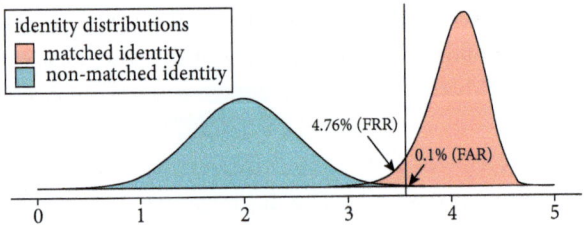

Figure 9.4 Hypothetical match and non-match distributions of a recognition system that would barely pass the criteria of the FRONTEX guidelines for passport recognition systems (FAR <= 0.1%, FRR <= 5%).

official. Interestingly, these recognition rates are quite liberal in comparison to those recommended for iris recognition (FAR = 0.001%). Independent tests of the ABC system are advised, and should preferably take place in the live environment because this may present new challenges that are not always included in algorithm testing procedures.

It is recommended that ABC e-gate systems should include 'live-ness' detection systems to check that a person has actually presented their face to the e-gate camera rather than a photograph or a mask (see Sanders & Jenkins, this volume). Camera quality is recommended to be at least 2 megapixels, with a minimum frame rate of 10 frames per second. Suggested lighting conditions are also reported in the FRONTEX report. As the above are recommended, rather than required, it follows that image capture systems may differ substantially across location.

9.3.2 Policing Scenarios (1:N Matching)

In policing scenarios, an officer may be tasked with trying to identify a person from an image, such as a CCTV image from a crime scene. This can be a difficult task, and there may be a large database of known offenders to compare the image against. An algorithm can *assist* the investigation by narrowing down the number of possible identity matches in a database. The target image is compared against database images, and the most similar images returned in a candidate list—a list of the most similar *x* number (number determined by the human operator) of identities to the input image (see Davies et al., 2018). While it is time-consuming for an officer to search a large database of potential suspects, an algorithm can perform such a task very quickly. But, because algorithms are not 100% accurate, a human operator is required to view the output image(s) and decide if a match is present.

Several police forces have trialled face recognition technology. However, there are few reports of the effectiveness of these systems in practice. Often, the ground truth (true identity) for face identifications is unknown, making it difficult to assess the accuracy of these systems in practice. In the few reports that exist, the human operator's verdict is often taken as ground truth. This is problematic, because we know that human face matching is error prone (see Fysh, this volume).

Davies et al. (2018) provide a report of South Wales Police's usage of automated face recognition systems. Their report explains two uses of algorithms in police investigations, which are termed 'Locate' and 'Identify'. The Locate mode is used in live face-matching situations. A camera scans a live crowd and compares the faces against custody images from a police database. If a match is identified, the police officer is alerted. If the officer believes that the match is 'true', then the person may be stopped by an officer and asked for their name and ID.

The Identify mode is used in police investigations to compare a single input image (such as a CCTV image) against a database to generate a candidate list of the most similar images ($N = 200$). The report emphasises that the algorithm is used as a tool to assist officers in their investigations. To help clarify the algorithm's role in investigations, the authors refer to the system as 'assisted face recognition' rather than 'automated face recognition'.

Algorithms search databases far faster than the human eye, making it possible to compare an input image against a large number of potential matches. This increases the likelihood that a correct match will be returned. However, the latest algorithms may return multiple faces that are of high visual similarity both to the target and to each other. The increase in algorithm accuracy has resulted in a challenging image comparison task for the human operator when selecting the target from the returned candidate list (see White, Dunn, et al., 2015).

9.4 Review of Face Recognition Accuracy

Automatic face recognition systems are most useful if they increase not only the speed of face recognition, but also the accuracy of facial identifications above that of human performance. This section begins with a brief review of the strengths and limitations of human face recognition and is followed by a review of algorithm face recognition performance from the early 2000s to the present day.

9.4.1 Human Face Recognition Accuracy: The Alternative to Algorithms

Prior to the invention of automatic face recognition systems, human operators controlled all levels of the face identification procedure. Nowadays, verification can be performed by humans and by algorithms. In many countries, the prevalence of face recognition technology in policing and security scenarios has increased. However, the use of face recognition technology has been met by a recent backlash of privacy concerns (e.g., the San Francisco face recognition ban)[1]. The choice to remove machines from the identification process results in the use of the only alternative to algorithm-human systems: An entirely human-based system. Before the identification accuracy

---

[1] https://www.bbc.co.uk/news/technology-48276660 (accessed 1 May 2020).

of algorithms is reviewed, human face recognition performance must be considered, because this provides a baseline against which algorithm accuracy can be compared.

Humans are extremely accurate at recognising the faces of people whom they know well, such as the faces of friends and family members. Identification and matching scenarios are much more challenging when the face is unknown (unfamiliar) to the viewer (Burton et al., 2010; Jenkins et al., 2011). In unfamiliar face-matching tasks, humans make errors on approximately 20% of trials under optimised conditions (Burton et al., 1999; Burton et al., 2010). Training does little to improve performance (Dowsett & Burton, 2014; Towler, White, et al., 2014, 2017; Towler, Kemp, et al., 2019; White, Kemp, Jenkins, et al., 2014; Woodhead et al., 1979), and passport officers perform with comparable accuracy to undergraduate students on these tasks (White, Kemp, Jenkins, Matheson, et al., 2014). There are, however, some professional groups, such as forensic facial examiners with access to the tools used for casework (Phillips et al., 2018) and specialist passport officers (White, Phillips, et al., 2015), who as a group, outperform student control groups (for a review, see White, Towler, & Kemp, this volume).

There are large individual differences in face recognition ability, which falls on a normal distribution spectrum. One method to increase face recognition performance in security contexts is therefore to recruit people from the top end of this distribution (often referred to as 'super-recognisers') into jobs where this skill is important (Noyes et al., 2017). However, the consistency of performance of super-recognisers across time, and across tasks, is yet to be established (see Bate, Mestry, & Portch, this volume; see also Bate et al., 2019; Ramon et al., 2019; Young & Noyes, 2019).

In addition, human face recognition performance is impaired by several factors (see Fysh, this volume). These include low image quality (Bindemann et al., 2013; Burton et al., 1999) and differences in image properties between the target and comparison images (e.g., pose, illumination, camera-to-subject distance) (Hill & Bruce, 1996; Noyes & Jenkins, 2017; O'Toole et al., 1998). Human performance also deteriorates when conducting face recognition tasks for long periods of time (Fysh & Bindemann, 2017) and is subject to a race bias, known as the 'other-race effect', whereby faces of races other than one's own are harder to recognise (Feingold, 1914; Malpass & Kravitz, 1969). A predominant theory to explain the other-race effect is the experience or 'contact' hypothesis (Carroo, 2011; Chiroro & Valentine, 1995). According to the experience model, human face recognition ability is fine-tuned to the faces with which we have most experience during childhood (cf. Kelly et al., 2005, 2007).

In sum, even people who are very skilled at unfamiliar face identification make errors on these tasks. Human performance is impaired by factors such as image quality, fatigue, and the other race effect (Burton et al., 1999; Fysh & Bindemann, 2017; Kelly et al., 2007). Moreover, given the large volumes of digital image evidence generated in criminal investigations via CCTV, social media, and smartphone cameras, there is an increasing demand by police agencies for tools that use this evidence effectively. Humans are simply unable to process these images in large volumes. Algorithms make it possible to make use of this data because they can rapidly compute identity decisions for large databases of faces.

9.4.2 Assessing Algorithm Accuracy

Algorithms address several human shortcomings in face recognition. They can process large databases quickly, and are immune to some factors that affect human error, such as fatigue. But how accurate are these algorithms? And are they really better than humans?

There are several challenges associated with evaluating the accuracy of face recognition algorithms in a general and objective way. Meaningful comparisons across algorithms require comparisons to be made on the same task, and on the same image database. In the 1990s, the US Government sponsored competitions to measure algorithm accuracy on the same tasks and images. Data from these competitions now span decades and demonstrate large improvements in algorithm accuracy across time (Phillips et al., 2000, 2005, 2012). Recent years have seen an increase in formalised objective comparisons across machines, and between humans and machines (Huang et al., 2008; Kemelmacher-Shlizerman et al., 2016; O'Toole et al., 2012; Phillips et al., 2015, 2018). The Government-sponsored competitions have typically attracted commercial competitors. University-led competitions have also become popular among a largely academic audience (e.g., Huang et al., 2008; Kemelmacher-Shlizerman et al., 2016).

In these competitions, tasks can include 1:1 image matching, 1:N image matching, or image classification. The databases used in these competitions have changed across time to reflect improvements in camera quality, and also to encompass greater image variability. Early databases consisted of frontal images (Phillips et al., 2000), whereas later datasets introduced factors such as varied illumination, pose, 3D images (Phillips et al., 2005), and uncontrolled images (e.g., 'images in-the-wild') (Huang et al., 2008). Such competitions have led to the creation of highly challenging image databases (e.g., IJB-C, see Maze et al., 2018).

9.4.3 Early Algorithms

The algorithms that competed in the early government challenges (Phillips et al., 2000, 2003, 2005) fall into the category of 'early algorithms' that we described in Section 9.2. In 2005, the state-of-the-art for these algorithms was high accuracy on highly controlled frontal-to-frontal image-matching tasks, but these algorithms did not fare well on unconstrained images. Algorithm performance progressed over time, and later versions of these early algorithms rivalled humans on 1:1 image comparison tasks that involved highly controlled frontally posed datasets (Jenkins & Burton, 2008; O'Toole, Phillips, et al., 2007; O'Toole et al., 2012). Notably, the accuracy of these algorithms was greatly reduced for face images that varied in pose, illumination, or expression (O'Toole et al., 2012; Phillips et al., 2012, 2015; Sankaranarayanan et al., 2016; Sengupta et al., 2016). By 2012, some early algorithms were comparable to, or better than, humans at matching frontal images across changes in illumination (indoor versus outdoor lighting) (O'Toole et al., 2012). However, this was the limit of their capability. Several more recent studies have tested algorithms of these early designs on more natural image types, known as 'in the wild' images. Early algorithm accuracy is far lower for these uncontrolled images than for controlled images (Sankaranarayanan et al., 2016; Sengupta et al., 2016).

9.4.4 State-of-the-Art Performance

Whereas the effective operation of early algorithm performance is limited to good quality, front-facing images, newer algorithms based on DCNNs perform well across a range of image scenarios (Taigman et al., 2014). This is reflective of the varied image sets that they are trained on (see Section 9.2). Ranjan et al. (2018) report face identification results for highly challenging datasets (IJB-A, -B, and -C) and Challenge Set 5 (most recent). The galleries in Ranjan et al. (2018) each consisted of over 1 million 'in the wild' face images. Results are reported for various false accept cut-off points. However, here we report results at the 0.1% false accept rate, because this is consistent with the false accept rate for ABC e-gates discussed in Section 9.3.

The challenges spanned two types of task. These were 1:1 verification tasks in which the algorithm decided if two probe images were of the same identity, and a 1:N mixed search, sometimes referred to as a '1:many' task. In 1:N tasks, the algorithm receives a probe (input) image, and creates a candidate list of N possible matches, ranked in order of similarity to the probe. On the 1:1 verification task, the top-performing algorithm performed with over 94% with a true accept rate (TAR) of over 94% on all three versions (IJB-A, -B, and -C) at the 0.1% false accept rate. It also performed at over 98% TAR for this task on the Challenge Set 5 dataset. On the 1:N task, this same algorithm returned the correct rank 1 candidate (i.e., the image with the highest similarity to the input) over 95% of the time in all but one of six tasks (accuracy was at 91% in the exception case). For the latest dataset (Challenge Set 5), accuracy rose to 97%. Across all datasets, the algorithm returned the correct match within the top 10 candidates over 98% of the time. These results demonstrate that the latest algorithms can achieve very high levels of performance accuracy on uncontrolled images.

9.4.5 Fusion

Accuracy was amplified by combining the results of *different* algorithms through fusion (Ranjan et al., 2018). This process mirrors that of a phenomenon known as 'wisdom of the crowds', which is when the collective opinion of a group of people is more accurate than the opinion of the individual. This effect has also been observed for fusing identity judgements from humans in matching tasks (Jeckeln et al., 2018; White et al., 2013).

9.4.6 Link Between Size of Training Database and Performance

Zhou, Cao, and Yin (2015) report a noteworthy pattern in the data on DCNN face recognition: The link between the size of the training database and the performance of the DCNN. As noted in Section 9.2, DCNNs are trained on a staggering number of images (millions, consisting of thousands of identities). Increasing the size of the training dataset appears to increase the performance of the algorithm. In other words, an algorithm performs better if it has been trained on more data.

Three conclusions can be made for DCNN performance: 1) State-of-the-art algorithms perform with very high accuracy on tasks that involve 'in the wild' faces, 2) fusing similarity scores of multiple algorithms can increase identification accuracy even further, and 3) increasing the size of the training data also increases DCNN performance.

9.4.7 Algorithm Bias

It is important to note that algorithms demonstrate several patterns of image bias. For example, identification accuracy of male faces is often higher than identification accuracy for female faces (e.g., Blanton et al., 2016). Additionally, Phillips et al. (2011) report an 'other-race effect' for both humans and early algorithms. In their study, half the human participants were Caucasian and the other half were East Asian. A Caucasian algorithm (made by fusing similarity scores of eight algorithms made in Western countries) and an East Asian algorithm (made by fusing five algorithms created in East Asian countries) were also tested. Performance was measured on recognition of highly controlled images of Caucasian and East Asian faces. Humans performed more accurately on faces of their own race. Algorithms performed best on the predominant race where the algorithm was developed (Phillips et al., 2011).

These published findings are based on older class algorithms. However, bias has also been reported for DCNNs (El Khiyari & Wechsler, 2016; Krishnapriya et al., 2019). This may reflect bias in training data (Klare et al., 2012) and/or differences in image quality (Krishnapriya et al., 2019). A very recent assessment of algorithm performance from the Face Recognition Vendor Test reports that the four top-performing algorithms made the least errors for Black male faces when compared against performance for White male, White female, and Black female faces (Klare, 2019). Demographic differentials were observed in the majority of algorithms tested in the NIST Face Recognition Vendor Test (Grother et al., 2019). The extent of these differences depended upon both the algorithm and the task at hand. It is therefore critical that users know the capabilities and limitations of their algorithm and set appropriate criterion thresholds to minimise bias (Cavazos, Phillips, Castillo, & O'Toole, 2019).

9.4.8 Comparison of Human and Algorithm Accuracy

Algorithm and human face recognition is a topic that spans both the psychology and the computer science literature. Several computer science papers include data on human face recognition accuracy. However, the methods used to assess human performance in the computer science literature are often inconsistent with those used in the psychology literature. The following points must be kept in mind when making conclusions on human and machine performance from the computer science literature. Psychologists tend to compute the average accuracy of each participant as derived from their individual (i.e., non-aggregated) response. O'Toole and Phillips (2017) argue that computer science reports of human face recognition accuracy are often inflated through misuse of fusion. Instead of averaging the overall performance of each human participant on a task, the classification accuracy of humans is often derived by averaging each judgement across all participants. This inflates accuracy due to the 'wisdom of the crowds' phenomenon. Computer science papers often report this fused human score, when the *average* human score should be reported. Computer science studies also often fail to account for factors such as face familiarity, the other-race effect, and access to information other than the face (e.g., body or clothing), all of which can influence human performance (O'Toole & Phillips, 2017).

O'Toole et al. (2012) provide the first direct comparison of human and algorithm 1:1 face-matching performance. In their study, humans (undergraduate students) and algorithms were tested on their ability to match a subset of images from the Face Recognition Grand Challenge image set. The images were carefully selected to contain 'easy' (constant illumination) and 'difficult' (varied illumination) image pairs. Algorithms consistently outperformed these untrained human lay observers on the easy image pairs. Moreover, three out of the four algorithms that were tested also outperformed humans on the difficult image pairs (O'Toole et al., 2012).

Earlier in this section, we noted that some individuals are better at recognising faces than others. Super-recognisers and forensic examiners with access to their tools perform particularly well on face recognition tasks (see White, Towler, & Kemp, this volume). Phillips et al. (2018) compared the performance of four DCNNs (state-of-the art in 2015, through to 2017) against undergraduate students, super-recognisers, and forensic examiners with access to their tools on a difficult face-matching task involving 20 frontal-facing face image pairs. The images varied in illumination and—to a lesser degree—in expression. The results showed that algorithms have made dramatic accuracy gains between 2015 and 2017. The 2015 algorithm performed with accuracy levels that were comparable to the score of the median undergraduate student, whereas the 2017b algorithm performed at a comparable level to the median forensic examiner and medium super-recogniser. This means that some examiners and some super-recognisers were better than the algorithm and some were worse, but the algorithm was equal to the 'middle value' of forensic examiners.

9.4.9 Accuracy of Algorithms Out in the Field

Thus far, we have covered algorithm accuracy as tested in controlled experimental settings. If these algorithms are to be used in real-world applications, it is important to test accuracy of algorithms 'in the field'. Davies et al. (2018) provide a report of South Wales Police's usage of automated face recognition systems. Their report explains two modes of usage of algorithms in police investigations. These are termed 'Locate' and 'Identify' (explained in 9.3.2).

A field test was designed to test accuracy of the Locate system. In this test, images of police officers were added to a watchlist, and the system was tested on how accurately it flagged these officers when their live face image was captured by the system. The ground truth of the officers was known, making it possible to assess algorithm accuracy. The algorithm flagged a true match between the officer and the image on the watchlist on between 76% and 81% of trials. In practice, a human officer would be required to review and verify the match.

The report also includes accuracy of the Locate system in operational deployments. There were 1,200 database images, made up of traditional police custody 'mugshot' images and other 'non-custody' images, which had been taken outside. Despite the relatively high accuracy of the system in the field test reported above, in applied practice the system flagged many faces that were deemed as false positives by the human operator. In initial usage of the algorithm, just 3% of flagged images were considered to be a true match. However, this number rose to 46% in later deployments (Davies et al., 2018). Arguably, the remaining 54% of identifications cannot be considered false positives because the human reviewer will ultimately decide whether to follow up the flagged identity to make a positive identification. Notwithstanding, the algorithm deployment resulted in a small number of arrests.

The report outlines several challenges experienced with the Locate system—namely, image quality, lighting, occluded features, and operational issues. The algorithm required good-quality database images in order to compute accurate similarity scores. Lighting affected matching accuracy, with the system performing poorly in dim lighting. Additionally, certain clothing and accessories, which obscured parts of the face when worn, reduced algorithm accuracy. And in live matching scenarios, the system often lagged, froze, or crashed, when dealing with images of crowds (Davies et al., 2018).

The success of the Identify system was also evaluated. Here, database images consisted of around 45,000 police custody images (mugshot-style images). The exact number increased over time. The quality of the probe image had a substantial effect on system accuracy. Between the end of October 2017 and March 2018, the algorithm rejected 60% of all input images because of poor image quality. Many of these rejected images were mobile phone images of CCTV footage. In this same time frame, 73% of the images that were accepted by the algorithm returned a possible true match within the candidate list, as confirmed by a police operator. Within these cases, the true match was listed as the rank 1 candidate 60% of the time, and listed within the top 10 ranked candidates 90% of the time. Notably, the 'true match' here cannot necessarily be considered a ground truth because humans also make face-matching errors.

9.5 Interactions Between Algorithms and Humans in Face Recognition

In this section, we consider the advantages and disadvantages of interactions between algorithms and humans. Specifically, we discuss the benefits of combining the response of algorithms and humans through fusion, and also consider the influence that an algorithm's identification may have on the human decision-making process.

9.5.1 Fusion of Algorithm and Human Similarity Scores

It is well documented that accuracy of human face recognition can be improved by wisdom of the crowds—fusing the decisions of multiple people on an item-by-item basis or, simply put, the combined judgement of many is better than the decision of an individual (Jeckeln et al., 2018; White et al., 2013). There is a similar benefit from fusing the performance of multiple algorithms (Ranjan et al., 2018). In addition, fusing the response of humans with that of algorithms has also led to large performance gains over the response of either humans or algorithms alone (O'Toole, Abdi, et al., 2007; Phillips et al., 2018). O'Toole, Abdi, et al. (2007) report that fusion of human and algorithm similarity scores resulted in near-perfect accuracy on images from the Face Recognition Grand Challenge (Phillips et al., 2005). Additionally, Phillips et al. (2018) report that highest identification accuracy was achieved by combining the decisions of the top-performing humans (forensic examiners) with the identifications provided by the algorithm. Fusion of human and machine identification decisions works in boosting overall performance, because humans and algorithms most likely use different methods to compute their similarity calculations. For example, some images that are challenging to an algorithm are not similarly challenging to humans, and vice versa (O'Toole et al., 2012). Fusion therefore utilises the individual strengths of both humans and algorithms.

9.5.2 Interference of Systems

In applied face identification scenarios that involve both humans and machines, humans act as check and balance against algorithm identification. In an ideal operational scenario, the human and algorithm would agree on correct identification verdicts. When the algorithm is incorrect, the human must catch and correct the algorithm error. In practice, the human operator may receive the algorithm output (similarity score) prior to reaching their identification decision. This raises an important question of whether the human operator is influenced by the algorithm's verdict.

Fysh and Bindemann (2018) tested whether human face matching is influenced by the presence of a pre-assigned identification label, such as that provided by an algorithm. In their study, participants viewed pairs of face images and made same/different identity responses to each image pair. Each pair of faces had been assigned a label of 'same identity', 'different identity', or 'unresolved' (representing no answer from the algorithm). Participants were told that the assigned label would often be accurate; this was true and reflected the high accuracy rates of current algorithms. The result was that the label influenced the identification: Incorrect identifications were made most often for image pairs that had an incorrect label. Instruction to ignore the label made no difference to the label's influence. Performance on the trials labelled 'unresolved' was in line with performance on standardised face-matching tasks (e.g., Burton et al., 2010). Additionally, Heyer, Semmler and Hendrickson (2018) report that candidate list length affects accuracy of a human reviewer. Candidate lists of over 100 items produced more false accepts, fewer true accept, and lower confidence in identifications than smaller candidate lists. Further testing is necessary to assess the effect of algorithm output on the accuracy of the human reviewer in practice.

9.5.3 When Humans Are the Weak Link in the System

The accuracy of any human-algorithm system is limited by the accuracy of each of these components—the human and the algorithm. If the human operator holds authority over the final identification, then the algorithm's performance is capped by the accuracy of the human operator.

Algorithms regularly return a true match to an input image within a candidate list. However, it is up to a human to select and confirm a match from this list. White, Dunn, et al. (2015) argue that humans may be the weak link in this process. They tested accuracy of undergraduate students and passport officers for selecting a match, or for identifying a target as absent, from a candidate list generated by an algorithm. In White, Dunn, et al. (2015), participants made errors in selecting the correct match from a candidate list on 50% of trials. Furthermore, there was no difference in the performance of undergraduate students and passport officers. However, a specialist group of face examiners made 20% fewer errors. The results from White, Dunn, et al. (2015) demonstrate that, even if algorithms are highly accurate at returning a correct match within a candidate list, humans are not always accurate at selecting the match from the list.

9.6 Summary

State-of-the-art face recognition algorithms modeled on DCNNs are far more accurate than their predecessors, and can operate accurately over greater image variation. This is because DCNNs leverage deep architectures and are often trained with millions of images of thousands of identities. Between the years of 2015 and 2017, algorithm face-matching accuracy increased from that of the median undergraduate student to that of the median forensic examiner (Phillips et al., 2018). It is likely that DCNN performance will continue to rise as training datasets become larger and algorithm developers begin to tackle more challenging image scenarios.

Algorithm accuracy is increasing at such a rapid rate that the literature that reports state-of-the-art performance quickly becomes outdated. The latest algorithms perform with very high accuracy on image-matching tasks involving front-facing images (Phillips et al., 2018), and also on much more challenging, naturalistic images (Ranjan et al., 2018). Ranjan et al. (2018) report impressive return rates of true matches within top 10 (and increasingly rank 1) images on candidate lists.

How do algorithms compare with humans? Algorithms perform more accurately than the average human on many frontal 1:1 and 1:N image-matching tasks. Algorithms' and humans' performance on images 'in the wild' has not yet been compared directly. However, we know that this is often a difficult task for humans, and algorithms are scoring with increasingly high accuracy on these types of task. In terms of speed and breadth of search scope, algorithms far outweigh humans. Algorithms can search databases of millions of images and return a list of possible matches within seconds. However, despite the impressive accuracy rates of algorithms, human verification remains an important part of the face identification process. In operational settings, humans are most often required to inspect and review the algorithm output. Face recognition algorithms have been described as a tool that can be used to assist investigations (Davies et al., 2018).

While algorithms have several strengths, it is also important to consider their limitations. Studies have revealed both gender and race biases in algorithm face identification (Blanton et al., 2016; Phillips et al., 2011). It is important to remember that humans also exhibit an other-race effect in their face recognition performance: Typically, performance is higher for recognising faces of own than other races (Carroo, 2011; Malpass & Kravitz, 1969). The experience hypothesis explains this in terms of fine-tuning face recognition expertise to races experienced mostly during childhood (Kelly et al., 2005, 2007). Analogously, algorithm race bias might be linked to an imbalance in faces of certain races represented within training data (Klare et al., 2012; Zhang & Deng, 2020).

Algorithms also experience several challenges in live deployment scenarios. Many of the issues with live deployment have been linked to poor image quality. Additionally, a large number of false positive responses result in a large workload for the human operator (Davies et al., 2018). Lighting and clothing can also affect algorithm accuracy (Davies et al., 2018). Despite these issues, the use of algorithms in live deployment scenarios has resulted in a small number of arrests. It is important to also investigate more deliberate attempts to deceive the system, including by using masks (Sanders et al., 2017), morphs (Robertson et al., 2017), and disguise (Noyes & Jenkins, 2019).

Face recognition systems rely on the accuracy and efficiency of both humans and algorithms. At times, the accuracy of one may be capped by accuracy of the other (Fysh & Bindemann, 2018; White, Dunn, et al., 2015). However, both humans and machines can contribute to the identification effort. Indeed, the best systems may result from fusing the judgements of the best-performing humans with the scores of algorithms. This resulted in the most accurate performance in a recent face-matching test for frontal images (Phillips et al., 2018). It is not yet known whether the benefit extends to more challenging images.

Accurate algorithm performance is dependent upon well-considered policy for the use of machines in face identification. The scientific evidence supports the use of face recognition algorithms for front-facing images, and also for naturalistic images that vary in pose, illumination, expression, and so forth. Just like humans, each individual algorithm has its own strengths and limitations. As these technologies continue to evolve and grow, it is important to understand their strengths and weaknesses to ensure the appropriate use of them. Operators need to know their algorithm in order to understand its capabilities and to set appropriate thresholds to reduce bias. The science should drive the use of face recognition algorithms and their role in human-machine face identification systems.

9.7 Conclusions

Going forward, as machines become more accurate and more integrated into our daily lives, there will be important questions to consider. If algorithms consistently outperform humans, then what role should humans play in the face recognition process? Perhaps the role of the human will change from that of an equal partner to the algorithm, to that of 'error catcher', or a system manager who knows the capabilities of the algorithm and sets appropriate parameters. For example, does the image quality meet the requirements for accurate identification? Is the criterion threshold appropriate for the demographics? If humans and algorithms perform identifications in different ways, then there will always be a role for humans to catch the errors made by machines. Therefore, we expect that the most accurate identification systems will include a role for both top-performing humans and top-performing algorithms.

This work was supported by the NIH under grant R01EY029692. Thank you to Professor Alice J. O'Toole for helpful comments on a draft of this chapter.

References

Alenezi, H. M., Bindemann, M., Fysh, M. C., & Johnston, R. A. (2015). Face matching in a long task: Enforced rest breaks and desk-switching cannot maintain identification accuracy. *PeerJ, 3,* e1184. doi:10.7717/peerj.1184

Bate, S., Portch, E., Mestry, N., & Bennetts, R. J. (2019). Redefining super recognition in the real world: Skilled face or person identity recognizers? *British Journal of Psychology*, 110, 480–482. doi:10.1111/bjop.12392.

Beattie, L., Walsh, D., McLaren, J., Biello, S. M., & White, D. (2016). Perceptual impairment in face identification with poor sleep. *Royal Society Open Science*, 3(10), 160321. doi:10.1098/rsos.160321

Bindemann, M., Attard, J., Leach, A., & Johnston, R. A. (2013). The effect of image pixelation on unfamiliar face matching. *Applied Cognitive Psychology*, 27, 707–717. doi:10.1002/acp.2970

Blanton, A., Allen, K. C., Miller, T., Kalka, N. D., & Jain, A. K. (2016). A comparison of human and automated face verification accuracy on unconstrained image sets. *IEEE Computer Society Conference on Computer Vision and Pattern Recognition Workshops*, 229–236. doi:10.1109/CVPRW.2016.35

Burton, A. M., White, D., & McNeill, A. (2010). The Glasgow Face Matching Test. *Behavior Research Methods*, 42, 286–291. doi:10.3758/BRM.42.1.286

Burton, A. M., Wilson, S., Cowan, M., & Bruce, V. (1999). Face recognition in poor-quality video: Evidence from security surveillance. *Psychological Science*, 10, 243–248. doi:10.1111/1467-9280.00144

Cadieu, C. F., Hong, H., Yamins, D. L. K., Pinto, N., Ardila, D., Solomon, E. A., et al. (2014). Deep neural networks rival the representation of primate IT cortex for core visual object recognition. *PLoS Computational Biology*, 10(12), e1003963. doi:10.1371/journal.pcbi.1003963

Carroo, A. W. (2011). Other race recognition: A comparison of black American and African subjects. *Perceptual and Motor Skills*, 62, 135–138. doi:10.2466/pms.1986.62.1.135

Cavazos, J. G., Phillips, P. J., Castillo, C. D., & O'Toole, A. J. (2019). Accuracy comparison across face recognition algorithms: Where are we on measuring race bias? Poster presented at the 16th International Summer School for Advanced Studies on Biometrics for Secure Authentication: Biometrics and Forensic science in the Deep Learning Era, Alghero, Italy, 2019.

Chiroro, P. & Valentine, T. (1995). An investigation of the contact hypothesis of the own-race bias in face recognition. *Quarterly Journal of Experimental Psychology Section A*, 48, 879–894. doi:10.1163/_q3_SIM_00374

Davies, B., Innes, M., & Dawson, A. (2018). An evaluation of South Wales police's use of automated facial recognition. Universities' Police Science Institute Crime and Security Research Institute, Cardiff University. Available at: https://www.statewatch.org/news/2018/nov/uk-south-wales-police-facial-recognition-cardiff-uni-eval-11-18.pdf (accessed 1 May 2020).

Dowsett, A. J. & Burton, A. M. (2014). Unfamiliar face matching: Pairs out-perform individuals and provide a route to training. *British Journal of Psychology*, 106, 433–445. doi:10.1111/bjop.12103

El Khiyari, H. & Wechsler, H. (2016). Face verification subject to varying (age, ethnicity, and gender) demographics using deep learning. *Journal of Biometrics & Biostatistics*, 7, 1–5.

Feingold, G. A. (1914). The influence of environment on identification of persons and things. *Journal of the American Institute of Criminal Law and Criminology*, 5, 39–51. doi:10.2307/1133283

FRONTEX. (2015). *Best Practice Technical Guidelines for Automated Border Control (ABC) Systems*. Available at: https://books.google.co.il/books?id=bYONnQAACAAJ (accessed 1 May 2020).

Fysh, M. C. & Bindemann, M. (2017). Effects of time pressure and time passage on face matching accuracy. *Royal Society Open Science*, 4(6), 170249. doi:10.1098/rsos.170249

Fysh, M. C. & Bindemann, M. (2018). Human-computer interaction in face matching. *Cognitive Science*, 42, 1714–1732. doi:10.1111/cogs.12633

Grother, P., Ngan, M., & Hanaoka, K. (2019). Face Recognition Vendor Test (FRVT) Part 3: Demographic effects. *NISTIR 8280, December*. doi:10.6028/NIST.IR.8280.

Heyer, R., Semmler, C., & Hendrickson, A. T. (2018). Humans and algorithms for facial recognition: The effects of candidate list length and experience on performance. *Journal of Applied Research in Memory and Cognition*, 7, 597–609. doi:10.1016/j.jarmac.2018.06.002

Hill, H. & Bruce, V. (1996). Effects of lighting on the perception of facial surfaces. *Journal of Experimental Psychology: Human Perception and Performance*, 22, 986–1004. doi:10.1037/0096-1523.22.4.986

Huang, G. B., Ramesh, M., Berg, T., & Learned-Miller, E. (2008). Labeled faces in the wild: A database for studying face recognition in unconstrained environments. *Workshop on Faces in 'Real-Life' Images: Detection, Alignment, and Recognition*, 1–11.

Jeckeln, G., Hahn, C. A., Noyes, E., Cavazos, J. G., & O'Toole, A. J. (2018). Wisdom of the social versus non-social crowd in face identification. *British Journal of Psychology, 109*, 724–735. doi:10.1111/bjop.12291

Jenkins, R. & Burton, A. M. (2008). 100% accuracy in automatic face recognition. *Science, 319*:5862, 435. doi:10.1126/science.1149656

Jenkins, R., White, D., Van Montfort, X., & Burton, A. M. (2011). Variability in photos of the same face. *Cognition, 121*, 313–323. doi:10.1016/j.cognition.2011.08.001

Kelly, D. J., Quinn, P. C., Slater, A. M., Lee, K., Ge, L., & Pascalis, O. (2007). The other-race effect develops during infancy. *Psychological Science, 18*, 1084–1089. doi:10.1111/j.1467-9280.2007.02029.x

Kelly, D. J., Quinn, P. C., Slater, A. M., Lee, K., Gibson, A., Smith, M., Ge, L., & Pascalis, O. (2005). Three-month-olds, but not newborns, prefer own-race faces. *Developmental Science, 8*, 31–36. doi:10.1111/j.1467-7687.2005.0434a.x

Kemelmacher-Shlizerman, I., Seitz, S. M., Miller, D., & Brossard, E. (2016). The MegaFace benchmark: 1 million faces for recognition at scale. *Proceedings of the IEEE Computer Society Conference on Computer Vision and Pattern Recognition, December 2016*, 4873–4882. doi:10.1109/CVPR.2016.527

Klare, B. F. (2019). *Race and face recognition accuracy: Common misconceptions.* Available at: https://blog.rankone.io/2019/09/12/race-and-face-recognition-accuracy-common-misconceptions/ (accessed 1 May 2020).

Klare, B. F., Burge, M. J., Klontz, J. C., Vorder Bruegge, R. W., & Jain, A. K. (2012). Face recognition performance: Role of demographic information. *IEEE Transactions on Information Forensics and Security, 7*, 1789–1801. doi:10.1109/TIFS.2012.2214212

Krishnapriya, K. S., Vangara, K., King, M. C., Albiero, V., & Bowyer, K. (2019). Characterizing the variability in face recognition accuracy relative to race. In *Proceedings of the IEEE Conference on Computer Vision and Pattern Recognition Workshops.*

Krizhevsky, A., Sutskever, I., & Hinton, G. E. (2012). Imagenet classification with deep convolutional neural networks. *Advances in Neural Information Processing Systems, 60*, 84–90. doi:10.1145/3065386

Malpass, R. S. & Kravitz, J. (1969). Recognition for faces of own and other race. *Journal of Personality and Social Psychology, 13*, 330–334. doi:10.1037/h0028434

Maze, B., Adams, J. C., Duncan, J. A., Kalka, N. D., Miller, T., Otto, C., et al. (2018). IARPA Janus Benchmark-C: Face dataset and protocol. *2018 International Conference on Biometrics (ICB)*, 158–165. doi:10.1109/ICB2018.2018.00033

Nech, A. & Kemelmacher-Shlizerman, I. (2017). Level playing field for million scale face recognition. *Proceedings of the IEEE Conference on Computer Vision and Pattern Recognition*, 7044–7053.

Noyes, E. & Jenkins, R. (2017). Camera-to-subject distance affects face configuration and perceived identity. *Cognition, 165*, 97–104. doi:10.1016/j.cognition.2017.05.012

Noyes, E. & Jenkins, R. (2019). Deliberate disguise in face identification. *Journal of Experimental Psychology Applied, 25*, 280–290. doi:10.1037/xap0000213

Noyes, E., Phillips, P. J., & O'Toole, A. J. (2017). What is a super-recogniser? In M. Bindemann & A. M. Megreya (eds), *Face processing: Systems, disorders and cultural differences* (pp. 173–201). New York: Nova Science Publishers.

O'Toole, A. J., Abdi, H., Jiang, F., & Phillips, P. J. (2007). Fusing face-verification algorithms and humans. *IEEE Transactions on Systems, Man, and Cybernetics, Part B: Cybernetics, 37*, 1149–1155. doi:10.1109/tsmcb.2007.907034

O'Toole, A. J., An, X., Dunlop, J., & Natu, V. (2012). Comparing face recognition algorithms to humans on challenging tasks. *ACM Transactions on Applied Perception (TAP), 9*, 1–13. doi:10.1145/2355598.2355599

O'Toole, A. J., Edelman, S., & Bülthoff, H. H. (1998). Stimulus-specific effects in face recognition over changes in viewpoint. *Vision Research, 38*, 2351–2363. doi:10.1016/S0042-6989(98)00042-X

O'Toole, A. J. & Phillips, P. J. (2017). Five principles for crowd-source experiments in face recognition. *IEEE International Conference on Automatic Face and Gesture Recognition*, 735–741. doi:/10.1109/FG.2017.146

O'Toole, A. J., Phillips, P. J., Member, S., Jiang, F., Ayyad, J., & Pe, N. (2007). Face recognition algorithms surpass humans matching faces over changes in illumination. *IEEE Transactions on Pattern Analysis and Machine Intelligence*, 29:9, 1642–1646. doi:10.1109/TPAMI.2007.1107

Phillips, P. J., Beveridge, J. R., Draper, B. A., Givens, G., O'Toole, A. J., Bolme, D., et al. (2012). The good, the bad, and the ugly face challenge problem. *Image and Vision Computing*, 30, 177–185. doi:10.1016/j.imavis.2012.01.004

Phillips, P. J., Flynn, P. J., Scruggs, T., Bowyer, K. W., Chang, J., Hoffman, K., et al. (2005). Overview of the face recognition grand challenge. *IEEE Computer Society Conference on Computer Vision and Pattern Recognition*, 947–954. doi:10.1109/CVPR.2005.268

Phillips, P. J., Grother, P., Micheals, R., Blackburn, D. M., Tabassi, E., & Bone, M. (2003). Face recognition vendor test 2002. *IEEE International SOI Conference. Proceedings*, 44. doi:10.1163/_q3_SIM_00374

Phillips, P. J., Hill, M. Q., Swindle, J. A., & O'Toole, A. J. (2015). Human and algorithm performance on the PaSC face recognition challenge. *IEEE 7th International Conference on Biometrics Theory, Applications and Systems*, 1–8. doi:10.1109/BTAS.2015.7358765

Phillips, P. J., Jiang, F., Narvekar, A., Ayyad, J., & O'Toole, A. J. (2011). An other-race effect for face recognition algorithms. *ACM Transactions on Applied Perception (TAP)*, 8:2, 14.

Phillips, P. J., Moon, H., Rizvi, S. A., & Rauss, P. J. (2000). The FERET evaluation methodology for face-recognition algorithms. *IEEE Transactions on Pattern Analysis and Machine Intelligence*, 22, 1090–1104.

Phillips, P. J., Yates, A. N., Hu, Y., Hahn, C. A., Noyes, E., Jackson, K., et al. (2018). Face recognition accuracy of forensic examiners, superrecognizers, and face recognition algorithms. *Proceedings of the National Academy of Sciences*, 115, 6171–6176. doi:10.1073/pnas.1721355115

Ramon, M., Bobak, A. K., & White, D. (2019). Super-recognizers: From the lab to the world and back again. *British Journal of Psychology*, 110, 461–479. doi:10.1111/bjop.12368

Ranjan, R., Bansal, A., Zheng, J., Xu, H., Gleason, J., Lu, B., et al. (2019). A fast and accurate system for face detection, identification, and verification. *IEEE Transactions on Biometrics, Behavior, and Identity Science*, 1:2, 82–96.

Robertson, D. J., Kramer, R. S. S., & Burton, A. M. (2017). Fraudulent ID using face morphs : Experiments on human and automatic recognition, 1–12. Available at: https://doi.org/10.1371/journal.pone.0173319 (accessed 1 May 2020).

Sanders, J. G., Ueda, Y., Minemoto, K., Noyes, E., Yoshikawa, S., & Jenkins, R. (2017). Hyper-realistic face masks: A new challenge in person identification. *Cognitive Research: Principles and Implications*, 2, 43. doi:10.1186/s41235-017-0079-y

Sankaranarayanan, S., Alavi, A., Castillo, C. D., & Chellappa, R. (2016). Triplet probabilistic embedding for face verification and clustering. *IEEE 8th International Conference on Biometrics Theory, Applications and Systems*, 1–8. doi:10.1109/BTAS.2016.7791205

Sengupta, S., Chen, J. C., Castillo, C., Patel, V. M., Chellappa, R., & Jacobs, D. W. (2016). Frontal to profile face verification in the wild. *IEEE Winter Conference on Applications of Computer Vision*, 1–9. doi:10.1109/WACV.2016.7477558

Taigman, Y., Yang, M., & Ranzato, M. A. (2014). Deepface: Closing the gap to human-level performance in face verification. *CVPR IEEE Conference*, 1701–1708. doi:10.1109/CVPR.2014.220

Towler, A., Kemp, R. I., Burton, A. M., Dunn, J. D., Wayne, T., Moreton, R., et al. (2019). Do professional facial image comparison training courses work? *PLoS ONE*, 14(2), e0211037. doi:10.1371/journal.pone.0211037

Towler, A., White, D., & Kemp, R. I. (2014). Evaluating training methods for facial image comparison: The face shape strategy does not work. *Perception*, 43, 214–218. doi:10.1068/p7676

Towler, A., White, D. & Kemp, R. (2017). Evaluating the feature comparison strategy for forensic face identification. *Journal of Experimental Psychology: Applied*, 23, 47–58. doi:10.1037/xap0000108

Turk, M. & Pentland, A. (1991). Eigenfaces for recognition. *Journal of Cognitive Neuroscience*, 3, 71–86. doi:10.1162/jocn.1991.3.1.71

White, D., Burton, A. M., Kemp, R. I., & Jenkins, R. O. B. (2013). Crowd effects in unfamiliar face matching, 27, 769–777. doi:10.1002/acp.2971

White, D., Dunn, J. D., Schmid, A. C., & Kemp, R. I. (2015). Error rates in users of automatic face recognition software. *PLoS ONE, 10*(10), e0139827. doi:10.1371/journal.pone.0139827

White, D., Kemp, R. I., Jenkins, R., & Burton, A. M. (2014). Feedback training for facial image comparison. *Psychonomic Bulletin & Review, 21*, 100–106. doi:10.3758/s13423-013-0475-3

White, D., Kemp, R. I., Jenkins, R., Matheson, M., & Burton, A. M. (2014). Passport officers' errors in face matching. *PLoS ONE, 9*(8), e103510. doi:10.1371/journal.pone.0103510

White, D., Phillips, P. J., Hahn, C. A., Hill, M., & O'Toole, A. J. (2015). Perceptual expertise in forensic facial image comparison. *Proceedings of the Royal Society B: Biological Sciences, 282*(1814), 20151292. doi:10.1098/rspb.2015.1292

Woodhead, M. M., Baddeley, A. D., & Simmonds, D. C. V. (1979). On training people to recognize faces. *Ergonomics, 22*, 333–343. doi:10.1080/00140137908924617

Young, A. W. & Noyes, E. (2019). We need to talk about super-recognizers: Invited commentary on: Ramon, M., Bobak, A. K., & White, D. 'Super-recognizers: From the lab to the world and back again'. *British Journal of Psychology, 110*, 492–494. doi:10.1111/bjop.12395.

Zeiler, M. D. & Fergus, R. (2014). Visualizing and understanding convolutional networks. *European Conference on Computer Vision*, 818–833.

Zhang, Y., & Deng, W. (2020). Class-Balanced Training for Deep Face Recognition. In *Proceedings of the IEEE/CVF Conference on Computer Vision and Pattern Recognition Workshops*, 824–825.

Zhou, E., Cao, Z., & Yin, Q. (2015). Naive-deep face recognition: Touching the limit of LFW benchmark or not? *arXiv preprint arXiv:1501.04690.*

10

Realistic Masks in the Real World

Jet G. Sanders and Rob Jenkins

10.1 Introduction

Experimental research has confirmed that deliberate disguise can impede face recognition by humans and machines (Dhamecha et al., 2014; Noyes & Jenkins, 2019). This vulnerability has implications for person identification in both security and forensic settings. With traditional disguises, such as balaclavas or hoodies, viewers can readily distinguish between a disguised individual (whose face is plainly obscured) and an undisguised individual (whose face is plainly visible). A new generation of masks that look like real faces has altered this dynamic (see Figure 10.1). Masks that pass for human not only obscure the wearer's face—they do so without rousing suspicion.

In the past 10 years, fabrication of hyper-realistic masks has become increasingly commercialized. A range of products can be bought online for around £400 to £2,000 (Bernstein, 2010), with different manufacturers offering different variants (e.g., CFX/ Composite Effects, Hyperflesh, Immortal masks, Real-F, RealFlesh, SPFX, Studio135, Trxmask). To our knowledge, only one company has published sales figures (SPFX; Becker, 2010). Assuming that companies' sales are proportional to their Google Search results, we estimate total annual global sales of hyper-realistic masks to be around 2,000 to 4,000 units.

Modern hyper-realistic masks typically comprise a single layer of flexible silicone that covers the whole head, neck, and upper shoulder area without any joins. Some are constructed from stiffer materials and only cover the head (e.g., http://hyperflesh. com) or face (e.g., http://real-f.jp). These stiffer materials allow less facial movement and often have a single fixed facial expression. However, in recent years, whole-head silicone masks have become more structurally advanced. Many now include an integrated nose bridge, eyeholes that tuck seamlessly under the eyelids, and a 'mouth-cupping system' that allows the mask to fit around the lips into the mouth, with the aim of improving the mask's facial expression. High-end masks are typically hand-finished with detailed paintwork and punched human hair.

10.1.1 Wearing Realistic Masks

Hyper-realistic silicone masks allow the wearer to completely transform their appearance in seconds. For example, CFX/Composite Effects mask manufacturers found that,

Jet G. Sanders and Rob Jenkins, *Realistic Masks in the Real World* In: *Forensic Face Matching*. Edited by: Markus Bindemann, Oxford University Press (2021). © Oxford University Press. DOI: 10.1093/oso/9780198837749.003.0010.

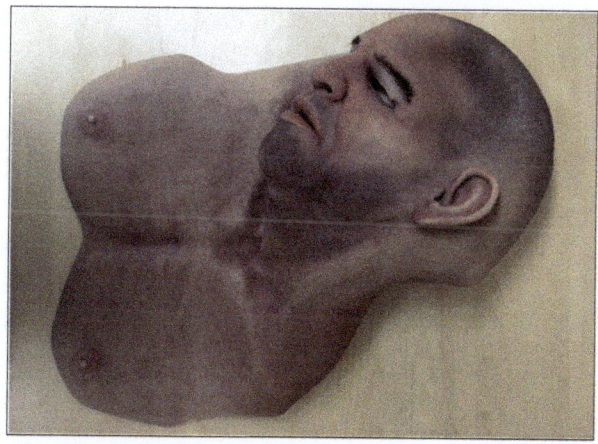 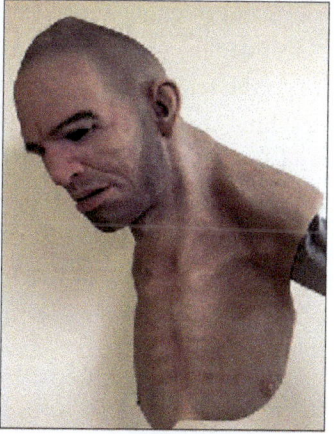

Figure 10.1 Example of a hyper-realistic face mask. Collapsed on flat surface (left) and held upright (right).

Source: Reproduced from Sanders & Jenkins (2018) 'Individual differences in hyper-realistic mask detection' *Cognitive Research: Principles and Implications, 3,* 24, Figure 1. https://doi.org/10.1186/s41235-018-0118-3 © 2018 The Authors.

in three minutes, an experienced mask wearer was able to make 21 mask changes—an average of just nine seconds per mask (Mazzuki et al., 2015; see http://bit.ly/2d293zD for a demonstration). A book on professional use of disguise describes the experience of wearing masks as follows: 'For an extended time, one of the authors wore a full-head human-like silicone mask while sitting in a dental office waiting room with a magazine in hand. Nobody using the room looked upon him with curiosity' (Mazzuki et al., 2015; p. 134). Mask users on social media echo this experience, substantiated by videos and pictures of mask wearers in everyday locations such as supermarkets (http://bit.ly/2czUkHF), hairdressers (http://bit.ly/2d28qFV) or outdoor public places (http://bit.ly/2cCR8OU). In these examples, no bystanders show any awareness that the protagonist is wearing a mask, despite some incongruous contexts (e.g., an elderly male playing football). The popular science television programme, *Mythbusters*, set up a more elaborate demonstration, appearing to show that a mask wearer can pass for a completely different person, even a person that the viewer knows (http://bit.ly/2lHmCtG). These demonstrations, and others like them, raise the unsettling possibility that individuals evading their own identity, or impersonating others, could be going undetected.

10.1.2 Mask Wearers

According to Facebook, Twitter, and Instagram, the population of mask users is estimated to be between 5,000 and 10,000 at this time. Popular forums include Realistic Silicone Masks, Silicone Mask Sickos, Silicone Mask Addicts, Silicone Mask Community, Silicone Maskerade, #compositeeffects, #realisticmasks, and #siliconemasks. Realistic masks seem to be used in three main ways. The first covers a range of professional applications. For example, hyper-realistic masks have been used for undercover investigations (Mazzuki et al., 2015), for quick Hollywood makeovers (e.g., the television series *Game of Thrones*; https://bit.ly/3945umo), for interactive teaching that involves role play (Frost & Reid-Searl, 2017; Reid-Searl et al., 2014), and for medical reasons such as protecting the wearer from sun allergy (Roberts, 2017) or facilitating face transplants (Mäkitie et al., 2016). Second, realistic masks are used to adopt an alternate identity, for Halloween parties and for cosplay (Malone, 2014). Finally, realistic masks have been used to conceal identity in criminal settings to thwart facial recognition. This chapter focuses on the use of masks for criminal purposes only.

10.1.3 Realistic Masks as Facial Identities

In principle, a mask can be cast from any face. Some companies do offer entirely personalized casts, though set-up costs are relatively high (see the 2013 episode of the television programme, *Mythbusters*, http://tiny.cc/k64q8y). For most manufacturers, the number of casts is limited. Based on the range of masks on offer, production companies seem to use 10 to 40 base casts at a time. However, variants of a single base mask can be adapted to the point where they are perceived as distinct identities. Several companies offer customization of skin colour and texture, and options for scars, moles, hair colour, hairstyle, facial hair, and chest size (on female masks), or chest hair. After-market modifications include prosthetic adhesives and facial silicone glue (Mazzuki et al., 2015). In addition to these inherent variations, the mask interacts with the facial structure of the wearer to determine apparent face shape. The masked face can be further modified by paraphernalia such as hats, wigs, sunglasses, and clothing to add character (see http://tiny.cc/k54q8y for an example). In sum, a single realistic mask can give rise to many perceived identities. The implication is that criminal misuse of realistic masks is unlikely to be tackled by cataloguing or memorizing specific mask types. Instead, a more general solution to mask detection may be required.

10.2 The Problem in Theory

10.2.1 Identification from Face Matching is Highly Error Prone

Face identification refers to the use of facial appearance to verify the identity of a specific individual. Face identification is the most common means of identification in security and forensic settings, but it is also highly error-prone. For example, the investigation into the disappearance of Malaysian Airlines flight MH370 from Kuala Lumpur in 2014 revealed that two passengers who had boarded the plane were travelling with false passports (Hodal et al., 2014). Evidently, these passengers had cleared the standard passport checks. Based on the sample of a single plane, it is hard to know whether or not this error rate is representative. What is clear is that such errors are not confined to unusual situations. Instead, they reflect a fundamental difficulty in identifying unfamiliar faces. Even under highly favourable conditions, human performance in photo-to-photo matching (comparing two face images; Burton et al., 2010) and person-to-photo matching (comparing an image to a live face; Kemp et al., 1997) is highly error-prone. Professional experience (White et al., 2014; see White, Towler, & Kemp, this volume) and training do not appear to improve performance (Towler et al., 2014; Towler et al., 2019; see Towler, Kemp, & White, this volume). Moreover, errors are almost certainly more common in real-world settings than in experimental settings. Experiments typically do not capture the changes in appearance a face can undergo in the 10-year period for which a passport is valid (Jenkins et al., 2011). Nor do they capture effects of observer fatigue, as when observers monitor for rare targets in the context of daily work (Alenezi et al., 2015). More importantly for this chapter, most face recognition studies only address situations where individuals make no deliberate attempt to change their appearance (Noyes & Jenkins, 2019).

10.2.2 Effects of Disguise on Face Matching

A meta-analysis of factors contributing to eyewitness accuracy by Shapiro and Penrod (1986) confirmed that facial transformations such as disguises clearly impair performance. Facial disguises do not need to be complex in order to be effective. Studies of traditional disguises have shown that adding or removing simple props, such as glasses, sunglasses, or facial hair can have a drastic impact on recognition memory for faces (Dhamecha et al., 2014; Patterson & Baddeley, 1977; Righi et al., 2012; Terry, 1993, 1994). These studies provide an interesting starting point for understanding disguise. However, traditional disguises all work by *occluding* facial features. They are not themselves mistaken for facial features that carry identity information. In fact, being aware of the disguise may encourage viewers to focus on undisguised regions of the face, or to conclude that the suspect cannot be identified unless the disguise is removed.

In other cases, it may be less obvious that a disguise is being used. Noyes and Jenkins (2019) investigated more naturalistic disguises that conformed to photo-ID guidelines, precluding the use of hats, hoods, sunglasses, and balaclavas. They found that evasion disguise (trying not to look like oneself) was more effective than impersonation disguise (trying to look like a specific other person). Interestingly, informing viewers about the disguise manipulations in the experiment did not improve their performance. These findings have several implications for hyper-realistic masks. First, when it is not obvious to viewers that a particular face is disguised, they may have little reason to try to foil the disguise—for example, by directing attention to diagnostic parts of the face. Second, even when viewers are alerted to the possibility of disguise, they may not have effective counter-strategies to deploy. Third, hyper-realistic masks offer much more extreme transformations of appearance, extending to changes in basic face shape and texture. If a superficial disguise can easily thwart identification, a silicone mask is likely to be even more effective—provided that the mask is not detected.

10.3 The Problem in Practice

10.3.1 Are Realistic Masks in the Real World Going Undetected?

In a number of high-profile criminal cases, protagonists have used hyper-realistic face masks to conceal their own identities or those of their victims. On separate occasions, white male Conrad Zdrierak targeted four American banks and a pharmacy wearing a black male mask. Eyewitnesses confirmed that the perpetrator was black, and some even identified a black suspect based on a security photograph (Damani, 2014; Gardner, 2010). Another US case concerns a wanted bank robber known as the 'Geezer Bandit', who committed 16 bank robberies between 2009 and 2011 (Perry, 2011). Based on eyewitness testimony and camera footage, police were originally looking for a man in his seventies. However, based on the speed at which he fled the scene of his final crime, some have suggested that the culprit was a younger person wearing an old male mask.

Hyper-realistic face masks have been used for other criminal activities besides robbing banks. For example, Swedish doctor Martin Peter Trenneborg used two hyper-realistic masks and matching passports to disguise himself and a sedated victim for a 350-mile car journey during a kidnapping (Ahlander, 2016). Hyper-realistic masks have even been used during international travel. In 2010, an Asian passenger boarded a flight from Hong Kong to Vancouver wearing an old white male mask and carrying a fraudulently obtained passport (Zamost, 2010). The mask wearer passed several identity checks at Hong Kong airport, only to be discovered when he took the mask off mid-flight. More recently, con-artists used a hyper-realistic face mask to impersonate French minister Jean-Yves Le Drian in a series of video calls (Schofield, 2019). The perpetrators succeeded in defrauding businesses of an estimated €80m before arrests were made.

Together, these examples show that hyper-realistic masks have been used for both evasion and impersonation disguise in several countries around the world. In all these cases, the masks appear to have been accepted as real faces by onlookers—that is, the use of masks was not detected directly, but was instead inferred from the incongruous behaviour of the wearer, or disclosed by another person who knew of the deceit. This pattern raises the interesting question of how frequently such masks have been used in criminal settings. It is difficult to answer this question definitively, partly because the number of *undetected* cases is, by definition, unknown. Nevertheless, a survey of reported cases can provide some insights by setting a lower bound, and by revealing any trend over time. To this end, we entered silicone, mask keywords as Google News search terms to identify separate cases. The search revealed 41 cases between 2009 and 2019 (see Table 10.1). The steady increase over this period—from one case in 2009 to

Table 10.1 Typology of criminal cases where hyper-realistic face masks were were used based on non-exhaustive search terms combining: 'silicone, latex, realistic, mask, Hollywood, old man, old woman, black man, white man, white woman, disguise, crime, robbery, border control, plane, asylum seeker' from 'Google News'.

Case	Year	Country	Crime	Wearer demographics	Mask demographics	Mask detected?	Culprit caught?	Link
1	2009	U.K.	Jewellery heist	Young white males	Young white males	No	No	https://bit.ly/2LbsJlY
2*	2010	U.S.A.	6 bank robberies	Young white male	Young black male	No	Yes	https://dailym.ai/1eq9vwa
3*	2010	Hong Kong / Canada	Illegal border crossing	Young Asian male	Old white male	No	Yes	https://bit.ly/2uFrHEr
4*	2011	U.S.A.	16 bank robberies	Unknown, profiled	Old white male	Yes	No	https://bit.ly/2O7A04c
5	2011	U.S.A.	11 bank robberies	Young white male	Young white male	No	Yes	https://cbsloc.al/2L9XRlT
6*	2012	U.S.A.	Bank robbery	Young black males	Young white males	No	Yes	https://dailym.ai/2mzGXOR
7	2012	U.K.	14 bank robberies	Young black male	Young white male	Unknown	Yes	https://bit.ly/2LuZx8K
8	2013	U.S.A.	False imprisonment	Young white male	Old white male	No	Yes	https://bit.ly/2Lf8GDh
9	2014	U.S.A.	Bank robbery	Unknown, profiled	Old white male	Yes	No	https://bit.ly/2LbakFU
10	2014	U.S.A.	Bank robbery	Unknown, profiled	Old white male	Yes	No	https://bit.ly/2A0XIvS
11	2014	U.S.A.	Bank robbery	Young white male	Old white male	Unknown	Yes	https://bit.ly/2JIUooH
12	2014	U.S.A.	Bank robbery	Young white male	Young Asian male	No	Yes	https://bit.ly/2LBrSY1
13	2014	U.S.A.	Bank robbery, assault, murder	Young black male	Old white male	No	Yes	https://bit.ly/2LuKOLc
14	2015	U.S.A.	Bank robbery	Young black male	Old white male	No	Yes	https://bit.ly/2uGdsPD
15	2015	U.S.A.	Bank robbery	Unknown, profiled	Old white male	Yes	No	https://bit.ly/2uRHW0s
16	2015	Canada	3 bank robberies	Young black male	Young white male	No	Yes	https://bit.ly/2JGVZvp
17	2015	France	Jewellery heist	Unknown, not profiled	Old white male	Yes	No	https://bit.ly/1cg2HaO

(Continued)

Table 10.1 Continued

Case	Year	Country	Crime	Wearer demographics	Mask demographics	Mask detected?	Culprit caught?	Link
18*	2015	Brazil	Prison escape	Young Hispanic male	Old white female	Yes	Yes	http://bit.ly/2bnHbo7
19	2015	U.K.	Jewellery heist	Young white male	Young white male	Yes	Yes	https://bit.ly/2myhKEf
20	2016	U.S.A.	5 bank robberies	Young white male	Old white male	No	Yes	https://bit.ly/2O5IF72
21	2016	U.S.A.	Fugitive, drug trafficking	Young white male	Old white male	Unknown	Yes	https://bit.ly/2mweNUR
22	2016	U.S.A.	2 bank robberies	Unknown, profiled	Old white male	Yes	No	https://bit.ly/2zWJjRc
23	2016	Australia	ATM scam	Unknown, not profiled	Unknown	Yes	No	https://bit.ly/2uV5S31
24*	2016	Sweden	Kidnapping	Young white male; Young white female	Old white male; Old white female	No	Yes	https://bbc.in/2O7oAxl
25	2017	U.S.A.	Bank robbery	Unknown, profiled	Old white male; Old white male	Yes	No	https://bit.ly/2OazB0S
26	2017	U.S.A.	Bank robbery	Young white male	Old white male	No	Yes	https://bit.ly/2LBV94O
27	2017	U.S.A.	2 bank robberies	Young Asian male	Old black male	Unknown	Yes	https://bit.ly/2O7ZUES
28	2017	U.S.A.	2 bank robberies	Unknown, profiled	Old black male	Yes	No	https://on-ajc.com/2uElFnp
29	2017	U.S.A.	Store robbery	Unknown, profiled	Old white male	Yes	No	https://bit.ly/2Lfl0TR
30	2017	U.S.A.	Conspiracy; kidnapping	Young white female	Old white male	No	Yes	https://bit.ly/2JH7G5c
31	2017	Israel	7 robberies	Young white male	Old white male	No	Yes	https://bit.ly/2uPMUuI
32	2017	U.S.A.	Murder	Old white male	Old white male	No	Yes	https://bit.ly/2JHVctW
33	2018	U.S.A.	2 bank robberies	Unknown, not profiled	Old white male	Yes	No	https://bit.ly/2LERFOL
34	2018	U.S.A.	4 bank robberies	Young white male	Old white male	No	No	http://bit.ly/2Uf8Iw8

#	Year	Country	Crime	Suspected profile	Actual profile	Detected	Caught	Link
35	2018	Austria	2 bank robberies	Young males	Young females in hijab	No	Yes	http://bit.ly/2L6EEQm
36	2019	U.S.A.	Bank robbery	Unknown, not profiled	Old white male	Yes	No	https://lat.ms/2L9do3E
37	2019	Brazil	Prison escape	Young Hispanic male	Young white female	Yes	Yes	http://bit.ly/32eHlzt
38*	2019	France	Impersonation, money scam	Old white male	Old white male	Yes	Yes	https://bbc.in/2NH8bC2
39	2019	U.S.A.	Bank robbery	Unknown, profiled	Old white male	Yes	No	http://bit.ly/32dPUA1
40	2019	U.S.A.	4 bank robberies	Young white male	Young black male	Yes	Yes	http://bit.ly/2zx3BOi
41	2019	Brazil	Bank robbery	Young Hispanic male	Old white male	No	No	https://dailym.ai/2L8gQLN
Most common	**41% 2017–2019**	**56% U.S.A.**	**76% robberies**	**94% young wearers 61% white wearers 94% male wearers**	**70% old masks 89% white masks 90% male masks**	**56% not detected**	**61% caught**	

Key: *High-profile criminal cases described in text.

Notes: (1) Web searches were only performed in English. (2) For realistic masks to be covered by a media outlet, they had to have been detected or caught. This is not representative of the number of cases that have gone undetected and uncaught. (3) Percentages for the most common categories are based on known statistics only.

Source: Jet G. Sanders and Rob Jenkins.

six cases in 2019—could be explained by increased prevalence or increased reporting or both.

10.4 How Could Realistic Masks Pass for Real Faces?

It is evident from the real-world cases in Table 10.1 that realistic masks can pass for real faces in some situations. One possible explanation for this is inattention on the part of observers. A long tradition of research has shown that people can fail to notice objects that are in plain sight if their attention is engaged in another task (see Mack & Rock, 1998, for a review). In a well-known demonstration of this phenomenon, people who were asked to count the number of passes in a basketball game failed to notice a man in a gorilla suit walking among the players (Simons & Chabris, 1999). These viewers were so focused on the ball that they overlooked a gorilla staring them in the face.

Continuing the primate theme, Drew et al. (2013) found that 83% of radiographers missed a gorilla image planted in a radiograph, while they were inspecting the same radiograph for anomalies. Given that such glaring intrusions can be missed when in view, it may not be surprising that relatively subtle differences between a realistic mask and a real face might also escape our notice. Part of the explanation is that expectations bias perception. Real faces are commonplace and expected in social settings. Realistic masks are rare and unexpected in social settings. Of course, the influence of expectation on perception is limited. As a general rule, the more realistic the mask, the more likely expectations can bridge the gap; the less realistic the mask, the less likely expectations can make up the distance.

10.5 How Realistic Are 'Hyper-Realistic Masks'?

10.5.1 Realism Test 1: Incidental Viewing of Realistic Masks

Imagine you are going about the world in a normal alert state, but not expecting to see a mask. If you looked at someone who was wearing a mask, would you notice it? In the first experimental test of mask realism, we devised a live viewing task to answer this question (Sanders et al., 2017). An experimental confederate wearing a high-realism mask, a low-realism mask, or no mask at all, sat at an outdoor table reading a book (Figure 10.2). At a distance of either 5 or 20 metres from the reader, experimenters stopped over 400 individual passers-by, and asked them what they thought of the reader's appearance. They were then asked whether they noticed anything unusual. Finally, participants were faced with a straight choice: Whether the person was wearing a mask or not. To our surprise, almost no one volunteered that the confederate was wearing a hyper-realistic mask (~1% hit rate). Even when pushed to a straight choice (mask or no mask), many viewers (30%) denied that the confederate was wearing a mask.

   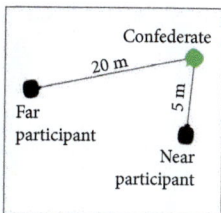

Figure 10.2 Illustration showing (from left to right) author RJ in the Low-realism mask, High-realism mask, and Real face conditions from Sanders et al. (2017), and the spatial arrangement of confederate and participants.

Source: Reproduced from Sanders et al. (2017) 'Hyper-realistic face masks: A new challenge in person identification' *Cognitive Research: Principles and Implications*, 2, 43, Figure 4. https://doi.org/10.1186/s41235-017-0079-y, © 2017, Springer Nature.

In a separate study, 54 visitors at the London Science Museum viewed a mask wearer at close range (2 metres) as part of a mock passport check (Robertson et al., 2020). Viewers answered a series of questions designed to assess mask detection, while the masked traveller was in full view. In an identity-matching task, 8% of viewers accepted the mask as matching a real photo of someone else, and 82% accepted the match between masked person and masked photo. These error rates are comparable to those seen in standard face-matching tasks such as the Glasgow Face Matching Test (Burton et al., 2010). When asked if there was any reason to detain the traveller, only 13% of viewers mentioned a mask. Only 11% more picked disguise from a list of suggested reasons that included suspicious luggage or travel destination. Even after reading about the use of masks in criminal cases, 10% of viewers judged that the traveller was not wearing a mask. This pattern implies that hyper-realistic face masks could already be sufficiently realistic to go undetected during an identity check.

One possible objection to these live viewing experiments is that participants may have been reluctant to comment on the face of a person nearby—and particularly to suggest that the face might not be real. To eliminate this possibility, we adapted the same basic design for a computer-based laboratory task that removed any social context (Sanders et al., 2017). In the computerized version, more than a hundred participants were asked to inspect 20 face photos, one at a time, and to rate each face for age, attractiveness, dominance, and trustworthiness. Participants were not informed that one of the photos showed a person wearing a hyper-realistic mask. Once they completed the rating task, participants were asked the same graded detection questions that were used in the live viewing experiment. None of the participants spontaneously mentioned the mask, even when prompted to report 'anything unusual'. This observation is particularly interesting given the impressions that participants did mention. The numerous comments on visual details such as freckles, wrinkles, and glasses suggest that attention was not the problem. Instead, it appears that the mask was accepted as a real face. This interpretation is strengthened by responses in a follow-up task. Participants were asked to look at the photos again in an array (Figure 10.3), and to pick out any

Figure 10.3 Example array challenge from Sanders et al. (2017).

Note: Participants were asked to indicate any photos that show a mask. The array always contained 19 real face photos and 1 mask photo. In this example, image 9 shows author Rob Jenkins in an old male mask.

Source: Reproduced from Sanders et al. (2017) 'Hyper-realistic face masks: A new challenge in person identification' *Cognitive Research: Principles and Implications*, 2, 43, Figure 2. https://doi.org/10.1186/s41235-017-0079-y © 2017, Springer Nature.

that showed a mask. Even then, only 70% of participants picked out the mask from the array, and those who did picked out some real faces too.

10.5.2 Realism Test 2: Discrimination and Categorization of Realistic Masks

The studies above tended to emphasize ecological validity over experimental control. To provide the complementary emphasis, we sought to develop a discrimination test for photographed faces, which follows the logic of a Turing test (Turing, 1950). This test offers a simple means to gauge the success of an imitation. In the original test, a human evaluator is engaged in natural language conversations with a real human and a computer designed to generate human-like responses. The evaluator knows that one of the two conversation partners is a computer, and is asked to determine which one it is. If the evaluator cannot reliably distinguish the computer from the human, the computer is said to have passed the test. The logic of this test provides a means for assessing the maturity of imitation technologies generally: Given the imitation alongside the real thing, can an observer tell which is which?

In a recent study (Sanders et al., 2019), we borrowed this logic to assess the success of imitation faces under photographic conditions (see Figures 10.4 and 10.5). Participants viewed pairs of face photographs, each consisting of one real face and one artificial face (a hyper-realistic mask). For each pair, the task was to decide which

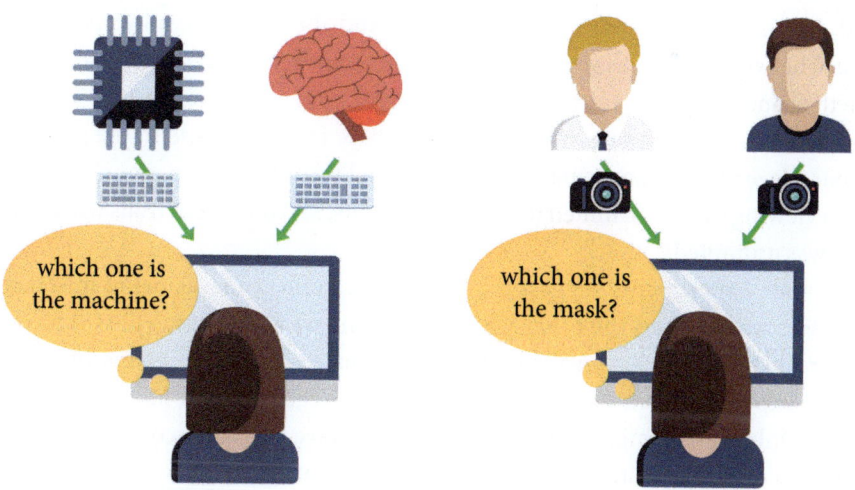

Figure 10.4 Schematic illustrating parallels between the standard Turing Test (left) and a similar test for artificial faces (right).

Note: In both cases, an evaluator is given the task of trying to determine which presentation is the genuine article and which is the imitation. The evaluator is limited to using a computer interface to make the determination.

Source: Reproduced from Sanders et al. (2019) 'More human than human: A Turing test for photographed faces' *Cognitive Research: Principles and Implications*, 4, 43 , Figure 1. https://doi.org/10.1186/s41235-019-0197-9 © 2019 The Authors.

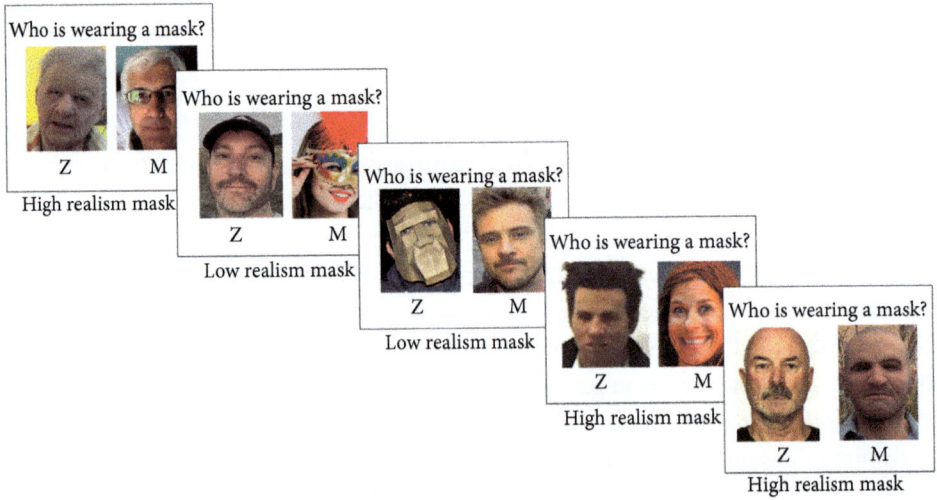

Figure 10.5 Example trials from Sanders et al. (2019).

Note: Each mask image was randomly paired with one real face image from the set, independently set for each participant. Correct answers from left to right: Z, M, Z, Z, M.

Source: Reproduced from Sanders et al. (2019) 'More human than human: A Turing test for photographed faces' *Cognitive Research: Principles and Implications*, 4, 43, Figure 2. https://doi.org/10.1186/s41235-019-0197-9 © 2019 The Authors.

image was the mask. This arrangement makes it much easier for viewers to distinguish hyper-realistic masks from real faces. The task instructions ensured that participants were aware in advance that masks would be presented. Social influence was minimized, because the task was computer based. And the task always involved a forced choice between two images. This meant that, even when participants were uncertain whether one of the images was the target, they could still solve the task indirectly if they were certain about the other image. All these factors worked in the participant's favour. Nevertheless, participants judged the real face to be the mask on 34% of trials when viewing time was limited to 500 milliseconds, and on 18% of trials when viewing time was unlimited.

Separate experiments suggest that such errors reflect masks being mistaken for real faces, rather than the other way round. Sanders and Jenkins (2018) presented high-realism masks, low-realism masks, and real faces one at a time in a computerized experiment, and asked participants to categorize each image as a mask or a face. Only 40% of high-realism mask images were classified correctly, compared with 96% of real face images. One possible explanation for these results is that the low-realism masks were very different from both the high-realism masks and the real faces, perhaps encouraging participants to group the latter categories together. However, removing the low-realism mask images did not eliminate the problem. Classification accuracy only reached 74% for masks and 91% for real faces. In all these tests, viewers had difficulty distinguishing photos of hyper-realistic masks from photos of real faces.

10.6 Eight Proposals for Improving Detection

10.6.1 Consciousness Raising

In a simple metacognition study, we asked participants to read a description of the live viewing experiment reported by Sanders et al. (2007). After reading the description, participants were asked to estimate how well people performed. Estimates of performance were much higher than actual performance. For the question, 'What do you think of this person?', estimated detection rate exceeded actual detection rate by 12%. For the follow-up question, 'Did you notice anything unusual?', estimates were 26% above actual rates. For the final question, 'Do you think you are in the mask condition, yes or no?' estimates were 10% higher than in the actual experiment. Interestingly, these overestimates were almost entirely corrected by showing participants what a hyper-realistic face mask looks like. The implication is that raising awareness of hyper-realistic masks—by showing them rather than describing them—were a simple way to correct complacency about mask detection.

10.6.2 Diagnostic Features

Sanders and Jenkins (2018) analysed visual differences between high-realism masks and real face images to determine which cues high-performing individuals might be using. The analysis revealed that mask and face stimuli were most strongly differentiated in the region below the eyes (see Figure 10.6). Interestingly, high-performing participants seemed to make use of differential information in this area, while low-performing participants did not. This pattern suggests that performance may be localized to specific image cues. If so, there may be a straightforward path for training differentiation between hyper-realistic masks and real faces.

10.6.3 Social Inference Cues

Analysis of social inference ratings such as trustworthiness, dominance, and attractiveness (Oosterhof & Todorov, 2008; Sutherland et al., 2013) hints at another potential mechanism for mask detection (Sanders et al., 2017). Viewers rated photographs of hyper-realistic face masks as significantly less attractive and less trustworthy than photographs of age-matched real faces. This suggests that low trustworthiness and low attractiveness could serve as cues to mask detection. It should be noted, however, that these cues were not used explicitly. First, none of the participants reported being aware that they had rated any masks when prompted to report on anything unusual. Second, real faces that were rated low in trustworthiness were more likely to be miscategorized as masks. To be clear, social inference ratings are not by themselves decisive, but they

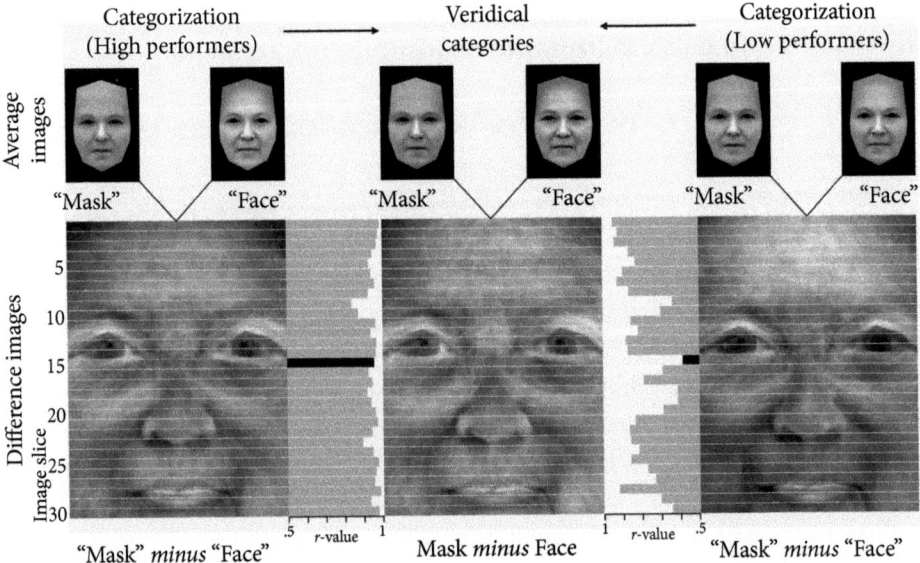

Figure 10.6 Summary of image analysis from Sanders and Jenkins (2018).

Average images show mean pixel intensities across images for Mask and Face images, separately for High performers (Left), Low performers (Right), and veridical categories (Centre). Difference images are subtractions of pixel intensity (Mask minus Face; rescaled for visualization). Lighter colours indicate larger differences. Note the light region around the eye in the veridical difference image. The y-axis shows 30 horizontal image slices. Correlations between difference images (gray bars) are shown for each image slice. The largest discrepancy between High and Low performers is shown at Slice 15 (black bars). High performers closely tracked categorical differences in this region. Low performers did not.

Source: Reproduced from Sanders & Jenkins (2018) 'Individual differences in hyper-realistic mask detection' *Cognitive Research: Principles and Implications*, 3, 24, Figure 9. https://doi.org/10.1186/s41235-018-0118-3 © 2018 The Authors.

may be useful in combination with other cues in the context of training. For example, trustworthiness ratings could be used to narrow down a pool of images or real-world encounters that merit further inspection.

10.6.4 Smile Intensity

Previous studies have shown that low attractiveness and trustworthiness ratings, and high dominance ratings, are associated with low smile intensity (Sutherland et al., 2013). In our own experiments, we found that smile intensity ratings were significantly lower for mask images than for real face images. One explanation for this pattern is that facial movements of the mask wearer are partly constrained or absorbed by the silicone, such that emotional expressions are no longer at full strength when they reach the surface of the mask. We also found a significant negative correlation between smile intensity and false alarms to real face images. That is, real faces were more likely to be mistaken for masks when smile intensity was low.

This correlation suggests that smile intensity—or facial animacy more generally—could be another useful cue to mask detection. For example, faces that seem unusually low in animacy could be triaged for additional scrutiny. Smile intensity also suggests a straightforward test for live interactions: A mask wearer should have difficulty complying with the instruction to smile.

10.6.5 Incongruent Perceptual or Behavioural Cues

The case of the Geezer Bandit poses an interesting challenge. If we accept that the perpetrator was wearing a mask, can we infer anything about the perpetrator's actual facial appearance? To address this question, we examined how much people can tell about the face beneath the mask. In a series of live viewing experiments conducted in the UK and Japan, we asked participants to guess the age, gender, and race of a confederate who was wearing a hyper-realistic face mask. Unsurprisingly, error rates were high across all these demographic traits. However, accuracy was above chance for judgements of gender and age, owing to cues from body shape and posture. Drawing attention to conflicting cues from outside the face area could potentially boost mask detection rates.

One advantage of this approach is that it should be relatively impervious to further advances in mask realism. Improvements in materials or fabrication techniques could feasibly improve the fit of the mask around the eyes, and its responsiveness to facial movement. However, they would not make it more aligned with the wearer's body shape, posture, or gait.

10.6.6 Speech Sounds and Lip-Reading

In most hyper-realistic silicone masks, the lips of the mask go over the lips of the wearer and tuck inside the wearer's mouth. This construction has a number of implications for speech and lip-reading. First, it introduces a physical barrier between the wearer's upper and lower lips, presumably impeding production of phonemes that require contact between the lips (e.g., /b/, /p/, /m/), or between the teeth and the lower lip (e.g., /f/, /v/). Second, it reduces the pliability of the whole mouth area, presumably impeding articulation more generally. Reduced lip movement implies reduced visual support for speech understanding (Campbell, 2008). It also suggests that hyper-realistic masks may affect the auditory stream in distinctive ways. This raises the possibility that masked speech may have a signature that could be exploited for mask detection (Fecher & Watt, 2011). Ironically, auditory information may provide the best hope of solving this difficult visual task.

10.6.7 Individual Differences

Several suggestions in this section concern training as a means to enhance mask detection. An alternative approach would be to exploit individual differences in ability. The aim here would be to identify and select individuals who have a natural aptitude for distinguishing masks from real faces. This approach has already been used for other face tasks, notably face identification (Robertson et al., 2016; Russell et al., 2009; Wilmer et al., 2010; see White, Towler, & Kemp, this volume). However, its success is predicated on large individual differences in the relevant ability.

To investigate the scale of individual differences in mask detection, we presented participants with a series of face images, and asked them to categorize each image as a mask or a real face (Sanders & Jenkins, 2018). This task revealed a wide range of classification accuracy (5% – 100%) for high-realism masks among low-realism masks and real faces. Even when the low-realism condition was removed, substantial individual differences remained. Accuracy ranged from near chance (43%) to near ceiling (91%) for the high-realism masks, and from 65% to 100% for real faces. As with face identification tasks, hyper-realistic mask detection gives rise to large individual differences in performance. Some very recent results suggest that performance on face identification tasks and mask detection tasks are not strongly related (Robertson et al., 2020). If individual differences in mask detection prove to be stable over time and across test conditions, it may be possible to single out individuals with unusual talent for this very specific task.

10.6.8 Machine Vision

Recent decades have seen tremendous advances in automatic face recognition (Masi et al., 2018). At the same time, machine vision has become more closely integrated with security and surveillance infrastructure (Mabrouk & Zagrouba, 2018). A few recent papers have examined the possibility of training neural networks to distinguish hyper-realistic silicone masks from real faces (Bhattacharjee et al., 2018; Manjani et al., 2017). Although these studies demonstrate the applicability of neural networks to this classification problem, performance is currently limited by the availability of training data.

Another possibility for machine vision is to image parts of the electromagnetic spectrum that are not visible to humans. Although hyper-realistic silicone masks are designed to resemble real faces in the visible light range, they are not designed to resemble real faces in the infrared range. Given that silicone is an excellent insulator, it may not be surprising that a silicone mask can alter the thermal signature of the wearer's head (Bhattacharjee & Marcel, 2017). Thermal imaging is already used by some border agencies to differentiate between animate and inanimate objects (Kong et al., 2005), and to assist in screening for fever (Mercer & Ring, 2009). Repurposing the same technique may be an efficient means to screen for hyper-realistic masks in the context of border crossings (Zamost, 2010).

10.7 Implications

Hyper-realistic silicone masks are easily mistaken for real faces. That much is clear from dozens of real-world incidents and a growing body of experimental research. The implications of this development are still being absorbed. Masks that pass for human break the usual connection between facial appearance and personal identity. Breaking this connection raises some difficult questions for identification procedures that rely on it—particularly in the context of security and crime prevention.

For now, any threat from misuse of these masks is likely small scale. Hyper-realistic face masks are difficult to make, expensive to buy, and can be uncomfortable to wear for extended periods (Bhattacharjee & Marcel, 2017). These factors naturally limit their spread. However, the first criminal cases involving hyper-realistic masks only emerged around 2009. In the decade since, the number of mask manufacturers has increased, construction techniques have become more sophisticated, and reports of their use in criminal settings have become more frequent. We see no reason to expect these trends to halt.

Against this backdrop, we find that spontaneous detection of hyper-realistic masks is highly unreliable, and that even guided detection is poor. These limitations leave plenty of scope for improving performance. The first step is recognizing the problem, which is not a problem that people grasp intuitively. In our studies, respondents who had never seen a hyper-realistic face mask greatly over-estimated the ease of detection tasks. However, merely seeing example photographs improved their estimates. This exposure effect suggests that, when it comes to raising awareness, showing the problem is likely to be more effective than describing it.

The second step is to actually elevate detection rates. We outlined several broad approaches to this, encompassing training, personnel selection, and machine vision. Although training in identification tasks has generally had disappointing results (Towler et al., 2014, 2019; White et al., 2014), this does not necessarily mean that training in mask detection is a lost cause. Training in detection of other synthetic items, such as money, drug, and gems, has been comparatively successful (Fernandez et al., 2008; Jonker et al., 2006; World Health Organization, 1999). Success in those domains suggests that training in mask detection might be worth pursuing.

Proposing interventions raises the question of how much effort should be devoted to improving detection of hyper-realistic face masks. In our view, the answer depends on whether misuse of these masks remains a small problem or continues to grow. At this stage, it is difficult to make confident projections. On the one hand, the total number of recorded incidents is low. On the other hand, it is climbing. To complicate matters, the number of *unrecorded* incidents is completely unknown. Given the trajectory over the past decade, it seems plausible that criminal misuse of hyper-realistic face masks will increase. The rate of change will be determined partly by the quality and availability of the masks themselves, and partly by people's incentives to use them.

References

Ahlander, J. (2016). *Martin Peter Trenneborg: Swedish doctor who abducted and imprisoned woman is jailed for 10 years*. Available at: https://www.independent.co.uk/news/world/europe/

martin-peter-trenneborg-swedish-doctor-who-abducted-and-imprisoned-woman-is-jailed-for-10-years-a6891881.html (accessed 1 May 2020).

Alenezi, H. M., Bindemann, M., Fysh, M. C., & Johnston, R. A. (2015). Face matching in a long task: Enforced rest and desk-switching cannot maintain identification accuracy. *PeerJ*, *3*, e1184. doi:10.7717/peerj.1184

Becker, S. (2010). *He gives 'making faces' a whole new meaning. Today News*. Available at: https://www.today.com/news/he-gives-making-faces-whole-new-meaning-1C9014890 (accessed 1 May 2020).

Bernstein, S. (2010). *Masks so realistic they're arresting the wrong guy*. Available at: http://articles.latimes.com/2010/dec/08/business/la-fi-mask-20101209 (accessed 1 May 2020).

Bhattacharjee, S. & Marcel, S. (2017). What you can't see can help you—extended-range imaging for 3D-mask presentation attack detection. In *Proceedings of the 16th International Conference on Biometrics Special Interest Group*. (No. EPFL-CONF-231840). *Gesellschaft fuer Informatik eV* (GI). doi:10.23919/BIOSIG.2017.8053524

Bhattacharjee, S., Mohammadi, A., & Marcel, S. (2018). Spoofing deep face recognition with custom silicone masks. In *2018 IEEE 9th International Conference on Biometrics Theory, Applications and Systems (BTAS)* (pp. 1–7). IEEE.

Burton, A. M., White, D., & McNeill, A. (2010). The Glasgow Face Matching Test. *Behavior Research Methods*, *42*, 286–291. doi:10.3758/BRM.42.1.286

Campbell, R. (2008). The processing of audio-visual speech: Empirical and neural bases. *Philosophical Transactions of the Royal Society of London B: Biological Sciences*, *363*, 1001–1010. doi:10.1098/rstb.2007.2155

Damani, S. (2014). *The white robber who carried out six raids disguised as a black man (and very nearly got away with it)*. Available at: https://www.codewit.com/north-america/16184-the-white-robber-who-carried-out-six-raids-disguised-as-a-black-man-and-very-nearly-got-away-with-it (accessed 1 May 2020).

Dhamecha, T. I., Singh, R., Vatsa, M., & Kumar, A. (2014). Recognizing disguised faces: Human and machine evaluation. *PLoS ONE*, *9*(7), e99212. doi:10.1371/journal.pone.0099212

Drew, T., Võ, M. L. H., & Wolfe, J. M. (2013). The invisible gorilla strikes again: Sustained inattentional blindness in expert observers. *Psychological Science*, *24*, 1848–1853. doi:10.1177/0956797613479386

Fecher, N. & Watt, D. (2011). Speaking under cover: The effect of face-concealing garments on spectral properties of fricatives. In *International Congress of Phonetic Sciences* (pp. 663–666). Available at: researchgate.net/publication/228766449 (accessed 1 May 2020).

Fernandez, F. M., Green, M. D., & Newton, P. N. (2008). Prevalence and detection of counterfeit pharmaceuticals: A mini review. *Industrial & Engineering Chemistry Research*, *47*, 585–590. doi:10.1021/ie0703787

Frost, J. & Reid-Searl, K. (2017). Exploring the potential of Mask-Ed™ (KRS simulation) to teach both the art and science of nursing: A discussion paper. *Collegian*, *24*, 197–203. doi:10.1016/j.colegn.2015.11.003

Gardner, D. (2010). *The bank rubber ... Raider uses movie-style mask to disguise himself. Daily Mail*. Available at: http://www.dailymail.co.uk/news/article-1268215/White-robber-fools-police-weeks-elaborate-African-American-Hollywood-mask.html (accessed 1 May 2020).

Hodal, K., Topping, A., & Oltermann, P. (2014). *Italian's passport used to board flight MH370 was stolen in Phuket*. Available at: https://www.theguardian.com/world/2014/mar/09/italian-passport-malaysia-airlines-flight-mh370-stolen-phuket (accessed 1 May 2020).

Jenkins, R., White, D., Van Montfort, X., & Burton, A. M. (2011). Variability in photos of the same face. *Cognition*, *121*, 3, 313–323.

Jonker, N., Scholten, B., van Emmerik, M., & van der Hoeven, M. (2006). Counterfeit or genuine: Can you tell the difference? (Working Paper No. 121) Netherlands Central Bank, Research Department. Available at: https://www.dnb.nl/en/binaries/Working%20Paper%20121-2006_tcm47-146778.pdf (accessed 1 May 2020).

Kemp, R., Towell, N., & Pike, G. (1997). When seeing should not be believing: Photographs, credit cards and fraud. *Applied Cognitive Psychology*, *11*, 211–222. doi:10.1002/(SICI)1099-0720(199706)11:3<211::AID-ACP430>3.0.CO;2-O

Kong, S. G., Heo, J., Abidi, B. R., Paik, J., & Abidi, M. A. (2005). Recent advances in visual and infrared face recognition—a review. *Computer Vision and Image Understanding, 97*, 103–135. doi:10.1016/j.cviu.2004.04.001

Mabrouk, A. B. & Zagrouba, E. (2018). Abnormal behavior recognition for intelligent video surveillance systems: A review. *Expert Systems with Applications, 91*, 480–491.

Mack, A. & Rock, I. (1998). *Inattentional blindness.* Cambridge, Mass.: MIT Press.

Mäkitie, A. A., Salmi, M., Lindford, A., Tuomi, J., & Lassus, P. (2016). Three-dimensional printing for restoration of the donor face: A new digital technique tested and used in the first facial allotransplantation patient in Finland. *Journal of Plastic, Reconstructive & Aesthetic Surgery, 69*, 1648–1652. doi:10.1016/j.bjps.2016.09.021

Malone, L. (2014). *What men find behind female masks.* Available at: https://www.theatlantic.com/health/archive/2014/02/what-men-find-behind-female-masks/283972 (accessed 1 May 2020).

Manjani, I., Tariyal, S., Vatsa, M., Singh, R., & Majumdar, A. (2017). Detecting silicone mask-based presentation attack via deep dictionary learning. *IEEE Transactions on Information Forensics and Security, 12*, 1713–1723. doi:10.1109/TIFS.2017.2676720

Masi, I., Wu, Y., Hassner, T., & Natarajan, P. (2018). Deep face recognition: A survey. In *2018 31st SIBGRAPI conference on graphics, patterns and images (SIBGRAPI)* (pp. 471–478). IEEE.

Mazzuki, A., Siljander, R., & Mitchel, S. (2015). *Undercover disguise methods for investigators: Quick-change techniques for both men and women.* Illinois: Springfield.

Mercer, J. B. & Ring, E. F. J. (2009). Fever screening and infrared thermal imaging: Concerns and guidelines. *Thermology International, 19*, 67–69.

Noyes, E. & Jenkins, R. (2019). Deliberate disguise in face identification. *Journal of Experimental Psychology: Applied, 25*, 280–290. doi:10.1037/xap0000213

Oosterhof, N. N. & Todorov, A. (2008). The functional basis of face evaluation. *Proceedings of the National Academy of Sciences, 105*, 11087–11092. doi:10.1073/pnas.0805664105

Patterson, K. E. & Baddeley, A. D. (1977). When face recognition fails. *Journal of Experimental Psychology: Human Learning and Memory, 3*, 406–417.

Perry, T. (2011). *FBI officials 'strongly believe' Geezer Bandit committed 14th bank robbery.* Available at: https://latimesblogs.latimes.com/lanow/2011/05/fbi-officials-strongly-believe-geezer-bandit-committed-14th-bank-robbery.html. (accessed 1 May 2020).

Reid-Searl, K., Levett-Jones, T., Cooper, S., & Happell, B. (2014). The implementation of Mask-Ed: Reflections of academic participants. *Nurse Education in Practice, 14*, 485–490. doi:10.1016/j.nepr.2014.05.008

Righi, G., Peissig, J. J., & Tarr, M. J. (2012). Recognizing disguised faces. *Visual Cognition, 20*, 143–169. doi:10.1080/13506285.2012.654624

Roberts, J. (2017). *Man with sun allergy gets mask that looks exactly like him to stop skin frying.* Available at: https://metro.co.uk/2018/07/30/man-sun-allergy-gets-mask-looks-exactly-like-stop-skin-frying-7774918/?ito=cbshare. (accessed 1 May 2020).

Robertson, D. J., Noyes, E., Dowsett, A. J., Jenkins, R., & Burton, A. M. (2016). Face recognition by Metropolitan Police super-recognisers. *PLoS ONE, 11*(2), e0150036. doi:10.1371/journal.pone.0150036

Robertson, D. J., Sanders, J. G., Towler. A., Kramer, R. S. S., Spowage, J., Byrne, A., et al. (2020). Hyper-realistic face masks in a live passport-checking task. *Perception, 49*, 298–309. doi:10.1177/0301006620904614

Russell, R., Duchaine, B., & Nakayama, K. (2009). Super-recognizers: People with extraordinary face recognition ability. *Psychonomic Bulletin & Review, 16*, 252–257. doi:10.3758/PBR.16.2.252

Sanders, J. G. & Jenkins, R. (2018). Individual differences in hyper-realistic mask detection. *Cognitive Research: Principles and Implications, 3*, 24. doi:10.1186/s41235-018-0118-3

Sanders, J. G., Ueda, Y., Minemoto, K., Noyes, E., Yoshikawa, S., & Jenkins, R. (2017). Hyper-realistic face masks: A new challenge in person identification. *Cognitive Research: Principles and Implications, 2*, 43. doi:10.1186/s41235-017-0079-y

Sanders, J. G., Ueda, Y., Yoshikawa, S., & Jenkins, R. (2019). More human than human: A Turing test for photographed faces. *Cognitive Research: Principles and Implications, 4*, 43. doi:10.1186/s41235-019-0197-9

Schofield, H. (2019). *The fake French minister in a silicone mask who stole millions.* Available at: https://www.bbc.co.uk/news/world-europe-48510027 (accessed 1 May 2020).

Shapiro, P. N. & Penrod, S. (1986). Meta-analysis of facial identification studies. *Psychological Bulletin, 100,* 139–156. doi:10.1037/0033-2909.100.2.139

Simons, D. J. & Chabris, C. F. (1999). Gorillas in our midst: Sustained inattentional blindness for dynamic events. *Perception, 28,* 1059–1074. doi:10.1068/p281059

Sutherland, C. A., Oldmeadow, J. A., Santos, I. M., Towler, J., Burt, D. M., & Young, A. W. (2013). Social inferences from faces: Ambient images generate a three-dimensional model. *Cognition, 127,* 105–118. doi:10.1016/j.cognition.2012.12.001

Terry, R. L. (1993). How wearing eyeglasses affects facial recognition. *Current Psychology, 12,* 151–162. doi:10.1007/BF02686820

Terry, R. L. (1994). Effects of facial transformations on accuracy of recognition. *The Journal of Social Psychology, 134,* 483–492. doi:10.1080/00224545.1994.9712199

Towler, A., Kemp, R. I., Burton, A. M., Dunn, J. D., Wayne, T., Moreton, R., et al. (2019). Do professional facial image comparison training courses work? *PLoS ONE, 14*(2), e0211037. doi:10.1371/journal.pone.0211037

Towler, A., White, D., & Kemp, R. I. (2014). Evaluating training methods for facial image comparison: The face shape strategy does not work. *Perception, 43,* 214–218. doi:10.1068/p7676

Turing, A. M. (1950). Computing machinery and intelligence. *Mind, 59,* 433–460. doi:10.1007/978-1-4020-6710-5_3

White, D., Kemp, R. I., Jenkins, R., Matheson, M., & Burton, A. M. (2014). Passport officers' errors in face matching. *PLoS ONE, 9*(8), e103510. doi:10.1371/journal.pone.0103510

Wilmer, J. B., Germine, L., Chabris, C. F., Chatterjee, G., Williams, M., Loken, E., et al. (2010). Human face recognition ability is specific and highly heritable. *Proceedings of the National Academy of Sciences, 107,* 5238–5241. doi:10.1073/pnas.0913053107

World Health Organization (1999). *Counterfeit drugs: Guidelines for the development of measures to combat counterfeit drugs* (No. WHO/EDM/QSM/99.1). Geneva: World Health Organization.

Zamost, S. (2010). *Exclusive: Man in disguise boards international flight.* Available at: https://edition.cnn.com/2010/WORLD/americas/11/04/canada.disguised.passenger/index.html (accessed 1 May 2020).

Epilogue

Markus Bindemann

E.1 The Present and Future of Face Matching

This book has provided an overview of the latest developments and current understanding of forensic/unfamiliar face matching. Throughout this book, the scientific study of face matching has been contextualized through two important applied tasks—facial comparison at passport control and in police settings. These applied tasks are now considered in turn to draw together content from different chapters and highlight some of the key insights emerging from this book.

E.2 Implications for Person Identification at Passport Control

The world in the twenty-first century has become a highly interconnected place: air travel is at an all-time high, and widespread, high-volume, cross-border movement of people is now the norm in countries around the globe. At the time of writing, in early 2020, this has been underscored by the rapid global spread of Covid-19, while subsequent travel restrictions have served to further highlight our enormous reliance on international transport networks and people movement. In this context, facial comparison at passport control has become a security task of unprecedented scale and ubiquity. In the past, those seeking to enter other countries could have used forged travel or passport documents, into which their face photograph had been inserted. As laid out in Chapter 1, the development of sophisticated passport documents with more varied security features has greatly reduced the usage of such forged and counterfeit documents. In turn, however, this has given rise to a new security threat in the form of identity *impostors*—people who are using genuine documents of another, similar-looking person to gain entry into other countries. The problem of impostors continues to rise and now constitutes one of the biggest immigration control threats in many countries.

Three insights emerge from consideration of this impostor problem. One of these is that technological advances and improvements to security often create new threats, and sometimes some very low-tech approaches, such as that of identity impostors, can be used effectively to circumnavigate new security. Second, it is the frontline staff who ultimately have to deal with such changes, including the detection of new threats, in the

Markus Bindemann, *Epilogue* In: *Forensic Face Matching*. Edited by: Markus Bindemann, Oxford University Press (2021).
© Oxford University Press. DOI: 10.1093/oso/9780198837749.003.0011.

first instance. In the case of improvements in the security of passport documents, for example, the role of passport control personnel has evolved from checking documents for signs of tampering, such as the fraudulent insertion of a different face photograph, to greater emphasis on the facial comparison process, in order to detect cases where the bearer of a passport may not be the person shown in the document. Third, with such shifts in the role of security personnel, a corresponding need emerges to understand the scale of new threats. In the case of impostor detection at border control, it is remarkable that the first systematic study of the face-matching accuracy of passport officers was only published a few years ago.[1] It is only through a substantial international research effort by psychologists working at universities around the globe that understanding of this identification task has moved forward quickly since.

In psychology, we now understand that this task is surprisingly error-prone due to factors that affect the visual characteristics of faces (Chapter 2) and manipulate the resemblance of people through an intricate interplay of within-person variability and between-person similarity in appearance (Chapter 3). From a systematic evaluation of the available scientific evidence, it has also become clear that facial reviewers—the security personnel who are responsible for processing the volume of travellers at passport control (i.e., passport officers)—are not consistently better than untrained lay observers in performing this task (Chapter 4), and that short training programmes, of the type that these professionals may receive, are not effective in improving performance (Chapter 5). The picture that emerges from these studies is that the problem of identity impostors is not dealt with adequately at present.

Several avenues are available to address this situation. One is to simply contend with the problem: In the grand scale of people movement at airports and borders, the threat of identity impostors likely only reflects a highly infrequent occurrence. Of course, this is true of all security threats in these settings, but it is the consequences of a security breach that raise the associated risk, even if the likelihood of its occurrence is low. In addition, in large-scale operations such as passport control, incidents that represent only a very small percentage of travellers can still add up to a large number of cases. Simply contending with the possible occurrence of impostors is also a negligent approach considering that this problem appears to be on the rise, and in light of poignant examples such as flight MH370, which was boarded by two impostors before it went missing over the Indian Ocean while carrying 239 people (see Chapter 1).

A different approach, particularly in light of the limited success of courses to train people in face identification (Chapter 5), is to select personnel with a high aptitude for face matching. This has the potential to bring about rapid improvements in facial identification at passport control. However, it is now also emerging that observers are often inconsistent in their matching accuracy, fluctuating in performance both within the same and across different face identification tests (Chapter 6). In addition, it remains unclear how laboratory performance on face-matching tests translates into

---

[1] White, D., Kemp, R. I., Jenkins, R., Matheson, M., & Burton, A. M. (2014). Passport officers' errors in face matching. *PLoS ONE*, 9(8), e103510. doi:10.1371/journal.pone.0103510

real-world practice. Therefore, it is currently still unresolved how accurate and reliable personnel selections based on face-matching ability should be made. If such selections are made on incorrect premises, then this could *reduce* rather than improve security, so this issue must be treated with great caution. In light of this uncertainty surrounding personnel training (Chapter 5) and selection (Chapter 6), one clear recommendation that arises is that, if facial reviewers such as those performing passport control checks are not better than untrained observers, then it is important that they are deployed under circumstances that provide best-possible conditions for high matching accuracy. Such conditions could be provided, for example, through improved standardization of equipment to capture passport photographs, and to address the influence of variables such as lens distortion and lighting conditions, both at image capture and passport control (Chapter 2).

Another route to improving the identification process at passport control, which is currently being implemented by an increasing number of countries, is the application of Automated Border Control (ABC) points, which apply face recognition algorithms at e-gates to match travellers to their passport image. These algorithms can now achieve high accuracy across an increasing range of conditions (Chapter 9). The benefits that such algorithms can provide are likely emphasized further when other operational variables are taken into account that reduce accuracy of the human observer, such as fatigue from working long shifts and irregular day- and night-time hours. On the other hand, the accuracy of these face recognition technologies in the field is still lagging behind their test performance in the laboratory, and this technology also gives rise to some problems of its own. A key issue here is that ABC points remain supervised by human operators, and it is not clear whether this is best practice for maximizing identification accuracy. For example, when human observers are provided with the identification decision of an algorithm before making their own judgement, then they can be biased by this information, reducing their ability to catch and correct algorithm errors (see Chapter 9). One pertinent question, then, that arises for future research is how the interaction of human operator and face recognition algorithms should be structured to maximize the accuracy of the identification process, particularly as algorithms continue to improve even further.

The emerging threat of hyper-realistic silicone masks, which can be constructed to match the appearance of a specific passport identity with increasing realism, also points to a potential limitation of the ABC point in its current incarnation. Unless further technologies are added, such as thermal imaging technology, the detection of such masks might exceed the capabilities of ABC points. Chapter 10 outlines a series of eight proposals for improving mask detection in security scenarios. Most of these, such as usage of diagnostic facial features, lip-reading, emotion perception, social inferencing, and the detection of behavioural cues, represent strategies for mask detection for the human observer. While the development of ABC points for the facial identification of travellers therefore raises questions about the specific role that human observers should hold in future, the emergence of hyper-realistic masks also emphasizes the importance of the human operator for dealing with such new threats. Similarly, the detection of new security threats more generally is likely to continue to rest on human personnel for the foreseeable future (see Chapter 1).

E.3   Facial Comparison by Facial Examiners

A different group of observers whose responsibility is facial comparison are facial examiners. These are experts who often work with the police and produce written reports for legal proceedings (Chapter 4). While many of the factors that limit identification at passport control also apply to facial examiners (see Chapter 2), these professionals perform more rigorous identifications and under more challenging conditions—for example, by comparing ambient face images that display much greater variation in a person's appearance than one would expect to encounter at passport control.

In contrast to facial reviewers working at passport control, facial examiners outperform untrained lay observers in psychological studies (Chapter 4). The basis of this advantage is not clear, although it likely reflects substantial on-the-job mentoring and training (Chapter 5). One reason for why such extensive training might improve a person's face-matching ability when shorter training courses fail (see Chapter 5) is that it can be tailored to the idiosyncratic variation that faces exhibit in appearance. Considering this variation, multiple strategies must exist to solve this task (Chapter 3), and it is possible that only the flexibility that personal mentoring affords is sufficient to impart the multitude of knowledge and experience that is required to *truly* improve a person's face-matching performance.

In recent years, however, it has also become clear that substantial individual differences exist between facial examiners in their ability to identify faces. This variation is such that some examiners can perform rather badly in face matching, at a level that is substantially below many lay observers (see Figure 2 in Chapter 6). The problem of the deployment of facial examiners is therefore one of uncertainty: While these experts outperform lay observers as a group, such inferences of expertise are difficult to make on an individual basis. This *problem of uncertainty* also applies to the methods that facial examiners bring to bear on the identification process in occupational settings. Chapter 7 explains that a lack of standardization of techniques exists in this field, whereby facial examiners often develop their own procedures. Consequently, the validation that procedures have undergone is often unknown and, therefore, also the error rates that they might incur when identifications are made. This problem is compounded even further by the lack of databases that allow for a quantitative statistical evaluation of facial comparison evidence. Thus, there is no objective data to determine the probability that two faces depict the same person based on the judged similarity of specific facial features.

It would seem common sense to assume that the combination of these three aspects—the face-matching ability of a facial examiner, the validity of the method that they bring to bear on an identification, and the statistical database that is used to evaluate what the facial comparison method at hand indicates—is essential to establish the accuracy of an identification in occupational settings. In practice, however, an objective assessment of these aspects is typically absent. The methods of facial examiners, for example, are often accepted on the simple basis that they are already commonly used. In turn, the lack of scientific data to establish the validity of a presented method is often ignored in legal settings (Chapter 8).

Moving forward, these are complex issues to address and will likely be resolved only through better information sharing and collaboration between practitioners, researchers, and legal experts. Researchers, for example, require a better understanding of the different methods that facial examiners might apply so that each of these can be tested rigorously, and practitioners then need to know whether these methods provide consistent and reliable results under systematic scientific validation. Case examples, such as the forensic morphological analysis outlined in Chapter 7, may provide a useful starting point here. To be ultimately successful, such research also needs to systematically explore how variables that affect facial appearance impact on identification by facial examiners (see Chapter 2).

E.4 Super-Recognizers

Another group of experts in facial identification that receives coverage in several chapters of this book are super-recognizers—a terminology that refers to people who appear to have extraordinarily good face-recognition ability. In contrast to facial examiners, who are held to have improved face-matching ability as a consequence of their training, super-recognizers in organizations such as the police were already better at face identification prior to their deployment and were selected for their role on the basis of that ability. The systematic analysis of facial expertise in Chapter 4 indicates that such occupational selection is warranted, with super-recognizers—similarly to facial examiners—outperforming lay observers across several published studies. However, facial examiners and super-recognizers seem to achieve higher accuracy for different reasons. Whereas facial examiners are held to apply slow analytic processes, based on a piecemeal comparison of sets of specific features, super-recognizer expertise appears to draw on holistic analysis, for which faces are not perceived as individual features but a single integrated percept (Chapter 4). These differences point to a dual-route model for explaining expertise in face identification (Chapter 5). This idea draws on existing models of familiar face recognition and provides a useful concept for understanding differences between these expert groups.

The dual-route model is a positive development for understanding these different expert groups in face matching, but it might also raise concern for the deployment of super-recognizers in occupational settings. According to the UK Forensic Science Regulator, for example, a skill that is not based on specialist knowledge and training does not constitute forensic science (Chapter 7). Extending this reasoning to a dual-route model would imply that, if super-recognition ability arises naturally via typical face-processing mechanisms, then super-recognizers are inadmissible as experts in legal settings, even when these individuals operate in police units.

In parallel, concern about the concept of super-recognizers has also arisen among researchers. A thought-provoking demonstration of why caution should be exercised in the deployment of super-recognizers comes from research that demonstrates that these observers are *inconsistent* in their performance across tests of face memory and face matching, and, more pertinently, also across different tests of face matching (Chapter 6). There is currently no guidance on how the deployment of super-recognizers should proceed in occupational settings given these circumstances. In legal proceedings, however, reliability is a key criterion for the admissibility of facial identification evidence (see Chapter 8). If these standards are applied to super-recognizers, with (in)consistency of individual performance across different tasks taken as an indicator of reliability, then many of these observers are also unlikely to pass this threshold.

Some organizations are now invested heavily in super-recognizers, so it is unlikely that the concept of super-recognition is going to disappear. And such investment seems warranted to an extent by the demonstrable identification advantages of super-recognizers in psychological studies (Chapters 4 and 5). At the same time, applied interest in these observers is proceeding faster than scientific understanding of this ability, creating a worrying gap in knowledge, with potentially dangerous implications for important identification tasks in occupational settings (Chapters 6 and 7).

E.5 Theory, the Key to Progress

The pressing current questions that arise in the study of face matching, such as how a person's ability to perform this task can be established reliably, how people can be trained to be more effective at this task, how personnel should be selected to fill relevant identification roles, and how humans should interact with face recognition algorithms to maximize accuracy, all converge on a pivotal issue. To fully understand the problems associated with face matching, and to devise effective solutions, requires an understanding of the cognitive underpinnings of this task—a psychological theory of how unfamiliar face matching is *actually* performed.

Despite a substantial expansion of research effort in this domain in recent years, much of this work has been motivated by relatively applied questions, such as how specific visual characteristics of faces have an impact on the accuracy of this task (see Chapter 2) or how the performance of different types of professionals compares with that of control groups (see Chapter 4). This empirical development has not been accompanied by corresponding gains in the theoretical understanding of face matching, even though these will inevitably create further insight for practical application. An illustration of this point comes from a consideration of the relationship between match and mismatch accuracy in face matching. The application of face matching requires the correct detection of identity mismatches (such as impostors at passport control), but also an accurate appreciation of when two different images are of the same person (e.g., to match a suspect to a target person in police investigations). One of the most surprising findings in this field is that the classifications of matches and mismatches do not correlate, suggesting that separable abilities are required to resolve these complementary aspects of face matching (see Chapter 3). Unless this dissociation between match and mismatch classification is understood on a theoretical level, it is difficult to see how important practical developments, such as the design of effective training programmes for facial comparison, can be achieved in full.

To aid the development of a cognitive theory of face matching, several candidate processes are identified in Chapter 3. Considered broadly, these processes converge with the proposal of an analytical route to face matching described in the dual-task model in Chapters 4 and 5, but provide a considerably more detailed breakdown of how such an analytical process might operate by specifying attention, perception, evaluation, and decision-making components for this task. To substantiate this framework, or to disprove it, the scientific study of face matching must now move on to research questions that are posed in a stronger theoretical space.

Overall, it is remarkable that we do not have a cognitive model of face matching yet when theories of related processes, such as face recognition, have been in existence for decades. It is clear that current applications of face matching are facing substantial challenges and, while the applied task of facial comparison by humans is undergoing changes, it also seems here to stay. In this context, the need for a theoretical account of face matching, to underpin its practical application, is greater than ever.

Index

For the benefit of digital users, indexed terms that span two pages (e.g., 52–53) may, on occasion, appear on only one of those pages.

Tables and figures are indicated by *t* and *f* following the page number